Philosophy as Drama

Also available from Bloomsbury

Plato and Nietzsche, Mark Anderson
Parmenides, Plato and Mortal Philosophy, Vishwa Adluri
Health and Hedonism in Plato and Epicurus, Kelly E. Arenson
Rethinking Order, edited by Nancy Cartwright and Keith Ward
Aesthetics of Ugliness, Karl Rosenkranz
Plotinus the Platonist, David J. Yount

Philosophy as Drama

Plato's Thinking through Dialogue

Hallvard Fossheim, Vigdis Songe-Møller and
Knut Ågotnes

BLOOMSBURY ACADEMIC
LONDON • NEW YORK • OXFORD • NEW DELHI • SYDNEY

BLOOMSBURY ACADEMIC
Bloomsbury Publishing Plc
50 Bedford Square, London, WC1B 3DP, UK
1385 Broadway, New York, NY 10018, USA
29 Earlsfort Terrace, Dublin 2, Ireland

BLOOMSBURY, BLOOMSBURY ACADEMIC and the Diana logo
are trademarks of Bloomsbury Publishing Plc

First published in Great Britain 2019
Paperback edition first published 2021

Copyright © Hallvard Fossheim, Vigdis Songe-Møller, Knut Ågotnes and
contributors, 2019

Hallvard Fossheim, Vigdis Songe-Møller and Knut Ågotnes have asserted their right under the Copyright,
Designs and Patents Act, 1988, to be identified as Authors of this work.

Cover design by Maria Rajka
Cover image: Head and other parts of a life-sized bronze statue from ca 230 BC, called the
Antikythera Philosopher. Found in the Antikythera wreck in 1901. In the National
Archaeological Museum of Athens. Photo by Giovanni Dall'Orto.

All rights reserved. No part of this publication may be reproduced or
transmitted in any form or by any means, electronic or mechanical,
including photocopying, recording, or any information storage or retrieval
system, without prior permission in writing from the publishers.

Bloomsbury Publishing Plc does not have any control over, or responsibility for,
any third-party websites referred to or in this book. All internet addresses given
in this book were correct at the time of going to press. The author and publisher
regret any inconvenience caused if addresses have changed or sites have
ceased to exist, but can accept no responsibility for any such changes.

A catalogue record for this book is available from the British Library.

A catalog record for this book is available from the Library of Congress.

ISBN: HB: 978-1-3500-8249-6
PB: 978-1-3502-4367-5
ePDF: 978-1-3500-8250-2
eBook: 978-1-3500-8251-9

Typeset by RefineCatch Limited, Bungay, Suffolk

To find out more about our authors and books visit
www.bloomsbury.com and sign up for our newsletters.

Contents

List of Contributors	vii
A note on transcribed Greek versus Greek fonts	xi
Preface	xiii
Introduction *Knut Ågotnes, Hallvard Fossheim and Vigdis Songe-Møller*	1

Part 1 Genre and the Philosophical Dialogue

1 The Whole Comedy and Tragedy of Philosophy: On Aristophanes' Speech in Plato's *Symposium* *Drew A. Hyland* 15
2 A Praise of the Philosophical Written Speech? Ethics and Philosophical Progression in Plato's *Symposium* *Elena Irrera* 29
3 Socrates' Appeals to Homer's Achilles in Plato's *Apology of Socrates* and *Crito* *Hayden W. Ausland* 51
4 Plato's Ring of Gyges and *Das Leben der Anderen* *Jacob Howland* 79

Part 2 Virtue and Soul-shaping

5 Plato's Inverted Theatre: Displacing the Wisdom of the Poets *Paul Woodruff* 95
6 Gods, Giants and Philosophers: On Being, Education and Dialogue in Plato's *Sophist* 245e6-249d5 *Jens Kristian Larsen* 107
7 *Philotimia*. On Rhetoric, Virtues and Honour in the *Symposium* *Knut Ågotnes* 123

Part 3 Reason and Irrationality

8 The Significance of the Ambiguity of Music in Plato *Kristin Sampson* 143
9 Pleasure, Perception and Images in Plato *Cynthia Freeland* 161
10 The Limits of Rationality in Plato's *Phaedo* *Hallvard Fossheim* 179

Contents

Part 4 Place and Displacement

11 Place (*topos*) and Strangeness (*atopia*) in the *Phaedrus*
    Erlend Breidal — 191
12 Hunt: Method and Metaphor. A Reading of the *Sophist*
    216a1-226a6   *Gro Rørstadbotten* — 209
13 Plato's *Sophist*: A Different Look   *John Sallis* — 231

Index — 241

List of Contributors

Hayden W. Ausland is Professor of Classics at the University of Montana. His publications include: 'Socrates in the Early Nineteenth Century, Come to Be Young and Beautiful', forthcoming in *Brill's Companion to the Reception of Socrates*; 'The Treatment of Virtue in Plato's Protagoras', in *Plato's Protagoras. Essays on the Confrontation of Philosophy and Sophistry* (2017); 'The Decline of Political Virtue in *Republic* 8–9', *Proceedings of the Boston Area Colloquium in Ancient Philosophy* (2013); 'Socratic Induction in Plato and Aristotle', in *Dialectic and Dialogue. The Development of Dialectic from Plato to Aristotle* (2012); 'Proëmial Prolepsis in Plato's Politeia', *Symbolae Osloenses* (2008).

Erlend Breidal has been a philosophy teacher at the University of Bergen for more than a decade and wrote a PhD on Plato in 2015, entitled *The Intermediate Being of Socratic Philosophy and its Suppression in Plato's* Theaetetus, Sophist, and Statesman.

Hallvard Fossheim is Professor of Philosophy at the University of Bergen. He has published widely on Plato and Aristotle, focusing much of his work on their moral psychology, with inquiries into questions of motivation, interaction and identity. He also has interests in virtue ethics and research ethics, as well as questions of dialectic and dialogue. He has recently co-edited the anthology *The Quest for the Good Life: Ancient Philosophers on Happiness* (2015).

Cynthia Freeland is Professor Emerita of Philosophy at the University of Houston. She is past president of the American Society for Aesthetics (2015–17). Her publications include articles and books on ancient philosophy, feminist theory, film theory and aesthetics. Her book *But Is It Art?* (2001) has been translated into fifteen languages. Her most recent book was *Portraits and Persons* (2010).

Jacob Howland is McFarlin Professor of Philosophy at the University of Tulsa. His research focuses on ancient Greek philosophy, history, epic and tragedy; the Hebrew Bible and the Talmud; Kierkegaard; and literary and philosophical responses to the Holocaust and Soviet totalitarianism. His books are *Glaucon's Fate: History, Myth, and Character in Plato's Republic* (2018); *Plato and the Talmud* (Cambridge University Press, 2011); *Kierkegaard and Socrates: A Study in Philosophy and Faith* (2006); *The Paradox of Political Philosophy: Socrates' Philosophic Trial* (1998); and *The Republic: The Odyssey of Philosophy* (1993 and 2004).

Drew A. Hyland is Charles A. Dana Professor Emeritus at Trinity College in Hartford, CT. He has also taught graduate courses at University of Toronto, The New School for

Social Research, Boston University, and Suffolk University. His major research areas are Ancient Greek Philosophy, nineteenth and twentieth century European philosophy, and philosophy of sport. Among his major publications are *Finitude and Transcendence in the Platonic Dialogues* (1995), *Questioning Platonism: Continental Interpretations of Plato* (2004), and *Plato and the Question of Beauty* (2008).

Elena Irrera is Senior Research Fellow in Political Philosophy at the University of Bologna. She is also member of Instituto 'Lucio Anneo Séneca' of Universidad Carlos III de Madrid. Her research interests concern aspects of ancient philosophy and contemporary political thought. Her publications include two books: *Il bello come causalità metafisica in Aristotele* (Beauty as Metaphysical Causation in Aristotle, 2011) and *Sulla bellezza della vita buona. Fini e Criteri dell'agire umano in Aristotele* (On the Beauty of the Good life. Aims and Criteria of Human Agency in Aristotle, 2012), as well as several articles on Plato's and Aristotle's political thought.

Jens Kristian Larsen is a Marie Skłodowska-Curie Fellow at the University of Bergen. His primary area of research is ancient philosophy, with a particular emphasis on Socratic philosophy and Plato. He also works on the reception of themes from ancient philosophy in the phenomenological tradition and is currently co-editing an anthology focused on this reception. His most recent published papers are 'Measuring Humans Against Gods: On the Digression of Plato's *Theaetetus*' (2019), 'By What Is the Soul Nourished? On the Art of the Physician of Souls in Plato's *Protagoras*' (2017), and 'Plato and Heidegger on Sophistry and Philosophy' (2016).

Gro Rørstadbotten teaches philosophy at the Department of Philosophy, University of Bergen, Norway. She is the co-author of the books *Tidslinjer* (Time Lines, 2008) and *Fortiede alternativer* (Silenced Alternatives, 2015). Her most recent articles are 'Turning Towards Philosophy: A Reading of *Protagoras* 309a1-314e2', in *Plato's Protagoras. Essays on the Confrontation of Philosophy and Sophistry* (2017) and 'Socrates's Telling of the Truth: A reading of the Apology 17a1-35d9', in *Readings of Plato's Apology of Socrates. Defending the Philosophical Life*, (2018).

John Sallis is Frederick J. Adelmann Professor of Philosophy at Boston College. He has also held Chairs at Pennsylvania State University, Vanderbilt University, Loyola University of Chicago, and Duquesne University. He is the author of more than twenty books; among the most recent are *Logic of Imagination* (2012), *Senses of Landscape* (2015), *The Figure of Nature* (2016) and *The Return of Nature* (2016). His books have been translated into many languages including French, German, Spanish and Chinese.

Kristin Sampson is Associate Professor at the Department of Philosophy at the University of Bergen, Norway. She is working mainly within the areas of ancient Greek philosophy and feminist philosophy, with a special focus on Plato and early Greek thinking previous to him. Her later publications on Plato include articles on the *Sophist* (2015), the *Protagoras* (2017), and the *Apology* (2018).

Vigdis Songe-Møller is Professor Emerita at the Department of Philosophy at the University of Bergen, Norway. Her area of research is ancient Greek philosophy, especially the pre-Socratics and Plato, and Greek tragedy, as well as contemporary feminist philosophy. She is the author of *Philosophy Without Women. The Birth of Sexism in Western Thought* (2002) and co-author of *Sexuality, Death and the Feminine. Philosophies of Embodiment* (2010).

Paul Woodruff teaches philosophy and classics at the University of Texas at Austin. He has been working on ancient and modern theories of the virtues. His best-known book is *Reverence: Renewing a Forgotten Virtue* (2nd edition, 2014). He has recently edited a volume of essays by philosophers on Oedipus in the plays of Sophocles.

Knut Ågotnes is Associate Professor Emeritus at the University of Bergen. His main interests are Plato and Aristotle, especially the dramatic form of Plato's dialogues and his ethics. Recent papers are 'Plato's Socrates in the Apology: Speaking in Two Voices' in *Readings of Plato's Apology of Socrates. Defending the Philosophical Life* (2018), and 'Socrates' Sophisticated Attack on Protagoras' in *Plato's Protagoras. Essays on the confrontation of Philosophy and Sophistry* (2017).

A note on transcribed Greek versus Greek fonts

We have advocated a policy of transcription of Greek letters for the benefit of non-Greek readers, but allowed for exceptions in cases where the author strongly felt that Greek fonts were crucial to their work.

Preface

This book is a result of a research project, *Poetry and Philosophy: Poetical and Argumentative Elements in Plato's Philosophy*. The project, funded by the Research Council of Norway, was hosted by the University of Bergen's Department of Philosophy. In the course of a seven year period, well established and younger Plato scholars from European and US universities met in Bergen and elsewhere for symposia, seminars, and workshops. This book came out of those years of communal and individual effort. The editors wish to thank all the authors for their contributions and for their participation in the project.

Introduction

Knut Ågotnes, Hallvard Fossheim and Vigdis Songe-Møller

Plato wrote philosophical dialogues. He was among those who first developed the genre of Socratic dialogues, and certainly he brought it to perfection.[1] Although there have been attempts to emulate it, no one else has mastered the genre with the same literary and philosophical virtuosity as Plato himself.

One reason for this is undoubtedly the fact that few philosophers have found it worth their while to write in this vein. Philosophical writing has had a stronger affinity to the treatise or the scientific article than to the dialogue. This may also partly account for the lack of interest among generations of Plato scholars in the form of writing that Plato made use of. The dialogue form has been regarded as a side issue, often understood as a mere didactic device, with interpreters focusing instead exclusively on the theses and the positions they thought they could extract from the text. However, during the last fifty years or so, another approach has gained ground. This alternative approach takes as a starting point the assumption that other dimensions of the texts than their argumentative structure and the formulation of their theses are philosophically relevant. Furthermore, many Plato scholars who are writing today presume that Plato developed this genre because it was in tune with his idea of how to do philosophy. Accordingly, aspects of the dialogue form have been explored by, among many others, Michael Frede, Charles Griswold, Francisco Gonzales, Gerald A. Press, David Roochnik, Jill Gordon, G.R.F. Ferrari, Rosemary Desjardins, Diskin Clay, Marina McCoy, Andrea Nightingale and Arlene Saxonhouse. Other important figures in this transition, who also contribute to the present collection of essays, are Hayden W. Ausland, Jacob Howland, Drew A. Hyland, John Sallis and Paul Woodruff.

We naturally want to know what the interlocutors in Plato's dialogues are talking about and what they think about the problem under discussion, and so we try to identify claims and search for arguments for these claims. However, arguments in Plato's texts are seldom unproblematically clear and unambiguous. More often they are in need of interpretation. Such interpretive work may take two main avenues. One can try to isolate argumentative sequences from the rest of the text and reconstruct them with the help of logical tools. Another approach has been to examine the narrative context for clues to the meanings of statements and arguments. This approach, favoured by the contributors to the present anthology, teaches us that argumentation in the strict sense does not exhaust the philosophical meaning of a dialogue.

Most of the interlocutors in Plato's dialogues express opinions and reveal attitudes pertaining to philosophical problems, most often questions concerning goodness, happiness and knowledge. These opinions and attitudes are tightly interwoven with the characters' experiences, with desires and emotions, with motives, interests and wishes, with values, aims and the efforts needed to bring them about. These aspects of the dialogue form might be taken to indicate that Plato's philosophers have no other choice than to start trying to reach an understanding of justice, say, by investigating the extant opinions and attitudes to justice, as they are expressed by three-dimensional people in ordinary language.

Plato's work is characterized by a lack of technical terms. We rarely find carefully construed and articulated concepts or first principles, which have played such an important role in philosophy since Aristotle. One reason for the strong interest that Plato takes in the opinions of more or less ordinary people could be that these opinions represent indispensable cognitive resources; material that is necessary for a critical examination and clarification of, for instance, moral concepts.

Another reason for this interest in everyday and mundane opinions is probably that a broader context for philosophical work is established when Socrates, often through tenacious questioning, manages to get an interlocutor to articulate his views. Through such articulations, aspects of the character of the interlocutor are revealed, and both psychological and cultural foundations of his opinions can be taken into account, directly or indirectly. In this way we learn something of the complex connections between moral and political opinions on the one hand, and character and human nature on the other. We also get recurring glimpses of what seems to be a final aim of Plato's philosophy: philosophy should shape individual character as well as society.

It is also true that Plato's investigations, mundane as they may start out, point 'upwards', away from the changeability and mutability of everyday life. Accordingly, the shaping of character too should ideally take place on the basis of insight into timeless, universal truths. The aim is to approach the good, something which indicates the virtues while also pointing beyond the merely human sphere. Ultimately, what is indicated seem to be timeless, unchangeable entities. The ontological question we encounter here – what kind of existence these entities have – is discussed much less in the corpus than one should expect if Plato's philosophy is primarily a 'Theory of Ideas'. The question of their way of existing is never settled, and when it is discussed, this is mostly done with the help of images and allegories.

The philosophical dialogues Plato wrote appear as an original, almost unique genre. However, it is not easy to pinpoint its nature. Part of the reason for this is Plato's use of heterogeneous material from a variety of other genres. The perhaps most salient point, however, is how he integrates these varied features in the text as a new kind of whole, arranging them along a storyline that gives us individuals as they exist and act in a time and a place. Things happen and we understand that what is said and done is said and done because the story concerns just these characters, who have such and such relations to each other, are more or less wise or virtuous, love honour or money, are cowardly or courageous, are quick to learn or not, docile or opinionated. One of these persons is Socrates. A story conveys meaning between the lines, to a much greater degree than does a purely theoretical text. Even when the action consists only of verbal acts, the relationship between the speakers gives clues to the text's meaning, in addition to what is said in plain words. Moreover, the narrative frame makes room for the use of a variety of contextual material. We thus get an abundance of possible meanings. This situation surely makes the work of the interpreter difficult, but there is no shortcut if a desideratum is a fuller appreciation for each text's complexities. We find elements taken from poetry, tragedy, comedy and myth. Setting, irony, humour, parody, hyperbole, analogy, images, allegories, ambiguity, flattery, boasting, deception and emotional outbursts may all have philosophical meaning. Conflict and competition create tension and suspense, and may tell us what is at stake philosophically. In addition, the repertoire of rhetoric is exploited.

A premise for the described approach is that we regard the dialogues as vehicles of Plato's philosophical investigations, and not as true reports of conversations that Socrates and others had with their contemporaries. Even if the texts relate stories about people who lived in Athens in Plato's time, he treats them with large doses of poetic licence. The fictional character of the dialogue, like its narrative form, allows for a wider register of literary devices than a factual account would accommodate.

These features imply that the philosophical dialogue is less constrained by formal requirements than literary genres such as tragedy or comedy usually are. However, the choice of setting and interlocutors imposes limits on the inquiry, limits that have their own philosophical significance. Such a choice is one reason why provisional and even unsatisfactory results are reached in a given dialogue. We do, indeed, find that the same themes and problems are attacked again in other texts, in new ways and from new angles. Accordingly, Plato never begins a dialogue with a reference to results already gained in other texts and then proceeds to use them as secure ground for new investigations.

Among the many literary devices in the dialogues, irony has drawn quite a lot of attention. As a feature of Socrates' character, it can denote a perceived tendency to dissimulation in his relation to other characters. Irony more broadly construed, however, occurs in several forms. It may be used dramatically to show disparities between what a speaker says and what the narrative reveals about him. In such a case, the meaning can be rather easy to grasp, but this is not always the case. Very often irony is used to show up ambiguities rather than contradictions. On its most fundamental level, then, irony in Plato points to a deficiency of language as such. Language always conveys several meanings and levels of meaning, as well as lack of meaning. A display of awareness of this could be said to be a kind of philosophical self-irony, and this is a characteristic of Plato's Socrates, the ignorant one, who can give the impression that nothing of philosophical importance could be said in a completely satisfactorily fashion. The dialogue form itself could well reflect Plato's insight on this point.

The dialogues can be read as works of fiction. They contain elements of extant literary genres within a narrative framework. With this in mind, it seems strange that Plato should look so askance at the literary genres of his own time. However, Socrates often reminds us that poets and speechmakers imitate and recycle prevalent prejudices, and so we are given some reason to believe that this is Plato's view. A difference between this literature and his own could then be that Plato thinks *he* is conducting critical investigations, while *they* give the masses what they want.

Yet his use of them also suggests that Plato thought that other genres could contain points of contact with his philosophical problems. He digs into literature and other types of cultural expressions – literary genres, music and myth – for material as well as for sparring partners. However, when Plato refers to and exploits such resources, he gives them new meaning and makes them play new roles in accordance with the philosophical aims of his text.

Plato's use of myths is often understood as explorations into unknown areas where ordinary language is inadequate. While this view may contain some truth, we should also keep in mind that language, while remaining an inescapable point of departure, is *always* insufficient for Plato's purpose. Since Plato does not have ready concepts that directly denote the 'things' he is hunting for, he must constantly use images and metaphors. Ordinary language can give us a setting and a story. However, as soon as Plato lets Socrates (or anyone else) steer the conversation towards philosophical questions, we discover that he is trying to find the best images for a meaning that somehow also goes beyond the everyday. At this point we can return to the frame story and see how this too takes on added significance, giving us clues to the relation between character, emotion and virtue, for instance. Plato may articulate a radical criticism of the poets for their use of imitation (*mimêsis*), but his own writing is permeated by images and image-making. His purpose explains the difference between himself and other makers of linguistic mimetic works, in that Plato uses images in an effort to transcend language. Such an effort may never fully succeed, but the way the dialogues are composed seems to indicate that philosophy includes such efforts.

If we consider Plato's work as a whole, we get the impression of a philosopher who is constantly *en route*. He has found a sphere of problems and a direction for working on them, but he never presents us with final theoretical results on the nature of knowledge or morality. The context laid out in a given dialogue is always integrated in the on-going philosophical discussion. Plato thus shows us that the philosopher carries with him the situatedness of his endeavour. Both very concrete contexts and a historical/cultural horizon will necessarily inform the texts. How does this relate to the thought that the task consists in reaching something timeless and universal? A constructive response would sensibly start from the assumption that there is a connection between the timeless virtues he is searching for and the opinions and attitudes of ordinary people. Plato seems to think that human beings possess character traits in a more or less unsatisfactory, inconsistent and one-sided way. Still he seems to believe that these qualities contain something genuine that can be investigated, criticized and elaborated on philosophically in terms of virtue(s) and goodness.

A still common assumption in Plato studies is that the dialectical question-and-answer form of conversation that Socrates so often engages in is meant solely to display philosophical lines of argumentation. A conversation of this sort may look like the following. There are two people involved and one of them asks a question like: What do you think justice is? The other answers and is supposed to answer sincerely. Then new questions follow. The questioner, usually Socrates, tries to make the other contradict himself, by showing that he utters, or consents to, statements that are inconsistent. This basic procedure is deployed in different ways and with different purposes in mind. At one extreme, Socrates may be investigating a moral concept, such as justice, together with an interlocutor who is keen to participate in an inquiry into important philosophical problems. In this case, what is refuted is supposed to be the suggestion the respondent puts forward on the nature of justice, rather than the answerer himself, and Socrates' attempts at refuting it can be seen as a test of his main claim.

A refutation means that the claim or some of the other statements must be discarded, and we have to start anew. However, as a research method this procedure is fraught with difficulties. It presupposes that the main concepts used to a fairly great extent have an unambiguous and consistent meaning for both interlocutors. Moreover, the procedure does not take into account the arbitrariness that can and probably will occur both in the choice of questions and in the way of responding to them. Even so, such refutation serves an important function: it shows that further investigations are necessary, perhaps from another point of view.

At another extreme Socrates is set on refuting his interlocutor's character. The question-and-answer procedure is followed here too, but Socrates may be conducting the conversation with the purpose of exposing the moral flaws and the lack of self-knowledge on the part of the other person. The pivotal point here is to create a feeling of *aporia*, a state of perplexity and confusion that challenges the security and assuredness of the self. Added to this could be a feeling of shame over having lost the verbal contest, especially when an audience is present. This too is a form of help. In the best case, the respondent's *aporia* could lead him to re-examine both himself and the conventions in which he has been brought up. This pedagogical dimension can also be found in dialogues where the leading dialogue partner is someone other than Socrates, for instance the Stranger in the *Sophist*.

Usually these aspects of the philosopher's procedure – conceptual investigations and character exposure and formation – are in play simultaneously. To investigate the ways they are interwoven in the text in question is one of the main tasks of the interpreter.

In the Western philosophical tradition from Aristotle on, we seldom encounter the philosopher himself in the texts. Nevertheless, his person plays an important part. When he puts his name on the front page, he assures the reader that he is backing the theses presented in the text, and the ethos his name has achieved lends authoritative force to his conclusions. What we otherwise get to know of the nature of his character is in the main considered to be immaterial and will easily be regarded as anecdote.

The anonymity of Plato is more complete than this and has another function. We do not know a single thesis in the dialogues that Plato has put his name to. When he appears in the dialogues, he is silent. Why does he hide himself so thoroughly? One reason can be that he wants to counteract the impact of the philosopher's authority. Plato makes it harder for the reader to avoid engaging with the problems herself. Another reason could be that he wants to combat the perception that philosophy is pure, solitary thinking. As we suggested, the dialogues seem to be intended as exhibitions of how philosophical work can most genuinely be performed. Philosophical investigations should resemble the dialogues themselves, they should be carried out *in media res,* in a setting where ideas are confronted and where problems that concern real people are discussed.

This means that the philosopher also finds himself *in media res*; he himself is situated, part of the context. He too must be formed through the activity he partakes in, an activity that is at any one time preliminary and unsatisfying. To let the philosopher appear as someone who, in his superior wisdom, stays outside and above the life he is investigating, would be misguided. The dialogue form makes it possible for Plato to make a significant move in this respect. He can give the story a protagonist, warts and all, who is involved in the philosophical activity. As we know, he usually selects Socrates for this role. He lets Socrates say in the *Apology* that 'the unexamined life is not worth living', implying that, for Socrates, whom we would like to consider as Plato's model philosopher, philosophy is a way of living. If philosophy is under way, if it is always more or less preliminary, the character of the philosopher too is on the move. The Socrates we find in the dialogues is, as we should expect, a somewhat more than average wise and good person, but not a perfect human being.

Other thinkers play leading roles in some of the dialogues. In these cases, there is often less focus on dramatic and narrative aspects of dialogue than in many of the texts where Socrates is central. Sometimes, as in the *Timaeus*, the talk sounds almost like a lecture. How we should understand the relationship between these thinkers and Socrates is a controversial question among Plato scholars, and the contributors to this anthology express different views. Are the Stranger in the *Sophist* and the *Statesman* and Timaeus in the *Timaeus* philosophers who further develop the philosophy Plato has given us through Socrates? Is this another kind of philosophy, perhaps more suited to working with other problems than those Socrates concentrates on? Are they lesser philosophers than Socrates? Or are they not philosophers at all; are they sophists, perhaps?

In several dialogues, Plato lets Socrates draw a seemingly clear line of demarcation between philosophers and sophists. Plato tends to paint all the sophists with the same brush. They are more similar to the poets than to the philosophers, he lets Socrates say; they do not seek truth, but adoration, influence and money, all of which they get by operating – or pretending to be operating – within the prevailing consensus. In some dialogues, however, as in the *Sophist,* similarities between the philosopher and the sophist appear, and the thin line between them is pointed to, if not thoroughly discussed. As with the question of 'the other philosophers' above, we are here confronted with a problem for philosophy itself: the difficult question of its identity and delimitation. If philosophy is constantly under way, if it lacks and always will lack a sure foundation, then this will be a question that cannot be closed, but must always be raised as part of the philosophical activity itself.

The dialogues give us the impression that Socrates could involve all and sundry in philosophical discussions. This is, however, not quite accurate. We are not exposed to any instances where he discusses the nature of the virtues with artisans. He shows respect for their craft knowledge in the *Apology*, and he does not consider them to be less cultured than the poets, for instance. Nonetheless, it is primarily the elite, people with political and cultural influence, that Socrates engages in conversations. This alerts us to the element of social criticism in Plato's philosophy.

The cultural elite was concerned with the lack of social harmony, and they were apt to attribute some of the disruptive tendencies in the city to noncompliance with traditional *paideia*. People, especially young people, were not as virtuous as they should;

they gave too free rein to pleasure and desire, love of money, honour and power. A moral criticism along these lines is found in Xenophon, for instance.

Plato's moralism is different. He lets Socrates diagnose the moral and political problems on a deeper level. The virtues have not been adequately understood, and people's values and aims, such as money, power and honour, are not unproblematic even when they are kept within bounds. Plato finds it necessary to reconsider the views on human nature that the Greek *paideia* took for granted. He discusses man's complex soul, its desires and emotions. Is the soul unitary, does it have parts that work together in harmony, or is it basically an irrational entity filled with contradictions? Can the soul be made harmonious with the help of philosophy? Are its manifold desires susceptible to nurture and education? In what ways do desires and emotions promote certain aims or values in life?

As stated previously, there is not a single philosophical thesis that we know with confidence to be Plato's considered view. Yet we have said a lot about Plato's philosophy, partly in an assertive way. Such assertions can be made in spite of the open and inconclusive nature of the conversations, on the instances of returning to the starting point in order to try again, and on the situatedness of his investigations. While we do not know what Plato's ultimate philosophical theses are, we can assume with some confidence that he presents philosophy as an activity without a secure foundation and without an overly technical vocabulary. Without being able to state what Plato considered the best definition of (for instance) justice, we can assume that he is engaged in studying the nature of the virtues. These assumptions are insights on a meta-level, and it is possible to know something about Plato's thinking on these issues because they must have guided the composition of the dialogues.

Finally, Plato lets Socrates make critical claims about writing. Plato nonetheless writes, however. Maybe part of the project is to try to imitate genuine thinking, with its communicative dimension, its loose threads, intricacies, interruptions and withdrawals. Most of the dialogues certainly look like a compromise between an oral and a written performance. They are, however, compositions that are thoroughly thought through. Plato could, then, have chosen to make it easier for us as readers; he could have reduced the complexity of the work of interpretation. As it is, the argumentation is usually complex and often unclear, and it is difficult to ascertain the significance of the different textual elements and their interconnectedness. Plato does not give us any master key. It seems that he takes pains to make the texts non-transparent to the readers. In so doing, he forces the reader to engage with the text in a different way than if she had been reading a treatise. In hardly any other philosophical *oeuvre* is the reader's active, and even creative, presence 'in' the text so necessary for its proper functioning. One has to strive to understand, one has to ponder the problems by oneself, and one has to become one of the interlocutors; one has to go along with Plato, and sometimes one even has to go against him.

The authors of the articles in this anthology consider their texts as results of such an engagement with Plato's dialogues.

In line with what we consider to be four crucial perspectives on the question of Plato's philosophy seen in its fuller, literary width, the book is divided according to the following headings: 'Genre and philosophical dialogue', approaching Plato through reflections on the works' formal characteristics and their implications; 'Virtue and soul-shaping', dealing with the most central concern among the dialogues' characters and in the work as a whole; 'Reason and irrationality', providing discussions of an issue that has tended to divide readers of Plato as far as the quality and impact of his texts are concerned; and 'Place and displacement', concretizing the relations between place, position, and their absence on the level of argument and the level of drama.

Genre and the philosophical dialogue

Plato's philosophical dialogues, understood as a distinct literary genre, nevertheless have many formal similarities with drama and poetry. Finding out more about the philosophical impact of choosing the dialogue form and how it relates to other literary genres is of value not only for its own sake, but is also crucial for understanding the specificity of Plato's philosophy. Four of our contributors deal with problems in the intersection of mimetic poetry and philosophy in Plato's dialogues.

Drew A. Hyland, in 'The Whole Comedy and Tragedy of Philosophy: On Aristophanes' Speech in Plato's *Symposium*', treats of more than the title reveals: not only the speech as an isolated piece of text, but the wider implications in Plato concerning the complicated relationship between these two dramatic genres, philosophy, and human existence. Seeing Aristophanes' work as an illustration of conservative inklings (including a view of philosophy as a dangerous manifestation of *erôs*), Hyland offers a fresh reading of his speech in the *Symposium* according to which the apparent praise of homosexual couples is meant ironically, *erôs* is presented as an all too human phenomenon, and the comic playwright provides a more pessimistic view of humankind than does Plato's Socrates. In fact, only the absence of recognized greatness in us keeps Aristophanes from being a tragic rather than a comic poet.

The question of genre and form is relevant both on the level of what goes on inside the dialogue, and on the level of how the dialogue relates to its readership. In 'A Praise of the Philosophical Written Speech? Ethics and Philosophical Progression in Plato's *Symposium*', Elena Irrera argues that the literary structure, as well as the arguments and content of the speeches in the *Symposium*, convey the idea that this dialogue is written as a 'self-defending' *logos*, i.e. a *logos* that implants seeds of intellectual progression in the soul of the reader. Through detailed analyses of the first three speeches on love – by Phaedrus, Pausanias and Eryximachus – Irrera shows how the reader's understanding of virtue and beauty is gradually enriched and thus prepared for Socrates' discussion of Eros. Irrera finds several connections between the first three eulogies and the steps of Diotima's 'ladder of love', which confirms Plato's power as a pedagogical writer steering the reader towards virtue and knowledge.

Plato's frequent references to Homer's poems have given rise to much controversy among Plato scholars throughout the ages. For instance, how should the reader of the *Apology of Socrates* understand Socrates' use of Achilles' behaviour in the *Iliad* as a model? Hayden W. Ausland, in 'Socrates' Appeals to Homer's Achilles in Plato's *Apology of Socrates* and *Crito*', argues that Plato, unlike Xenophon, offers no direct reply to the literary allegation that Socrates interpreted passages from the poets in a perverse way, thus contributing to the corruption of the young with which he was charged at his trial. Instead, Plato displays the defendant appealing to the Homeric Achilles as a model for his own conduct in a manner that has occasioned its interpreters no little perplexity. This problem receives illumination from an allusion to the same literary work with which the *Crito* begins, which offers its own difficulties. These complementary appeals to the example of Homer's central character, once animated by reference to the greater plot of *Iliad*, reveal Socrates as invoking constructively that poem's key teachings.

Contemporary works of art may also help us see more clearly how goodness relates to some of its shadows. Jacob Howland actualizes central features of Plato's *Republic* by reading them through the lens of von Donnersmarck's 2006 film *Das Leben der Anderen* (*The Lives of Others*). The myth of the ring of Gyges displays to us limitations concerning how to relate to the Other, while the suppression of poetic imagination is at the heart of the issue of totalitarianism. *Das Leben der Anderen* makes a topic of these questions by depicting the conditions for art in the DDR, and as Howland brings out, it does so in ways that let us see more clearly potentials in Plato's text. What is the relation between technical expertise/technocracy and moral insight, lying and moral goodness, poetic production and knowledge? On Howland's reading, von Donnersmarck's film exposes not only the potential of Plato's *Republic*, but also dangers inherent in Kallipolis and later similar models.

Virtue and soul-shaping

Central to the discussions in Plato's dialogues is the question of ethical development and how one becomes good (or bad, as the case may be), while on another level, the dialogues themselves must be thought to have an ethical mission in this sense. The three authors in this section all address this side of Plato's *oeuvre*.

One of the most famous images of the soul's insight that we have from Plato, is the cosmic vision of the soul's journey in the *Phaedrus*. Paul Woodruff, in 'Plato's Inverted Theatre: Displacing the Wisdom of the Poets', fleshes out a new reading of the central myth of the *Phaedrus*. The cosmic setting for the soul's journey is presented by Socrates as an inverted theatre, thus subverting the central authority of the poets in favour of the new authority of divine philosophical insight. In this fresh vision of reality, the classical gods are no longer authorities in their own right, but moral exemplars in the striving for something beyond them. Woodruff ends his analysis by suggesting how the new philosophical vision relates to established ideals of love, compassion and good deliberation.

How may insight be engendered in the more mundane setting of the dialogue? In 'Gods, Giants and Philosophers: On Being, Education and Dialogue in Plato's *Sophist* 245e6-249d5', Jens Kristian Larsen analyses the significance of the 'battle' between the materialists and the idealists for understanding the philosophical function of the exchange between the visitor from Elea and the young Theaetetus. As a result of the fictive conversation between the corporealists and the friends of the Forms, the guest from Elea proposes that being is power. Larsen argues that this proposal is meant for

Theaetetus, not for any of the participants in the 'battle', as has been commonly assumed, and Larsen thus manages to show that this central section of the dialogue has a pedagogical aspect: through different styles of conversation the stranger aims at educating Theaetetus about the soul's relation to being.

Knut Ågotnes, in '*Philotimia*. On Rhetoric, Virtues and Honour in the *Symposium*', combines a focus on genre with the claim that Plato's subject in this dialogue is the relationship between virtues and values/aims. The speeches – including that of Diotima – are all in the rhetorical genre of the *encomium*. This means that due to the genre itself, the speeches eulogizing *erôs* are obliged to give an inflated view of the positive role of *erôs* in our lives. The analysis of the text, however, shows that *erôs* is prized because of the honour it contrives to give us. Diotima even says that *erôs* is a force that makes us strive for renown and immortality. Plato wants to show how the obsession with victory, honour and renown among Athenian men clashes with the hegemony of the virtues important to Socrates. In his portrayal of Alcibiades, Plato pushes this conflict to extremes.

Reason and irrationality

Contrary to a rather common preconception, the distinction reason/irrationality does not correspond to the distinction between what is good and what is not good in Plato's dramatizations of the real and the ideal. Among the arts, for instance, are found plenty of examples of partly irrational forces on the side of goodness. Accordingly, in 'The Significance of the Ambiguity of Music in Plato', Kristin Sampson aims at showing how music functions as a *pharmakon* that can be both a remedy and a poison, and how this ambiguity is significant in the thinking of Plato. Her point of departure being passages in the *Laws*, Sampson discusses the relation between music and philosophy on two levels: in the *polis* and in the divine sphere. This last level informs the former, in that the musical ordering of the cosmos echoes within every living creature and so forms a basis for music in education and politics. The philosopher, as a lawgiver and knowledgeable of both divine beauty and the human soul, is thus depicted as a master of music. But music also has a Dionysian, and thus potentially destabilizing, element. Through a discussion of passages in the *Phaedrus*, *Phaedo*, *Timaeus* and *Republic*, Sampson links this aspect of music to philosophy's relation to the divine as well as to the corporeal. As the highest form of music, philosophy is also charged with ambiguity.

Not only art, but aspects of human nature too can be seen to transcend simple dualism. Cynthia Freeland, in 'Pleasure, Perception and Images in Plato', details the gist of the theories of pleasure offered in dialogues as diverse as *Phaedo*, *Republic*, *Theaetetus*, *Timaeus* and *Philebus*. She distinguishes between two broad approaches to the analysis of pleasure: the replenishment model and the psychological model. While the replenishment model seems to fit the phenomena for a certain range of experiences, Plato has Socrates criticize it in other contexts, and provides the beginnings of theories that transcend its limitations not least when it comes to explaining higher pleasures (including the pleasure of philosophy itself). Freeland concludes that the more sophisticated analysis on Plato's part will also be able to allow for taking commendable, 'true' pleasure from, e.g., images in representational art.

While most of Plato's dialogues reserve a place for irrationality as an irreducible aspect of human psychology, the *Phaedo* has tended to stand out as building its case on the soul as a unified and wholly rational entity. Hallvard Fossheim, in 'The Limits of Rationality in Plato's *Phaedo*' aims to show that this text ultimately presents a picture of reason as weak, secondary and dependent on a framework of non-rational forces. The findings are relevant both to the level of the dialogue and to the level of the reader. After pointing out how Plato foregrounds the *Phaedo*'s quality as a story or fable as well as a collection of arguments, the import of the dialogue's first emphases on pleasure, pain and emotion is articulated. To these indications of a moral psychology not reducible to rationality are then added considerations of the text's allowance for a popular, secondary virtue which is profoundly bodily, and of the famous 'child inside'. The dialogue's major myth is then shown to indicate that reason remains doubly embedded in, and dependent on, irrational forces in the soul. Finally, the dialogue's acknowledgement of a mimetic impulse is presented as an added dimension of irrationality to which all except the ideal figure of Socrates are receptive.

Place and displacement

Plato's thinking in the dialogues is constantly and in various ways played out in the tension between place and displacement. This is partly a consequence of the drama in each dialogue, in that all thinking finds (or takes) place in the sense of having a concrete topological context, while on the other hand Plato's philosophy transcends any specific place. Moreover, the complex dramatic structure of the dialogues produces a constant displacement of metaphors, arguments, concepts and philosophical positions, which often results in the dialogue partners' – and the readers' – bewilderment, or *aporia*. This basic notion of a philosophical crisis is couched in terms of place (*topos*) and its lack (*atopos*), of being and non-being. In 'Place (*topos*) and Strangeness (*atopia*) in the *Phaedrus*', Erlend Breidal takes as his point of departure the relationship between the *topos* of the conversation between Socrates and Phaedrus – the sacred grove outside the city walls – and Socrates' feeling of being 'out of place' (*atopos*), or his state of strangeness (*atopia*). While this *topos*, where speeches of love occurred, signifies a place of transcendence, the state of *atopia* is one of perplexity, or *aporia*, and points to the human state of ignorance. In his reading of the *Phaedrus*, Breidal suggests that the interplay between the terms of *topos* and *atopia* can be interpreted as an image of the tension not only between transcendence and human finitude, but also between presence and absence, between pure Being and human embodiment, between original and image, and between self and other. Philosophical activity operates within these tensions, which cannot be resolved in the realm of human beings.

Another dialogue which is permeated by displacement is the *Sophist*. In 'Hunt: Method and Metaphor. A reading of the *Sophist* 216a1-226a6', Gro Rørstadbotten argues that the overall impact of the *Sophist* is confusion, caused by the Stranger's manipulation of Theaetetus. She sets out to show that the Stranger's proposed method for hunting down the sophist and his art (*technê*) and which is presented as a paradigm (*paradeigma*) is intentionally broken down and distorted in the first three applications of this method. Theaetetus, who does not realize what is going on, appears as the Stranger's prey, himself being hunted down by the Stranger, while the reader is starting to hunt for the Stranger's identity. The hunting metaphor is thus said to camouflage a metaphor for a threefold hunt: the reader's hunt for the Stranger, Theaetetus' belief of hunting the sophist, and the stranger's hunt for Theaetetus. The result is that the several definitions of the sophist's art point to the Stranger's own manipulative practice.

In a radically different way, John Sallis too addresses the inherent perplexity of the *Sophist*. In 'Plato's *Sophist*: A Different Look', Sallis discusses the complex relationship between central Platonic concepts, such as appearance, being, non-being, otherness and power. Sallis starts by analysing the opening scene of the dialogue, where the sophist, whom the Stranger aims at defining, is said to appear as a philosopher, i.e. he appears as what he is not, as something other than what he is. The hunt for the sophist thus involves a hunt for being and its interweaving with non-being, which leads to an understanding of being as *dynamis*: the power to bring something about and to be affected. The question of non-being, which, as Sallis puts it, 'has haunted the whole dialogue', is confronted in the discourse on the other: it is the other that installs non-being in being. Sallis concludes his guided tour through this multifaceted dialogue with an open question: Does the discourse of the other suffice to make the philosopher visible, or is a more perplexing alterity needed?

Note

1. We know little about the nature of the texts of authors who may have been forerunners. Diogenes Laertius writes: 'They say that Zeno the Eleatic was the first to write dialogues. But, according to Favorinus in his *Memorabilia*, Aristotle in his first book of his dialogue *On Poets* asserts that it was Alexamenus of Styra or Teos. In my opinion Plato, who brought this form of writing to perfection, ought to be adjudged the prize for its invention as well as for its embellishment.' Diogenes Laertius, *Lives of Eminent Philosophers*, trans. R.D. Hicks, The Loeb Classical Library, vol. III (Cambridge: Harvard University Press, 1972), 3.48.

Part One

Genre and the Philosophical Dialogue

1

The Whole Comedy and Tragedy of Philosophy: On Aristophanes' Speech in Plato's *Symposium*[1]

Drew A. Hyland

In the *Philebus*, the Platonic Socrates speaks of 'the whole comedy and tragedy of human life'.[2] The *Symposium* famously closes with Socrates convincing the presumably almost passed out Aristophanes and Agathon that 'the same man could know how to compose a comedy and a tragedy and that one skilled in tragedy could create comedies' (*Symposium* 223d). Yet in the *Republic,* famously criticizing poetry throughout the dialogue and operating on a strict construction of the 'one man one job' principle, Socrates convinces Adeimantus that the same man *could not* adequately compose both comedies and tragedies (*Republic* 395a). These three citations, clearly in a complicated tension with each other, by themselves establish what is in any case manifest throughout the Platonic dialogues: the relation of comedy and tragedy to human life and so to philosophy is one of those core issues that is a constantly recurring theme in Plato's work, even if it is one that, like beauty, like truth, Plato seems to have decided is best treated obliquely, in the context of other more explicit themes, rather than made themselves an explicit object of investigation.[3] That core issues such as these do not get treated thematically as explicit themes in no sense should suggest that they are in Plato's view less decisive. Instead, it should raise important questions about how certain kinds of themes are best raised for thought, whether the best way to consider an issue is in every case to isolate it as an explicit theme of investigation.[4]

At the risk of ignoring Plato's implicit suggestion, I want in this chapter to look more explicitly at the question of comedy and tragedy in relation to human life and philosophy as it plays out in one specific instance, the comic poet Aristophanes' speech supposedly[5] in praise of *erôs* in the *Symposium*. In doing so, I want to make a number of general points in addition to – hopefully – many more focused ones. First, that in Aristophanes' speech, Plato allows us to see something of just how complicated the relation of comedy and tragedy is to human life. Second, how that complicated relation gets implicated in the very nature of philosophy. Third, I want to argue that Plato beautifully captures the way these themes actually arise in Aristophanes' plays and so that the speech he gives Aristophanes is quite true to the spirit of Aristophanes' own work. And finally, I want to draw out, with occasional references ahead to Socrates' own speech on *erôs*, how Plato offers a kind of proto-Kantian 'critique' of Aristophanes' standpoint, allowing both his great insightfulness and the limitations of his position to emerge.

Let me begin with a brief account of the basic standpoint on these issues as they play out in Aristophanes' own plays. In doing so, I shall focus very narrowly on the themes in his plays that Plato allows to come to the fore in Aristophanes' speech at the *Symposium*. That will hardly amount to a fair or adequate treatment of the comedies as a whole.[6]

Aristophanes' plays advocate, hilariously but seriously, for a certain classical conservatism. This begins with a profoundly pessimistic view of the human situation: human beings, Aristophanes teaches us, are fools. Every one of Aristophanes' comedies demonstrates this view, the general point of which is that humans, if they are allowed to pursue their polymorphous and for the most part perverse desires in uninhibited ways, will inevitably ruin themselves and each other. This is the Aristophanic or pagan version of the Judaeo-Christian foundation of classical conservatism: the doctrine of original sin. One might say that the Judaeo-Christian formulation of this understanding of the human situation sees only the tragedy, whereas Aristophanes sees its comic consequences as well. Humans desire what they do not have the wherewithal to attain and in any case would often be better off without, and their pursuit of these ultimately unattainable goals results in calamity, a calamity that, from the standpoint of the untouched observer, is or can be hilarious. Perhaps there is no better example of this than Strepsiades of the *Clouds*, who leaves the farm for the city and a sophisticated 'city' wife, no doubt on the assumption that thereby he will attain wealth and happiness, only to have disaster ensue. But the same is true of the Socrates of the same play, whose pretentions of noble theoretical investigations into 'the things above and the things below', reduce in the end to self-interested sophistry.

Given this pessimistic view of the human condition, what, if anything, can we do about it? Aristophanes' answer will become the foundation of the classical conservative answer: if, as is surely true of Aristophanes, one holds this pessimism about the human condition and at the same time loves humans, a plausible – perhaps the most plausible – response is to recommend unflinching adherence to *nomos*, to the laws of the land, to religious tradition, to cultural tradition.[7] Perhaps the greatest sin of the Aristophanic Socrates is his impiety if not atheism. This disrespect for the traditional gods leads inevitably to disrespect for the law, and hence to disaster. It should be noticed here that Aristophanes' affirmation of traditional religion is based more on his conviction that it is *salutary* for people to believe the traditional religion than on any evidence of his personal belief that the claims of religion are *true*. The emphasis is regularly on the bad consequences of atheism, not on independent claims or arguments for the truth of orthodox religion.[8] We shall see how Plato captures this difference in the speech he gives to Aristophanes. Clearly, however, Aristophanes does recommend in his plays that it is better to uphold the traditional religious and cultural teachings (embodied in the *Clouds*, at least to an extent, in the older, 'just *logos*') and thereby stay out of trouble. This is connected to Aristophanes' (and traditional conservatism's) affection for life on the farm, embodied in Strepsiades' lament, early in the *Clouds*, that he should never have left the farm, come to the city, and married this wealthy city woman. Only then did *all* the trouble begin! We find the same originating impetus for Peithetaerus and

Euelpides in the *Birds,* who wish to leave the 'hustle and bustle' of Athens for a quieter, more peaceful life outside the city.⁹ What is so appealing to a conservative consciousness about the farming life? The answer is clear to anyone who has spent a summer working on a farm. One has to work from dawn to dusk, go to bed early, and so stay out of trouble!

Also related to all this is Aristophanes' manifest distrust of and contempt for the political life, not to mention the life of philosophy (encapsulated in the parody of Socrates in the *Clouds*). Virtually every politician in Aristophanes's plays is a charlatan and a would-be if not a real tyrant. Even Peithetaerus in the *Birds,* originally intending to *escape* the sordid politics of Athens, becomes a tyrant himself once presented with the opportunity. Moreover, the politicians – at least Aristophanes' politicians – are almost all homosexuals – another traditional conservative object of censure. Why, we need to ask, does Aristophanes so regularly associate and roundly condemn philosophy, politics, and homosexuality? I suggest that it is because they are all manifestations of *erôs* that are *dangerous* to tradition and the traditional religious and cultural values that Aristophanes wants to uphold, and therefore these activities need to be carefully controlled if not entirely condemned. But does not Aristophanes in his speech in the *Symposium praise erôs*? Only apparently, as we shall see, and only as long as it is very carefully limited in its scope. But we do not need to turn yet to Plato to see this point. In the *Birds*, Aristophanes reveals his suspicions regarding *erôs* when he gives his genealogy of the birds, who, with Peithetaerus and Euelpides (who grow wings and so in a sense become birds) are attempting to establish a tyranny over not only humans but the gods as well. For the birds are the progeny of *erôs*!¹⁰ *Erôs*, we are thus told, is the father of revolution, lawlessness, and tyranny. We learn, for example, that 'All that is considered shameful and illegal by humans is among the birds noble (*kala*)'.¹¹ This, we soon see, includes father beating, adultery, and treason and revolution, not to mention blatant impiety. Moreover, in a remarkable prefiguration of a decisive element in Socrates' own characterization of *erôs*, Aristophanes places the birds 'in the middle' between mortals and the gods, but with an utterly different consequence from the one Socrates, under Diotima's tutelage, will draw. For Socrates and Diotima, *erôs* 'in between' status means that the erotic human soul has partial access to both the divine and the mortal, and so can 'bind the two together into a whole' (*Symposium,* 202e-203a). But Aristophanes sees something much more sinister in this 'in between' status: the birds, in the middle between mortals and the gods, can *control* the passage of messages from the gods to humans and sacrifices from humans to gods. They are thus in a position to establish a tyranny not just over humans but over the gods as well! Since of course the *Symposium* was written significantly later than the *Birds* – the former probably about 385 BC and the latter performed first in 414 BC – it was clearly Plato who would have intended this difference. He thus has Socrates and Diotima 'correct' Aristophanes' quite negative interpretation of the consequences of *erôs*' intermediary status, substituting for this tyrannical implication the more positive one of partial access to both the mortal and the divine and thus the potential to 'bind the two into a whole'. Aristophanes' suspicion of *erôs* – as the potential source of lawlessness and tyranny – is why I believe Aristophanes in his plays tries to allow – and so praises – only one manifestation of *erôs*: heterosexual *erôs* which results in lots of children, the raising of whom is very time consuming, and hence will keep us out of trouble. The problem with the other manifestations of *erôs*, from homosexuality to politics to philosophy, is that, without the time-consuming consequence of children, they offer the leisure for all sorts of tyrannical and revolutionary impulses.

What, then, is the 'conservative' response to this tendency to uninhibited erotic aspiration in all its manifestations? Aristophanes' answer, as we have already limned, is implicitly and often explicitly to recommend the quiet, country life, away from the hustle and bustle of city life, away from its politics, its philosophy and its polymorphous perverse sexuality. This is the lament of Strepsiades early in the *Clouds,* that he never should have left the farm, and it is as we have seen the originating impetus of Peithetaerus and Euelpides in the *Birds,* to 'retire' from the city and the complex agitations of city life. Again, it is important to underline that the founding premise of this entire outlook is Aristophanes' conviction that humans are at bottom fools, that if allowed to pursue their desires freely, they will ruin themselves and each other. This conviction, whether in its pagan or its Judaeo-Christian manifestations, is the *archê* of classical conservatism.

This general discussion of Aristophanes' standpoint hopefully will prepare us to see how true Plato is to Aristophanes' convictions in the speech he gives the comic poet in the *Symposium,* and at the same time how he subtlety injects a proto-Kantian critique of that position into the very speech that advocates it. Let us turn then to Aristophanes' speech in the *Symposium.*

We should not begin our consideration of Aristophanes' speech without reminding ourselves that, following the order of their seating, he was supposed to speak immediately following Pausanias' speech. However, presumably during Pausanias' speech, he contracted a bad case of the hiccups, and Eryximachus the doctor agreed both to give him the cure (actually three cures) for his hiccups and speak in his place while he was recovering. There are at least two very comic aspects to this little interlude. First, we are invited to wonder why Aristophanes contracted such a bad case of the hiccups. Given the content of Pausanias speech, with its unqualified praise of pederastic love (unqualified because, despite the rhetoric of 'noble' vs. 'common' *erôs*, he gives license to the pursuing lover to behave in all sorts of shameful ways if only he succeeds), and given what we have seen of Aristophanes' negative view of pederasty in his plays, we can surmise that it was his revulsion at the content of Pausanias' speech that caused him to suffer as he does! Second, we have to imagine the hilarity of the scene during Eryximachus' typically pretentious speech, with Aristophanes (no doubt dramatically) holding his breath as long as he can, then gargling loudly, and finally, presumably towards the end, tickling his nose and emitting a loud sneeze – all this during Eryximachus' didactic praise of his own medical *technê*! Eryximachus' natural irritation at these interruptions in part explains the banter between him and Aristophanes that precedes the comic poet's speech, which he finally can give once the hiccups have subsided.

Aristophanes begins his speech by chastising the Greeks for not sufficiently appreciating the power of *erôs*, who, he claims, is the 'most philanthropic' of the gods, literally, the god who loves humans the most (189c). We shall have to see whether he stays true to this opening pious claim that *erôs* is a god and indeed the most philanthropic one.

He then seems – but only seems – to shift the subject: 'You must first learn of human nature and what it has suffered' (189d). It will turn out that this is no shift at all, that *erôs* as Aristophanes explains it *just is* human nature, at least, human nature as it is now. This is in fact an important step that will be shared by Socrates: *erôs* is not just an occasional experience that happens to us from time to time – now I fall in love, now I'm not in love – but something very close to the *human condition,* to 'human nature' as Aristophanes says. To explain *erôs* is to explain human nature. This is in part why the issue of *erôs* is so closely tied to the question of the comedy and tragedy of human life.

Aristophanes' account of 'human nature and its sufferings' is contained in his hilarious and rather ribald myth about our original status as 'double people'. As the story goes, we were originally double versions of what we are now, with two heads, four arms and hands, four feet, two sets of genitals, etc. That we were double versions of our present status meant that there were not two but three possible combinations: a double male, a double female, and a male-female combination, literally androgynous, which, says Aristophanes, no longer exists in our present split condition but remains as a term of reproach (189e). As such, we were much more powerful than we are now, capable, as he describes it, of whirling along on eight limbs when we wanted to go fast. Which is to say, our original nature was in principle far superior to our present condition. We in our present split condition are a 'fallen race'.

Aristophanes takes time to comment on where our original natures themselves originated. Obviously, we cannot have come originally from the Olympian gods, who are always portrayed, as we are now, as 'split'. Instead, we were literally cosmic creatures, our roundness in imitation of the roundness of our sources, the sun (for the double males), the earth (for the double females), and the moon (for the male-female combination) (190b). This is important for what ensues: as cosmic creatures, literally the children of the cosmos, we have no 'natural' relation to the Olympians. What kinship we have to them, physically and spiritually, seems in Aristophanes' myth to be accidental, not natural. There is no 'natural' basis for our piety to the Olympians.

Perhaps understandably, then, we did not obey the Olympians, indeed tried to overthrow them (as do Peithetaerus, Euelpides, and the birds in Aristophanes' play), and in our powerful double natures must have been a serious threat. There ensues an account of the gods that portrays them almost as, like us, comic fools. The gods were literally 'in *aporia*' about what to do about us! (190c). Moreover, they had no more affection for us than we for them. The only reason they did not simply kill us is that they did not want to do without our sacrifices. Their interest in us was entirely self-interest. Aristophanes' original, apparently pious claim that *erôs* was the 'most philanthropic' of the gods needs refining: he is the *only* god who loves us. Finally, 'with trouble' (*mogis*), Zeus comes up with an idea: split us in two, which will have two good effects: make us weaker and thus less threatening, and more numerous, hence increasing the number of sacrifices for the gods. But, once again comically, Zeus' original plan proves foolhardy: to be sure, he splits us in two, ties our skin around in a knot at the waist, and leaves wrinkles there so that we may look at it occasionally and be humble. But the first result is that we run around doing nothing but trying to join with our original halves, neither eating nor taking care of ourselves, and so we were dying off. Zeus is hardly omniscient or even wise! His original plan is a comic – or tragic – failure.

He thus has to come up with a second plan, which he does by having Apollo move our genitals around to the front (they were originally on the sides), so that at least when the originally androgynous pairings came together, they would generate in each other and the race would continue.

We will return to this situation in a moment, but first we must pause to reflect on what Plato's Aristophanes has already accomplished. Just as in his plays he recommends piety to the gods and a quiet life, so in this speech Aristophanes is setting out a fundamentally religious account of *erôs* or, as he says, 'human nature and its sufferings'. He begins by urging us to be pious towards the Olympians and towards the god Eros. He then gives an account of our original natures in which we were in a superior situation to our present one. However, even in that superior condition, we had an original flaw, the 'original sin' of *hybris*: we tried to overthrow the gods. So, we had to be punished, and our present situation is a result of that punishment. Still further, we are warned that if we continue to be impious, Zeus will punish us yet again, splitting us once more so that we have to hop around on one leg, etc. The extent to which this account incorporates so much of the religious view of the world as we now know it is remarkable. Plato is indeed granting to Aristophanes a position of historical importance.

With this second operation, the race is saved, but *only*, according to Aristophanes, thanks to the male-female originals, now heterosexuals.[12] Of the double males, now homosexuals, Aristophanes says rather abruptly that, when they join together 'at least they will get satiety (*plêsmonê*) from their union and stop (*diapauein*),[13] and return to their work and attend to the rest of life' (191c). About the double females now lesbians, he says nothing here, but presumably their situation would be similar to the male homosexuals: at least they would stop and get on with their lives. One can hear in these words quite clearly the preference that Aristophanes exhibits in his plays for heterosexuality and his suspicion of homosexuality. The heterosexuals literally save the race. The homosexuals will at least be satiated and stop.

'It is from this situation, then, that our natural *erôs* for each other developed in human beings' (191d). Aristophanes now makes explicit what is already implicit. *Erôs* is the natural (*emphytos*) desire for us in our split condition to join together and try to become whole again. Now we know why we take all those funny positions in our sexual experiences! We're trying to become whole beings again! Aristophanes' ribald comedy reaches its peak here. But underneath the hilarity, Aristophanes is again developing several remarkable points. First, for perhaps the first time in our literary tradition, he in fact presents a 'natural' – what we today call a 'genetic' – basis for sexual orientation. Our sexual orientation is not a 'lifestyle choice' – it is not 'sexual preference' – but a consequence of our original natures. Aristophanes thus legitimates, in the sense of 'makes natural' the three basic sexual orientations.[14] However, second, before this audience of almost exclusively homosexual men whose clear paradigm for *erôs* so far has been pederasty, Aristophanes seems to show a distinct preference for the male homosexual pairing and almost to denigrate the heterosexuals. He begins with the heterosexual pairings who, he has just quietly acknowledged, save the race. 'Those men who are split from the mixed nature, which was then called androgynous, are fond of women. Most adulterers come from this type, and those women who are fond of men and are adulteresses come from this type' (191e). Apparently appealing to the biases of the men present, Aristophanes mentions only the most negative instances of this pairing, failing to mention that from this group will also come the heterosexual couples who will save the race and whose lives he commends regularly if hilariously in his plays. Of the double females he simply mentions that they have no interest in men and become lesbians. But of the homosexual males he seems much more effusive. The passage is important enough to quote at length:

> Those who are split from the male pursue males. While they are boys, since they are a slice off the male, they are fond of men and enjoy lying with men and becoming entwined with them. These are the best of the boys and young men, and at the same time are the most manly in nature (*andreiotatoi ontes physei*). Anyone who says they are shameless is mistaken, for they do this not from shamelessness but from courage, manliness, and masculinity (*tharrous kai andreias kai arrenôpias*), welcoming what is like themselves. There is a definite proof of this: only men of this sort are completely successful in politics. When they become men, they are lovers of boys and by nature are not interested in marriage and having children, though they are forced into it by custom. They would be satisfied to live all the time with one another without marrying. This is certainly the sort of man who becomes a lover of boys, and as a boy is fond of such lovers, always welcoming a kinsman.
>
> 191e-192b

On the surface, this passage surely seems to praise the male homosexual type above the others, and so to be in strong contrast to the attitude exhibited by Aristophanes in his plays. But let us look more closely at this apparent praise, for I believe it is demonstrably ironic. First, he praises the double male pairing as distinguished by their 'manliness', then even more emphatically by their 'courage and manliness and masculinity'. All this while, sitting almost next to him, is the tragic poet Agathon, the beloved of Pausanias, who is so notoriously effeminate that Aristophanes himself has publicly mocked Agathon's effeminacy in his *Thesmophoriazusai*![15] Towards the end of his speech, Aristophanes will explicitly acknowledge that Pausanias and Agathon may be one of those natural male pairings who are 'both male by nature'! (193c). If so, to say the least, they hardly conform to his description here of the double males as 'courageous, manly, and masculine'! Much more likely, I suggest, that Plato's Aristophanes is continuing his mockery of Agathon that Aristophanes himself began in his play. In further support of this, Aristophanes adds that a 'proof' of their manliness is that when they become adults they successfully enter into politics. Yet even the most superficial consideration of Aristophanes' plays reveals clearly enough what he thinks of politicians! For him, they are a congress of scoundrels. Aristophanes can hardly be said to be praising the double males here! In sum, I submit that a careful reading of the irony of this passage makes clear that Plato is not having Aristophanes contradict his suspicion of homosexual *erôs* in his plays but rather sustaining it while at the same time ironically teasing the all-male and predominantly homosexual company he is keeping.

But much more is going on in this passage. Recall that Aristophanes had begun his speech by urging piety towards Eros and all the gods, and calling Eros the most philanthropic of the gods. Yet in the account he has just given of the origin of *erôs*, it is clear that *erôs* is an entirely *human* phenomenon! *Erôs* arises only after we have been rendered split beings, and is, as Aristophanes told us, the natural love for one another *among human beings* (191d). *Erôs* is thus the *human* desire to become whole again having been rendered incomplete. Yet at the beginning and the end of his speech, Aristophanes urges us to be pious towards the god Eros. But the core of his speech contains a very different teaching: *erôs* is not a god at all, but human nature after we are rendered incomplete. Just as in his plays, Aristophanes urges a piety and reverence for tradition that does not seem founded in a personal belief on his own part but is essentially 'pragmatic', so here, Plato, by having Aristophanes preach piety and reverence towards the god Eros at the beginning and end of his speech but present a very different teaching at the core of his speech, stays true to the complicated relation in his plays between what he believes it is best for 'the many' to believe and what he seems to believe personally. We may say that in both cases, Aristophanes' 'conservatism' is a *pragmatic* conservatism.

Perhaps most importantly, the passage we are considering presents a teaching concerning human erotic nature that implicitly at least goes far beyond the narrow focus of Aristophanes' actual account. Clearly, Aristophanes wants us to understand *erôs* as the human desire to join together with our original halves. It is thus a ribald explanation of our sexual behaviour. But as Aristophanes himself acknowledges a little later in his speech (192c), it is not *just* sexual behaviour that he is describing, but something else. As Aristophanes goes on to develop it, *erôs* seems to include something like a kinship of two souls, who want to spend their lives together. But let us see if his account of *erôs* cannot be generalized far more broadly, perhaps more broadly than even Aristophanes might want to acknowledge.

Human *erôs* as Aristophanes describes it seems to have three 'moments'. First, what might be called the 'ontological' moment is our present human condition as incomplete. We humans *are* as incomplete, partial. But second, humans *recognize* or *experience* that incompleteness. Rocks and trees may be incomplete too, but they are not erotic because they do not *suffer* that incompleteness, it is not an experience for them. Third, our *erôs* leads us humans to *respond* to that recognition of incompleteness by striving for wholeness. Being incomplete, recognizing that incompleteness, responding by striving for wholeness: implicit in this teaching is an account of all human aspiration as such. We might be and experience an incompleteness of wealth and strive for a fortune; that is our *erôs*. We might experience an incompleteness of political power and run for public office; that too is our *erôs*. Or, decisively, we might experience an incompleteness of *wisdom* and strive for wisdom; that is virtually definitive of Socratic philosophy, founded as it is in *aporia,* the recognition of the incompleteness of our knowledge and the striving for the wholeness of wisdom. I cite the last two examples pointedly: Aristophanes' account of *erôs* contains implicitly an account of human aspirations that Aristophanes himself may find dubious and may well even want to suppress, as he does in his plays. Plato's account here allows us to see something of the precarious complexity of Aristophanes' teaching. His insightful account of the human condition as erotic contains manifestations that Aristophanes himself finds dangerous and in need of control. He seems to want to allow only certain, relatively harmless manifestations of *erôs* to thrive – paradigmatically, personal love between (preferably) heterosexual humans who will get married, have children, and spend their lives together quietly and piously. But given the very nature of *erôs*, how can its manifestations be thus limited?

So far, Aristophanes' speech has certainly been comic in a certain sense. His hilarious account of the real source of our sexual unions should raise a good laugh with anyone. We have just seen that his implicit teaching has much more far reaching consequences that may point to a comic or a tragic view of the human situation. But nothing yet is explicit. In the rest of his speech, from 192c on, Aristophanes now makes explicit certain consequences of our erotic situation that bring to the fore these tragic and comic implications.

Aristophanes imagines (192c ff) two lovers who find their other halves and are overwhelmed with their 'friendship, intimacy and love', and do not want to be separated even for a moment – something perhaps like the 'love at first sight' experience. These are people, he says, 'who spend their entire lives with each other, *though they cannot say what it is that they want from each other*'.[16] He acknowledges that it cannot be simply sexual desire that motivates this intense feeling. 'On the contrary, it is clear that the soul of each wants something, *what it is it cannot say, but speaks prophetically and in riddles*'.[17]

Human beings do not know themselves. Their deepest experiences, indeed, their very natures as erotic, remain an unfathomable mystery to them. The pessimism about the human situation that we saw in Aristophanes' plays comes back in spades in the speech that Plato has Aristophanes present. Self-knowledge is impossible for humans on Aristophanes' view. We shall see presently that Socrates will be, in an appropriately qualified way, considerably more optimistic on this account than Aristophanes, and the reason why will have everything to do with what is missing in Aristophanes' speech.

As a replacement for our inability to know ourselves, Aristophanes recommends, not surprisingly, religion. If the Olympian god Hephaestus should come upon two such lovers, Aristophanes surmises, and ask them whether what they wanted was to be joined together so that they would spend their entire lives as one and even experience a common death, none would refuse but 'they would think they had discovered what they had really desired all along' (192e). Humans need the gods, need religion, to make sense of themselves. Religion furnishes us with answers regarding our natures and deepest experiences that we cannot attain on our own. Again we see the 'pragmatic' foundation of Aristophanes' affirmation of religious piety. And again, we shall see that Plato has his Socrates – under the tutelage of Diotima – furnish us with the basis for a more optimistic view of the human situation, both regarding self-knowledge and in other ways.

But the situation for humans, on Aristophanes' account, proves even more dire. As he nears the peroration of his speech, Aristophanes expresses an even more profound pessimism about the human situation. Beginning with what turns out to be an unfulfillable promise, Aristophanes first urges us to 'perfect love, and everyone must find their own beloved, thereby returning to our original nature'. But then he adds, '*If this is what is best, then the nearest thing to that is necessarily the best in the present circumstances, and that is to happen upon (tychein) a beloved who is suited naturally to one's own mind*'.[18] Aristophanes is here acknowledging an empirically verifiable result of his view that has profound consequences: after the first generation of split humans, we are *born* split, and *therefore no longer have a true 'other half' with whom to join*. Hence, 'under the present circumstances', that is, *without* a natural or original other half, the best we can hope to do is find a compatible mate – presumably one with a matching sexual orientation – settle down and try to behave ourselves.

What we desire in our deepest natures, what indeed it is our very nature to desire – a return to true wholeness with our original other half – we can no longer attain. Aristophanes' account places humans almost in the classic tragic situation: we do not and cannot know ourselves, but our natures are such that we are fated – by nature – to desire and strive after what we cannot have. Given our lack of self-knowledge, our striving after impossible goals will almost certainly end in . . . is it tragedy? Comedy? The only possible way to avoid this, says Aristophanes, is to take Pindar's advice: 'strive not to be a god'.[19] Get married, settle down, have a family, live a quiet, peaceful live and stay out of trouble.

To decide whether in the end Aristophanes' position is comic, tragic, or both, we must turn briefly to certain aspects of Socrates' speech which will furnish us the wherewithal, I think, to venture a response. Let us begin with the question of self-knowledge. As we have seen, Aristophanes claims in the speech Plato gives him that self-knowledge is impossible. Socrates, as always in a complicated way, is somewhat more optimistic about this possibility. In the *Apology,* Socrates develops perhaps his most famous statement of his self-knowledge in terms of his *aporia.* The reputed wise men whom he questions, as he discovers when he questions them, are not wise. This becomes for Socrates the definitive stance of real ignorance: thinking one knows what one does not. We might say that 'true ignorance', then, is not merely not knowing; it is, more strongly, thinking that one knows what one does not. The difference is crucial: not knowing, but *recognizing* that one does not know, can be the impetus to overcoming our lack. Thinking that one knows what one does not is inertial: there is no impetus, when one thinks one knows but does not, to overcome one's ignorance. Thus, Socrates decides that he is 'a little wiser' (*Apology* 21d) than these reputed wise ones insofar as he *recognizes* that he is not wise, and so strives to become wiser. Socrates, to state the implications of his *aporia* more positively, knows what he knows and what he does not know. This 'human wisdom', as he calls it (*Apology,* 20d), is manifestly a mode of self-knowledge, and to the extent that Socrates – or anyone for that matter – comprehensively knows what he or she does and does not know, it is a remarkable self-knowledge indeed. But it is important to understand its foundation; Socratic self-knowledge is founded in, and so is a manifestation of, his *aporia.* A brief consideration of this *aporia,* however, reveals something most remarkable: *aporia* is obviously located in our situation as *lacking* knowledge, our recognition of that lack, and so our subsequent effort to overcome that lack. But this is the very structure of *erôs* as we saw it in Aristophanes' account! Socratic *aporia,* and so Socratic self-knowledge, is thus itself a manifestation of *erôs.* Socrates himself draws out this implication in his brief dialogue with Agathon at the beginning of Socrates' speech. *Erôs,* Socrates shows Agathon, is always *of* something, and of something that it *lacks* (*Symposium,* 200b). Moreover, *erôs* is the *desire* for the possession of that which it lacks (200b). Not only is Aristophanes wrong to deny the possibility of self-knowledge; at least as Socrates understands it, the very possibility of self-knowledge is founded in the very *erôs* that Aristophanes is describing, though in a manifestation – philosophy – of which Aristophanes is deeply suspicious!

But, as Socrates' speech shows, there is an even stronger basis for his qualified optimism regarding the possibility of self-knowledge. In his supposed conversation with Diotima, Socrates at one point asks her, rather strangely, who *erôs*' parents are. Diotima responds with her mythical account of *erôs*' parentage: his mother was *Penia* ('poverty', 'lack') and his father *Poros* ('plenty', 'resourcefulness') (203b ff). This myth almost by itself constitutes a counter-myth, a 'critique' of Aristophanes' position. That *erôs*' mother is Penia nicely captures Aristophanes' account of *erôs* as characterized by incompleteness, by lack. He is surely right about this, as Socrates' brief dialogue with Agathon has already established 'logically'. But he is literally only half right! What Aristophanes misses is *erôs*' paternity, that he is also the child of Poros, of Plenty, of Resourcefulness.[20] This means that Aristophanes misses or cannot see the element of fullness, of positive power, in *erôs* that modifies or mitigates its undoubted element of incompleteness. Struck only by *erôs*' incompleteness, its lack, Aristophanes has too pessimistic an attitude regarding *erôs* and so human nature, fails to see its more positive capacity that would derive from its father. Or so Diotima's account would teach.

But something else is shown to be missing from Aristophanes' account that will prove to be of decisive importance for the question of whether his speech is comic or tragic: *kallos*, 'nobility' or 'beauty'. It comes as a stunning recognition that Aristophanes' is the only speech in the entire *Symposium* that does not so much as mention *kallos*. The word or any of its cognates is missing entirely from his speech and his speech alone. The issue of the intimate connection of *erôs* and beauty is developed by Agathon in his speech about to follow, and it plays a role in each of the speeches previous to Aristophanes. To be sure, Socrates and Diotima will significantly modify the connection that Agathon formulates, but nevertheless preserve the intimate connection between *erôs* and beauty or nobility. *Erôs*, Socrates will eventually be told by Diotima, desires to give birth in the beautiful (206b), and it must be profoundly significant that in the famous ascent passage of the young Socrates up to a form (210 ff), the form Diotima chooses is *not* 'Eros itself', 'the form *erôs*', but rather 'beauty itself'. And in perhaps the most striking passage in this regard, Diotima at one point unmistakably refers to Aristophanes speech, correcting him by observing that *erôs* cannot simply be the desire to become whole, for people will even cut off a part of themselves if they believe that doing so will be *good*.[21] This is precisely what is missing from Aristophanes' speech: goodness or beauty.

But if there is nothing of beauty or nobility in *erôs* and so in human life for Aristophanes, how can it be tragic? For surely a sine qua non of tragedy for the Greeks was that tragic experience contains an element of nobility. One difference between the comic demise of a comic fool like Strepsiades (or Aristophanes' Socrates) and the demise of a tragic hero like Oedipus or Antigone is surely an element of nobility in the latter pair. The Antigones and Oedipuses of Greek tragedy may fail and fail miserably in their intentions, they may or may not have a 'tragic flaw'; but there always remains something noble – and so for the Greeks, something beautiful – about their 'tragic' striving. This is no doubt why, as has often enough been observed, the heroes and heroines of Greek tragedy tend to come from 'nobility', whereas Aristophanes' comic figures tend to be more ordinary citizens.

What, then, might we venture regarding the question of whether Aristophanes' account is comic or tragic? The first important feature of Aristophanes' speech, I would suggest, is that it brings the question of the tragic or comic character of human life to the fore, and does so in such a way as to bring the two into an intimate connection. In his account of the human erotic situation as radically incomplete and as desiring a return to wholeness or completeness which it can never in the end attain, as well as in his account of humans as lacking – among other things – the self-knowledge to even adequately know what it desires and what it is doing, Aristophanes includes in his account many of the basic features of a tragic understanding of human life. But one crucial feature is missing, and that is the element of beauty, of nobility, that from time to time can characterize human erotic striving, even an erotic striving that is fated to fail. Aristophanes, both in his plays and in the speech that Plato gives him, seems unimpressed by or even oblivious to the element of beauty, of nobility, that characterizes for the Greeks tragic striving and even tragic failing. For this reason, in his speech in the *Symposium*, Aristophanes remains a comic poet, even if one whose position contains many of the ingredients of tragic experience within it.

At the beginning of this chapter, I referred in passing to the well-known line at the end of the *Symposium* in which Socrates is portrayed convincing Aristophanes and Agathon that the same person who can write a comedy can also write a tragedy. It may be possible, that is, to portray – at once and perhaps as a unity – the tragic and the comic character of human life and so of philosophy. Perhaps so; but this dialogue – and this chapter – suggests that the person who could do so will not be Aristophanes (nor, surely, will it be Agathon). Who then would do so? Can it be other than the author of the philosophic works of art, the tragicomic works of art, that are the Platonic dialogues? A question for another paper, for which, hopefully, this paper has been a partial preparation.

Notes

1 This text was originally published in *Norsk filosofisk tidsskrift* 48, no. 1 (2013): 6–18. Universitetsforlaget, Oslo, DOI: 10.18261/issn.1504-2901. https://www.idunn.no/nft/2013/01/the_whole_comedy_and_tragedy_of_philosophy_on_aristophanes.
2 Plato, *Philebus*, in *Platonis Opera*, volume II, edited by John Burnet (Oxford: Clarendon Press, 1946), 50b. Unless otherwise indicated, all translations in this chapter are my own.
3 For the application of this to the question of beauty, see my *Plato and the Question of Beauty* (Indianapolis: Indiana University Press, 2008).
4 To follow, as it were, the Aristotelian path for the pursuit of learning.
5 I say 'supposedly' because, as we shall see, neither in his plays nor in his speech in the *Symposium* is Aristophanes an unqualified affirmer of *erôs*, especially in its 'higher' manifestations.
6 Two excellent more detailed studies of the philosophic significance of Aristophanes are Leo Strauss' *Socrates and Aristophanes* (New York: Basic Books, 1966), and Bernard Freydberg's *Philosophy and Comedy: Aristophanes, Logos, and Erôs* (Bloomington: Indiana University Press, 2008). In important ways, these two insightful readings disagree with each other, and I shall disagree in various ways with each.

7   The trace of this view that remains in modern conservatism is that most conservatives advocate 'law and order' policies.
8   Strauss, *Socrates and Aristophanes*, points this out regularly in his analysis of the plays.
9   That and why their aspirations become more problematic constitutes the comedy of the play.
10 Aristophanes, *Birds*, in *Aristophanes 1: Clouds, Wasps, Birds*, translated by Peter Meineck (Indianapolis: Hackett Publishing, 1998), 696ff.
11 Aristophanes, *Birds*, line 754–5. See Strauss' *Socrates and Aristophanes*, 170–2, for Strauss' account of this origin, which ignores the implications of tyranny.
12 This may be interpreting a myth too far, but one problem with Aristophanes' myth here is that on the thesis of a 'natural' sexual orientation, always passed on through procreation, should not homosexuals have died out by now? My thanks to Kristin Sampson for this point.
13 The *dia* strengthens the force of the verb. *Liddell and Scott English Lexicon* says 'make to cease utterly. pass. To cease to exist.'
14 This is of course Plato's doing. I find no indication of this in Aristophanes' plays.
15 Aristophanes, *Thesmophoriazusai*, in *Aristophanes: The Eleven Comedies*, anonymous translator, volume II (New York: Tudor Publishing Company, no date), 273–336. In the play, Euripides, fearing that he is about to be punished by the assembly of women, tries to convince Agathon to go among the women and spy on them, the assumption being that Agathon is so effeminate that the women will not recognize that he is a man!
16 Plato, *Symposium*, 192c, my emphasis.
17 Plato, *Symposium*, 192d, my emphasis.
18 Plato, *Symposium*, 193c, my emphasis.
19 Pindar, *Olympian Ode 5*, in *The Odes of Pindar*, translated by Richmond Lattimore (Chicago: University of Chicago Press, 1947), 14.
20 Agathon in his speech is also half-right, but in the other direction. He sees only *erôs*' fullness, not its incompleteness. It should also be noted that – against Pausanias – this myth portrays Eros' parentage as *heterosexual*. But these are topics for another paper.
21 Plato, *Symposium*, 205e. To be sure, at the end of Socrates' speech (212c), Aristophanes tries to respond to something that Socrates said in his speech, but is interrupted by the entrance of Alcibiades, who changes everything. This is a 'Platonic provocation' if ever there was one: we are invited to reflect on how Aristophanes might try to respond to Socrates' account of *erôs*.

Bibliography

Aristophanes. *Aristophanes 1: Clouds, Wasps, Birds*. Translated by Peter Meineck. Indianapolis: Hackett Publishing, 1998.

Aristophanes. *Aristophanes: The Eleven Comedies*. Anonymous translator. Vol. II. New York: Tudor Publishing Company [no date].

Freydberg, Bernard. *Philosophy and Comedy: Aristophanes, Logos, and Erôs*. Bloomington: Indiana University Press, 2008.

Hyland, Drew. *Plato and the Question of Beauty*. Indianapolis: Indiana University Press, 2008.

Pindar. *The Odes of Pindar*. Translated by Richmond Lattimore. Chicago: University of Chicago Press, 1947.

Plato. *Apology.* In *Platonis Opera,* volume I, edited by John Burnet. Oxford: Clarendon Press, 1946.

Plato. *Philebus.* In *Platonis Opera,* volume II, edited by John Burnet. Oxford: Clarendon Press, 1946.

Plato. *Republic.* In *Platonic Opera,* volume IV, edited by John Burnet. Oxford: Clarendon Press, 1946.

Plato. *Symposium.* In *Platonis Opera,* volume II, edited by John Burnet. Oxford: Clarendon Press, 1946.

Strauss, Leo. *Socrates and Aristophanes.* New York: Basic Books, 1966.

2

A Praise of the Philosophical Written Speech? Ethics and Philosophical Progression in Plato's *Symposium*[1]

Elena Irrera

So if the way round is a long one, don't be surprised;
for it is for the sake of great things that the journey is to be made,
not for those you have in mind.

Plato, *Phaedrus* 274a2-4[2]

Plato's choice of the written dialogue as a suitable medium of philosophical communication has received a vast amount of scholarly attention over the past four decades, especially with regard to the nature of its specific contribution to our understanding of his thought. The themes he addresses in his written speeches are developed along paths of fictional conversations between Socrates and the characters he cross-examines,[3] conversations in which Plato himself seems to play an active role as a 'hidden', external interlocutor. By employing a rich battery of dramatic devices, ranging from his personal *mimêsis* of the characters to a number of ironic remarks put into Socrates' mouth, he virtually interacts with the fictional voices staged in his dialogues without using them as mouthpieces for the expression of his own stances.[4] Viewed from this perspective, then, the Platonic dialogue might appear as one whose main subjects are the philosopher and the characters he fictionalizes.

An alternative way of looking at Plato's dialogues is to understand them as forms of dialectical interaction whose protagonists are Plato's written speeches and his readers. A similar interpretive approach is premised on the assumption that written speeches ought to be considered as alive interlocutors rather than as inanimate documents, and that through them Plato invites the readers to critically engage with issues of high philosophical import.[5] In this chapter I shall adopt this approach as a guiding framework for a reading of one specific dialogue: the *Symposium*. My most general contention is that the dialogue at stake proves eminently suitable for shedding light on Plato's concern for the dialectic potentialities of the philosophical written speech. I shall suggest that the literary structure of the *Symposium* and some of its content-related points, particularly those referring to beauty and education, convey the idea of the Platonic dialogue as a 'self-defending' *logos*, i.e. one able to progressively flourish in the soul of those readers who approach the written text.[6] More specifically, by way of comparative analysis between the *Symposium* and the *Phaedrus*, I will propose that, throughout some of the eulogies of Eros[7] uttered in the *Symposium*, Plato enables his readers to autonomously establish an analogy between several distinctive features of *erôs* and a number of properties which in the *Phaedrus* are said to belong to a well-crafted philosophical writing.

In this chapter I will focus on some relevant aspects of the first three encomiastic speeches on Love and show how each of them, followed by the two speeches uttered respectively by the poets Aristophanes and Agathon, pave the way for the content of Socrates' account of Eros, i.e. a speech inclusive of Diotima's revelations. I will propose that the picture of *erôs* which takes shape throughout the whole dialogue (a) is inextricably linked to the concept of 'progression', both ethical and intellectual, towards the forms of beauty and goodness; (b) presents features which can be attributed also to the literary form adopted by Plato. The *Symposium*, in other words, would represent a paradigmatic case of a dialogue in which arguments, although *prima facie* unrelated to the issue of philosophical writing, offer significant clues about the nature and philosophical import of written speeches.

Love of honour in Phaedrus' speech: a stepping stone to love of virtue

The *Symposium*, one of Plato's best known and most influential dialogues, is an account of a banquet hosted by the tragic poet Agathon to celebrate his first victory at one of the two main Athenian dramatic contests, an event in which Socrates takes part alongside a comedy writer, a physician and two rhetoricians. The setting of the dialogue, the characters and their interlocking claims revolve around a well-defined central core: the nature of *erôs* and its effects on nature and human beings. However, as the reader gradually realizes, a complex constellation of themes enervates the dialogue, and their possible theoretical connections pave the way for increasingly deeper levels of interpretation. Through this written work, Plato suggests that an event like a symposium can be turned from a valueless amusement to a serious philosophical experience for those who participate in it. We might suppose that the narrative itself, as a good philosophical speech, becomes a delightful learning opportunity for Plato's readers. The series of eulogies crafted by the author sets them in the direction of a more profound understanding of human nature, happiness and the role played by philosophical *erôs* in the achievement of the latter ideal.

The first eulogy of love reported in the dialogue is the one delivered by Phaedrus, a character who, in other Platonic dialogues, is depicted as a learner in the field of rhetoric and an enthusiastic lover of speeches.[8] The language employed in his description of Eros and the very structure of his encomiastic speech express a cultural setting whose central tenet is the importance of honour in human life. For instance, at *Symposium* 178a6-7 we see Phaedrus presenting Eros as 'great and marvellous' (*megas . . . kai thaumastos*); a little later, he calls him most worthy of honour (*timiôtaton*,

180b2). He thus employs attributes used in laudatory speeches or epic poetry of the noblest and most audacious warriors.[9]

Despite this, Phaedrus' speech does not seem to be purely conventional,[10] for he enthusiastically presents *erôs* as a powerful motivation for virtuous action, a source that transcends mere desire for external recognition. This emerges at 178c5-d1, where we learn that the search for public honours cannot compete with Eros in inspiring virtuous human agency:

> What it is that should guide (*hêgeisthai*) human beings who mean to live beautifully (*kalôs*), in their whole lives: this, nothing – not kinship, or public honours, or wealth, or anything else – is capable of implanting (*empoiein*) so well (*houtô kalôs*) as love can.[11]

This passage, besides suggesting a devaluation of honour as a source of human agency, contains two points of interest. First, Plato seems to set the stage for later articulating a goal: living *beautifully*. As the conclusion of Phaedrus' speech will show more clearly (180b6-9), this goes along with a happy life, that is, one intimately linked to virtue. Second, Eros possesses an unparalleled excellence: instilling an efficient *guiding principle* for those who desire to live in a beautiful manner. Remarkably, Eros is not described as a guiding principle for human beings; he is rather presented as a force able to implant the criteria of good conduct in those beings who set the beautiful life as their ultimate goal. Should Eros guide them directly, the individuals steered by him would be prevented from acting autonomously and directing their emotional and intellectual inclinations towards happiness. In other words, should Eros be their principle of correct conduct, there would be no need of either ethical or philosophical education for human beings. Phaedrus proposes meaningful examples of the way in which love stimulates lovers to the accomplishment of beautiful deeds. He appeals to the cases of Alcestis, who sacrifices her own life for the sake of her husband's survival (179b5-d2), and to Achilles, who avenges the death of his beloved Patroclus at the cost of renouncing the privilege of immortality (179e1-180a4). As Plato puts it via Phaedrus' voice, Alcestis, although compelled by love, *willingly* (*ethelêsasa*, 179b7) *undertook* to die.[12] Plato's choice of the verb *ethelein* might suggest that the erotic passion which drives the woman affects and guides her deliberative capacity by infusing an appropriate sort of motivation for her actions, without forcing or overwhelming it. Similarly, Achilles, although moved by an unrestrained impulse for revenge, *dared to choose* (*etolmêsen helesthai*, 179e4) to go to his lover Patroclus' aid and avenge him.[13] Eros drives human beings by allowing them to draw on a variety of resources and options when engaged in action. If men and women must themselves decide, and love acts only as a motivating force, then the kind of love mentioned in 178c5-d1, which should guide those who want to live beautifully, will implant in them the seeds of virtuous activity. It is their own responsibility to bring such seeds to maturity.

In none of the examples advanced by Phaedrus do the protagonists seem to act out of love of honour, even though their noble actions receive human and godly praise. The remainder of his eulogy, however, contains clues suggesting that Phaedrus views honour as the ultimate goal of human action. For instance, just after claiming that honour cannot compete with love in the promotion of the beautiful life, Phaedrus identifies living 'beautifully' with practicing *philotimia* in respect of beautiful things, that is, with an ambitious desire for distinguishing oneself in the pursuit of fine deeds. Such a desire is inseparable from a sense of shame about performing bad actions, that is, shame at actions that might provoke censure in those who observe and assess them. As he makes clear at 178d1-4,

> [W]hat is it that I refer to? The feeling of shame at shameful things (*tên epi men toîs aischroîs aischynên*), and love of honour in the case of fine ones (*epi de toîs kaloîs philotimian*); without these it is impossible for either a city or an individual to enact great and fine actions.

At this stage of Phaedrus' speech, desire for self-distinction and recognition of one's fine actions outshines love of virtue in itself, and the beautiful things mentioned here are pursued only out of love of honour. This approach appears starkly at odds with the previous reference to Eros as a source of motivation and guiding principle for a 'beautiful life' distinguished from honour. Is Phaedrus offering two incompatible accounts of basic human motivation?

We can resolve the puzzle by hypothesizing that, within one and the same eulogy, two different voices can be traced, namely that of Phaedrus and that of Plato. Despite their differences, the view championing honour as the content of human happiness and the one defending the primacy of virtue can be reconciled by assuming that one's love for honour and sense of shame, when stimulated and nurtured by erotic love, set human beings on the correct road to virtue. Those who cultivate feelings of love will not only avoid mutual injustice, but will even perform good deeds. If the same motivational principles of action could be extended, reciprocal love among citizens, both rulers and ruled, might set the city on the road to virtuous political life and the wellbeing of all its members. This seems to be the import of Phaedrus' image of the city as an 'army of lovers':

> So if in some way it could be brought about that there was a city, or an army, of lovers and their beloveds, there is nothing that would enable them to govern their country better than their abstention from all shameful things and their rivalry with each other in pursuit of honour, and if they actually fought alongside each other, such men – even a few of them – could overcome practically all human opponents. A man in love would surely find it less acceptable to be seen either breaking ranks or throwing his arms away by a beloved than by anyone else, and rather than have that happen he would choose to die many times over.
>
> 178e3-179a5

The passage above, which resonates strongly with epic poetry,[14] expresses a crucial concept: reciprocal shame can form a principle of community for a group of people whose members, although performing different roles, operate with a view to a shared end.[15] With the inspiring support of Eros, reciprocal concern might be strengthened and pursued with less effort. If we apply this principle to the civic sphere, as Plato himself is asking his readers to do, shame and the risk of losing one's own honour might be adopted as educational values conditioning virtuous action.[16]

Through Phaedrus' speech, then, Plato makes accessible to his readers a specific way of thinking about moral beauty: one that, although rooted in the cultural code of honour, competition and military zeal, can at the same time be conceived as a stimulus of the soul to virtue. As shown at 178c5-d1, beauty appears connected to a distinctively human way of life, one led according to virtue, the prospect of which moves individuals to action. Beauty is introduced as a normative ideal, the mark of correct action. By stimulating individuals particularly sensitive to the sense of honour and shame, *erôs* becomes the occasion for virtuous human deeds.

From a different perspective, the first eulogy of love reveals Plato's ability as a philosophic writer. Concern for honour might be viewed as a suitable rhetorical platform for the practical worth of *erôs* and its role in the human achievement of *aretê* and of *eudaimonia*. By establishing a preliminary connection between beauty and honour in Phaedrus' speech, Plato manages to guide certain readers, specifically those sensitive to the lure of honour, towards the understanding of a philosophically richer and more complex *logos*. He seems to follow the prescriptions Socrates addresses to would-be rhetoricians at *Phaedrus* 271a3-272b2, where the power of speech is identified as a leading of the soul (*psychagôgia*, 271c9). A true expert in rhetoric must know not only how many forms the soul has, but also what people of differing kinds might find persuasive, so as to connect successfully each type of speech to the corresponding kind of soul (271b1-5). When an orator is able to match the most appropriate literary style to particular occasions, his craft is practised 'in a beautiful and accomplished fashion' (*kalôs te kai teleôs*, 272a7).

Socrates' aim, however (like Plato's), is not to persuade any and every reader. As he explains in the *Phaedrus* by way of an agricultural metaphor, there are speeches crafted by individuals in possession of the science of the just, the beautiful and the good (276c3-5). Such people, being keen on planting the seeds they most care for, will select the most suitable soil – that is, human souls – in the hope that such seeds bear fruit for them (276b1-d8). Just as Eros implants (*empoiein*) a guiding principle in lovers without acting as the principle itself, so the author of philosophical speeches sows seeds of knowledge and virtue in the soul of well-inclined readers, leaving them free to grow and be turned into a process of human development towards the good. Speeches of this kind are very different from those written discourses which have just an appearance of life, such as those that, being asked something by the reader, preserve a solemn silence (275d4-9). This does not necessarily mean, however, that only oral discourses can be 'fruitful' speeches. For, a serious composer of speeches will sow (*speirein*) and write 'literary gardens' (276d1-2), that is, gardens which, even when composed for amusement, enable anyone who is following the same track to be pleased as he watches their fresh growth.[17] It is in this respect that some of the powers attributed to Eros in the first eulogy of the *Symposium* might resonate with properties that, elsewhere, Plato presents as characteristic of well-crafted philosophical writings. Just like Eros, who is endowed with the power to stimulate men to virtuous agency, the Platonic dialogue is able to activate in philosophically receptive readers a reflection on the worth and the benefits of moral virtue. By offering original insights on beauty and moral education against the background of a well-known cultural horizon, Plato establishes a solid basis for philosophical dialogue between his readers and the *Symposium* itself, a discussion that will lead them to believe that happiness, virtue and beauty rise over and above the value of honour. Thus, already in the first eulogy of love we find nested a positive evaluation of the art of philosophical dialogue and its function.

Pausanias' speech: beauty as a way of acting

Pausanias' speech reflects on some problematic elements in Phaedrus' eulogy. His initial words do not seem to betray any inclination to mockery or sterile criticism.[18] Rather, he emphasizes the limits of Phaedrus' speech with a view to offering a chance for the discussion on the nature and the effects of *erôs* to progress, allowing the question of love to be explored in a properly philosophical, not simply encomiastic manner.[19] Like the eulogy delivered by Phaedrus, Pausanias' speech presupposes a specific cultural framework, focused on the social ethos of homosexuality as observed in Athens in particular.[20] Plato means to evoke a context that, being familiar to his contemporary readers, is particularly well suited to his aim of sowing the seeds of persuasion in them. His real centre of interest seems to be the 'beautiful way' of acting,[21] such as loving an individual or composing a speech. At 180c4-d1 Pausanias points out that Phaedrus has spoken about Eros in a univocal way, making unjustified generalizations. Phaedrus fails to speak in a beautiful way ('our subject seems to me not to have been put forward *kalôs*') due to failing to distinguish between a vulgar, mundane love and a celestial one (180d5-e2). By asserting that there are two kinds of love Pausanias does not say that there is a love endowed with a sexual component and another deprived of it. Rather, through the voice of Pausanias, Plato makes a different, yet crucial distinction: just as a sexual relationship is not bad or vulgar by itself, so actions by themselves are neither fine nor shameful. What makes an action fine is *the way* in which it is accomplished:[22]

> Every action is like this: when done, in and by itself it is neither fine nor shameful. So for example with what we are doing now. Whether we drink, or sing, or talk to each other, none of these things is in itself fine, but rather the manner in which it is done is what determines how it turns out, in the doing of it; if it is done in a fine way (*kalôs*), and correctly, it becomes fine, and if incorrectly, shameful. This is how it is with loving and with Love: not all of Love is fine, or a worthy object of encomium – only the Love who impels us to love in a fine way.
>
> 181a1-7

The 'beautiful way' of acting is connected to the human capacity to distinguish a celestial love from a vulgar one,[23] and the first should be chosen for the sake of its positive effects on the development of intelligence and an education to virtue. Unlike heterosexual love, which Pausanias connects to sheer carnal desire, homosexual love gives lovers opportunity for avoiding immoderation. He insists that the Love who belongs to 'Common Aphrodite' carries through with anything that happens to come his way, and that his is the love experienced by inferior people (*hoi phauloi*) (181a8-b3), people unable to discriminate between goodness and badness. To the contrary, the Love belonging to 'Heavenly Aphrodite' has no portion of lawlessness (*hybreôs amoirou*, 181c4).

In this way, Pausanias indirectly introduces the topic of moderation, which in Plato's thought emerges as a decisive virtue for the acquisition of knowledge and justice.[24] Those who are inspired by an *erôs* of such a kind long by nature for those who are stronger and more intelligent. This is why a lover (*erastês*) should never love young boys whose personality has not reached full maturity.[25] Of course, individuals who are already good spontaneously lay down this law for themselves; but the same sort of thing ought to be imposed on vulgar lovers too, so that they are prevented from displaying conduct that is shameful (181e3-182a3).

What emerges from Pausanias' speech is the idea that the power of laws is not merely coercive, but conducive to stability of mind and capacity for discrimination. Both lovers, who ought not to choose non-virtuous young boys, and the beloved boys themselves, who in their relationship to a temperate and wise lover find an opportunity for ethical and intellectual growth, must follow the path implied by the above distinctions. By examining the different kinds of laws in force in various parts of Greece, Pausanias shows that there is no universally recognized law, and also that not just any law can educate to virtue. The Athenian law, which Pausanias presents as the most righteous, prescribes it a beautiful thing for lovers to love openly, providing that one should love those who are exceedingly noble and good, even when physically less appealing (182d3-e1). Moreover, the beloved should confer his favours in a beautiful way (183d5-e3), that is, by following the rules inspired by the dictates of intelligence and temperance. As Pausanias declares, such a practice

> in and by itself is neither fine nor shameful (*oute kalon oute aischron*), but it is, rather, fine if it is done in a fine way, and shameful if done in a shameful way. Doing it shamefully consists in granting favour to a disreputable person and in a disreputable way, while doing it finely consists in granting favours to a person of the right sort (*chrêstô*) and in a fine way.
>
> 183d5-8

The beautiful way of loving, then, includes both the choice of a lover on whom it is proper to confer one's favours and the adoption of a particular attitude towards the chosen lover. The choice of the lover and the way of conceding favours are not necessarily connected to goodness, and the risk of loving in a shameful way is high, especially when the dispositions of character of young are not well trained. This is why fathers who care for the education of their *own* sons will entrust them to pedagogues, men tasked with accompanying and protecting them on their outings. What is needed is a type of education able to promote a 'beautiful way of acting', that is, one that develops and strengthens virtue of character. An explicit confirmation of Pausanias' concern for virtue is offered at 184b7-c7, where we learn that, if a beloved is to grant favours to a lover in a beautiful way, only one route is left by the rules in force in Athens: to adhere to a sort of 'slavery' that relates virtue:

> For it is our considered view that if someone wishes to be of service to someone because he thinks that through him he will be a better person, as measured by some kind of wisdom, or by any other part of excellence whatever, this kind of voluntary slavery is not shameful, nor is it obsequiousness.

Unlike Phaedrus' speech, in which the educational power of *erôs* seems to concern the lover rather than the beloved, Pausanias' eulogy pictures *erôs* as an educational force both for lovers and their beloveds:

> These two rules – the one about the loving of boys, and the one about the pursuit of wisdom, and about the other parts of excellence – need to be combined into one, if the beloved's granting of favours to the lover is to turn out a fine thing.
>
> 184c7-d4

The beautiful way of loving spelled out by Pausanias presents both connections relevant to, and points of analogy with, the art of philosophical writing as discussed by Socrates in the *Phaedrus*. In the first place,

> this much [...] is clear to everyone, that in itself, at least, writing speeches is not something shameful [...] what is shameful, I think, is speaking and writing not in an acceptable way, but shamefully and badly.
>
> 258d1-5

Given that not every speech is beautiful, it is necessary to consider in what way it is acceptable to make and write a speech, and in what way it is not (259e1-4). Socrates allows for the possibility of making speeches *in a beautiful way* (see *Phaedrus* 259e1-2).[26] An indispensable precondition for the successful accomplishment of such a task is the author's authentic knowledge of truth concerning the things discussed in the speech (*Phaedrus* 259e4-6; 260d3-9). A speech written in a beautiful way should not simply instil persuasion in the many, but also indicate a road to authentic goodness. In the second place, Pausanias' speech makes us aware of the importance of a correct assessment of the *erastês* by those who mean to grant favours in a beautiful way. Similarly, a valid author of speeches will not aim to please the multitude by offering them a deceitful appearance of what is just (cf. *Phaedrus* 259e7-260a4); on the contrary, he will try to speak to people well-prepared to understand authentic justice. This implies that a good speech, as Socrates points out, would carry an intrinsic awareness of those with whom it should communicate and of those with whom it should not (*Phaedrus* 276a1-7). This holds true even of written discourses. As already shown, Plato does not condemn any and every written speech in itself. So some of them may be endowed with the capacity to stimulate and guide the reader towards knowledge and virtue. Having the power to 'tap' the reader's mental energy and use it for the improvement of his or her philosophic discernment,[27] the written philosophical speech can be viewed as a *paidagôgos* able to set the reader on the correct road to virtue and philosophy.

Eryximachus' speech: the harmonizing power of craftsmanship

Unlike Pausanias, who criticizes Phaedrus for failing to speak in a beautiful manner, the physician Eryximachus admits that Pausanias has concluded his discussion beautifully by relying on a distinction between a celestial *erôs* and a vulgar one. Still, he declares, the issue has not been sufficiently explored, given that Pausanias has applied such a distinction only in relation to souls, whereas it should also work in the investigation of the realm of bodies of all the other animals, and, even in all the things that exist (185e6-186a7). Pausanias has clearly maintained that what makes a beautiful way of acting different from a shameful one is the moderate and critical attitude informing it. Plato seems to place Eryximachus' speech along the same road, by inviting the reader to consider the possibility of inquiring into the two opposed ways of loving in terms of 'love that exists in the healthy' and 'love that exists in the diseased' (186b7-8). As Eryximachus explains, the healthy and unhealthy parts of the body are by general consent different and unlike, and things unlike love unlike things. Thus, whoever loves in a state of moderation will love different things and in a different way from those who love in the opposite condition. Taking up the concepts spelled out by Pausanias and the lexicon of homosexual relationships highlighted in his speech (a strategy which, among other things, seems to reinforce the conceptual connection with the previous speeches), Eryximachus explains:

> [And] so just as Pausanias was saying just now that it was a fine thing to grant favours to those people who are good (*toîs agathoîs*), and shameful to gratify those who are immoral (*akolastoîs*)[28], so too in the case of bodies themselves it is a fine thing, and imperative, to favour the good and healthy things in each body, and this is what the name 'medical expertise' belongs to, whereas it is not only shameful to favour the bad and diseased things but imperative to disfavour them, if one is to be a true expert.
>
> 186b8-c6

The capacity for 'granting favours' in the right way is not introduced here as a prerogative of the *eromenos* in a loving relationship, but as the faculty of an expert in the medical craft. Eryximachus describes such a craft in terms of a science of the erotic affairs of the body in relation to filling up and emptying, adding that the person with the best claim to possessing the medical craft (*ho iatrikôtatos*) is the one who is able to distinguish the fine and the shameful love in these (186c6-d1).

By describing the physician as a good 'demiurge' (186d5), whose intervention consists in infusing order and harmony in elements, Plato calls to mind a crucial character of the *Timaeus*, namely the Demiurge who, having contemplated goodness and beauty itself, translates his own contemplative experience in the shaping of the cosmos by impressing on a pre-existing chaotic matter a harmonious order grounded in mathematical proportion (*Timaeus* 28a1-31a2). Eryximachus' view of beauty is undoubtedly linked to harmony and health. However, these are not presented as the outcome of a spontaneous tendency to reciprocal encounter between elements. It is a

God, Eros, that infuses such things as love and concord from outside, making sure that the different parts involved in the combination do not produce any harmful result.

As a good craftsman and doctor *par excellence*, Eros is able to instil a change in bodies and to cause them to acquire one tendency in the place of another. For – as Eryximachus explains:

> [W]hat is needed is the ability to make the things in the body that are most hostile to each other into friends (*phila*), and make them love one another (*hoîon t'eînai poieîn kai erân allêlôn*). The things that are most hostile to each other are those that are most opposed, cold to hot, bitter to sweet, dry to wet, everything like that.
> 186d5-e1

More specifically, the doctor skilfully creates a bond between parts of the body that are originally opposed to each other, and such a process is explained by Eryximachus in terms of *friendship* and *reciprocity* between them. Such a bond can be created not only by the craft of medicine, but also by gymnastics, music and agriculture, crafts which, despite their ontological inferiority,[29] are not merely mimetic, but capable of promoting a definite change in the life of entities on which they are practised. Music, for example, is a science of erotic matters in relation to harmony and rhythm (187c4-5). Like a clever physician, music implants in discordant elements love and unanimity with each other (187c3-4). Its laws and dynamics are paradigmatic of the requirements of a good moral education directed by an expert, as we learn at 187c5-d4:

> There is no difficulty in distinguishing what belongs to love in the structure itself of harmony and rhythm, nor is the double love yet present here; but when one needs to deploy rhythm and harmony in relation to human beings, whether one is composing, which they call musical composition, or making correct use of melodies and measures once composed, which is called education (*paideia*), here there really is something which is difficult, and which calls for a good practitioner (*agathoû dêmiourgoû*).

In the following lines Plato establishes a connection with Pausanias' speech by re-proposing the concept of granting favours to moderate people. As he has Eryximachus acknowledge,

> [T]he same theme as before comes back again: that it is those people who are orderly that one must gratify, and in such a way that those who are not yet orderly might become more so, and it is these people's love that should be cherished, and this is the beautiful Love, the heavenly one, the one who belongs to the Heavenly muse ...
> 187d5-e1

The idea of granting favours gives emphasis to the possibility that different parts are harmonized with one another under the guidance of a wise craftsman, in health as well as in cosmology and in music.

We might wonder what the frequent reference to a demiurge operating and intervening from an external position suggests. This reference may offer precious clues not only on how to understand education to moderation under the guidance of a wise teacher, but also about the power of the dialogue form and the role played by its writer. Plato himself might be regarded as a 'demiurge', given his capacity to compose a philosophical dialogue like the *Symposium*. Its component speeches, although separately offered, are delivered in a sequence and harmonized in a way that facilitates the reader's understanding of the issues examined: *erôs* and its connection to virtue and happiness. Thus, Plato might be compared to the physician described by Eryximachus, who makes a practical use of his art by establishing harmonious connections between dissimilar elements in the body.

What is more, the medical craftsmanship mentioned in Eryximachus' speech is an example of *technê* which, as Plato himself recognizes, is inferior to nature but not to figurative arts.[30] The art of philosophical writing might have a similar status. By infusing the soul of readers with thought-provoking clues and suggestions, the writing gives rise to living knowledge in the reader, even though it cannot reach the levels of dynamism found in living oral communication. By fitting each part of a written speech into an overarching literary and philosophical harmony, the author of a well-crafted philosophical dialogue creates a composition able to raise suggestions in the reader even when the author is not available for clarifying help. Thanks to Eryximachus' eulogy, the reader's understanding of virtue and beauty acquires a chance of further progression, being gradually enriched with new particulars on the virtue of moderation and the fine quality of the harmonization it requires.

Poetry and the art of speech writing: the eulogies of Aristophanes and Agathon

After Eryximachus' speech, the poets Aristophanes and Agathon are offered the opportunity to explore further aspects of the nature and power of *erôs*. As Socrates claims in many Platonic dialogues, poetry is by itself unable to produce authentically philosophical accounts of its subjects, and this occurs mainly for two reasons. In the first place, even when the poets express good and fine things concerning human nature and the relationships between human beings and the gods, the correctness of what they say (and, presumably, their insistence on the need to attain virtue) is not the outcome of real knowledge of the causes and the nature of the treated issues (cf. *Apology* 22c2-3; *Ion* 534b7-c1). The poets are interpreters (*hermênês*) of the gods only by divine inspiration (cf. *Ion* 535a1-2), not by possession of a real craft. Most crucially, the poets shape images which, albeit disclosing some relevant truth concerning human nature, do not necessarily stress the relevance of virtue in human life. The Platonic Socrates, by contrast, suggests that poems ought to be useful (cf. *Republic* III 386b8-c1), that is, that the stories (*mythoi*) that the young hear should be so composed to convey lessons of virtue (cf. *Republic* II 377d3ff., especially 378d6-e3).

Despite Plato's criticism of the poets, his art of philosophical writing makes extensive use of poetic images that appear designed to encourage virtuous behaviour,[31] and the speeches on Eros crafted by the poets in the *Symposium* embody aspects of philosophical love (for instance, the relationship between *erôs* and happiness and *erôs* and virtue) that will find a more philosophically informed treatment in Socrates' speech. In the present section of this chapter I will not provide a detailed analysis of the speeches respectively uttered by Aristophanes and Agathon. With particular reference to Aristophanes' speech, however, I propose that a poetic speech on *erôs* can supply Plato's reader with useful instructions on the way in which a philosophically fine speech ought to be constructed.

As Aristophanes explains, there was a time in which the original nature of human beings was not the same as it is now. In the first place, there were three types of human beings: male, female, and beings containing a combination of both sexes. In the second place, the form of each human being was round all over, with four arms, four legs, two faces on a single head and a cylindrical neck, and two sets of genitals (*Symposium* 189d5-190a1). They were exceptionally strong and vigorous, and their ambition brought them to conspire against the gods (190b5-c1). In the attempt to find a remedy against their arrogance, Zeus and the other gods decided to put their outraging inclinations to an end by cutting them into halves:

> With these words ['I shall cut them into two all over again, so that they'll move around by hopping on one leg'] he [Zeus] set about cutting human beings into two, like people who cut up sorb-apples before they preserve them, or like people cutting eggs with hairs; as he cut each one, he told Apollo to twist the face and the half-neck round towards the cut, so that the spectacle of his own cutting would make the human more orderly (*kosmiôteros*), and as for the rest, he told Apollo to heal everything up.
>
> 190d7-e5

In the following lines of the passage, Aristophanes explains that Apollo was entrusted to twist the faces round, to draw the skin from all sides over the belly, and to smooth away wrinkles, shaping the chest just as shoemakers smooth the wrinkles of leather, although he left there a few which we have just about the belly and navel, to remind human beings of their early fall. When the form of each had been cut into two halves, each half started to long for what originally belonged to it (190e5-191a5). This is why *erôs* can be identified as a desire to restore one's own original nature, that is, desire to become one with the being whom each sees as the 'missing half'.

Although Aristophanes' speech in the *Symposium* does not explicitly present *erôs* as an irrational desire, this idea seems to be implied by Aristophanes' belief that *erôs* brings the souls to death. The verb *epithymein* at *Symposium* 191a7 ('So, because their natural form had been cut in two, each half longed for what belonged to it and tried to engage with it'), being generally used by Plato to express a strive not necessarily rooted in goodness, might offer further support to this interpretation. The idea of *erôs* as an instinctive impulse disentwined from beauty and moral goodness is not a Platonic invention, but a distinctively Aristophanic theme.[32] Just to mention two comedies, in the *Ecclesiazouse* (the *Assemblywomen*, dating from 391 BC) Aristophanes portrays women committed to setting up a communist-like government, in which men are allowed to sleep with any woman, only on condition that they sleep first with every woman who is uglier than the one each desires.[33] Along a similar line, in the *Lysistrata* (performed for the first time in Athens in 411 BC), Aristophanes presents *erôs* as a motivational force that affects the decisions and actions of men and women, still with no specific regard for goodness and happiness based on virtue.[34] During the Peloponnesian War, Lysistrata, the main character, persuades her Greek female-fellows to refuse to have sex with their husbands as a way to induce them to negotiate peace.[35]

Similarly, by striving for their original unity, Aristophanic lovers in the *Symposium* lack the self-sufficiency which Plato notoriously ascribes to virtuous men and to their pursuit of an authentically happy life (cf. *Republic* III 387d9-e2). What is more, only a sense of fear, not virtue, can prevent such beings from being respectful of the gods. Only the gods can make them *kosmiôteroi* by cutting them into halves (*Symposium* 190e4), and the gods themselves find a means to guarantee the survival of dying lovers by giving them the possibility to reproduce themselves:

> [O]ut of pity for them Zeus came up with another plan, moving their genitals round to the front; for up till then they had these too on what was originally their outside, and they did their begetting and child-bearing not in each other but in the ground, like cicadas.
>
> *Symposium* 191b6-c2

If the corrective intervention illustrated above represents an exquisitely Platonic contribution, we might wonder whether the *mythos* narrated by Aristophanes is able to say something on the art of philosophical writing. I believe that substantial aspects of analogy can be detected between Aristophanes' speech and the section of the *Phaedrus* devoted to the possibility of a 'philosophical rhetoric' (that is, art rooted in knowledge of truth and goodness). In the first place, before talking about the suitable methodological criteria for composing a correct speech, the Platonic Socrates resorts to a *mythos* according to which some human beings, being overwhelmed by the song of the new-born Muses, sang and sang, forgetting to eat until they died (*Phaedrus* 259b5e-d8). A remedy for such an intense and deadly desire was put by the Muses, who created out of men the race of cicadas (presumably the same which, as we read in *Symposium* 191b6-c2, did reproduce themselves in the ground).

Given the continuity established by Plato between the myth of the Cicadas and the art of good speechwriting, we might suppose that this art is taken by the Platonic Socrates as a remedy against the risks entailed by the seductions of poetry, especially when poetry itself does not offer lessons concerning truth and the possibility of an authentically good life. Socrates points out that the orator, unlike the poet, must know and be able to distinguish good from evil (*Phaedrus* 260c6-d2), and he must speak only after having attained the truth (269d3-7). Most crucially, we might hypothesize that, just like Aristophanes' human beings, who get cut, corrected and restored by Zeus according to the due proportion, good speeches must be cut and modelled as a living being equipped with specific parts. This idea is introduced in *Phaedrus* 264c1-5, where Socrates explains that every speech should be put together like a living creature, as it were with a body of its own, so as not to lack either a head or feet, but to have both middle parts and extremities, so written as to fit both each other and the whole.

If viewed from this perspective, the role of the gods in Aristophanes' myth appears to resemble the activity and the craft of an expert in good rhetoric. For cutting human beings into halves and shaping the parts of their bodies somehow evokes the diaeretic method followed by the Platonic Socrates. This method includes two fundamental principles. The first consists in

> [P]erceiving together and bringing into one form itself that are scattered in many places, in order that one can define each thing and make clear whatever it is that one wishes to instruct one's audience about on any occasion.
> *Phaedrus* 265d2-5

The second principle involves

> [B]eing able to cut it up again, for by form, according to its natural joints, and not try to break any part into pieces, like an inexpert butcher.
> *Phaedrus* 265e1-3

Unlike a well-crafted speech, however, the whole from which single lovers proceed and into which they recompose is not the outcome of knowledge of the good and the bad, and the desire that inspires persons to it is not informed by moderate attitudes. The idea of a 'temperant' *erôs* is rather introduced by Agathon, whose speech contains several references to the relationships between this concept and happiness, beauty and the whole of virtue (inclusive of justice, courage and wisdom; cf. *Symposium* 195a4). As it is generally believed by scholars, Agathon's speech is embellished with mythological allusions and the rhetorical flourishes of his day,[36] and his idea that Eros is the happiest, most beautiful and best god is not epistemologically serious.[37] Despite the absence of a rigorous treatment of the issue of *erôs*, Agathon's speech contains helpful material for a philosophically informed view on the nature of *erôs* and its relationship to human well-being (such as the one that will subsequently be proposed by Socrates). Eros is described as a god dominating pleasures and desires, one who has nothing to do with the excesses of exceedingly ambitious persons.

As it is interesting to observe, a further aspect of Aristophanes' speech that Socrates will take up in his discussion of *erôs* is his consideration on the correct method to perform a eulogy. While arguing with those who spoke before him that their praising the happiness of human beings who enjoy the benefits of the god Eros rather than eulogizing Eros itself, he says

> There is one correct method for any praise of any subject, namely to describe in speech what sort of character whoever is the subject of the speech has in virtue of which he is actually responsible for what.
> *Symposium* 195a1-3

It is plausible to suppose that, despite his failure to comply to the same methodological principles he utters in his speech, Agathon paves the way for the idea that an authentic philosophical treatment of *erôs* requires knowledge of its causes and effects. On the one hand, Plato supposedly invites his readers to identify flaws and deficiencies in Agathon's speech; on the other, Plato himself seems to offer a display of a positive way in which poetry can be incorporated in a philosophical investigation still in progress.

The ultimate proof of Plato's power as a writer. Diotima's ladder of love

Through their emphasis on beauty and education into virtues like courage, moderation, and intellectual discrimination, the previous eulogies of *erôs* in the *Symposium* prepare the ground for Socrates' discussion of the deep connection between *erôs* itself, human nature and happiness. By reporting the words of the priestess Diotima, Socrates adds to the discussion the idea that human beings desire to incorporate beauty in their lives and preserve it forever (204d3-7; 206a3-13). Desire for immortality unleashes a creative urge that can be expressed either in the generation of new human beings or in the invention of beautiful speeches. *Erôs* acts as a stimulating force whose distinctive activity is described by Diotima as 'giving birth in beauty' (206b7-8). Beauty is not primarily treated an object of desire, but rather as a reality that discloses the generative potential of human beings and their opportunities for development towards goodness.[38]

We might postulate that *erôs* is stimulated by a vision of beauty – physical, psychical or intellectual – and that the effects of such a stimulus do not disappear once the lover's reaction is 'activated'. The stimulus itself might become a 'territory', so to speak, that allows and accompanies the progressive pursuit of the object of love. Conceived in this way, the idea of giving birth in beauty has important implications for our examination of the philosophical written speech. Perhaps this might provide the dimension of literary beauty in which the philosophical pursuits of mindful readers originate. By implanting profitable seeds of knowledge and virtue, the philosophical written speech might act as a midwife for the readers at issue. We might suppose that their pregnancy is carried into effect in response to their experiencing the beauty of good speeches. The beauty at issue seems to reside not only in their content (theoretical and/or ethical), but also in the arrangement of their constitutive parts. Understood this way, we get a better appreciation of the *Symposium* as a beautifully crafted progression of arguments that flourishes in Diotima's revelation, thus creating a well-structured 'get-together' (*synousia*) of speeches.[39] Such a *get-together* does not simply emerge in the intellectually stimulating order of presentation of the speeches set up by Plato, but also in the effectiveness of the last speech to sum up the main tenets of the earlier ones. My suggestion is further confirmed by considering Diotima's illustration of the so-called 'ladder of love', in whose progressive steps we find significant references to the first three eulogies of Eros. Such a ladder might rather be viewed as the peak of a more complex ladder, the initial steps of which are represented by the messages conveyed by the first three eulogies on virtue and the education of the soul to goodness. The initial steps, by expressing the importance of virtue of character as the basis for the erotic tension, show how an individual's soul should begin with a suitable emotional and motivational preparation.

Diotima's revelation takes its departure from the idea that lovers can generate not only physical offspring, but also beautiful speeches. She hints at the presence of a guide (*ho hêgoumenos*) to the steps of such an initiation, who directs the young towards a correct expression of their erotic tension. In the first stage of the ladder, this guide helps them to produce *kaloi logoi*, laudable speeches inspired by *erôs* for a single body (210a4-8). This initial passage has an embryonic pre-figuration in the first eulogy, where cases of love for a single individual, like those of Alcestis and Achilles, are offered as paradigmatic of the virtuous agency inspired by Eros. The benefits of *erôs* for a single person are so strong that Phaedrus proposes to extend its sphere of action to the city, thus effecting an almost imperceptible move from love of an individual to love of a multiplicity of human beings. A similar move from the particular to the general occurs also at the first stage of the ladder of love, where Diotima explains that a shift should occur from attention to the physical beauty of one beloved object towards recognition that beauty belongs also to other such objects (210a8-b6).

In the second stage of the ladder, lovers are led to concentrate on psychic beauty, and to promote the ethical amelioration of their beloved by producing speeches, which, to be effective, must presuppose an exploration of laws and social practices (210b6-c2). We can trace here a resonance with Pausanias' eulogy, where the erotic relationship emerged as an experience endowed with profound educational value. Lovers find in human activities and laws a suitable teaching material, and an exploration of such aspects will reveal to them that the beauty they see in the soul of their beloved lies also and especially in activities and laws themselves. Thus, the teacher becomes a learner in matters of beauty. The ladder of love, however, tells us something more. While Pausanias sought to explain a specific way of loving in a beautiful manner, namely a virtuous homosexual relationship, any reference to homosexuality in Diotima's speech appears overshadowed by a more poignant interest in the process of education to virtue. This process commits human beings not only to ethically good behaviour, but also and especially to knowledge under an expert guide. The subject who accompanies the lover's education since his youth acts from outside the relationship, as a pedagogue.

The guide continues to operate in the next step of the ladder, by turning the lover to address his interest to sciences and help him climb the third step of the ladder of love. Once more, we can find a reference to Eryximachus' eulogy of Eros and his illustration of the role that *erôs* plays in sciences like the medical craft, music and astronomy. From this new perspective, beauty can be seen as a wider power (though one that is craft-like), one that transcends individual entities and extends over various aspects of human knowledge, stimulating new, and more profound speeches (210c6-e1). This will be the last stage before the achievement of the top of the ladder, in which the lover is finally enabled to look at beauty itself.

In conclusion, I have argued that, by inviting his readers to draw meaningful connections between the first five eulogies and the steps of Diotima's ladder of love, Plato means to implant in them (i.e., in us) the seeds of an intellectual progression, one which matches the stages to be traversed by a lover directed to an authentically philosophical experience. Thus, the *Symposium* draws on Plato's own magisterial arrangement of speeches, themes and clues, to enact a pedagogical function in setting the readers on the right road to virtue and knowledge. Besides supplying meaningful normative indications on how to steer one's own path of investigation towards truth and goodness, it also exemplifies how a written speech ought to be crafted so as to instil in readers a true love for knowledge and dialectical confrontation.[40]

Notes

1 This chapter is a substantially revised and expanded version of 'A Eulogy of the Written Dialogue? – Education, Beauty, and Progression in Plato's *Symposium*', *Norsk filosofisk tidsskrift*, 48, no. 1 (2013): 44–56.
2 Christopher J. Rowe, trans., *Plato: Phaedrus* (Warminster: Aris & Phillips, 2000) from which all the mentioned passages of the *Phaedrus* will be taken.
3 One notable exception is represented for instance by Plato's *Laws*, where Socrates is absent and the leading role in the discussion is held by the Athenian. Also, in the *Sophist*, the *Statesman* and the *Parmenides*, Socrates is not the person who undertakes the cross-examination.
4 On the nature and the role of *mimêsis* in Plato's literary craft see Aryeh Kosman, 'Silence and Imitation in the Platonic Dialogues', in *Methods of Interpreting Plato and his Dialogues*, Oxford Studies in Ancient Philosophy, supplementary volume, ed. James C. Klagge and Nicholas D. Smith (Oxford: Clarendon Press, 1992). Beginning from the conceptual distinction between narration and imitation expounded by Socrates in *Republic* III, 392d-394c, Kosman argues that the dialogues are *mimêseis* in which the author does not withdraw from speech, but acts as a silent partner by concealing himself in the mimetic mode and expressing views in an indirect fashion, leaving his readers free to discover the truth by themselves.
5 This approach is endorsed for instance by Sayre in Kenneth Sayre, *Plato's Literary Garden: How to Read a Platonic Dialogue* (Notre Dame: University of Notre Dame Press, 1995). By devoting special attention to the *Phaedrus*, Sayre proposes that Plato sets up a contrast between the written speech and a kind of communication which, being described as living and animated, is plausibly identified with oral speech. The latter speech, contrary to the first one, would be perfectly able to defend itself and be aware of those with whom it should be silent (cf. *Phaedrus* 276a1-7).
6 Many debatable issues revolve around the question of Plato's audience. For an enumeration of such issues see Hallvard J. Fossheim, 'On Plato's Use of Socrates as a Character in his Dialogues', *Rhizai. A Journal for Ancient Philosophy and Science* V. 2 (2008): 241, footnote 3. In the first place, as Fossheim explains, it is not clear whether there are different intended audiences for different dialogues. Second, it is difficult to establish whether such an audience ought to be thought of as individual readers, or groups of listeners, or even as observers of dramatic spectacles – as James A. Arieti instead does in 'How to read a Platonic Dialogue', in *The Third Way: New Directions in Platonic Studies*, ed. Francisco J. Gonzales (Lanham, MD: Rowman & Littlefield, 1995). Third, it is not possible to establish how broad the notion of 'reader' might have been for Plato. Like Fossheim, I shall think of 'the audience' in an all-encompassing sense, that is, as including contemporary readers.

7   I shall refer to the god as 'Eros' (with initial capital letter), whereas I will use the word *'erôs'* primarily to indicate the passion which Eros implants in humans. I assume, however, that both 'Eros' and *'erôs'* can be understood along the various eulogies as a motivational force for human beings.

8   Cf. *Phaedrus* 228a1. On this point see Jonathan Hecht, *Plato's* Symposium. *Eros and the Human Predicament* (New York: Twayne, 1999), 38.

9   See Arthur W.H. Adkins, *Merit and Responsibility: A Study in Greek Values* (Oxford: Clarendon Press, 1965). The Greek moral universe investigated by Adkins is presented in the light of the category of a 'shame-culture' (which he adapted from Ruth Benedict, who used it to explain the Japanese to Westerners).

10 See Alexander Nehamas and Paul Woodruff, *Plato: Symposium* (Indianopolis: Hackett, 1989), xv: 'None of these speeches, however, is purely conventional. Phaedrus' passionate emphasis on virtue and self-sacrifice, for example, goes beyond common practice. His style is simple, but carefully balanced and concise. His enthusiasm, however, carries him to say extravagant things: that love is the best guide to virtue and that virtue is most valuable when connected with love.'

11 Christopher J. Rowe, trans., *Plato: Symposium* (Warminster: Aris & Phillips, 1998), from which all the mentioned passages of the *Symposium* will be taken (and quoted exclusively by use of Stephanus numbers).

12 As the Liddell & Scott's Greek Lexicon suggests, *ethelein* is usually employed to indicate an aware willingness, and not an irrational wish, although, as Hayden Ausland has pointed out to me, the verb at issue comes to refer to the will only in Christian times. As he suggests, an alternative translation is 'being prepared to'. I do not find his suggestion totally incompatible with the idea of an aware agency. Being ready for action does not imply a denial of individual deliberative autonomy.

13 On the self-determination of the Homeric hero see Bernard Williams, *Shame and Necessity* (Los Angeles and Berkeley: University of California Press, 2008), particularly chapter IV.

14 An indirect example of the socializing power of shame might be represented by Homer's *Odyssey* (2.64-65), in which we see Telemachus inviting his fellow-citizens to feel shame, and having regard to the neighbours who dwell roundabout. By asking each member of the community to take on an attitude of shame before the other members of the army, Telemachus is substantially inviting them to a reciprocal consideration. With the inspiring support of *erôs* as motivating force, reciprocal concern might be strengthened and pursued with even less effort.

15 On shame as an emotion which serves to bind people together in a community of feeling see Williams, *Shame and Necessity*, 80.

16 See Pierre Hadot, *What is Ancient Philosophy?* (Cambridge, MA: Harvard University Press, 2002), 11. Hadot explains that military education is a restricted part of a wide project of moral education. On the relation between Eros and courage see Leo Strauss, *Leo Strauss on Plato's Symposium*, ed. Seth Bernadete (Chicago: University of Chicago Press, 2001), 49: 'Eros, then, produces a sense of shame, bringing about virtue in general but manliness in particular. How does this show? In which case does he prove it? In the case of the lover, the beloved, or both? In the lover. Let us, then, make the thesis more precise: Eros produces a sense of shame in the lover which makes him courageous. This is the emphasis of the speech. How does this effect come about, how does it appear? When the lover is seen by the beloved.'

17 I subscribe to Rowe's position in his commentary to the last sections of the *Phaedrus*; cf. Ferrari, *Listening to The Cicadas. A Study of Plato's* Phaedrus (Cambridge:

Cambridge University Press, 1990), 221; Trabattoni, *Scrivere nell'anima*, chapters II and III. By contrast, R. Hackforth, *Plato's Phaedrus. Translated with Introduction and Commentary* (Cambridge: Cambridge University Press, 1952), 162–4, and Gerrit J. de Vries, *A Commentary on the Phaedrus of Plato*. (Amsterdam: Hakkert, 1969), 20–2, argue that Plato rules out the possibility of a written speech presenting the same qualities of a good oral speech. For a detailed treatment of the debate see Ferrari, *Listening to The Cicadas*, 204–22.

18 In this respect I do not agree with James M. Rhodes, *Eros, Wisdom and Silence. Plato's Erotic Dialogues* (Columbia, London: University of Missouri Press, 2003), 226.

19 See Gerhard Krüger, *Ragione e passione. L'essenza del pensiero platonico* (Milano: Vita e pensiero, 1996), 101. As Krüger points out, it is only beginning with Pausanias' speech that the problem of *erôs* is critically explored.

20 See Richard B. Rutherford, *The Art of Plato* (London: Duckworth, 1995), 181. Cf. Kenneth J. Dover, *Greek Homosexuality* (London: Duckworth, 1978), and Hecht, *Plato's Symposium*, 37.

21 The adverb 'beautifully' frequently occurs in Pausanias' speech (180c4, c6, 181a4, b6, 183d6, d8, 184a1, a7).

22 As Krüger (*Ragione e passione*, 102) explains, the ground of the distinction between the two kinds of love does not reside in experience of a supposed difference in power between the two kinds of *erôs*, but in human conduct. This is a properly moral issue.

23 For an indirect reference to this theme see *Symposium* 181b1-c1, where Pausanias, while talking of young boys who love bodies more than souls, explains that they tend to love people with scant intelligence and to have their eye on achieving what they want, not caring whether the way in which they get it is fine or not.

24 Given the impossibility of offering an extensive treatment of the notion of *sôphrosynê*, I confine myself to referring the reader to *Republic* IV, where such a virtue is presented as crucial for the attainment of justice, and to books I–III of the *Laws*, where such a virtue is often mentioned as opposed to *hybris*. Cf. Hendrik Lorenz, *The Brute Within. Appetitive Desire in Plato and Aristotle* (Oxford: Clarendon Press, 2006).

25 In this respect, Plato seems to offer a theoretical justification for a belief that appears well-rooted in his culture. See Félix Buffière, *Eros adolescent. La pédérastie dans la Grèce antique* (Paris: Société d'Édition Les Belles Lettres, 1980), 7.

26 In Greek culture, writing beautiful speeches was regarded as an example of noble activity. See for instance Plato's *Hippias Major*, 286a4-c2, where the sophist Hippias declares to have gained a reputation in Athens by recounting noble and beautiful pursuits (*epitêdeumatôn kalôn*), describing what those of a young man should be and, most importantly, insisting that he compose a very beautiful discourse (*pagkalôs logos*) about them, well arranged in words and other respects. With regard to this passage see Drew Hyland, *Plato and the Question of Beauty* (Bloomington: Indiana University Press, 2008), 11: '...Hippias's uses of the term [*to kalon*] point both to his claim to know what "beautiful pursuits" are for the young, and also to be able to articulate them "beautifully".

27 Cf. Sayre, *Plato's Literary Garden*, xii.

28 I believe that a better translation of the substantive adjective is 'immoderate'.

29 As Strauss points out at *Leo Strauss on Plato's Symposium*, 101: '[T]hese three arts – medicine, gymnastics, and farming – are mentioned together also in the tenth book of the Laws (889b-e) in the context of a representation of the doctrine of the subversive people. Art is lower than nature, and the most respectable arts are, therefore, medicine, farming, gymnastics, because these are the arts which most

cooperate with nature.' Medicine, gymnastics and farming are here regarded as superior to painting, music and those arts subsidiary to the latter.
30 See footnote above.
31 On the positive role played by poetry in Plato's philosophy see F.M. Giuliano, *Platone e la Poesia. Teoria della composizione e prassi della ricezione* (Sankt Augustin: Academia Verlag, 2005).
32 Cf. Bernard Freydberg, *Philosophy and Comedy. Aristophanes, Logos, and Eros* (Bloomington & Indianapolis: Indiana University Press, 2008).
33 Cf. Freydberg, *Philosophy and Comedy*, 111–57.
34 Cf. Freydberg, *Philosophy and Comedy*, 158–95.
35 Cf. Freydberg, *Philosophy and Comedy*, 158–95.
36 Cf. Frisbee C.C. Sheffield, *Plato's* Symposium: *The Ethics of Desire* (Oxford: Oxford University Press, 2006), 25. Cf. Kenneth J. Dover, *Plato: Symposium* (Cambridge: Cambridge University Press, 1980), 123–4, who considers Agathon's speech 'a display of Gorgianic rhetoric'; Rowe, *Plato. Symposium*, 161.
37 Cf. Rhodes, *Eros, Wisdom, and Silence*, 283.
38 See Gabriel Richardson Lear, *Happy Lives and the Highest Good. An Essay on Aristotle's Nicomachean Ethics* (Princeton: Princeton University Press, 2004), appendix. By the same author see also 'Permanent Beauty and Becoming Happy in Plato's *Symposium*', in *Plato's Symposium: Issues in Interpretation and Reception*, eds James H. Lesher, Debra Nails and Frisbee Sheffield (Washington DC: Center for Hellenic Studies, 2006). Cf. Hyland, *Plato and the Question of Beauty*, 50–2.
39 On the *Symposium* as a dialogue in which the narrative figures as an object of love and appreciation, see David M. Halperin, 'Plato and the Erotics of Narrativity', in *Methods of Interpreting Plato and His Dialogues*, Oxford Studies in Ancient Philosophy, Supplementary Volume, ed. James C. Klagge and Nicholas D. Smith, (Oxford: Clarendon Press, 1992).
40 I would like to thank Professor Vigdis Songe-Møller for her very constructive criticism of the new version of my paper.

Bibliography

Adkins, Arthur W.H. *Merit and Responsibility: A Study in Greek Values*. Oxford: Clarendon Press, 1965.
Arieti, James A. 'How to read a Platonic Dialogue'. In *The Third Way: New Directions in Platonic Studies*, edited by Francisco J. Gonzales, 119–32. Lanham, MD: Rowman & Littlefield, 1995.
Buffière, Félix. *Eros adolescent. La pédérastie dans la Grèce antique*. Paris: Société d'Édition Les Belles Lettres, 1980.
De Vries, Gerrit J. *A Commentary on the* Phaedrus *of Plato*. Amsterdam: Hackert, 1969.
Dover, Kenneth J. *Greek Homosexuality*. London: Duckworth, 1978.
Dover, Kenneth J. *Plato: Symposium*. Cambridge: Cambridge University Press, 1980.
Ferrari, Giovanni R.F. *Listening to The Cicadas. A Study of Plato's* Phaedrus. Cambridge: Cambridge University Press, 1990 (first published 1987).
Fossheim, Hallvard J. 'On Plato's Use of Socrates as a Character in his Dialogues'. *Rhizai. A Journal for Ancient Philosophy and Science* V. 2 (2008): 239–63.

Hackforth, Reginald. *Plato's* Phaedrus. *Translated with Introduction and Commentary.* Cambridge: Cambridge University Press, 1952.

Hadot, Pierre. *What is Ancient Philosophy?* Cambridge: Harvard University Press, 2002.

Halperin, David M. 'Plato and the Erotics of Narrativity'. In *Methods of Interpreting Plato and His Dialogues.* Oxford Studies in Ancient Philosophy, Supplementary Volume, edited by James C. Klagge and Nicholas D. Smith, Oxford: Clarendon Press, 1992, 93–130.

Hecht, Jonathan. *Plato's* Symposium. *Eros and the Human Predicament.* New York: Twayne, 1999.

Hyland, Drew A. *Plato and the Question of Beauty.* Bloomington: Indiana University Press, 2008.

Kosman, Aryeh. 'Silence and Imitation in the Platonic Dialogues'. In *Methods of Interpreting Plato and His Dialogues.* Oxford Studies in Ancient Philosophy, Supplementary Volume, edited by James C. Klagge and Nicholas D. Smith, Oxford: Clarendon Press, 1992, 73–92.

Krüger, Gerhard. *Ragione e passione. L'essenza del pensiero platonico.* Milano: Vita e pensiero, 1996 (first published 1939).

Lorenz, Hendrik. *The Brute Within. Appetitive Desire in Plato and Aristotle*, Oxford: Clarendon Press, 2006.

Nehamas, Alexander and Paul Woodruff, trans. *Plato: Symposium.* Indianapolis: Hackett, 1989.

Rhodes, James M. *Eros, Wisdom and Silence. Plato's Erotic Dialogues.* Columbia, London: University of Missouri Press, 2003.

Richardson Lear, Gabriel. *Happy Lives and the Highest Good. An Essay on Aristotle's* Nicomachean Ethics. Princeton: Princeton University Press, 2004.

Richardson Lear, Gabriel. 'Permanent Beauty and Becoming Happy in Plato's *Symposium*'. In *Plato's Symposium: Issues in Interpretation and Reception*, edited by James H. Lesher, Debra Nails and Frisbee Sheffield, 96–123. Washington DC: Center for Hellenic Studies, 2006.

Rowe, Christopher J., trans. *Plato:* Symposium. Warminster: Aris & Phillips, 1998.

Rowe, Christopher J., trans. *Plato:* Phaedrus. Warminster: Aris & Phillips, 2000.

Rutherford, Richard B. *The Art of Plato.* London: Duckworth, 1995.

Sayre, Kenneth M. *Plato's Literary Garden: How to Read a Platonic Dialogue.* Notre Dame: University of Notre Dame Press, 1995.

Sheffield, Frisbee C.C. *Plato's* Symposium: *The Ethics of Desire.* Oxford: Oxford University Press, 2006.

Strauss, Leo. *Leo Strauss on Plato's Symposium*, edited by Seth Bernadete. Chicago: University of Chicago Press, 2001.

Trabattoni, Franco. *Scrivere nell'anima. Verità, dialettica e persuasione* in Platone. Firenze: La Nuova Italia, 1994.

3

Socrates' Appeals to Homer's Achilles in Plato's *Apology of Socrates* and *Crito*

Hayden W. Ausland

Martin Schanz commences his edition of 1893 with the sensible observation that an adequate interpretation of the *Apology of Socrates* presupposes a familiarity as exact as possible with the charges leveled against Socrates.[1] Knowledge of these is complicated by the work's fictional character, however. On the one hand, the work is virtually alone in the *Corpus Platonicum* in depicting an event that cannot have been invented, Socrates' defense speech in reply to specific formal charges. On the other, it is evidently but one instance of a genre of more or less free compositions using the striking historical event of Socrates' trial as their literary hypothesis. These compositions included not only other defense speeches like Plato's, but reportedly also a speech of accusation written by a pupil of Gorgias named Polycrates. Of the contents of Polycrates' work very little is recorded, but conjectural reconstructions have been attempted on the basis of literary statements made in Socrates' defense. C.G. Cobet had, in 1858, concluded that it was chiefly Polycrates' fictional accusation, rather than the speeches of Socrates' historical accusers, to which Xenophon replied in the overtly apologetic first two chapters of the *Memorabilia*.[2] Following Cobet in this, Schanz considers the further possibility that Plato has Polycrates in mind as he is writing his version of Socrates' defense speech.[3]

Schanz reconstructs the charges Polycrates will have made as follows:

1. Socrates taught his associates to despise the laws and the existing constitution;
2. his pupils Alcibiades and Critias did great harm to the Athenian community;
3. he encouraged his associates to treat their parents with disrespect; and
4. he mis-interpreted to damaging effect passages taken from reputable poets.[4]

The last is of special interest in a study of Plato's relation of philosophy to poetry in his *Apology of Socrates* and *Crito*. The portion of Schanz's source-passage in Xenophon pertaining to Homer in particular reads as follows:

> The accuser said he often recounted the passage of Homer to the effect that Odysseus:

> Whenever he encountered some king, or man of influence,
> he would stand beside him and with soft words try to restrain him:
> 'Excellency! It does not become you to be frightened like any
> coward. Rather hold fast and check the rest of the people.'
> When he saw some man of the people who was shouting,
> he would strike at him with his staff, and reprove him also:
> 'Excellency! Sit still and listen to what others tell you,
> to those who are better men than you, you skulker and coward
> and thing of no account whatever in battle or council.'
>
> tr. Lattimore

> These lines he allegedly explained as the poet's praise for striking the common and poor. But Socrates did not say these things, ... rather that those who are neither in word nor deed beneficial, and who are sufficient for coming to the aid of neither army nor city nor the commons itself, when in need, especially should they in addition be bold, ought to be restrained, even should they be quite wealthy. Socrates, however, was manifestly their opposite in these respects, being both a man of the people and of humanistic inclination.
>
> Xen., Mem. 1.2.58-60[5]

That Socrates should be accused of perverting the meaning of these lines from Homer's *Iliad* prompts us to distinguish various questions pertinent already within the literary hypothesis:

(a) How did Homer intend this passage?
(b) How did Socrates understand or explain it?
(c) How did the accuser hold that Homer understood it?
(d) How did the accuser hold that Socrates understood or explained it?

If we take Schanz's supposition into account, however, we may further ask:

(e) How did Polycrates intend this element of his literary accusation?
(f) How does Plato mean to respond to it in his fictional defense speech?

To hazard some possible answers for the first four: (a) In the *Iliad* and the *Odyssey* alike, Homer depicts Odysseus as the consummate diplomat, expert at tailoring his words to the occasions and persons he must address. In this early and perhaps programmatic scene, we see him acting to stop a general military retreat by admonishing men of lower rank while more gently persuading those of higher – as either kind probably would expect. (b) One may imagine that both Plato's and Xenophon's Socrates understood the passage as exemplifying a more general principle they share that a rhetorically adept philosopher will know how to address different kinds of souls in different ways.[6] (c) Except to the extent that he claims that Socrates chose 'the basest passages from the most reputable poets' to use as witnesses when teaching his associates to be malefactors and tyrannically inclined (1.2.56), Xenophon's accuser omits to mention his own understanding of Homer's lines, (d) relying instead on the democratic character of the Athenian court system to brand Socrates' appeal to this passage as an anti-democratic political sermon.

In regard to the authors' literary intentions, it is relevant to observe that: (e) the tradition remembers Polycrates as a 'sophist', i.e. as one competent rhetorically and apt to produce persuasive literary compositions designed to make some particularly clever or even paradoxical case.[7] His literary burden at the level of details was to invent or elaborate arguments that Socrates' accusers either will or might have made so as to effect his condemnation and execution. But this was subservient to the larger goals of his literary activity as a sophist. The task of his professional opponents, including writers like Plato and Xenophon, will have been to devise effective responses to his particular arguments, while indicating their own fundamental alternatives to the sophist's governing aims. Xenophon does not deny that Socrates appealed to poetry in his conversations but denies the substance of the charge, asserting that Socrates never interpreted Homer's poetry in the way the accusation alleged, but rather in a benign fashion, and further that he was on the contrary a man of the people and a friend of mankind. Correspondingly, one may allow that (f) Plato's Socrates makes mention of his having subjected 'poets' – presumably men like the Ion of the Platonic dialogue so styled – to the same kind of inquiry and refutation he does political men and craftsmen (*Apology of Socrates* 22a8-c8), but also ask whether he has any kind of response to the charge that he misinterprets the most reputable poets.

Socrates' use of Homer's poetry in the *Apology of Socrates*

In Plato's *Apology of Socrates*, the defendant appeals to the poetry of Homer most notably not in responding to any known element of the accusation mentioning poetry or Socrates' use of it, but when replying to a hypothetical question he himself poses. Socrates repeats his earlier point that his more difficult task is to address previously existing prejudices, which he here calls 'the slander and envy of the many'. He then supposes: 'one of you might say, "Are you not ashamed, pursuing a pursuit of a kind from which you run the risk of now dying?"' His reply is to the effect that the difference between life and death is a consideration negligible relative to the question of acting justly or unjustly or of being a good or a bad man. To illustrate his point, he appeals to the case of 'the demigods who died at Troy, in particular the son of Thetis'. Socrates outlines Achilles' situation as follows, in the process quoting a few lines from the *Iliad*:

> [Achilles] despised death to such an extent compared to enduring something shameful that, when his mother, goddess as she was, spoke to him to some such effect as the following, as I believe, 'My child, if you really mean to avenge the death of your companion Patroclus and to kill Hector, you yourself will die – for immediately,' she said, 'your fate is ready after Hector' – but he upon hearing this made light of his death and his jeopardy, and with much more fear for living a base man and for failing to avenge his friends, said 'Immediately, then, may I die, upon exacting a penalty of the wrongdoer, in order that I should not remain here a

laughing-stock beside the hollow ships, a burden on the land.' Do you think he gave thought to death and jeopardy?

Apology of Socrates 28c2-d5; cf. Homer, *Iliad* 18.94-104

In an associated but distinguishable point, Socrates next compares his own role as a philosopher to a quasi-military assignment either self-imposed, since understood as best, or enjoined on one by a ruler. It is obligatory for him to undergo danger by remaining at his station, giving no consideration either to death or to anything else in preference to what is shameful (cf. *Apology of Socrates* 38e5-39b1). Socrates illustrates the principle put into practice by recalling his own past military service, saying that he would act dreadfully inconsistently should he abandon the philosophical service enjoined on him by the god, when he, even at the risk of his death, stood firm as ordered by those placed in charge through election when serving in the military on various campaigns. To do so, he says, would in truth merit a charge of impiety.

The example of Achilles

Characteristic pitfalls await modern readings of Socrates' appeal to the example of Achilles, of which certain interrelated cases merit mention here. During the second half of the twentieth century, approaches to classical literature and thought came under the influence of various styles of analysis proper to modern social science, among which numbered a distinction between two stages, or kinds, of culture, in accord with which a hypothesis was introduced of a development from a Homeric 'shame' culture to a classical 'guilt' culture. According to this view in its fully stated form, characters in the Homeric poems are motivated by purely external considerations – how they will appear to others in the terms of a putative 'heroic code' – whereas Greeks of the age of classical philosophy have come to appreciate an inner sense of morality, to which they will look for guidance in questions of conduct.[8] In the face of such a strain infecting classical scholarship, it is best to use caution when assessing Socrates' attribution of the thought to Achilles that the avoidance of death is something shameful. It seems likely that Plato has made the term he employs at 28c3, which is usually translated 'shame', thematic in the *Apology of Socrates*, where it or related noun- or verb-formations are used no fewer than fourteen times, and in a variety of connections.

Thus Socrates opens his speech by saying that his accusers should be ashamed for having accused him falsely, inconsistently, or unjustly. In comparing his questioning to Achilles' returning to battle – the passage quoted above – he uses 'what is shameful' to refer to a course of action that is safer but wrong. When explaining why he refrains from begging the jury for mercy (a conventional forensic *praeteritio* one finds already in Gorgias' defense of Palamedes), he speaks of the shame attaching to a city whose citizens would respond to such appeals, but also concludes by saying that his conviction will flow from his own 'shamelessness' – which he seems to explain as his unwillingness to tell the members of the jury what would be most pleasant for them to hear. He says he asks Athenians whether they are not ashamed at inverting the right hierarchy of life goals (money, fame, virtue). He only once uses the verb in the first person singular, and this in reference to what he says must be said nevertheless, viz. that he found that ordinary men had more to say about the things he asked about than did the men most reputed for wisdom. What Socrates appears to hold worthy of shame, then, includes:

(a) falsely and unjustly accusing others of injustice;
(b) failing to do what is right because it is easier not to;
(c) elevating lower over higher goods; and
(d) demeaning oneself relative to one's reputation or speaking with a view primarily to a jury's pleasure;

but the only thing he says he himself feels ashamed of is:

(e) having to say what he found out about men reputed to be wise.[9]

Socrates employs the terminology fully four times when comparing his own case with that of an Achilles who feels the force of shame, but never with a view to contrasting anything that might be termed his own sense of 'guilt'. Quite the contrary: Socrates explains his own sense of shame by comparing it directly to that given voice by Achilles.[10]

The last observation brings to mind a second pitfall apt to confront readings of Plato's *Apology of Socrates*. During the seventeenth century there developed a peculiarly modern conception of the literary 'hero', who has enjoyed a prodigious history in all manner of applications since. The one that concerns us here is in the first instance its being introduced into interpretations of ancient poetry, both epic and tragic, but secondarily the transferred use of this anachronism in talk of the Platonic Socrates as himself being a kind of literary 'hero'.[11] The subject is extensive, deserving of fuller and more careful treatment than it has hitherto received, but for the present purpose it will be sufficient to advert to one or two facts directly pertinent to the present study. It should be noted first that, although the modern term derives from a similar Greek noun,[12] neither Homer nor Plato uses this with the connotations 'hero' has for moderns. Indeed, Homer has no term whatever with such connotations, for the very good reason that the notion is unknown to him and his epic dialect. The same goes for Classical Attic Greek, in which a regular term for referring to a Homeric character like Achilles is the equivalent of the English 'demi-god',[13] which Socrates uses accordingly to refer to men of his kind at 28c1. The Greeks certainly understood the idea of a paradigmatic human case, but of the affective modern variety they had no notion. A man beset with a passion they naturally enough viewed as a case of potentially damaging pathology – interesting to analyze, perhaps, but never as a model for admiration or imitation. This is why the various ancient attempts to account for Socrates' ostensibly self-destructive behavior at the end of his life all seek reasons susceptible of a rational explanation. Many modern treatments, by contrast, speak openly in terms of his heroism – or at least his instantiation of some special variation of this term's meaning peculiar to his own case. Such approaches one way or the other are all reducible to an anachronistic reading of the primarily romantic notion into ancient thinking and literature, and should accordingly be avoided.

A third and final pitfall we shall mention arises from the quasi-Hegelian reading of Greek intellectual history put forward by Bruno Snell in a number of his writings, according to which what we call the mind or spirit (*Geist*) was not coeval with humanity, but rather 'discovered' (scholars of today might prefer to say 'constructed') in the course of a development traceable from the earliest Greek poetry to the thought of classical philosophy. An early corollary anticipatory of Snell's general theory has it that Homer's characters show no signs of being conscious of their own capacity to make choices, relying instead on outside influences like gods to represent what later Greeks came to think of in terms of a human soul, which made decisions based upon the influence of factors internal to it. At an extreme, this approach approximates to denying moral agency as such to a character like Achilles, which needless to say confounds any attempt to draw a direct comparison between his actions and those of the paradigmatic classical philosopher Socrates. Snell holds that one can see some development underway already in Aeschylean tragic action, which depicts the decisions of characters placed under various kinds of pressure in ways noticeably different from supposedly parallel cases in the poems of Homer, but the process he has in view culminates only in the explicit, articulate psychology of Plato's dialogues.[14] In illustration of the importance of his overall thesis, he adduces, among many others, the very context presently under consideration:

> At 9.393, Achilles hopes to return (sc. home to Phthia), but not in earnest. Achilles even contemplates returning, but without inner conflict; likewise, at the opening of 18, in the lines cited in the *Apology*, there is nothing about a decision of Achilles. That people later interpreted the passage so ... is an instructive example of the legend's instinctive further development, and shows how cautious one must be in order not to read later thoughts into a narrative.[15]

One sharply critical review of Snell's thesis resulted in a swift re-statement, where he held that it had been fundamentally misunderstood and sought to clarify exactly what he meant by it.[16] In the course of the idea's own further development, a criticism implied in the passage quoted above of the Platonic Socrates' appeal to the Homeric Achilles becomes more explicit in both his works and those of several scholars adopting the principles of his history of the human psyche.[17] This did not stop competent criticism of his views, however,[18] and nearly forty years later, Snell would address the matter once again in preparing to interpret fragmentary evidence for Aeschylus' now lost Achilles-trilogy; by this time, his idea has become implicated both with the romantic notion of the hero and with the social-scientific shame-guilt apparatus already mentioned:

> For Plato, Achilles is a great hero (*Apol.* 28 D, *Symp.* 179 E) because he chooses to die young for the sake of immortal glory. Ever since, we think of him in much the same way as Goethe, for example, describes him in his *Achilleîs* (515):
>
> Alle Völker verehren Deine treffliche Wahl des kurzen rühmlichen Lebens, 'All nations venerate/Thy seemly choice of the short and glorious life.'
>
> We are inclined to read this picture of Achilles into Homer as well, although he never mentions Achilles' choice. In the Iliad, it is true, we experience at first hand the slowly developing certainty that he will die young. We also hear that he is

destined either to die a young and glorious death or to live a long and inglorious life, but nowhere does Homer mention Achilles' own conscious decision to make the nobler choice.[19]

While it is true that moderns tend to think of Achilles in terms of the kind expressed by Goethe, Snell's implication that this way of seeing him as a romantic hero originates already in classical times is unlikely.[20]

Bearing in mind the standard pitfalls just sketched, we may turn with a better instructed interest to a claim more recent in kind that Socrates mis-applies Homer in the *Apology of Socrates*. It has been remarked and considered within the confines of the Straussian school of political philosophy how Socrates' appeal to the example of Homer's Achilles might seem to be of limited application. Not only was Achilles young when he made the decision depicted in the Homeric scene the aged Socrates recalls, but the hero's immediately previous actions fit ill with Socrates' subsequent explanation in terms recalling the philosopher's own military service, insofar as Achilles was so far from standing at his post as to have caused the Greeks great woes by refraining from fighting as expected of him, out of anger at his treatment by his superior, Agamemnon.[21]

Yet Socrates seems to have different points in mind with the two illustrations. For the first, it will be useful to recall for closer consideration the greater context of the scene in the *Iliad* to which he appeals; for the second, we can advert briefly to the illustrative value of the Athenian military engagements Socrates calls to mind.

To be understood, Achilles' statements in *Iliad* 18 must be viewed against the background of the poem's main theme, the development of which it will be useful here briefly to recall.[22] This theme is neither Achilles' own person nor any choice he makes – much less the Trojan war – but a particular passion with which Achilles is beset.[23] As passions will, this wrath has a beginning and ending, between which it runs a course, and it is these limits and this course that determine the extent and articulation of the poem. Thus, the *Iliad* begins and ends together with the wrath of Achilles, but in order for this to be clear, his wrath needs to be viewed under more than a single aspect. According to one, it is a feud in a legal sense, a sense sanctioned by custom. But Achilles' passionate state runs deeper than this, as becomes evident especially on the occasion he refuses the generous offer of restitution Agamemnon makes through the embassy in book 9. The stages in the poem's action proceed according to the stages by which he comes to grips with his own condition. His several attempts lead him to occupy opposite extremes before he is able to achieve the equilibrium seen in his interview with Priam in book 24. At one of these extremes, he seeks to make an exception of himself by gaining immortal glory in his present life. His carefully calibrated plan to achieve this by re-entering the war only when the Greeks are on the very brink of losing everything is directed to this end. He cuts matters too finely, however, and unsuccessfully risks the life of his best friend. What he intended as the last stage in a build-up to his own glorious reappearance as savior becomes his loss of Patroclus. A kind of tragic effect is heightened by the way he can be seen to be coming around after he has turned away the embassy in book 9; thus in book 11, he shows concern for the healer Machaon in a fashion that bespeaks his own healing process. And it is by a miscalculation, rather than by virtue of any grand new design, that he loses his friend and with him all prospect of a more decorous re-entry into the war. This experience brings him back to the realization of his proper role in the general Greek effort, and it is on this occasion he has the conversation with his mother that is invoked by Socrates in the *Apology of Socrates*. Viewed in its Homeric context, then, Socrates' example of the Achilles of *Iliad* 18 brings to mind a warrior's overcoming an extraordinary passion that has caused him shamefully to omit actions in some way obligatory.

To consider whether Socrates invokes this passage in a way faithful to Homer's intention, it will be useful first to dispose of a question regarding an apparent discrepancy. What Socrates reports in our text of Plato reads somewhat differently in the received text of Homer: where our text of Homer reads 'I must die soon, then; since I was not to stand by my companion when he was killed' (18.98f.) and then, after several intervening lines, 'but sit here beside my ships, a useless weight on the good land' (18.104), the text of Plato modifies and compresses these into 'may I die forthwith, in order that I not stay laughable by the hollow ships, a burden for the land' (28d3f.);[24] in addition, Socrates attributes to Achilles directly after 'may I die forthwith' a thought framed emphatically in terms of an application of justice – 'once I have done justice to a perpetrator of injustice'[25] – with no obvious correlate in Homer's version. These differences have occasioned some comment, most tending to assume a definite text or meaning in Homer as a basis for trying to explain Plato's divergence from these.

Some have inferred that Plato used a different text from ours, but this is generally judged inadequate as a full explanation. Noting Socrates' qualification 'in some such words as these',[26] and in view of the dialogues' general readiness to modify some words and phrases in such contexts, others have ascribed the phenomenon to a habitual looseness on Plato's part. Subtler critics have even considered the possibility that he deliberately alters the meaning of the Homeric text in a way significant for his own purposes, and that careful readers will understand this significance.[27] Noteworthy among the last group are Thomas G. and Grace Starry West, who delineate as follows what they see as the key differences:

> Homer's Achilles chooses to avenge Patroclus out of grief and anger, while Socrates' Achilles, more concerned with how he looks to others, fears doing anything shameful and appearing 'ridiculous'. Further, in Homer the death of Patroclus is for Achilles the private loss of his dearest friend, while Socrates transforms it into a crime that deserves punishment (and so Hector rather than Patroclus is dwelt upon): Patroclus' death is a 'murder' and Achilles will 'inflict a penalty [*dikê*, also the word for justice] on the doer of injustice.'[28]

The interpretation exhibits several flaws common in creative understandings of the words Socrates seems to quote directly (viz. *Iliad* 18.96, 98, and 104). Insofar as it might attribute to Achilles a heroic 'choice' between a short, glorious life and a short obscure one, it runs afoul of the second pitfall mentioned above: as one can see from Snell's reading, what is actually said in Homer is quite compatible with an interpretation of a different kind. But while it is unnecessary to hold with Snell that Achilles has no consciousness 'yet' of internal decision-making, it will be useful to consider one sense in which Achilles explains to his mother that he *has no choice* but to slay Hector.[29]

Here we must confront the question of Achilles' motivation for his decision – a related area of weakness in the interpretation quoted above, which offers no grounds whatever for asserting that Homer's Achilles 'chooses to avenge Patroclus out of grief and anger'. In the immediate context, Achilles makes no mention of anger at all. He is experiencing sorrow, but this is not the reason he gives for having to act, which is his determination to make Hector pay for having killed and stripped Patroclus, a duty he conceives in the light of his own failure previously to defend his friend. It is also true that Socrates frames the issue of retributive justice in a manner that the cited Homeric lines do not. But Plato's allusion can be seen hereby to explain points that are made thematic by Homer just earlier and right afterward. To see this requires considering the entire scene between Achilles and his mother, which runs 18.70-137 and includes five distinct speeches, as set out in the following discussion.

First, Thetis initially asks her son the reason for his sorrow, pointing out that he has achieved the object for which he prayed at the outset. Second, Achilles replies that, although Zeus has indeed brought about disaster for the Achaeans, this can now hold no pleasure for him, since his dear companion has perished. Achilles has lost him, and his killer Hector has stripped away the great armor that the gods gave his father Peleus on the occasion of his wedding to Thetis. Expressing the first of two wishes he will give voice to within this scene – that they had never married (i.e. that he had never been born) – he mentions the sorrow his mother must feel at the prospect of her son perishing, never to return home,

> since the spirit within does not drive me
> to go on living and be among men, except on condition
> that Hektor first be beaten down under my spear, lose his life
> and pay the price for stripping Patroklos, the son of Menoitios.
>
> 18.90-93

The language used in the last line quoted indicates that he is moved to kill Hector in order that the latter 'pay the price' for the two sources of sorrow he has just mentioned: killing his dear friend and taking the divine armor Achilles inherited from his father Peleus – the poetic term he uses comprises both aspects.[30] In this first speech in reply to his mother, then, Achilles nowhere mentions anger and his references to his sorrow are not made in order to explain his plan to kill Hector, which seems to be purely a matter of settling scores.

Third, when she next informs her son that he is to die soon after Hector, Thetis' tears confirm what he has said about the sorrow she must feel. Fourth, in his second reply to her – the speech from which Socrates quotes or paraphrases lines 18.98 and 104 – Achilles now allows that then he might die soon:

> since I was not to stand by my companion
> when he was killed. And now, far away from the land of his fathers,
> he has perished, and lacked my strength to defend him.
> Now, since I am not going back to the beloved land of my fathers,
> since I was no light of safety to Patroklos, nor to my other

companions, who in their numbers went down before glorious Hektor, but sit here
beside my ships, a useless weight on the good land, ...

18.98-104

Achilles here twice states his understanding of the reason for the action that will lead to his death. He has been useless, letting down his friend Patroclus – just as he did all his companions when they needed him, even though he is the best fighter the Achaeans have. The clear implication is that he is ashamed of the way he has been acting, and so must now do what he can to rectify this. And this is rather different from acting 'out of grief and anger'.

Achilles at this point mentions anger as a cause, but it is in the context of his second wish, that strife and bitter anger[31] should cease to exist, exemplifying these with the way Agamemnon angered him. But so far from invoking his anger as a reason for his urge to kill Hector, Achilles now says he will *suppress* his anger with a view to this very object:

Still, we will let all this be a thing of the past, and for all our
sorrow beat down by force the anger deeply within us.
Now I shall go, to overtake that killer of a dear life,
Hektor; then I will accept my own death, ...

18.112-115

Here, he offers a mythological *exemplum*: not even Herakles could escape his death, brought about the anger (*cholos*) of Hera. So too will he die when the time comes, but:

Now I must win excellent glory
and drive some one of the women of Troy, or some deep-girdled
Dardanian woman, lifting up to her soft cheeks both hands
to wipe away the close tears in her bursts of lamentation,
and learn that I stayed too long out of the fighting.

18.121-125

What Achilles here says he will bring some bereft woman to learn clearly enough alludes to what he himself has learned by his loss of Patroclus: that he has failed his companions by staying out of the fighting past the point at which it would have been appropriate for him to re-enter it, the occasion of the embassy in book 9. Fifth, Thetis responds accordingly, allowing:

Yes, it is true, my child, this is no cowardly action,
to beat aside sudden death from your afflicted companions.

18.128-130

and moving to the matter of his acquiring new god-given armor for the purpose. Not waiting for another answer from Achilles, she leaves to see to this, at which Homer turns our attention to the battle raging over the body of Patroclus.

In the scene between Achilles and his mother excerpted above, the overarching mood is sorrow, first signaled in Thetis' question to Achilles, concluding with his plan to cause sorrow to some woman bereft of a man, and surfacing explicitly on several occasions in between. Anger is mentioned twice: as the *regrettable* cause for Achilles' abstention from battle for too long, and as a divine cause for the death of Herakles, in the light of whose example he can accept his own impending demise. In speaking of his reasons for planning to slay Hector, Achilles mentions only his intention to make Hector pay for what he has done, which deed Achilles articulates into two parts: (a) killing his dear friend Patroclus, and (b) stripping from his corpse the armor that the gods gave Peleus when he married Thetis. That at least Achilles regards his making Hector 'pay back' for these deeds as a matter of doing justice, rather than satiating a continuing fury, is clearly indicated by the terminology he here uses.[32]

The ungrounded claim to the contrary in the second part of the reading quoted above relies in part on an anachronistic distinction between private offense and public crime. Not only does Homeric language and thought recognize no such distinction – the word often translated 'murder'[33] in fact always means simply 'killing' or 'slaughter' (as e.g. in Thetis' prediction at 18.133 to Hector's coming death at the hands of Achilles) – but even the Classical Attic used by Plato's Socrates lacks any equivalent for what we call 'murder' and regard as a public 'crime'. In Athenian legal parlance, the same term refers to homicide generally, comprising, among other cases, a man's being killed by a horse's delivering him a fatal kick or a deadly weight falling on his head from the cornice of a building. Although homicides were treated as a public concern insofar as they could incur religious pollution, their prosecution was a kind of private complaint, open only to parties directly affected, not a public indictment,[34] such as the charge of impiety that it was open to any citizen to make against Socrates. It is this very feature of Athenian homicide law that gives rise to the paradox of Euthyphro's charging his own father with homicide on behalf of a day-laborer.[35] It was Euthyphro's father's personal responsibility to take remedial action against the man who had killed his slave, but given the circumstances, he wanted to inquire first about the religious proprieties of the case. When the man meanwhile died of exposure, it would be expected of Euthyphro to defend his father against any attempt on the part of an interested party connected with the killer to exact vengeance on the father. Since, however, the killer worked for his keep as a free laborer[36] and as such enjoyed no family support-structure at all,[37] this issue would normally have been moot.[38] That Euthyphro should disregard all the mentioned familial connections (or lack of them) and instead prosecute his own father would at the time have been considered an extreme of impiety. Hence the emphatic surprise Socrates expresses when he learns the nature of Euthyphro's action (4a7-b6).[39]

Thus, even in the thought and terminology of Classical times prosecuting a homicide under the law comes far closer to avenging it privately than does a public prosecutor's charge in modern times. That Homer's Achilles regards himself as prosecuting a killing in the formal sense available in his day is clear from his words at 18.91-93, where he explains that he is unwilling to continue living, 'except on condition that Hektor first be beaten down under my spear, lose his life and pay the price for stripping Patroklos, the son of Menoitios'.[40] It is this formulation to which Homer's Thetis then refers when she says, 'Then I must lose you soon, my child, by what you are saying, since it is decreed your death must come soon after Hektor's.'[41] (18.95f.) Plato's Socrates brings both statements together in recalling for the jury that, 'when Achilles was eager to kill Hector, Thetis spoke to some such effect as "O child, if you avenge the slaughter of your companion Patroclus and kill Hector, you yourself will die – for directly after Hector your fate stands ready."'[42] Socrates thus reports at least Homer's Achilles quite accurately as intending to make Hector pay back for his deeds as a matter of exacting justice from him by avenging his friend.[43]

Whether this exhausts Homer's entire meaning once the passage is viewed within the larger plot of the *Iliad*, is another question, the answer to which must be sought in an interpretation of the poem as a whole. Here it will be enough to recall that, viewed against the basic action of the *Iliad* as a whole, Socrates' appeal to the example of Achilles in book 18 recalls a warrior's overcoming an extraordinary passion that has caused him shamefully to omit actions in some way obligatory. Socrates' comparison of his own comparatively pedestrian military service seems, by contrast, meant to explain the basis on which certain actions are to be regarded as obligatory. Socrates allows two ways in which a man might come to occupy a quasi-military post: through self-assignment on the basis of a conviction that it is best, and through assignment by someone placed in charge of him. He describes his own past military service in terms that conform to the latter alternative, but, in the light of what else we know of him (also from other dialogues like the *Euthyphro*), it is easy enough to imagine that he means his stated reliance upon the oracle at Delphi ironically, and that his philosophical way of life is something he has imposed on himself through his own conviction that it is the best way of life for a man (cf. *Apology of Socrates* 37e3-38a8). This part of what he says to the jury is sometimes drawn into attempts to understand his appeal to the example of Achilles, but this study will regard it as a distinct, if ostensibly related kind of argument in support of the complementary point mentioned.

Someone might still, however, wonder whether there is supposed to be some analogue in his own case for Achilles' inhuman anger and consequent behavior. Is there a sense in which Socrates' previous activity has been the result of a passion that has led him to go beyond socially sanctioned limits? Someone might further consider whether there is some further parallel for Achilles' fixation on slaughtering everyone and everything coming in his path until he can kill Hector, and even beyond this on defiling his corpse, for it is this unseemly series of events, and not the divinely sanctioned moment of peace between Achilles and Priam or Hector's funeral, as described in book 24, that is initially set in motion by the hero's return to the fray. Who or what might be the agent of wrongdoing for Socrates' choice to fight things out rather than play it safe by leading a quiet life at home? And how might his choice for such an action constitute a kind of vindication on behalf of his otherwise injured friends? Various answers might suggest themselves,[44] but ones that have been put forward all presuppose a definite sense of the primary meaning of Socrates' use of the Homeric example. Rather than address such endless speculations, we shall here concentrate on isolating this basic meaning by considering hypothetically the alternative path Achilles toys with earlier in the *Iliad*. As an aid to this consideration, there is a thematically related Platonic dialogue that illustrates its own main problem by alluding to this very possibility.

Socrates' allusion to Homer's poetry in the *Crito*

The *Crito* depicts a conversation between Socrates and his old friend, who urges him to take advantage of what will be his last opportunity to escape into exile rather than undergo his sentence of death. Socrates offers him arguments against this course of action, certain underpinnings of which he attributes to 'the laws', which he personifies in a hypothetical conversation he rehearses for Crito's benefit. Whether it is intended or not, this complication has occasioned certain misunderstandings. Like readers who conflate Plato's fictional character Socrates with the author himself, some scholars have been insufficiently attentive to the way Socrates distances himself from some arguments by attributing them to 'the laws'. It is in this connection well to remember the hypothetical purpose delimiting the character of Socrates' greater argument in this dialogue, which is to set his old friend Crito's mind at ease. Crito is of course sad to think that he will be losing his friend, but this is not the concern that gives rise to their conversation. What does is a concomitant worry that he will have nothing effective to say to people who blame him for having failed to rescue his friend Socrates from death in the way that people would have expected him to, viz. by arranging for Socrates to slip out of prison and quit Attica before his sentence can be carried out. Socrates' burden, then, is to provide Crito with something he can in good conscience say to people who might blame him in this way.[45] For such a purpose, the arguments Socrates requires need not be congruent with his own reasons for staying and submitting to his execution. It is sufficient that he offer considerations that his friend Crito can himself believe and people of conventional outlook will find adequate to explain Crito's acquiescence. It is in this connection worth noting that Crito is not one of Socrates' many younger philosophical companions, but his coeval and oldest friend. For Socrates, he is perhaps like someone with whom we went to school and to whom we remained good friends many years later, even though our vocational paths diverged in critical respects. Crito may thus be the kind of man for whom what the laws have to say is decisive. This can help explain why one premise on which Socrates' own reasoning rests, viz. the principle that one must never commit an injustice, although tolerably consistent with the principle he invokes in the *Apology of Socrates* that a man assigned a post by a superior is obligated to remain at it, here apparently leads him to adopt a position deferential to the laws of Athens rather than defiant of them, as his behavior at his trial might have led one to expect.[46] Still, the larger argument he states in his own person for Crito's benefit, reduced to its essentials, is that he cannot take an opportunity to escape, since to do so would be to commit an injustice. How might the case of Achilles exemplify this principle?

The dialogue begins with Crito's visiting Socrates quite early on a day shortly before his execution is to take place, the imminent prospect of which Crito has inferred from the approach of a ceremonial ship whose arrival the authorities must await before proceeding with any executions. Socrates recounts a dream that leads him to think he has not one, but two days left to live:

> I thought a woman who was approaching me, beautiful and comely of form, and wearing white garments, called me and said, 'Socrates, on the third day you might reach fertile Phthia.'
>
> Crito 44a10-b2

Crito calls the dream strange, but when Socrates says he thinks its meaning clear enough, Crito admits it is all too clear. Neither of them explains its meaning, however, so we cannot be sure how either interprets it or know whether the meaning it has for them both is the same.

In Socrates' dream, the anonymous woman states the potential for Socrates' reaching Phthia two days hence. Viewed in the light of his execution two days hence, 'Phthia' would appear to refer to a place he will be once he is dead. But when Greeks die, they go to the house of Hades (see *Apology of Socrates* 41a1). Phthia is the place-name of the home of Homer's Achilles, and the words spoken by the anonymous woman adapt a verse Achilles himself utters in book 9 of the *Iliad*, as he has been staying aloof from the action for some days and is toying with the idea of leaving Troy altogether.

> But, now I am unwilling to fight against brilliant Hektor,
> tomorrow, when I have sacrificed to Zeus and to all gods,
> and loaded well my ships, and rowed out to the salt water,
> you will see, if you have a mind to it and it concerns you,
> my ships in the dawn at sea on the Hellespont where the fish swarm
> and my men manning them with good will to row. If the glorious
> shaker of the earth should grant us a favouring passage
> on the third day thereafter we might raise generous Phthia.
>
> Iliad 9.356-363

These lines occur in a speech Achilles makes in response to Odysseus' representations on behalf of Agamemnon, who is now willing to make full and even generous restitution. In his reply, Achilles sharply rejects the offer, offering, among others, the argument that no offer of recompense could possibly make up for the loss of his own life, which he (as he tells the embassy) knows will follow on the basis of a prophesy his mother has made. Let us briefly return to the action of the *Iliad*, so as to elaborate on this and some related points outlined above in reference to the *Apology of Socrates*.

The proem of the *Iliad* announces the subject matter as the wrath of Peleus' son Achilles, qualifying this by adding that 'the plan of Zeus was fulfilled' (*Iliad* 1.5). The course taken by Achilles' wrath is not identical with the fulfilment of the plan of Zeus. Anger of the sort that Achilles initially shows toward Agamemnon is a socially and divinely sanctioned matter: when one man violates another man's possessions or honor, the victim reacts with anger that is directed toward inflicting damage on the other that will compel him to make formal compensation and to recognize publicly the rightful relation between them. Custom supports this anger up until the point at which proper restitution is made, and just such a resolution is the aim of Zeus' plan. Achilles' exceptional persistence in his anger delays this resolution beyond its natural place in the action of book 9, until book 19 – traditionally styled the 'unsaying of the wrath'.[47] As matters develop beyond even that point, it will emerge that neither Zeus' nor Achilles' plan is quite the same as Homer's plan, which animates also the action of the remaining books in a way to be indicated shortly. But the passage alluded to in the *Crito* occurs at a much earlier stage, in book 9.

As just mentioned, a *cholos* is a socially sanctioned anger up until a violator moves to make his victim whole. What if the victim refuses this for some reason? Thereafter the burden will fall socially on him. The *nemesis*, or righteous indignation, felt earlier toward the perpetrator of the original indignity, will now be transferred onto a victim unwilling to have things made right once more. This is the situation in which Achilles finds himself when he refuses Agamemnon's offer of recompense in book 9, as first Phoenix hints and then Ajax makes quite clear. But Achilles cannot help himself: already his answer to Odysseus has betrayed a deeper reason for his unrelenting anger: it is his fear of death.

>   For not
>   worth the value of my life are all the possessions they fable
>   were won for Ilion, that strong-founded citadel, in the old days
>   when there was peace, before the coming of the sons of the Achaians;
>   not all that the stone doorsill of the Archer holds fast within it,
>   of Phoibos Apollo in Pytho of the rocks. Of possessions
>   cattle and fat sheep are things to be had for the lifting,
>   and tripods can be won, and the tawny hides of horses,
>   but a man's life cannot some back again, it cannot be lifted
>   nor captured by force, once it has crossed the teeth's barrier.
>   For my mother Thetis the goddess of the golden feet tells me
>   I carry two sorts of destiny toward the day of my death. Either,
>   if I stay here and fight beside the city of the Trojans,
>   my return home is gone, but my glory shall be everlasting;
>   but if I return home to the beloved land of my fathers,
>   the excellence of my glory is gone, but there will be a long life
>   left for me, and my end will not come to me quickly.
>   9.400-416

This fear is something he will be ashamed to admit by book 16, when Patroclus asks him whether there may be some prophesy of his mother's which is keeping him from the fighting. But meanwhile, he remains the only Greek who openly toys with the idea of desertion, even though the dual destiny he knows of is in a sense every other soldier's probable lot. As mentioned already, it is important that we not fall for the notion that Achilles is made aware of this alternative as a romantic 'hero' who will make a free choice for a short but glorious life. Achilles is beset with a pathology: his detestable self-image as a 'vagabond' (*Iliad* 9.648) leads him to ignore all sense of communal responsibility for the sake of the vain hope of achieving immortal fame in the present life. The vanity of his aspiration surfaces repeatedly but is perhaps clearest in the words he speaks to Patroclus as he sends him out to battle (see 16.97-100). Yet even this aspect of Achilles' pathology seems over with by book 19, when Patroclus' death has brought him back to his senses.

At this point, however, a newly brutish condition arises in Achilles emanating, as it would seem, from the combination of his regret at having indulged his *cholos* too long and his sorrow at Patroclus having been killed by Hector. Like his *cholos*, however, it in turn goes too far as he challenges divinities – first directly on the battlefield and then implicitly, by showing an undue disrespect for the dead.[48] The last is what moves Zeus to intervene at the beginning of book 24, where his plan finally diverges from that of Achilles. Only if we see that Achilles' passion for killing, taken to the extent of even defiling the dead, is a further immoderate extension of his *mênis*, does it make sense that the *Iliad* should end only with the burial of Hector. The scene between Priam and Achilles depicts concretely their negotiation of the conditions necessary for this to occur, and only in the course of this scene will Achilles show himself fully restored.[49] But this additional dimension of the *Iliad* would seem to extend beyond the scope of this study.

Like the Delphic Oracle, Socrates' dream is ambiguous. In its Homeric context, the statement recalled by the anonymous woman in Socrates' dream represents a real, if remote, possibility Achilles entertains as he is approached in book 9 with an offer of restitution he should, by all applicable standards, accept. Should he abandon his military obligations altogether, he might avoid the attendant risks, in favor of living a long if uneventful life back on his family farm. This is any fighting man's basic choice, but in the light of his divine mother's prophesy, for the demigod Achilles, reaching Phthia represents escaping an otherwise certain sentence of death – the very prospect he will only later have come to see he cannot pursue as he in book 18, in the exchange recalled in the *Apology of Socrates*, informs his mother that he must go back into battle nonetheless. Phthia is of course in Thessaly, where Crito has local connections (*Xenoi*) to whom he suggests Socrates can go, should he choose exile in preference to death.[50] But the dream might just as well allude to his companions' sense that he is abandoning them.

Tentative conclusion

In his depiction of Socrates' final days, Plato tends to confirm the charges against him in a literal sense while elaborating their meaning in a way justifying his life. In his conversation with *Euthyphro*, Socrates is shown subordinating the gods of the city to the form of piety; in his defense speech, he speaks of the measures he has taken to cross-examine the oracle of Apollo; and in the *Crito* he even seems to let down his family and friends for the sake of an abstract kind of justice. It is likewise clear why sophists and scholars alike can accuse the Platonic Socrates of misusing quotations from the poets. In both the *Apology of Socrates* and the *Crito*, Plato depicts Socrates invoking the case of Achilles. But Plato designs his teacher's distortions of Homer's poetry in interestingly complementary ways. In the *Apology of Socrates*, the defendant explains his lack of shame at the prospect of undergoing a death sentence for standing his ground by appealing to a Homeric passage in which a hero who has spent much of the poem shirking his duty is now ready to resume fighting in order to avenge a friend for whose death he with good reason feels personally responsible. In the *Crito*, he opens a conversation aimed at persuading a friend that he has no choice but to undergo his death sentence by alluding to an earlier Homeric context in which the same hero reveals to his friends that his reluctance to go back into battle at bottom rests on his fear of his own death. But perhaps one can respond to accusations of misuse by adverting to a more general level of meaning in Socrates' appeals to Homer. The allusion in the *Crito* to the *Iliad* is to the critical occasion on which Achilles makes clearest the choice he faces between what is sanctioned by right and what is more convenient but shameful, an occasion forming the critical turning point after which he begins his arduous return to a full sense of responsibility. The passage recalled in the *Apology of Socrates* occurs later during the course of this return, and at exactly the point in the *Iliad* where Achilles make clear that he has realized – perhaps for the first time in his short life – the meaning of the shame that attaches to a man who makes it a priority to avoid death. His use of these two poetic passages is necessarily susceptible to misrepresentation in an accusation of Socrates, but to anyone recalling the poem well, they are probably the clearest illustrations in the *Iliad* of these two principles, neither of which – like the two passages themselves – is properly intelligible when considered in abstraction from the other. Plato has characteristically reversed their Homeric sequence in his literary presentation of them, and both are fully understood only in the light of the greater plot of the *Iliad*, inasmuch as neither passage recalls Achilles' having finally overcome his anger and most fully realized his humanity, which occurs only in book 24 when he yields up the body of Hector so as to allow for the proper funeral with which the entire poem ends. For a Platonic equivalent to the classic Homeric scene in which Achilles consoles Priam by recalling him to the limitations under which humanity as such labors, we may look forward to a suitable reading of the *Phaedo*.[51] But this must be reserved for some future occasion.

Appendix: Polycrates' *Accusation of Socrates* and its critics

In the mid-nineteenth century there developed a scholarly practice of tracing the courses of professional feuds supposed as having occurred between ancient literary figures. The style was one phase in a longer-standing fascination with authorial developments imagined on the model on romantic literary fashions: it was accordingly thought that one might better understand the works of ancient authors if only one could recover the biographical particulars attending their literary activities. Since classical writers rarely give any – much less exact – information about the occasions, sequence, or overall chronology of their writings, pursuit of this line of research necessarily required a generous measure of hypothetical reconstruction, including conjectures regarding the contents of lost works seemingly implicated in one or another such ongoing quarrel. Noteworthy for the study of Plato's works, for instance, is the way he and Isocrates were held to have carried on a lengthy dialogue about the nature of philosophy, rhetoric and education, which will have conditioned discoverable features of both their works, thus enabling the scholar to construct a skeletal chronology within which to interpret their several related literary efforts. More particularly, it was in the course of this pursuit that a still-popular practice of assigning dates to the works of Plato based on their stylistic characteristics was initially conceived.

As one part of this scholarly tendency a supposition was entertained that certain writings incorporating or implying a defense of Socrates against allegations of a kind that will have figured in his trial were inspired less directly by the event itself than by a now lost fourth-century BC *Accusation of Socrates* attributed to a sophist named Polycrates. Such writings included Isocrates' *Busiris* and a lost *Apology of Socrates* attributed to Lysias, as well as the opening chapters of Xenophon's *Memorabilia* (1.1-2). Efforts aimed at reconstructing Polycrates' *Accusation* then came to rely heavily on a notion that categorical arguments addressed by the late rhetorical writer Libanius in his own *Apology of Socrates* derive from this work, whether directly or otherwise.

Since first being aired, the last notion has been explored or adopted by a number of scholars, but there have been sceptics too, whose consideration of the matter seems fuller and informed by comparison. That Libanius' speech and Xenophon's apologetic treatment in the *Memorabilia* reply in differing ways to specific charges that one may guess featured Polycrates' speech shows at most that the charges were topical in literary works based on Socrates' trial, but by the same token fails to establish that Xenophon or Libanius relied significantly, much less directly, on Polycrates in composing their treatments. Whether specific charges of the kind figured in Socrates' actual trial can hardly be known, but for literary purposes it is sufficient they be charges of a kind that might well have figured in such a trial. Indeed, only so could they conveniently serve as the common premise for various authors' competing treatments of the same general theme. The peculiarly modern obsession with tracing the genetic development of thought – of which hypothetical literary 'feuds' are a sub-species – tends to distract scholars from the otherwise obvious fact that ancient writers were as a rule masters of a highly developed literary craft. An advantage close students of ancient rhetorical theory and practice can enjoy is in being intrinsically less apt to make this mistake.[52]

Notes

1. *Sammlung ausgewählter Dialogen Platos mit deutschem Kommentar*, von M. Schanz. 3 Bändchen. *Apologia* (Leipzig: Tauchnitz, 1893), 5.
2. C.G. Cobet, *Novae Lectiones* (Leiden: Brill, 1858), 661–82.
3. The broader context for the scholarly views mentioned is outlined in an Appendix *infra*.
4. Schanz, *Apologia*, 36–45.
5. Translations are the author's own, except for extended passages of the Homeric text, which are taken from Richmond Lattimore's versions.
6. See Pl., *Phdr.* 271c10-272b6 and Xen. *Mem.* 4.1.3.
7. On Polycrates, see E.M. Cope, 'On the Sophistical Rhetoric', *Journal of Classical and Sacred Philology* 3 (1857): 281–3.
8. According to Douglas L. Cairns, *Aidōs. The Psychology and Ethics of Honour and Shame in Ancient Greek Literature* (Oxford: Clarendon, 1993), 29, the underlying conceptualization can be traced to Margaret Mead, *Cooperation and Competition*

among Primitive Peoples (New York: McGraw-Hill, 1937). A rigid terminology was popularized by Ruth Benedict, who during the Second World War adapted ideas current in cultural anthropology and psychology to help 'guilt-culture' Americans better understand their supposedly 'shame-culture' Japanese enemy (*The Chrysanthemum and the Sword. Patterns of Japanese Culture*, Boston: Houghton Mifflin, 1946), 222–7. The conceptual apparatus can be seen spreading to various disciplines shortly afterward. Erik Erikson would shortly employ it in his theory of psycho-social development, according to which there are 'eight ages of man', the second of which runs from eighteen months to three years, and the third from three to six years (*Childhood and Society*, New York: Norton, 1950). According to Erikson, during these two stages children characteristically sense shame, and then guilt, respectively. The following year, Benedict's scheme was introduced into classical studies by E.R. Dodds who viewed the development from the culture depicted in the Homeric poems to that of Classical times in analogous terms (*The Greeks and the Irrational*, Berkeley: University of California Press, 1951, chapter II: 'From Shame Culture to Guilt Culture'). One may contrast the enthusiastic reception of Norman O. Brown ('Psychoanalysis and the Classics', *Classical Journal* 52 (1957): 41–5) with the relative caution expressed by Friedrich Solmsen, among others (*American Journal of Philology* 75: 190–6; cf. other reviews by H.W. Parke, *Hermathena* 80 1952, 82–4 and J. Myers, *Annals of the American Academy of Political and Social Science* 1953, 203f. and 285). To judge from Cairns' conclusions (*Aidōs*, 47), the opposition between shame and guilt cultures within a generation outgrew its usefulness within classical studies even for approaches framed in terms proper to the social sciences. But one finds it still – if by now somewhat mechanically – applied in the interpretation of classical texts. The distinction has affinities with a slightly older one – sometimes employed in tandem with it – between what are termed 'competitive' and 'cooperative' virtues (or 'values'). Having recently outlined the origins of this apparatus elsewhere, I shall here add only that the mythical picture of cooperative virtues superseding competitive ones in ancient times was encouraged by a modernizing historical analysis that saw a development from comparatively exclusive aristocracy to a more inclusive democracy, and nicely dovetailed with the supposed development from a 'shame' culture of the Homeric poems to a 'guilt' culture of classical times. In an example of psychological speculation relying upon such categories, Graham Zanker – the utter lack of any corresponding Greek terminology notwithstanding – understands Achilles to be referring to his sense of guilt at 18.90–95 and 101-113 (*The Heart of Achilles. Characterization and Personal Ethics in the Iliad*, Ann Arbor: University of Michigan Press, 1994), 17; cf. 59–64.

9   The terminology of shame (αἰσχύνομαι, τὸ αἰσχρόν) is used as follows: (a) five times: as Socrates wonders at his accusers' shamelessness (17b1, b3, 24d8, 31b8, b9); (b) four times: where Socrates compares his sense of shame to that of Achilles (28b3, c3, d10, 29b7); (c) three times: when Socrates speaks of proper behavior in an Athenian court (35a3, a8, 38d7); (d) once: when Socrates speaks of Athenians' distorting the right priorities (29d9); (e) once: where Socrates speaks of the deficiencies of those reputed wise (22b5).

10 A more germane sense of shame, albeit to the exclusion of much else, has been aptly clarified and traced through the argument of the *Apology of Socrates* by Robert Metcalf, 'Socrates and Achilles', in *Reexamining Socrates in Plato's Apology*, eds. P. Fagan and J. Russon (Evanston, IL: Northwestern University Press, 2009), 62–84. In considering whether Socrates' comparison with Achilles 'speaks to the vigilant sense of

shame, or *aidos*, at the heart of Socrates' philosophical activity' (ibid. 80) it should perhaps be noticed that αἰδώς and etymologically related terms, which carry connotations of reverence or respect lacking to αἰσχύνη, occur nowhere in the *Apology of Socrates*. This and multiple analogous reservations would hold for Arlene Saxonhouse, 'A Shameless Socrates on Trial in Democratic Athens', in *Readings of Plato's* Apology of Socrates. *Defending the Philosophical Life*, eds. V.V. Haraldsen, O. Pettersson and O. Tvedt (Lanham, MD: Lexington, 2018), 17–36, where the principal's alleged shamelessness before democratic norms and expectations somehow transforms an ostensibly forensic speech into a tragi-comedy.

11 A tendency to treat Socrates as a literary 'hero' comes to sight at the outset of the century. Compare Lord Shaftesbury's analytic treatment, *Soliloquy: or Advice to an Author* (London: Morphew, 1710), 42, with a poetic application in Samuel Catherall, εἰκὼν Σωκρατική. *or, A Portraiture of Socrates*, Extracted out of Plato. In Blank Verse (Oxford: Litchfield, 1717), 52:

But now th' unwelcome Tragick Hour drew nigh,
Big with the Fate of Socrates and Athens
Oh! see the Vertuous Man pierc'd thro' with Pains,
And struggling in the Agonies of Death!
The potent Poyson overpowr's his Blood, –
And boils thro' ev'ry Vein. How wan His Looks!
How swoln his Legs, which can no more support
Th' envenom'd Mass! See, how he panting lies,
Pale, and half dead! Life quivers on a Point!
By slow Degrees the dire Infection rolls
Nearer, and nearer to his spotless Heart.
And shiv'ring Death creeps cold thro' ev'ry Limb.
See! He, unvails his Face, and sets his Eyes
On Crito, eager now to vent his last;
When the remaining Breath, which Life supply'd,
Broke out in Words like these: Crito, 'tis done.
The Cure is wrought; and let that early Bird,
Which crowing first Salutes the Light, be slain
A Victim due to great Apollo's Son.
I charge thee by those Sacred Shades below,
And all the unbody'd Ghosts, that wander there,
Remember Æsculapius!
Then Crito thus reply'd. It shall be done:
And hast thou more to Say, Majestick Soul?
Ah! Not a word! – Ev'n now he groans, and dies:
There goes the Hero, and Philosopher,
The Greatest, Athens ever bred! oh Friend!
Oh Socrates! _____
Thus Speaking, He drew nigh, wept o'er the Corps,
Beheld the Clay divested of its Soul,
The immortal Socrates for ever fled,
And own'd the Truth of all His Reas'nings clear.

Worthy of Seneca, perhaps, but hardly of Plato. Yet before too long the category had turned up in scholarly works on Plato. (See Floyer Sydenham, *A Synopsis Or General*

View of the Works of Plato, (London: Richardson, 1759), 21 and Ebenezer Macfait, *Remarks On the Life and Writings of Plato*, (Edinburgh: Millar, 1760), 86.) This romantic notion, later amalgamated with an equally creative social-scientific conception (best known though its popularization by Joseph Campbell, for the full-blown version of which, see *The Power of Myth* (New York: Doubleday, 1988)), has recently come to inform book-length 'literary-philosophical' treatments of Plato – among which one by Angela Hobbs, *Plato and the Hero. Courage, Manliness and the Impersonal Good* (Cambridge: Cambridge University Press, 2000), might have qualified, did it not in fact devote so much space to familiar the quodlibets apt to bewilder contemporary philosophical readings of Socrates' comparison of Achilles' case with his own – on which see 178–86. Apparently, we may reasonably demand of Socrates even on a critical forensic occasion that he avoid statements demonstrably at odds with sundry 'theses' that analytic philosophers have contrived to extract from Plato's literary dialogues.
12 ἥρως.
13 ἡμίθεος.
14 Bruno Snell, *Aischylos und das Handeln im Drama*, Philologus Suppl. 20, no. 1 (Leipzig: Dieter, 1928), 20. Cf. id. *Die Entdeckung des Geistes. Studien zur Entstehung des europäischen Denkens bei den Griechen* (Hamburg: Claassen & Goverts, 1946) (Eng. trans. of 2nd ed. of 1948 as: *The Discovery of the Mind; The Greek Origins of European Thought*, trans. T. Rosenmeyer, Oxford: Blackwell, 1953) (4th German ed. Göttingen: Vandenhoeck und Ruprecht, 1974, where see 104–5 and 304 nn12–14.).
15 I 393 hofft Achill auf Rückkehr, aber nicht ernsthaft. Achill erwägt auch die Rückkehr, aber ohne inneren Kampf; ebenso steht im Anfang des Σ, in den versen, die in der Apologie zitiert werden, nichts von einer Entscheidung des Achill. Daß man später die Erzählung so gedeutet hat . . . ist ein lehrreiches Beispiel für unwillkürliche Weiterentwicklung der Sage, und zeigt, wie vorsichtig man sein muß, um nicht spätere Gedanken in einer Erzählung einzutragen. (Snell, *Aischylos*, 22)
16 E. Wolff, *Gnomon* 5, no. 7 (1928): 386–400. The same author had lately published his doctoral dissertation on the *Apology of Socrates* (*Platos Apologie*, Neue Philologische Untersuchungen Heft 4, Berlin: Weidmann, 1929), a central chapter of which ('Prohairesis', 34–66) was partly undercut by Snell's interpretation. Snell replied to Wolff's criticisms in 'Das Bewusstsein von eigenen Entscheidungen im frühen Griechentum', *Philologus* 85 (1930): 141–58.
17 Snell's views had considerable influence on various subsequent treatments: F. Mehmel, 'Homer und die Griechen', *Antike und Abendland* 4 (1954), 16–41; Chr. Voigt, *Überlegung und Entscheidung: Studien zur Selbstauffassung des Menschen bei Homer* (Meisenhaim am Glan: Anthon Hain, 1972).
18 See in particular Albin Lesky, *Göttliche und menschliche Motivation im homerischen Epos* (Heidelberg: Winter, 1952) and Snell's reply in 'Göttliche und menschliche Motivation im homerischen Schriften', *Sitz.-Ber. Heidelb. Akad. Wiss. Phil-hist. Kl.* 4. Abt. (reprinted in id. *Gesammelte Schriften*, Göttingen: Vandenhoeck und Ruprecht, 1966), 55–61. For an interesting attempt to question Snell's findings via the methods of ordinary-language philosophy, see R. Gaskin, 'Do Homeric Heroes Make Real Decisions?' *Classical Quarterly* 40, no. 1 (1990): 1–15.
19 Snell, 'Shame and Guilt: Aeschylus' Achilles', in id. *Scenes from Greek Drama*, 1 (Berkeley: University of California Press, 1964). In a revised and augmented German version of these Sather Lectures, Snell's quotation from Goethe is corrected to read, not 'treffliche', but 'treffende Wahl' – i.e., a 'striking' or even 'touching', rather than

'excellent' or 'admirable' choice. ('Achill bei Aischylos', in id., *Szenen aus griechischen Dramen*, 1 (Berlin: De Gruyter, 1971).

20 The premise for Goethe's fragment – only the initial scenes for a longer work never continued – is suggestive: Achilles stands contemplatively in the pit made ready to receive the freshly incinerated remains of Patroclus, when, after some discussion among the gods on Olympus, Athene appears to him in the guise of Antilochus. The quoted lines occur in a *consolatio* in which the goddess explains the poetic fame that will be his, spoken with a view to encouraging his resolution in the face of the inevitable. External evidence indicates that Goethe's plan was for Achilles to be distracted from Athene's purpose by falling in love with the Trojan Princess Polyxena, varying a myth developed by Ovid and Seneca in Roman imperial times. It is unclear whether his love was to be requited, with the two hopeless lovers succumbing in Shakespearean fashion, or rather Polyxena would reject his advances, expose him to the Trojans, and therewith help bring about his demise at the hands of Paris. See G. Brandes, *Wolfgang Goethe*, 3rd ed. (Copenhagen: Gydendal, 1920, II.72-74 (German trans. *Goethe*, 4th ed. (Berlin: Reiss, 1922), 402–5; Eng. trans. *Wolfgang Goethe*, from the 2nd ed. of 1916 (New York: Crown, 1936), II.173-177.))

21 See L. Strauss, 'On Plato's *Apology of Socrates* and *Crito*', in id., *Studies in Platonic Political Philosophy*, 44 and 55 (Chicago: University of Chicago Press, 1983); cf. T.G. West, *Plato's Apology of Socrates. An Interpretation with a New Translation* (Ithaca: Cornell University Press, 1979), 157–9. Elaborations or modifications of this line of interpretation include Alan Bloom, *The Republic of Plato*, (New York: Basic Books, 1968), 353–8 (2nd ed. 1991, 354–9); Metcalf, 'Socrates and Achilles'; and Saxonhouse, 'A Shameless Socrates'. As an extreme instance of the tendency, Saxonhouse holds Socrates' comparison of himself to Achilles 'a truly shocking image that can be read as either a completely laughable or tragic analogy' (27), one that is 'curious' (ibid.), 'most awkward' and 'weird' (29).

22 For the main lines of the analysis of the *Iliad* premised here, see Eric Voegelin, *The World of the Polis* (Baton Rouge: University of Louisiana Press, 1957), 83–92.

23 μῆνις.

24 That is, where our text of Homer reads αὐτίκα τεθναίην, ἐπεὶ οὐκ ἄρ' ἔμελλον ἑταίρῳ κτεινομένῳ ἐπαμῦναι (18.98f.) and then, after several intervening lines, ἀλλ' ἧμαι παρὰ νηυσὶν ἐτώσιον ἄχθος ἀρούρης (18.104) Plato's modifies and compresses these into αὐτίκα τεθναίην, ἵνα μὴ μένω καταγέλαστος παρὰ νηυσὶ κορωνίσιν ἄχθος ἀρούρης (28d3f.).

25 δίκην ἐπιτιθεὶς τῷ ἀδικοῦντι (28d2).

26 οὑτωσί πως (28c5).

27 See Diskin Clay, 'Socrates' Mulishness and Heroism', *Phronesis* 17 (1972): 59f. with n13.

28 Thomas G. West and Grace S. West, *Four Texts on Socrates. Plato's Euthyphro, Apology, and Crito and Aristophanes' Clouds* (Ithaca: Cornell University Press, 1984), 79 n50. This work builds on Thomas G. West, *Plato's Apology of Socrates. An Interpretation with a New Translation* (Ithaca: Cornell University Press, 1979), in relation to which (where see 59f.) it elaborates on, or restates, certain points.

29 For a development of this thought along somewhat different lines from those pursued in this paper, see Wolfgang Schadewaldt, 'Die Entscheidung des Achilles', *Die Antike* 12 (1936): 173–210 (reprinted in id. *Von Homers Welt und Werk. Aufsätze und Auslegungen zur homerischen Frage*. (Leipzig: Koehler & Amelang, 1944); 2nd ed. 1951; 3rd ed. 1959; 3., erw. Aufl. 1965, 162–95), which speaks of a 'necessity' under which Achilles labors.

30 ἕλωρα is the accusative plural of the Epic neuter ἕλωρ, a noun derived from ἑλεῖν (to take, or sieze). In the singular it regularly refers to unburied corpses under their aspect as spoils or prey for the enemy or animals. Liddell and Scott are less than consistent on the exact force of the plural ἕλωρα here, its only use in Homer. The 7th edition (1883), on which the Intermediate currently in use is based, rendered the whole phrase 'pay the penalty for the slaughter of Patroclus' (s.v. ἕλωρ), but in another place 'may atone for making a prey of Patroclus' (s.v. ἀποτίνω). But the abridged edition, last revised in 1871, renders the phrase 'pay for leaving Patroclus a prey to all dishonour', possibly reflecting older editions like the 5th (1864), which rendered the word with its accompanying genitive 'an atonement for slaying and despoiling' (s.v. ἕλωρ), but also the whole phrase with the verb as 'may atone for making a prey of Patroclus' (s.v. ἀποτίνω). Whatever the reason for the change seen in the 7th edition, given that the word concretely refers to things dragged off (ἑλκύσματα), rather than animal nourishment (βρώματα – see Aristonicus Gramm. *de sign. Iliad.* ad 18.93), and that Homer is about to describe the fight over his corpse, it seems best to understand it to refer here to the booty constituted by Patroclus' – and thereby prospectively, Hector's (see Eustathius *In Iliad.* 4.140.2-12) – still-armored person.
31 Achilles' terms here are ἔρις and χόλος.
32 ἀποτίνω means primarily 'to repay', whence also 'to atone for', as at 18.93. Achilles' announcement that he intends to exact such atonement at 90–94 is what Thetis responds to at 95f., which Socrates paraphrases as her predicting that he will die if he avenges (εἰ τιμωρήσεις) Patroclus' slaughter by killing Hector (28c6f.). Cf. further her words at 128f. (οὐ κακόν ἐστι, τειρομένοις ἑτάροισιν ἀμύνεμεν αἰπὺν ὄλεθρον) with Socrates' phrasing at 28d1: δείσας τὸ ζῆν κακὸς ὢν καὶ τοῖς φίλοις μὴ τιμωρεῖν, where the καὶ is epexegetical.
33 φόνος.
34 δίκη and γράφη, respectively.
35 πελάτης; the term suggests 'someone drawing near, or nearby' (4c3).
36 ἐθήτευεν (3c4); cf. θής (15c5).
37 A θής is not at all a 'slave', as is often carelessly held, but he is not even the same as a 'serf' (as often translated, e.g. in Bloom, *The Republic of Plato*, 63 and 195). An unattached laborer lacked the support every Athenian's slave or Spartan's Helot enjoyed from a larger family. This is why when the shade of Achilles wants Odysseus to understand how unfortunate he feels to be dead, he does so by contrasting being lord over all the dead and gone (πᾶσιν νεκύεσσι καταφθιμένοισιν ἀνάσσειν) not with being a slave or a serf, but with ἐπάρουρος ἐὼν θητευέμεν ἄλλῳ, ἀνδρὶ παρ' ἀκλήρῳ, ᾧ μὴ βίοτας πολὺς εἴη, i.e. with doing farm work for someone else of limited means for lack of property (*Od.* 11.489-91). Relative to the administration of justice (a driving issue for both main characters), the lord occupies the most authoritative position, while a θής holds the weakest one imaginable. See Burnet's notes ad 5d6 and c4.
38 On the unlikely supposition that, as a patron, Euthyphro could have legitimately felt some responsibility for his πελάτης, see Burnet's note ad 4c3.
39 For the relevant facts of law and custom, see Burnet, 2f. and notes ad 2a5, 3e5, 4a7, b4, b9, b10, c1, c2, c6, and d7.
40 αἴ κε μὴ Ἕκτωρ πρῶτος ἐμῷ ὑπὸ δουρὶ τυπεὶς ἀπὸ θυμὸν ὀλέσσῃ, ... ἕλωρα ... ἀποτίσῃ (18.91-93).
41 ὠκύμορος δή μοι τέκος ἔσσεαι, οἷ' ἀγορεύεις· αὐτίκα γάρ τοι ἔπειτα μεθ' Ἕκτορα πότμος ἑτοῖμος. (18.95f.)
42 εἰ τιμωρήσεις Πατρόκλῳ τῷ ἑταίρῳ τὸν φόνον καὶ Ἕκτορα ἀποκτενεῖς, αὐτὸς ἀποθανῇ, αὐτίκα γάρ τοι ... μεθ' Ἕκτορα πότμος ἑτοῖμος (28c6-8).

43 τοῖς φίλοις ... τιμωρεῖν ... δίκην ἐπιθεὶς τῷ ἀδικοῦντι 28d1f. Cf. Achilles' words to Hector as he is on the point of throwing his spear at him (22.271f).
44 For speculation along such lines, see West, *Plato's Apology*, 155–62.
45 See Strauss, 'On Plato's *Apology*', 55f. and 66.
46 Relying on a notion of 'sovereignty' peculiar to modern political thought, Gregory Vlastos would in his lectures allege an inconsistency between Socrates' statement that he would decline a bargain by which he could live provided he give up his philosophical questioning and his position that he is legally bound to abide by the verdict of the jury. A 1974 article then spawned an extensive and correspondingly tinged scholarly discussion. For some useful observations, see Grace S. West, 'Socrates in the *Crito*: Patriot or Friend?', in *Essays in Ancient Greek Philosophy* 3, eds. J. Anton and A. Preus, (Albany: State University of New York Press, 1989), 71–83.
47 μήνιδος ἀπόρρησις.
48 This phase of the course of Achilles' μῆνις is signalled, among other ways, by Homer's repeated use of the verb μενεαίνειν, which means something like 'to be in a fury'. The verb is used eleven times in the first fifteen books – normally of eagerness on the part of a warrior to overcome an enemy, and never of Achilles. In the last nine books, it is used twelve times – all but once of Achilles. At 19.67f., he makes a direct connection with his earlier anger, saying, as he is renouncing his wrath, 'Now I will make an end to my anger (χόλον). It does not become me unrelentingly to rage on (μενεαίνεμεν).' But this is just what he now does in another form.
49 Saxonhouse makes some observations pertinent to understanding the greater course of Achilles' wrath ('*Thymos*, Justice and the Moderation of Anger in the Story of Achilles', in *Understanding the Political Spirit: Philosophical Investigations from Socrates to Nietzsche*, ed. C. Zuckert (New Haven: Yale University Press, 1988), 30–47). Unfortunately, her characterization of Homer's Achilles blends several inapplicable ideas. Postulating a crisis of confidence in the principle of distributive justice observed in a heroic society, and lending a palpably Christian cast to the humanity gained by Achilles in the course of his anger, she conflates Homer's θυμός with Plato's θυμοειδές – in keeping with the aims of an anthology designed to elaborate yet further on some remarks Leo Strauss made about the significance of 'spiritedness' for Plato's philosophy. Cf. Bloom, *The Republic of Plato Republic*, 353–8, with Strauss 'The Problem of Socrates: Five Lectures', in id., *The Rebirth of Classical Political Rationalism* (Chicago: University of Chicago Press, 1989), 164–8. For a perceptive analysis more germane to Homeric thought, see Katherine Callan King. *Achilles. Paradigms of the War Hero from Homer to the Middle Ages*. Berkeley: University of California Press, 1987, 28–32.
50 See Strauss, 'On the *Apology*', 55.
51 Cf. *Phaedo* 70b1-7 with 115d2-6.
52 The supposition of an influence was first explored in any detail by Rudolf Hirzel ('Polykrates' Anklage und Lysias' Vertheidigung des Sokrates', *Rheinisches Museum* 42 (1887): 239–50), who concluded that Libanius had what he did from Polycrates only through a lost *Defense of Socrates* attributed to Lysias, while others would hold to a hypothesis of direct dependence. Attempts to reconstruct Polycrates' speech out of Xenophon and Libanius culminated with Jean Humbert, 'Le Pamphlet de Polycrates et le Gorgias de Platon', *Revue de philologie* (1931): 20–77. Humbert's questionable conclusions will be cited uncritically as givens even today; for salutary remarks informed by close acquaintance with Libanius' actual methods, see D.A. Russell, *Libanius: Imaginary Speeches: a Selection of Declamations* (London: Duckworth, 1996), 17f.

Bibliography

Benedict, Ruth. *The Chrysanthemum and the Sword. Patterns of Japanese Culture.* Boston: Houghton Mifflin, 1946.
Bloom, Allan. Trans. *The Republic of Plato.* New York: Basic Books, 1968 (2nd ed. 1991).
Brandes, Georg. *Wolfgang Goethe*, 3rd ed. Copenhagen: Gydendal, 1920. (German trans. *Goethe*, 4th ed., trans. Erich Holm & Emilie Stein. Berlin: Reiss, 1922; English trans. *Wolfgang Goethe*, from the 2nd ed. of 1916, trans. Allen W. Porterfield. New York: Crown 1936).
Brown, Norman O. 'Psychoanalysis and the Classics'. *Classical Journal* 52 (1957): 41–5.
Burnet, John. *Plato's* Euthyphro, Apology of Socrates, *and* Crito. Oxford: Clarendon, 1924.
Cairns, Douglas L. *Aidōs. The Psychology and Ethics of Honour and Shame in Ancient Greek Literature.* Oxford: Clarendon, 1993.
Campbell, Joseph. *The Power of Myth.* New York: Doubleday, 1988.
Catherall, Sam. εἰκὼν Σωκρατική. *Or, A Portraiture of Socrates, Extracted out of Plato. In Blank Verse.* Oxford: Litchfield, 1717.
Clay, Diskin. 'Socrates' Mulishness and Heroism'. *Phronesis* 17 (1972): 53–60.
Cobet, C.G. *Novae Lectiones*, Leiden: Brill, 1858.
Cope, E.M. 'On the Sophistical Rhetoric'. *Journal of Classical and Sacred Philology* 3 (1857): 34–80 and 253–88.
Dodds, E.R. *The Greeks and the Irrational.* Berkeley: University of California Press, 1951.
Erikson, Erik. *Childhood and Society.* New York: Norton, 1950.
Gaskin, Richard. 'Do Homeric Heroes Make Real Decisions?' *Classical Quarterly* 40, no. 1 (1990): 1–15.
Hirzel, Rudolph. 'Polykrates' Anklage und Lysias' Vertheidigung des Sokrates'. *Rheinisches Museum* 42 (1887): 239–50.
Hobbs, Angela. *Plato and the Hero. Courage, Manliness and the Impersonal Good.* Cambridge: Cambridge University Press, 2000.
Humbert, Jean. 'Le Pamphlet de Polycrates et le Gorgias de Platon'. *Revue de philologie* (1931): 20–77.
King, Katherine Callen. *Achilles. Paradigms of the War Hero from Homer to the Middle Ages.* Berkeley: University of California Press, 1987.
Lesky, Albin. *Göttliche und menschliche Motivation im homerischen Epos.* Sitzungsberichte der Heidelberger Akademie der Wissenschaften, Philosophisch-Historische Klasse, 4. Abh., 1961.
Macfait, Ebenezer. *Remarks on the Life and Writings of Plato.* Edinburgh: Millar, 1760.
Mead, Margaret. (ed.) *Cooperation and Competition among Primitive Peoples.* New York: McGraw-Hill, 1937.
Mehmel, Friedrich. 'Homer und die Griechen'. *Antike und Abendland* 4 (1954): 16–41.
Metcalf, Robert. 'Socrates and Achilles'. In *Reexamining Socrates in the Apology*, edited by P. Fagan and J. Russon. Evanston, IL: Northwestern University Press 2009, 62–84.
Myers, John L. Review of Dodds, *The Greeks and the Irrational. Annals of the American Academy of Political and Social Science* 285 (1953): 203f.
Parke, H.W. Review of Dodds, *The Greeks and the Irrational. Hermathena* 80 (1952): 82–4.
Russell, D.A. *Libanius: Imaginary Speeches: a Selection of Declamations.* London: Duckworth, 1996.
Saxonhouse, Arlene. '*Thymos*, Justice and the Moderation of Anger in the Story of Achilles'. In *Understanding the Political Spirit: Philosophical Investigations from Socrates to Nietzsche*, edited by C. Zuckert, 30–47. New Haven: Yale University Press, 1988.

Saxonhouse, Arlene. 'A Shameless Socrates on Trial in Democratic Athens'. In *Readings of Plato's Apology of Socrates. Defending the Philosophical Life*, edited by V.V. Haraldsen, O. Pettersson and O. Tvedt, 17-36. Lanham, MD: Lexington, 2018.

Schadewaldt, Wolfgang. 'Die Entscheidung des Achilles'. *Die Antike* 12 (1936): 173-210 (reprinted in id. *Von Homers Welt und Werk. Aufsätze und Auslegungen zur homerischen Frage*. Leipzig: Koehler & Amelang 1944 2nd ed. 1951; 3rd ed. 1959; 3., erw. Aufl. 1965, 162-95).

Schanz, Martin. *Sammlung ausgewählter Dialogen Platos mit deutschem Kommentar*, von M. Schanz. 3 Bändchen. *Apologia*, Leipzig: Tauchnitz, 1893.

Shaftesbury, Lord (A.A. Cooper, 3rd Earl of Shaftesbury). *Soliloquy: or Advice to an Author*. London: Morphew, 1710.

Snell, Bruno. *Aischylos und das Handeln im Drama*. Philologus Suppl. 20, no. 1. Leipzig: Dieter, 1928.

Snell, Bruno. 'Das Bewusstsein von eigenen Entscheidungen im frühen Griechentum'. *Philologus* 85 (1930): 141-58.

Snell, Bruno. 'Göttliche und menschliche Motivation im homerischen Schriften'. In: *Argumentationen. Festschrift für Josef König*, edited by H. Delius and G. Patzig, 249-55. Göttingen: Vandenhoeck und Ruprecht (reprinted in id. *Gesammelte Schriften*, 55-61. Göttingen: Vandenhoeck und Ruprecht, 1966).

Snell, Bruno. *Die Entdeckung des Geistes. Studien zur Entstehung des europäischen Denkens bei den Griechen*, Hamburg: Claassen & Goverts, 1946. (Eng. trans. of 2nd ed. of 1948 as: *The Discovery of the Mind; The Greek Origins of European Thought*, trans. by T. Rosenmeyer, Oxford: Blackwell, 1953) (4th ed. 1974, Göttingen: Vandenhoeck und Ruprecht).

Snell, Bruno. 'Shame and Guilt: Aeschylus' Achilles'. In id., *Scenes from Greek Drama*, 1-22. Berkeley: University of California Press, 1964.

Snell, Bruno. 'Achill bei Aischylos'. In id., *Szenen aus griechischen Dramen*, 1-24. Berlin: De Gruyter, 1971.

Solmsen, Friedrich. Review of Dodds, *The Greeks and the Irrational*. *American Journal of Philology* 75 (1954): 190-6.

Strauss, Leo. 'On Plato's *Apology of Socrates* and *Crito*'. In: *Essays in Honor of Jacob Klein*, edited by S. Kutler, 155-60. Annapolis: St. John's College Press, 1976. (Reprinted in id. *Studies in Platonic Political Philosophy*, edited by T. Pangle, 38-66. Chicago: University of Chicago Press, 1983.)

Strauss, Leo. 'The Problem of Socrates: Five Lectures' In id., *The Rebirth of Classical Political Rationalism*, 103-83. Chicago: University of Chicago Press, 1989.

Sydenham, Floyer. *A Synopsis Or General View of the Works of Plato*. London: Richardson, 1759.

Voegelin, Eric. *The World of the Polis*. Baton Rouge: University of Louisiana Press, 1957.

Voigt, Christian. *Überlegung und Entscheidung: Studien zur Selbstauffassung des Menschen bei Homer*. Meisenhaim am Glan: Anthon Hain, 1972.

West, Grace Starry. 'Socrates in the *Crito*: Patriot or Friend?' In *Essays in Ancient Greek Philosophy* 3, edited by J. Anton & A. Preus, 71-83. Albany: State University of New York Press, 1989.

West, Thomas G. *Plato's* Apology of Socrates. *An Interpretation with a New Translation*. Ithaca: Cornell University Press, 1979.

West, Thomas G. and Grace Starry West (trans.). *Four Texts on Socrates. Plato's* Euthyphro, Apology, *and* Crito *and Aristophanes'* Clouds. Ithaca: Cornell University Press, 1984.

Wolf, Erwin. *Platos Apologie*. Neue Philologische Untersuchungen Heft 4. Berlin: Weidmann, 1929.

Wolff, Erwin. Review of Snell, *Aischylos und das Handeln im Drama. Gnomon* 5, no. 7 (1929): 386–400.

Zanker, Graham. *The Heart of Achilles. Characterization and Personal Ethics in the* Iliad. Ann Arbor: University of Michigan Press, 1996.

4

Plato's Ring of Gyges and *Das Leben der Anderen*

Jacob Howland

At the very beginning of Plato's *Republic* II, Socrates remarks that his defence of justice in Book I 'was, as it seems, only a prelude' (357a).[1] The real action of the *Republic* evidently begins when Glaucon 'renew[s] the argument of Thrasymachus' (358b–c). The core of this renewal is a well-known myth. An anonymous ancestor of Gyges the Lydian (or perhaps Gyges himself) is working as a shepherd when the earth splits open. He goes down into the underworld and steals a ring from the finger of a giant corpse. Upon discovering that the ring makes him invisible, he uses it to sleep with the queen, kill the king, and usurp his office. Thinking through this myth, Glaucon asserts, will show that all human beings would commit injustice if given the 'license' to do so (359b–c). When Glaucon is finished speaking, Adeimantus argues that the mythological tradition inaugurated by Homer and Hesiod, particularly in conjunction with rituals of sacrifice and religious initiation, teaches intelligent young men to behave unjustly. He reiterates his brother's request that Socrates genuinely persuade them that it is preferable to be just rather than unjust.

Taken together, Glaucon's praise of injustice and Adeimantus's indictment of the poeticoreligious tradition determine the overall course of the rest of the dialogue. 'Like men mythologizing in a myth' (376d), and thus like poets, Socrates and his companions proceed to weave a philosophical story about city and soul that is designed to clarify the nature of justice and demonstrate its superiority to injustice. Looking back over the conversation from the vantage point of Book X, Socrates concludes – and Glaucon agrees – that 'the soul must do the just things, whether it has the ring of Gyges or not' (612b).

Socrates does not, however, acknowledge (although Plato surely wishes us to perceive) that the central political myth of the *Republic* – the myth of Kallipolis, the Noble and Beautiful City – is itself Gygean. The philosopher-kings are godlike in their supposed wisdom (540a-c; cf. 521c), but also in their hiddenness: 'most precise guardians' who share in a 'most precise education' (503b, d), they unite Thrasymachus's conception of ruling as an exact and infallible technical expertise with Gyges' seemingly divine power of invisibility (340e, 360b). In fact, the rulers possess a political *technê* that falls short of genuine wisdom.[2] In Kallipolis, the ideal of absolute social control for the sake of justice furthermore eclipses, but does not replace, the totality of self-satisfaction exemplified in the figure of Gyges. The regime's founders aim to control *erôs* and *thymos*, or erotic longing and aggression – forces, to paraphrase Freud, that rule the world[3] – by deploying the political equivalent of the metal web in which Homer's Hephaestus ensnares the adulterous Ares and Aphrodite, the gods of war and love (*Odyssey* 8.266-366). Unfortunately, the rulers who wield this web must stand outside of it, even though they are produced within it and bear its impress, which is to say that Kallipolis suffers from an essential contradiction. This contradiction is reflected in the regime's incoherent combination of licence and restriction, a combination that virtually guarantees corruption among the rulers.

Gyges' ring, Glaucon observes, would allow one 'to take whatever he might want from the marketplace without fear, and to go into the houses and have intercourse with whomever he wants, and to kill or release from bonds anyone he wants, and in all other things to act as an equal to a god among human beings' (360b-c). It is not often noted that the bravest warriors in Kallipolis would enjoy similar satisfactions, including frequent and even incestuous intercourse with multiple partners, the legal discharge of violent aggression (there being no laws against assault or insult), the choicest cuts of meat, celebratory encomia in poetry and music, and worship after death as deities, to say nothing of freedom from the need to care for relatives or labour for wages.[4] Their life, Socrates says, will be 'more blessed than the most blessed one the Olympic victors live' (465d); and while he subsequently qualifies this claim (466a), he does not mention that the near-divinity of this existence is in certain respects indistinguishable from bestiality. The regime nevertheless embraces Glaucon's guiding idea that injustice flourishes only when it is invisible. Hence the auxiliaries are allowed no private property beyond the bare necessities, and no 'house or storeroom into which whoever wishes cannot enter' (416d). It need hardly be said that such entry would sometimes have to be unobserved in order to be fully efficacious, which is to say that the regime will spy on its citizens – in this, too, following the example of Gyges, who first uses the ring to eavesdrop while others are discussing him (359e-60a). What is more, the rulers of Kallipolis will censor poetry, deploy politically useful lies, suppress politically inconvenient truths, and secretly manipulate the sexual lives of citizens. In brief, the regime addresses the problem of injustice by confronting individuals as an anonymous, faceless, and therefore utterly irresponsible totality of power. Its citizens will be propagandized and constantly monitored by rulers whose work is largely covert, and who are in essential respects accountable to no one but themselves.

Incoherent as it may be, the idealistic ambition of Kallipolis is boundless. Thrasymachus states that tyranny is perfect injustice, which 'by stealth and force takes away what belongs to others, both what is sacred and holy, private and public, not bit by bit, but all at once' (344a). *Hiera kai hosia* seems to refer to sanctified property associated with religious rites;[5] the tyrant's greed, in other words, is in no way moderated by religious awe. The founders of Kallipolis, however, are still more comprehensive – and more subtle – in exercising power over things divine as well as human. Socrates inaugurates the inquiry into the education of young children by remarking that 'the beginning is the greatest part of every work' (377a). The 'beginning' in question is poetry, the ensuing discussion of which incorporates the first known occurrence (and the only one in the Platonic corpus) of the word 'theology'. As used at 379a, *theologia* means simply 'speech about the gods'. Socrates introduces the word in the course of establishing models to which all such speech, especially including poetic myths, must conform. He goes on to propose two models that transform the amoral and protean gods of the poetic tradition into perfect and unchanging entities, much like the Platonic Ideas. The first is that 'the god is not the cause of all things, but [only] of the good'; the second, that the god 'remains forever in his own shape', neither transforming himself nor misleading others 'by lies in speech or deed' (380c, 381c, 382e–83a). These theological principles are legislative enactments, not philosophical conclusions; Socrates embraces them not because they are true – for he admits that 'we don't know where the truth about ancient things resides' – but because they are of great utility in educating citizens to be as 'god-revering and divine as possible' (382d, 383c).

The regulation of theology in Kallipolis raises a closely related question on which Socrates is largely silent, namely, the regime's control of poetic speech about *itself*. Such control is presupposed by the Noble Lie of Book III, a myth about the brotherhood of the citizens that would be rendered useless by an honest account of its purpose and origins, and by Socrates' statement in Book X that 'only so much of poetry as is hymns to gods or celebration of good men should be admitted into a city' (607a). In other words, the models of theological speech in Kallipolis would seem to apply to the regime as well: speech that publicly calls into question the goodness of its laws and customs, or the decency and truthfulness of its founders and rulers, must be suppressed (cf. 377b with 537d–39a). The issue of falsity is irrelevant in this context; even some truths, Socrates explains, are to be regarded as 'unspeakable secrets' (378a). But everyone knows that poets imitate and produce speeches about human existence as a whole, irrespective of its goodness or badness. From this we may draw two conclusions. First, because poets are naturally inclined to observe and portray human behaviour in all of its forms, and because their speech will be closely regulated in Kallipolis, they are well positioned to communicate base truths as well as noble lies about the regime. Second, the rulers will have to spy on the poets in order to ensure that they do not do so.

These conclusions have been amply confirmed by the actual practices of totalitarian regimes in the twentieth century. This brings me to my topic, which is in the broadest sense the relationship between poetic imagination and quasi-philosophical or ideological totalitarianism. We shall see in the next section that poetic imagination has the potential to reveal fundamental moral truths, but that there is nothing necessary about this sort of revelation: for those like Glaucon, the Ring Myth establishes the universality of injustice; for others, it discloses the moral impossibility of radical injustice. Similarly, in another passage with decisive consequences for the development of the dialogue, Socrates regards as 'true' and 'healthy' the simple city in speech of book 2 that is produced (*poiêsei* 369c) by basic human needs, while Glaucon dismisses it as a 'city of pigs' (372d-e). Socrates initially replaces the true and healthy city with a regime that results from the introduction and subsequent political purgation of the sickness of unrestrained desire, one ruled by ostensibly courageous and moderate guardians (but see Socrates' doubts at 416b). This austere product of political medicine, however, does not satisfy Socrates' manly and erotic interlocutors: Adeimantus asserts the guardians will be unhappy, and everyone wants to hear more about relations with women (419a-20a, 449a-50a). The dissatisfaction of his interlocutors causes Socrates to modify his defence of justice in a manner that ultimately leads to the construction of Kallipolis, a decayed simulacrum of the true and healthy city in which political artifice attempts to replace natural necessity, even in the education of its rulers.[6] If, as these passages suggest, poetry speaks to people in different ways according to differences in the disposition of their souls, Socrates' attempt to banish equivocal myths from the city in speech (378d-e) would seem to be doomed to fail. In fact, the *mythos* of Kallipolis is itself revealingly equivocal: it looks noble and beautiful to Glaucon, who can easily imagine himself as a richly rewarded member of its ruling elite, but ugly and base to those who (like Socrates) are able to divine, or (like us, and Plato when he wrote the *Republic*) are already familiar with, the morally and intellectually destructive effects of totalizing politics.[7] Read within the broader context of the *Republic*, the story of Kallipolis thus reflects the potential of poetry to seduce and mislead the soul as well as to guide it towards truth and justice – a potential that in any case serves, in the hands of philosophers like Socrates and Plato, as a tool for assessing our moral and intellectual condition.

To my knowledge, the first literary exploration in the modern era of the relationship between poetic imagination and totalitarianism is Yevgeny Zamyatin's 1921 novel *We*, which was denied publication by the censors of the Soviet Union.[8] Equally substantial, and much more recent, is Florian Henckel von Donnersmarck's *Das Leben der Anderen*, a film about the secret monitoring of writers by the Stasi, the East German *Ministerium für Staatssicherheit*. *The Life of Others* is especially pertinent to the *Republic*. In dramatizing the Gygean character of the Stasi – whose declared goal, as the film informs us, was 'to know everything' – the film indirectly illuminates the connection between the Ring Myth of Glaucon and the political myth of Kallipolis. Surprisingly, however, it refutes Glaucon's argument for the universal appeal of injustice. It does so by connecting Gygean invisibility with poetic education, convincingly imagining that, in extraordinary circumstances, the power of the ring could lead even a servant of tyranny onto the path of nobility and justice. The key to this liberating education is the example of the poets themselves, whose difficult struggle to articulate and transmit freely chosen ideals of truth and beauty ultimately undermines the communist regime's indoctrination of its citizens and aggressive suppression of dissent. In the end, the greatest danger to the systematic imposition of abstract social justice proves not to be the predictable debasement of desire through the corruptive effects of power, but its moral and aesthetic purification and sublimation – a process that operates on the single individual by means of erotic and mimetic mechanisms.

I begin with a brief reflection that aims to illuminate the connection between poetic imagination and moral receptivity in the Ring Myth. We will then be prepared to consider the ways in which the educative power of poetry operates in and through *The Life of Others*.

Gyges and the imagination of the other

In Book II, Glaucon explains that he has not yet learned from Socrates what justice and injustice are, 'and what power each has all by itself in the soul' (358a). He asks about their powers in the soul because he wants to know what it is to *be* purely and simply just or unjust. Glaucon recognizes that this experience cannot be conveyed by a philosophical definition or *logos*. To the extent that it is available at all to one who is neither perfectly just nor perfectly unjust, it requires an act of imagination, and is accessible only by way of a story – a *mythos*, in the broad sense of the word. His myth is a thought-experiment specifically designed to establish a point that he attributes to 'Thrasymachus and countless others', namely, that those who practice justice do so 'unwillingly, from a lack of power to do injustice' (358c, 359b). Were we to give both the just and the unjust man the 'license to do whatever he wants', and to 'follow and watch' each as he is led by his desire – something he proposes to do within the space opened up by imagination – we would catch the just man, he claims, 'going the same way as the unjust man' (359c). This way of putting the matter emphasizes that narrative, like Gyges' ring, can involve a kind of undetected hearing and seeing, whether metaphorically (as in reading) or literally as well (as in film). The poetic imagination, however, is in one sense more powerful than the ring of invisibility: its deepest purpose is not to make available ordinarily forbidden pleasures, but to turn one's perceptions around by allowing one to see the world – including oneself – through the eyes of others, and to experience what they experience. Socrates thus remarks in Book IX that the proper judge of the misery or happiness of the tyrant is 'he who is able in thought to enter into a man's character and to see through it' (577a) – a trick that involves constructing stories, as he himself does in the *Republic*, that give one access to the internal lives of others.

With the foregoing reflections in mind, it is clear that Glaucon's myth does not show what he claims it does. Glaucon says that the ring would make it possible to steal, rape, murder, 'and to do other things as an equal to a god among human beings' (360c), but it would do so only if one were incapable of experiencing the fundamentally ethical turnabout of the soul that I have just described. Virtually everyone, no doubt, would be tempted to take small liberties with a ring of invisibility. But could one envision looking into the astonished and terrified face of one's victim – to whom one is, after all, invisible – while raping or murdering her? Those who are unable to take matters quite so far (and there are certainly some) can be said to have imaginatively experienced what Emmanuel Levinas describes as the interruption of 'totality' by the 'infinity' of an 'Other ... [who is] irreducib[le] to the I, to my thoughts and possessions', an irreducibility that he names the 'face' of the Other or the Stranger.[9] For these readers, the myth incorporates a powerful symbol of the moral impenetrability that would be required to follow in the footsteps of Gyges. We are told that he steals the ring from a corpse and then slips it on his finger. This relatively petty theft, which establishes that he is already inclined to injustice, resembles a rite of initiation for membership in a gang of criminals. One senses that the ring is the sign of the corpse, so that to wear it is to take the place of the corpse. Indeed, it becomes clear in the sequel that the shepherd is alive to his own self-image, but dead to the inner experience of others. The terror of his victims is for him a surface without depth; it is a mirror in which the face of the other is entirely occluded by the reflection of his own power.

I have suggested that the Ring Myth does not, as Glaucon asserts, establish the injustice of supposedly just individuals.[10] Rather, thinking through the myth can help to reveal the existence or nonexistence of the other as an absolute limit on the satisfaction of one's desires. This thought experiment is admittedly not probative; some who cannot imagine raping or murdering anyone might actually be capable of such deeds, while others who can might actually be incapable of them. Glaucon's myth furthermore abstracts completely from all social bonds of affection, loyalty and the like; he imagines an utterly isolated individual, a barbarian nobody at the margins of society, with no meaningful relationship to any other human being. Given the connection I have begun to develop between the Ring Myth and the myth of Kallipolis, what remains is to test Glaucon's thesis about the universality of injustice by trying to imagine how a ruling elite that possesses Gygean powers would behave within the concrete context of a society like Kallipolis. This is precisely the accomplishment of Henkel von Donnersmarck's poetic interpretation of the actual history of East Germany.

The Life of Others

The title *Das Leben der Anderen* emphasizes the shared life of unnamed 'others', not their multiple individual lives.[11] This is our first hint that the film presents a drama that is played out between two groups of human beings distinguished by very different, yet intimately intertwined, ways of life: the Stasi, guardians of the state and protectors of its socialist ideology, and the poets, the East German playwrights and writers who attract a fair share of the Stasi's professional attention. The protagonists of this drama are Gerd Wiesler, a dedicated and principled functionary and true believer who brings ideological zeal to his first encounter with the theatre; Georg Dreyman, a celebrated and officially approved artist who enjoys the rare privilege of being, it is said, the only non-subversive East German writer who is also read in the West; and Christa-Maria Sieland, a prominent actress (and Dreyman's girlfriend). The film tells the story of the moral development of Dreyman, who undergoes a political education, and of Wiesler, who undergoes a poetic one. Dreyman discovers that, if he is to live up to his vocation, he must act in concert with his friends – writers who have been persecuted by the regime – to oppose the oppressive and corrupt system that masquerades as a *demokratische Republik*. Wiesler's education is more radical: his secret, continual observation of Dreyman and Sieland leads him to care about them enough to betray his professional mission as well as the Party to which he swore an oath. These men's recognition that they are complicit in an inhuman political system causes them to combine poetry with politics in unsanctioned ways: Wiesler scripts and plays the deceptive roles of dedicated spy and interrogator and loyal fan, while Dreyman covertly writes and delivers an anonymous exposé of the problem of suicide in the DDR that is published in *Der Spiegel*.

The Life of Others is a profound, beautifully composed, and extraordinarily rich film, and I must limit my discussion to the concepts of human being and humanity (*Mensch* and *Menschlichkeit*) that structure the film's dramatic action. Like Kallipolis's philosopher-kings, the Stasi men fall short of genuine wisdom, for which they substitute a technical or applied-scientific approach to its study of human beings. In the film's opening scene, Wiesler details for a class of operatives-in-training the principles that will allow them to determine when the subject of an interrogation is lying. A liar, he asserts, can be counted on to repeat the same alibis, word for word, under the stress of cross-examination. Wiesler's boss Grubitz later tells him about a PhD thesis that specifies prison conditions for subversive artists based on their character profile. There are, he explains, five types of artist, of which Dreyman is type four: a 'hysterical anthropocentrist'.[12] 'Is that not scientific?' Grubitz asks. The basic assumption of this technicism is more seriously articulated by Hempf, the corrupt Minister of Culture: 'human beings [*Menschen*] do not change' – a claim that is supported by his own unrepentant abuse of power, but belied by the moral growth of Wiesler and Dreyman. Hempf's characterization of the poet as 'the engineer of the soul' (a phrase he borrows from Stalin) furthermore implies that human beings can effectively be made to order; human souls, including those of the poets, could not be successfully 'engineered' if they were free to alter their ideologically constructed identities. But Dreyman, who is awakened to the human cost of this engineering by the suicide of his friend Albert Jerska, and Wiesler, at first a true believer who puts a black mark beside the name of a student who asserts that Stasi interrogation techniques are 'inhumane' (*unmenschlich*), ultimately prove to be free in just this way. In liberating themselves from the intellectual and moral control of the regime, they exemplify a simultaneously strong and vulnerable humanity that opens itself up to the nobility and suffering of other individuals.

The emancipation of Dreyman and Wiesler unfolds in stages, and involves a complex set of attachments and rivalries. After the premiere of his play *Faces of Love*, Dreyman – whom Grubitz describes as a 'good man' (*ein guter Mann*), meaning that he is politically reliable – urges Hempf to reconsider the blacklisting of Jerska, a playwright who is being punished for having signed a statement of protest against the regime. 'Put yourself in his place', he pleads, not realizing that Hempf – who is in fact blackmailing Sieland for sex, having used his office to discover her addiction to illegal drugs – is completely closed (like Gyges) to the capacity of sympathetic identification that he takes for granted as a dramatist. Hempf replies that Dreyman's love of human beings is admirable, but naïvely idealistic; *Menschen verändern sich nicht* – 'human beings do not change'. And in fact, Dreyman and Sieland do suffer from bad faith in relation to reality. When a despairing Jerska later tells him that he is nothing if he cannot direct plays, Dreyman transparently lies to him about his prospects; Sieland subsequently asks Dreyman to remain strong for her, and not to let his sadness about Jerska into his life – as though moral strength were equivalent to emotional obtuseness. At Dreyman's birthday party, however, his friend Paul Hauser, another writer who has fallen afoul of the regime, accuses him of being wilfully ignorant of the actual conditions of their existence as artists. Hauser delivers an ultimatum: if he does not take a stand against those who ruined Jerska, he is not a *Mensch* and need not have anything further to do with him. In the end, it is Jerska's suicide, a violent act of self-liberation – the Germans call it *Freitod*, freely-chosen death – that forces Dreyman to abandon his beautiful illusions. When he receives the shocking news that Jerska has hanged himself, Dreyman performs the *Sonate vom guten Menschen*, a piano score that Jerska had given him for his birthday. 'You know what Lenin said about Beethoven's "Appassionata"?' he asks Sieland. 'If I keep listening to it, I won't finish the revolution. Can anyone who's heard this music – I mean truly heard it – be a bad person [*ein schlechter Mensch*]?'

Unbeknownst to Dreyman, Wiesler, who planted electronic bugs throughout his apartment immediately after attending his play, is moved to tears by what he is hearing. Wiesler's decision to monitor Dreyman perhaps reflects a certain rivalry in relation to Sieland, with whom he seems to be somewhat smitten after seeing her in the leading role of Marta in the play *Faces of Love*. One furthermore suspects that his decision to alert Dreyman to what he calls 'the bitter truth' of Sieland's affair with Hempf, which he does by opportunely using a doorbell as a sort of stage-prop, is motivated by jealousy of both men, as well as at least mild indignation at Hempf's abuse of power. Up to this point, Wiesler's machinations look like small steps along the path of corruption that Hempf himself has followed. But while Hempf's sexual appetite for Sieland leads him crudely to force himself on her, Wiesler begins to be moved by a higher *erôs*. He is visited in his apartment by a prostitute – his first time, at least with this particular woman – and he urges her to stay, which suggests that he longs not simply for sexual pleasure, but for human intimacy. At the same time, his attraction to Sieland as an actress and a person begins to open him up to her suffering and that of her friends. In an attic, Wiesler chalks the exact floor-plan of Dreyman's flat; surrounded by recording machines in this virtual apartment, he looks and acts like a sound and light man for the theatre. Through his earphones, however, flows a real life-story of individuals who relate essentially to art. Wiesler thus begins to learn what it means to live a life in which poetry, drama and music are potent moral forces – sources of inspiration as well as consolation. More than this, his unique position allows him also to intercede in, and in a real sense to direct, the action he is professionally obliged strictly to register and record. And it is in crossing the line from the acquisition of knowledge to the production of poetry that he directly experiences the extreme pleasure, and finally the great moral power, of artistic creation.

Socrates teaches in the *Republic* that we imitate what we admire (500c). Wiesler proves to be an excellent student of poetic imitation, because he is capable of genuine admiration. Having stolen into the intimate centre of the lives of others, Wiesler transforms the reality he has witnessed into a dramatic performance with a deep core of emotional honesty. His debut as playwright and actor alike, combining the activities of both Dreyman and Sieland, occurs immediately after he taps into an argument between the couple. As Sieland prepares for a tryst with Hempf, Dreyman reveals that he knows where she is going. 'You don't need him,' he insists; 'you are a great artist, and your audience knows it too.' 'And you?' she replies, incidentally revealing her strong dependence on his example, 'You get in bed with them too. Why do you do it? Because they can destroy you too, despite your talent and your faith.' 'You're right about so many things, and I want to change so much,' Dreyman admits – but he is not able to stop her from leaving. He does, however, supply Wiesler with raw material for the role he fabricates in order to convince Sieland to break off with Hempf. Encountering her in a bar as if by accident, Wiesler introduces himself as 'your audience' and declares that 'many people love you only because you are as you are'. 'An actor is never as he is [*nie so, wie er ist*],' she says. 'You are,' he insists. 'I saw you on stage – you were then more who you are [*wie Sie sind*] than you are now ... You are a great artist – don't you know that?' 'And you are a good person [*ein guter Mensch*],' she replies. In this remarkable exchange, Wiesler is himself both more 'as he is' and less than he appears. Less, because he is dissimulating and concealing his identity as an agent of the Stasi; more, because his sincere encouragement represents a morally significant expansion of his previous identity, and because he discovers a greater fulfilment as an artist than he ever knew as a spy.

Wiesler's performance is in fact far more consequential, both aesthetically and morally, than it first appears to be. He effectively produces his own version of *Faces of Love*: Sieland, who is deeply moved by his heartfelt appeal, passionately reconciles with Dreyman and permanently renounces Hempf – an outcome that gives Dreyman the strength to write his anonymous article and that immensely pleases Wiesler, who reads his assistant's report the next morning with the enthusiasm of a playwright basking in rave reviews. The supreme importance of this dramatically satisfying cascade of moral influences is suggested by their location at the exact centre of the film, which is also its point of maximum happiness for this little love triangle. Things immediately begin to go downhill, as Wiesler has unwittingly set in motion a genuine human tragedy. For Sieland, the flawed heroine of this drama, the moment of moral salvation is also the beginning of professional and personal destruction: stood up by her, Hempf retaliates by having her arrested for illegally purchasing prescription drugs. What is more, Wiesler is forced to become an agent of her downfall. It is true that she capitulates immediately to Grubitz, offering her body in exchange for her career, but any resistance she might still have mustered against his demand that she inform on Dreyman collapses when her most enthusiastic fan turns out to be her interrogator – her *real* audience, not her imagined one. This is the mimetic cascade in reverse; as nobility breeds nobility, baseness breeds baseness. Sieland is once again the audience to which Wiesler must play, and in her presence he experiences his professional activity as a role of which he is deeply ashamed. But it is a role he is condemned to play by the presence of Grubitz, who watches from behind a one-way mirror. Nor is his shame morally sufficient, for his profound violation of her trust is far more crushing than Hempf's sexual blackmail. Wiesler atones for his betrayal of Sieland by removing the typewriter that would have incriminated Dreyman, a desperate act that ends his career; Sieland atones for her betrayal of Dreyman, into whose eyes she can no longer bear to look, by committing suicide. Such is the poetic justice of life in the DDR, in which blood and tears are the price of beauty and goodness.

In the end, art serves once again as a vehicle of moral truth. After the fall of the Wall, Wiesler graduates from steaming open letters – the menial work to which he had been demoted – to delivering them. This, too, is poetic justice: the erstwhile interceptor of private communications is now an official public bearer of them. Dreyman reads his Stasi file and discovers the fictions Wiesler invented to protect him and Sieland. He subsequently memorializes Jerska, Wiesler, and Sieland in a book entitled *Die Sonate vom Guten Menschen*, which he dedicates to HGW XX/7 – the code name by which agent Wieser once signed his reports. The quiet eloquence of this gesture is not lost on Wiesler, who has learned to appreciate art as a language of goodness. *Es ist für mich*, he tells the store-clerk who hands him Dreyman's book – a statement that strikes the viewer as an acknowledgment of what his secret life as a poet was all about: it was 'for *me*', the single individual, a good man who became such through the power of poetic imitation to stimulate longing, inspire admiration, and compel decency.

Here comes the sun: Gyges and the poets

Towards the end of *The Life of Others*, Hempf encounters Dreyman at a theatrical revival of *Faces of Love*. Compared to life in the new Germany, he remarks, 'it was beautiful in our little republic'. The echo of Plato in the mouth of an East German Gyges seems more than coincidental. *The Life of Others* involves so many of the *Republic*'s thematic oppositions – technical expertise and moral insight, erotic passion and aggression, body and soul, publicity and privacy, lying and truth-telling, reality and ideality, image and original, poetic production and the acquisition of knowledge, the political suppression of injustice and the philosophical love of truth – that it is hard to believe Henckel von Donnersmarck did not have the dialogue in mind when he made the film.[13] Our conviction that he did is strengthened by his brilliant use of the *Republic*'s image of the Sun to represent the scope of totalitarian aspiration and the struggle of poetry against ideology, as well as to convey, in microcosm, the essential structure of the film's action. I refer to the joke that Grubitz cruelly encourages an underling to finish telling about Erich Honecker, the Head of State and Party General Secretary:

> Honecker comes to his office early in the morning and opens the window. He sees the sun and says: 'Good morning, dear sun.' The sun replies: 'Good morning, dear Erich.' Honecker works and goes at noon to the window and says: 'Good day, dear sun.' The sun replies: 'Good day, dear Erich.' In the evening Erich closes up and goes once more to the window and says 'Good evening, dear sun.' The sun does not respond. Honecker again says: 'Good evening, dear sun. What's the matter with you?' The sun answers: 'Lick my ass, I'm in the West now.'

This joke captures the unlimited aspiration of late-modern totalitarianism, which seeks to control even the heavenly bodies. In the *Republic*, the sun – the source of light and life on Earth which was worshipped as a god by the Greeks – is the likeness of the Good, the ultimate principle of order and intelligibility in the cosmos and the highest object of philosophical aspiration. Socrates, one should note, does not profess knowledge of the Good, but mere opinion. The laughable yet tragic arrogance of the communist ideologues of East Germany lies in their claim to have grasped the Good intellectually, or to have transcended philosophy in the actual achievement of wisdom – a claim Socrates makes on behalf of the philosopher-kings of Kallipolis (540a–b).[14] What is more, they forcefully insist that they can bring the Good down from the heavens of philosophical abstraction and into everyday human existence. Their revolutionary transformation of society follows the paradigmatic example of the rulers of Kallipolis, whose political work, on the analogy of the crafts (*technai*), is fundamentally poetic and productive – a process accomplished in large part by the Stalinist soul-engineering that is, according to Hempf, the proper vocation of the poets.[15]

While Honecker, so the joke goes, is so pompous that he expects servility from a heavenly body, the DDR's combination of force and debased philosophy is so fearsome that he receives it. This artful bit of humour is itself a persuasive response to Hempf:

inasmuch as it dares to speak the truth about the *hybris* of the regime, the moral and intellectual darkness of the East, and the ideal significance of the free West in the minds of those who suffer under the yoke of communism, it furnishes an example of anti-ideological poetry. This is not all. In *The Life of Others*, Dreyman and his friends, who conspire to deliver his article on suicide to *Der Spiegel*, trace the path of the sun as it travels from east to west. Dreyman is moved to write the article by the *Freitod* of Jerska, who can find no other way than suicide to liberate himself from the darkness of his professional oppression. As an image of the poets' resolute commitment to artistic creation and the communication of truth, the sun's movement once again functions as a rebuke to the regime's exclusive and univocal claim to wisdom. Finally, the ascent and descent of the sun through morning, noon, and evening anticipates the dramatic arc of *The Life of Others*, which peaks, as we've seen, at the film's midpoint.[16]

Erôs and understanding

I have suggested that the behaviour of the Party and Stasi members in Henckel von Donnersmarck's film exposes the incoherence of the idealism of the late-modern imitators of Kallipolis – and so, indirectly, of Kallipolis itself. Hempf, officially the chief guardian of culture in the DDR (!), uses the political equivalent of the licence of Gyges much as Glaucon would have predicted: as a means to satisfy sexual and aggressive impulses, punish perceived enemies, and consolidate personal power. Grubitz, a careerist with a streak of sadism, manages to refuse Sieland's sexual bribe, but neither political indoctrination nor technical and bureaucratic training provides him with the inclination, much less the capacity, to resist Hempf's corruption. On the contrary, he tells Wiesler that they both have much to gain, or to lose, from what he cynically describes as the 'love story' (*Liebesgeschichte*) of Hempf and Sieland. The only real surprise is Wiesler, who at one point uses his office to steal, of all things, a book of poems by Bertolt Brecht. While neither Hempf nor Grubitz seem to be in any way familiar with the erotic longing for transcendence, Weisler is drawn into a kind of aesthetic reverie as he reads Brecht's 'Erinnerung an die Marie A', a poem in which a cloud floats high above the head of a lover – a cloud so high, or so insubstantial, that it suddenly disappears.

Kallipolis, as we have seen, aims permanently to liberate human beings from the corrupting effects of ignoble poetry, including well-known stories and verses about the difficulty of virtue, the ease of vice, and the violence and bribability of the gods (363e-66b). The regime's guiding assumption that the human soul can be successfully engineered, or that a political community could be designed in which both rulers and ruled are carefully and deliberately constructed from the ground up, rests on the further presupposition that what has long been regarded as intransigent human nature is in fact a predictable consequence of inadequate social control. To be sure, the recent history of fascist and communist states offers abundant evidence of the power of ideological indoctrination. But this history also testifies to the power of erotic desire to resist indoctrination. Glaucon's Ring Myth, in which Gyges immediately uses his newfound power to rape and murder, Socrates' description in Book V of the philosopher, who is moved by a passionate love of truth and beauty (474c-76c), and Socrates' own example of dialectical care for the souls of others are reflections of the spontaneity of *erôs* in its basest and most noble manifestations. And it is this uncontrollable erotic liberty that dooms Kallipolis, as Socrates makes clear in attributing the decline of the city to unsanctioned births (546a-47a).

The erotic turning of Wiesler's soul in *The Life of Others* makes the same point in a higher, more philosophical register. The unsanctioned births of Henckel von Donnersmarck's film are not physical, but artistic, intellectual and moral. Wiesler is saved from injustice and opened to a spiritually richer individual existence by an *erôs* that responds to the beauty of souls and poems as well as bodies. This is the *erôs* that is summoned by Plato's dialogues, and in the light of which – indeed, *only* in the light of which – it is possible to understand the *Republic*'s nuanced critique of radical revolutionary idealism.

But if *Das Leben der Anderen* affirms the morally educative power of art that is latent even in Glaucon's Ring Myth, the ease of Wiesler's transformation from a spy into a dramatist seems also to contain a warning about poetry. How, exactly, are we to understand this warning? There is no doubt that the soul-engineering or political poetry of totalitarianism does violence to human beings. Gygean metaphors, however, also describe the creative activity of the poetic imagination as such: it engages in literary theft – as Henckel von Donnersmarck certainly does in relation to Zamyatin's *We*, which fully anticipates the Platonic opposition he portrays in his film between poetic and technical ways of knowing; it ransacks life for the sake of art; it steals into the character of others. In the case of Wiesler's dramatic craft, in fact, these are more than metaphors. Have we really grasped the implicitly Gygean character of anti-ideological poetry, including that of the *Republic* as well as *The Life of Others*? Does genuinely liberating poetic imitation involve the violation of more than just unreflective certainties, after the fashion of Socrates? These are some of the many questions with which Henckel von Donnersmarck's remarkable film leaves us.[17]

Notes

1 The translation by Allan Bloom, *The Republic of Plato*, 2nd ed. (New York: Basic Books, 1991), is used throughout.
2 See in this connection Roslyn Weiss's discussion of the erotic and intellectual limitations of the philosopher-kings in *Philosophers in the Republic: Plato's Two Paradigms* (Cornell University Press, 2012). Weiss shows that the 'natural' philosophers Socrates describes in Books V and VI (specifically, 473c–490d and 496a-502c) love wisdom, learn with delight, and show no aversion to ruling (should the chance arise) because they are eager to help others and improve their souls. But the 'artificial' philosopher-kings of Book VII (502c–543c) – 'hardened men, products of coercion' (103) who are produced by the regime because it cannot count on nature to furnish an adequate supply of philosophical rulers – do not love wisdom, are unconcerned with the welfare of others, and must be compelled both to learn and to rule. I develop Weiss's insights in *Glaucon's Fate: History, Myth, and Character in Plato's Republic* (Philadelphia: Paul Dry Books, 2018).

3   Sigmund Freud, *Civilization and its Discontents*, trans. David McLintock (New York: Penguin Books, 2002), 45 (where Freud quotes Schiller).
4   460a–b, 461b–c, 464e, 465b–c, 468c–69b.
5   Thus G.M.A. Grube, *Plato's Republic* (Indianapolis: Hackett Publishing Company, 1974) translates this phrase as 'sacred objects or temple property'.
6   See above, n. 2. Although Socrates is gravely concerned that he might deceive his companions about 'noble, good, and just customs' (451a), he finally decides in book 5 vicariously to gratify the appetites and ambitions of his interlocutors in what appears to be an oblique attempt to lead them towards the just life of philosophy. Enticed by the strange mixture of Spartan rigor and Athenian self-indulgence that characterizes the life of the warrior elite of Kallipolis, Glaucon in particular may be ready to embrace philosophy as a means to the regime's realization, and then – perhaps! – as an end in itself. I argue in *Glaucon's Fate* that this risky pedagogical strategy fails spectacularly.
7   See Plato's reflections in the *Seventh Letter* (324b-25c) on the regime of the Thirty that held power in Athens in 404–403, as well as my discussion of the significant resemblances between the ideological tyranny of the Thirty, Sparta, and the Kallipolis in *Glaucon's Fate* (83–5).
8   In the Preface to her 1972 translation, Mirra Ginsburg described *We* as 'a searing satire, among other things, on schematic – hence, necessarily totalitarian – society'. Yevgeny Zamyatin, *We*, trans. Mirra Ginsburg (New York: Harper Voyager, 2012), xiii.
9   Emmanuel Levinas, *Totality and Infinity: An Essay on Exteriority*, trans. Alphonso Lingis (Pittsburgh: Duquesne University Press, 1969), 43, 50. On 39, Levinas speaks of 'the Stranger who disturbs the being at home with oneself'.
10 I offer an extended discussion of the Ring Myth, including reflections on its connection with Herodotus's story of Gyges, in Jacob Howland, 'Storytelling and Philosophy in Plato's *Republic*', *American Catholic Philosophical Quarterly* 79.2 (2005): 213–32. See also *Glaucon's Fate*, 141–53.
11 The English title *The Lives of Others* is thus misleading.
12 In quoting and translating dialogue from the film, I have referred to Florian Henckel von Donnersmarck, *Das Leben der Anderen: Filmbuch* (Frankfurt: Suhrkamp Verlag, 2007).
13 The suppression of injustice in Kallipolis and in the DDR is a consequence of the hatred of falsehood that Socrates attributes to lovers of truth (484c), combined with the claim of wisdom advanced by the rulers of both regimes (more on which below) – for only this claim, notwithstanding its spuriousness, could justify their severely repressive measures.
14 The rising sun is a common symbol of fascist and communist regimes, including the USSR.
15 In Kallipolis, the citizens' souls are first metaphorically wiped clean (as for example by a violent purge of everyone over the age of ten) and then stamped, molded, tuned, dyed, and painted (377b–c, 412a, 430a–b, 501a–c).
16 Interestingly, Plato's *Republic* has an analogous dramatic structure. The erotic high-point of the dialogue occurs when Socrates introduces the philosopher at the exact center of the text (calculated in Jacob Howland, 'The *Republic*'s Third Wave and the Paradox of Political Philosophy', *The Review of Metaphysics* 51.3 (1998): 633–4 n. 2.) But the process by which the philosopher decays into the philosopher-king begins almost immediately.

17 I wish to thank Vigdis Songe-Møller for inviting me to Bergen in 2013 to speak on Gyges and *Das Leben der Anderen*, and the members of the Philosophy and Poetry Project for significantly enriching my understanding of Henckel von Donnersmarck's film.

Bibliography

Bloom, Allan. *The Republic of Plato*, trans., 2nd ed. New York: Basic Books, 1991.

Freud, Sigmund. *Civilization and its Discontents*. Translated by David McLintock. New York: Penguin Books, 2002.

Grube, G.M.A. *Plato's Republic*. Indianapolis: Hackett Publishing Company, 1974.

Henckel von Donnersmarck, Florian. *Das Leben der Anderen: Filmbuch*. Frankfurt: Suhrkamp Verlag, 2007.

Howland, Jacob. *Glaucon's Fate: History, Myth, and Character in Plato's Republic*. Philadelphia: Paul Dry Books, 2018.

Howland, Jacob. 'Storytelling and Philosophy in Plato's *Republic*'. *American Catholic Philosophical Quarterly* 79, no. 2 (2005): 213–32.

Howland, Jacob. 'The *Republic*'s Third Wave and the Paradox of Political Philosophy'. *The Review of Metaphysics* 51, no. 3 (1998): 633–57.

Levinas, Emmanuel. *Totality and Infinity: An Essay on Exteriority*. Translated by Alphonso Lingis. Pittsburgh: Duquesne University Press, 1969.

Weiss, Roslyn. *Philosophers in the Republic: Plato's Two Paradigms*. Ithaca: Cornell University Press, 2012.

Zamyatin, Yevgeny. *We*. Translated by Mirra Ginsburg. New York: Harper Voyager, 2012.

Part Two

Virtue and Soul-shaping

5

Plato's Inverted Theatre: Displacing the Wisdom of the Poets

Paul Woodruff

In the great speech of the *Phaedrus*, Plato has Socrates deliver a myth that has the power to displace what the poets have been saying on a number of points. Poets have powers that Plato considers dangerous, and they use those powers to instil in their audiences values that Plato has reason to reject. Poets use language that lodges like a virus in the memory, they manipulate a captivating body of mythology, and with this they invoke emotions that disable the ability of their hearers to use reason, turning their hearers into passive, uncritical receivers. The poets in question composed a body of work that functioned as the wisdom literature of the ancient Greeks. In his own time, the principal creators of this literature were the tragic poets, and these are Plato's main target, but Plato takes Homer as their leader, also rejecting Hesiod and the major lyric poets.

Socrates in the *Phaedrus* aims to bring his companion to the study of philosophy, explicitly turning him away from the traditional teaching of rhetoric, and, at the same time, pulling him away from the poets. Although he compliments the poets at one point, his overall message is thoroughly subversive of the poets and of the venues they used. In the *Phaedrus*, Socrates implicitly condemns the poets' claim to wisdom, just as he does explicitly in the *Republic*.

A possible theatre image in the *Phaedrus*[1]

Classical poetry was created to be performed, and tragic poetry was composed for performance in the Theatre of Dionysus, which had a well-known shape: a central hearth in the centre of a circle, from which rose tier on tier of seats, leading at the top to a rim of the highest seats. From the circle radiated pathways with steps. Since the action was mainly in the circle (with perhaps some action on a stage behind it), the best seats were at the bottom, and we can easily imagine the rush of an audience racing on entering the space to take the seats with the best view of the spectacle.

This race Plato will invert in an image that can be visualized at least partly on the model of an ancient theatre. The language Plato uses allows (but does not require) this visualization, and the larger context is suggestive of the *ponos* and *agôn* of theatre.

Plato's heaven is indeed a place where the most important and difficult work is watching, but with the mind's eye – taking in the timeless truths of the reality that lies beyond heaven:

> T1. Inside heaven are many wonderful places from which to look (*theai*) and many aisles (*diexodoi*) which the blessed gods take up and back (or to and fro) ... When they go to the [visual] banquet they have a steep climb to the high tier at the rim of heaven (*akran epi tên hypouranion hapsida*) ...
>
> Phaedrus 247a4-b1[2]

The space will look much like an Athenian theatre, in having aisles and a high rim, though its circle completely surrounds the audience.[3] Those inside have no access to external reality except by ascending to the topmost tier and looking out. In effect, the meaning and use of this space has been turned upside down. The spectacle will be outside the theatre, to be seen only by those who look outside the theatre altogether. In this new kind of theatre, there will be a new sort of thing to watch, and a new way to be a watcher.

Watching something different

A theatre is a place for watching. In Athens, plays were composed, as Aristotle rightly noted, to represent action by means of action in the orchestra and on the platform behind it. In Plato's theatre, the action belongs entirely to the watchers; what they watch is utterly still and unchanging.

Athenian theatre often shows a contest, an *agôn*, in which speakers compete by means of words. The *agôn* may serve to amuse the audience, but its goal is often life or death. Helen contends for her life in Euripides' *Helen*, Haemon argues for the life of Antigone (in Sophocles' *Antigone*), Hecuba for the life of her daughter, and later for vengeance against the man who killed her son (in Euripides' *Hecuba*). A human life is no small prize for winning a contest, but Plato turns even this around. In his theatre, the contenders are members of the audience, and human life is the penalty for failure. The prize is knowledge – a prize far more valuable, to Plato, than mere human life, which after all entails a deprivation of knowledge:

> T2. If ... it does not see anything true because it could not keep up, and by some accident takes on a burden of forgetfulness and wrongdoing, then it is weighed down, sheds its wings, and falls to earth.
>
> Phaedrus 248c5-8

In effect, the prize for good watching is the privilege of remaining in the theatre as a disembodied soul; not having bodies, Plato's audience will be able to stay in the theatre and continue to see what they are there to see.

Moreover, what the audience sees will be different. An Athenian audience came to the theatre to see representations of action; Plato's audience will be eager to see actual entities that are eternally at rest. For Athenians, the space outside the theatre would be Athens itself – a better place to look than the theatre according to the teaching of the *Republic*, as Athens is only at second remove from the reality of the Forms. For the souls in heaven, the plain on which they may gaze, if they climb to the highest row of seats and look out, is the space in which the transcendental Forms are to be seen, most notably the Forms of virtues and of Beauty:

> T3. On the way around [the soul] has a view of Justice as it really is; it has a view of Sound-mindedness; it has a view of Knowledge – not the knowledge that is close to change ...
> *Phaedrus* 247d5–e2

Virtues are precisely the subjects of which the poets are most notably ignorant, according to Socrates in the *Republic*:

> T4. So shouldn't we declare that all mimetic poets, starting with Homer, are copying images of virtue and their other subjects, and have no grasp of the truth?
> *Republic* 600e4–6

Plato's audience will see the truth about the virtues, and they will see it for themselves, without the mediating influence of teachers of any kind – no poets, no diviners, not even philosophers are in the picture. This is a theatre for pure learning.

Gods are in the picture, but they have nothing to tell us. Plato gives the gods new roles as moral exemplars, changing their character, with consequences for the sorts of stories that may be told about them. Athenian theatre was ambivalent about the ethical role of the gods; although they are often represented as enforcers of justice, they are also shown behaving in ways that are forbidden to human beings. And although their messages through oracles always seem to come true, they send them in ways that often confuse human beings and lead them astray.

In the Kallipolis of the *Republic*, gods are to be consulted on matters of religious observance, but on matters of policy and day-to-day management of the city, the philosopher rulers will act in accordance with the knowledge they have acquired themselves of Forms such as the Form of Justice. A traditional view in the fifth century was that a city should consult the gods before making important decisions. One sign of Oedipus' *hybris*, in the opening scene of the *Oedipus Tyrannus*, is his insistence that he had been able to solve the riddle of the sphinx without divine help:

> T5. This wasn't to be known from the gods; instead, I arrived, Oedipus, who didn't know a thing, and I stopped her.
> I solved the riddle by using my mind (*gnômê*), not from omens or oracles ...
> *Oedipus Tyrannus* 396–98[4]

Of course, he does inquire of Delphi through Creon and he also asks Tiresias for information, but he relies on his own resources to infer that Creon and Tiresias are lying, because (he thinks) they are agents in a plot against him. By contrast, when

Creon takes power at the end of the play, he will show his reverence by declining to take the obvious step of exiling Oedipus until he has consulted the gods. Oedipus' claim at lines 396–98 to be able to go it alone, without the gods, is one of the clues to his *hybris* in the play. He will learn what the audience believes already – that the claim is arrogant and false.

A second traditional view was that a city should be guided by fundamental laws that have been sanctioned by the gods. That concept too is absent from the Kallipolis. In *Phaedrus* as in *Republic*, human seekers must see the truth for themselves. The gods are never treated in Plato as sources for ethical or political wisdom. If they were, Socrates could claim wisdom by virtue of his special information from the *daimonion* or from the oracle that reported no one wiser than he. But he does not do so.

In the *Phaedrus*, the gods provide some guidance for human souls in heaven. Their guidance is analogous to that of chorus leaders, and their human followers are called *synopadoi*, companions or attendants (248c3). Apparently, each god sets a kind of style for his or her chorus, but is not showing them where to go. Each human soul is already frantic to reach the goal at the top of the theatre and see the Forms (248b5-c2). They all seem to know where to go as they race each other to the high rim. The image of a chariot race erases that of an orderly chorus of stately dancers following the lead of their principal. Racers know where they are headed; they have no need to fall in behind their leaders.

Plato's theatre takes the gods off their pedestal as sources of knowledge. Gods too are seekers of knowledge. They are more effective than we are, because they always reach their goal. But we cannot wait at the bottom of heaven for the divine knowledge-seekers to return and tell us what they have seen. We must see for ourselves. They differ from us mainly in being exemplary seekers. The first effect of this displacement is that the gods influence us in other than the traditional ways – not through oracles, physical interventions, or legislation, but through the ways in which they exemplify goodness for us. As both Plato and the poets have noticed, the gods of myth do not exemplify goodness, at least not very often.

Plato sounds this theme of emulating gods in a number of dialogues. The texts below come from Socrates' long speech in the *Phaedrus*. Human souls before birth have travelled with the gods in heaven, from which they looked out onto the truth of the Forms. Those who remember what they saw before birth are prepared afterwards both for philosophy and for the best kind of love – a love that expresses itself in a common project of emulating the appropriate god:

> T6. So it is for each of the gods: everyone spends his life honouring the god in whose chorus he danced, and emulates that god in every way he can, so long as he remains undefiled and in his first life down here.
>
> *Phaedrus* 252d1–3

Although there appears to be no competition or other cause for disagreement among the gods,[5] they exemplify a range of good qualities, and differences among these play out on earth through a range of good pursuits. Zeus, for example, shines in a nobility that is homonymous with his name:

T7. Those who followed Zeus (*Dios*), for example, choose someone to love who is a Zeus himself in the nobility of his soul (*dios . . . tên psychên*).

Phaedrus 252e1–2

Socrates says that a lover who follows Ares may turn murderous (252c3–7), but this seems inconsistent with the view of the gods he takes elsewhere, and strikes me as a crumb thrown to disciples of traditional mythology. Socrates does not believe that a human being can go wrong by emulating the gods. Once lovers have found the right boys to love, their ethical course is mapped by the attributes of the relevant god:

T8. They [the philosophers] are well equipped to track down their god's true nature with their own resources because of their driving need to gaze at the god, and as they are in touch with the god by memory they are inspired by him and adopt his customs and practices, so far as a human being can share a god's life.

Phaedrus 252e5–53a5

The traditional view of the gods showed them only sporadically exemplifying qualities or behaviours that human beings ought to cultivate. Plato's inversion entails a radical revision of myth, which is not consistent with Socrates' disingenuous disclaimer, when asked about naturalistic explanations for myth:

T9. [Phaedrus:] Do you really believe that legend is true? [Socrates:] Actually, it would not be out of place to reject it as our intellectuals do. . . . But I have no time for such things. . . . I accept what is commonly believed, and, as I was just saying, I look not into them but into my own self.

Phaedrus 229c5–230a2

Socrates does not in fact accept what is commonly believed. It cannot be true of the gods of Plato, as it is of the gods of the poets, that they sometimes do wrong. The poets do show uneasiness about injustices done by the gods (T10, below), but they stick to their stories.

A puzzle arises: If I have seen the Form of Justice before birth, and am able to recover some memories of it, why should these memories not be enough? Knowing the Form sufficed for the philosopher rulers of Kallipolis. Why should I need to recollect (for the *Phaedrus*) the god as well as the Form? Plato does not say; a speculative answer would be that visualizing the god and his customary behaviour is a valuable pedagogical device in the relation between philosopher lover and young beloved. But advice to emulate the gods goes beyond the love story of the *Phaedrus*. The gods are evidently ideal knowers of the Forms and as such are objects of emulation apart from their role in the *Phaedrus* myth.

The gods are better philosophers than we are, mainly because they have more time to see the Forms and would have more time to develop an account of a difficult matter.[6] Moreover, the gods appear to be more accessible to us than are the true objects of knowledge; in that case, contemplating gods would be a way station on the journey towards contemplating the Forms.[7]

Watching differently

Besides seeing something different in Plato's theatre, his audience will watch in a different manner – actively and without emotion. The Athenian audience (Plato says in the *Republic*) fed its emotions on what it saw; Plato's audience will feed their powers of reason, represented in his image by wings. An Athenian audience watched, vibrating with emotions that were aroused in them by the performances, and in their emotions they were led by a chorus that showed them how to feel after each scene through appropriate dancing and singing. Plato's audience is led by the gods, who show by example how to maintain control of the emotion-related powers that move the soul, represented in the myth by horses.

Although led by the gods, Plato's audience is composed of active watchers. They must work hard to see what they see. Athenian audiences are passive, packed into rows of seats from which they cannot easily move. And the work is done for them; the chorus tells them what to think about the action and models the appropriate emotional responses. Plato's audiences see for themselves; individuals who see well are permitted to stay and see more; those who fail are ejected from the theatre.

In this we can see the most profound of the inversions in Plato's theatre. Athenian audiences knew they would be released from the theatre and allowed to go home. They saw a play once, and that was enough for them. Plato's audience members are allowed only temporary respites from watching. Even the gods must return to watching what lies outside the theatre. The learning that takes place in Plato's theatre is never complete; no matter how well I have seen Justice in the plain outside heaven, I must return to see it again and again. An occasional glimpse will not suffice. I must rise to the top level and stay long enough to see well. A modern thinker would say that Plato's audience actively contemplates the Forms, and must do so at frequent intervals to remain capable of such contemplation.

Love

Love is a god in ancient Greek mythology. Ordinarily, this would entail that Love is immortal, powerful and able to know the future. But not necessarily good or virtuous. The gods of the poets use their powers for good or ill, without apology to mortals. A character in Euripides makes this complaint to Apollo:

> T10. If – it will never happen – but let's suppose –
> You paid us what justice demands for raping women,
> You and Poseidon and Zeus who rules heaven,
> Then you'd empty the treasuries of your temples, paying for injustice.
>
> Euripides, *Ion* 444–47

On the subject of love, the poets are almost unanimous. In lyric, tragic, and epic verse, they show love as a powerful and usually calamitous force in human affairs. Sometimes, as in Anacreon and a fragment of Pindar, a poet's lament about love rings hollow; he seems really to be delighted by his plight.[8] But on the whole the poets treat love as a disaster for which the best image is the sudden onset of a plague. Here is the entire third stasimon of Sophocles' *Antigone* 786–98, where the chorus plausibly attributes the quarrel between Creon and his son to the son's having been emasculated and defeated by love for Antigone:

> T11. In battle, the victory goes to Love;
> Prizes and properties fall to Love.
> Love dallies the night
> On a girl's soft cheeks,
> Ranges across the sea, [790]
> Lodges in wild meadows.
> O Love, no one can hide from you:
> You take gods who live forever,
> You take humans who die in a day,
> And they take you, and go mad.
>
> Destroyer Love, you seize a good mind,
> And pervert it to wickedness:
> This fight is your doing,
> This uproar in the family.
> And the winner will be desire, [795]
> Shining in the eyes of a bride,
> An invitation to bed,
> A power to stand against the bounds of right and wrong.

The chorus has anticipated the quarrel in the stasimon that precedes the scene between father and son, where they represent love as deceptive:

> T12. But many are fooled by a light-headed love,
> And deception stalks those who know nothing
> Until they set their feet in fire, and burn.
>
> Sophocles, *Antigone* 617–19

The lyric poets represent love as deadly, as a madness that is to be avoided or for which one should seek a cure:[9]

> T13. Love again! Limb-loosener, he makes me shake,
> The bitter-sweet, the impossible creeping thing!
>
> Sappho 130

> T14.　　　　　　　there's a swarm
> Of desiccating furies in my mind.
> Love chews away my heart
> From the roots, in the dark.
>
> Ibycus 286, lines 12–15[10]

> T15. Oh, I'm in love again and not in love,
> I've gone mad and I'm not mad.
>
> Anacreon 428

Plato's Socrates will agree with the idea that love is a form of madness, but not with the claims that it is both destructive and immoral. That may be part of why he mentions poets of love in positive terms in criticizing the speech of Lysias:

> T16. I'm sure I've heard better somewhere; perhaps it was the lovely Sappho or the wise Anacreon or even some writer of prose.
>
> *Phaedrus* 235c2–4

I understand him to mean that attacks on love have been delivered better by the poets than by Lysias. He will defend love in the great speech:

> T17. If Love is a god or something divine, as he is, then he is not at all bad.
>
> *Phaedrus* 242e2–3

Plato vehemently resists the poetic wisdom on the amorality of divine power. The unstated premise here is that no god can be bad, a premise emphatically not supported by the poets. Socrates' defence of love goes beyond this simple argument. His image of love as the awakening of wings on the soul is far more captivating than the poets' image of love as disease, and by this image he must hope to eclipse the poets' clichéd images of disease and death.

Virtue

The distinctly human virtues celebrated by the poets are displaced by Platonic virtues that can be shared among gods and human beings. The virtues most celebrated by tragic poets survive, if at all, in subordinate positions. The first effect of displacing the gods is a radical revision of stories told about them; a second effect is a decisive but implicit move away from those virtues the poets have celebrated as specifically human. These traditional virtues could not belong to gods, and so they will have to be displaced or replaced by those that can – if, that is, the goal of a moral life for a human being is to be as godlike as possible.

Plato will not ask humans to cultivate virtues that gods cannot have. These are the virtues of imperfection, virtues that would have no place in a god (as Plato understands the gods). The displacement of these virtues is not explicit; we must infer it from the difference between Plato's virtues and those of the wisdom literature (especially Athenian tragedy) that represents traditional views. The three most obvious cases are reverence, good judgement and compassion. These three virtues are based on a felt recognition of the huge difference poets observed between human beings and the gods of their stories. We humans are mortal, ignorant and vulnerable to tragic blindness, say the poets. The gods are not. In this section I summarize discussions of these virtues that I have published elsewhere.[11]

Reverence

Reverence (*hosiotês, eusebeia*) was understood by the poets to be a felt recognition of the difference between the divine and the human. This virtue was to be shown in an acceptance of human limitations, as well as in capacities for awe and shame. Reverence helps guard against the dangers of arrogance that beset successful people, especially tyrants (*hybris*). One may violate reverence by failing to show respect for the gods, but in tragic poetry violations of reverence generally consist in a powerful figure showing too much confidence in his own power or knowledge. Reverence, in tragic poetry, is more about how we treat ourselves and each other than it is about how we treat the gods. It is an ethical virtue, but it is a virtue to which gods would not aspire. After all, they do not suffer from limitations, and they have little to fear from overconfidence.

Now Plato did of course list reverence among the virtues; it is one of the five that Socrates argues in the *Protagoras* are one in essence, and it is the subject of the famous short dialogue *Euthyphro*. Reverence plays no explicit part, however, in the *Republic*. The four remaining virtues appear to be sufficient for an ethically healthy city. Whatever happened to reverence in Plato? The answer must be speculative; we cannot infer much with certainty from an author's silence. But the *Euthyphro* supplies an important clue. There, Socrates easily persuades his partner that reverence is a proper part of justice – that is, all reverent actions and persons are just, but not vice versa. Successful definition then depends on identifying a feature that differentiates reverence within justice. Such a feature, however, Socrates fails to find. He leaves us, then, with the idea that once we know what justice is, we know everything we need to know about reverence, apart from the important point that Plato's gods cherish justice so much that we serve the gods by cultivating justice and other virtues in ourselves.[12]

Good judgement

Good judgement (*euboulia*) is the virtue on which we depend to make good decisions in the absence of determinate knowledge. You show good judgement by consulting other people and carefully considering all the things that might go wrong with a course of action before you embark upon it. People who fail in reverence also often fail in good judgement, owing to overconfidence in their knowledge. Creon in *Antigone*, for example, refuses to listen to advice from his son and from Tiresias.

Now Plato's gods, being perfect, have no need of good judgement, and human beings should not seek it either. They should, instead, seek the knowledge that the gods have. In the myth of the *Phaedrus* Plato shows us in the same circumstances as the gods – needing to look on reality in order to sustain our wings. The only difference is that we are less well equipped to maintain our knowledge, having a mixed pair of horses only one of which responds well to the reins.

Compassion

Compassion illustrates the rift between Plato and the poets sharply. A sense of potential kinship with the divine, in Plato's work, displaces the sense of common human frailty, which (according to the poets) is the basis of compassion for fellow human beings.[13] Gods are not frail, and therefore the poets show them as immune to compassion, on the whole.[14]

By 'compassion' the poets seem to mean a developed capacity to understand human suffering with appropriate affect – for example, to feel pity when that is called for. This is not quite the same as what we now call empathy or sympathy.[15]

The tragic poets often illustrate compassion in the way their choruses interact with the main characters. Often, too, a character shows exemplary compassion, especially in the work of Sophocles. Odysseus in the *Ajax*, for example, and Neoptolemus in the *Philoctetes*. In the last lines of the *Women of Trachis*, the son of Heracles calls for compassion from the chorus and audience, while recognizing that he cannot expect compassion from the gods.

We will find few traces of compassion in Plato, for three main reasons. First, if the gods are not compassionate, and we are to be like the gods, then we should not be compassionate either. And Plato's gods are no more given to compassion than are the gods of the poets, and for the same reason: the gods are not vulnerable in the way the Greeks thought one must be in order to feel compassion.

Second, when justice displaced reverence in Plato's system, it displaced compassion as well (compassion being a consequence of reverence as the poets, but not Plato, understood it). Like many thinkers, Plato holds that compassion tends to lead people to violate justice.[16]

Third, compassion is closely allied to grief: we feel compassion for people who have something to grieve about, such as death, or physical injury, or loss of power. These are indeed subjects of grief for the poets, but not for Plato. We should not be surprised, then, to find no place for compassion in Plato's inverted theatre: no grieving chorus, no mourning heroes, no poetry of sadness. In the place of such sadness, Plato's inward looking theatre gives us only the joyful race for knowledge, in which we must do our best to keep up with the gods.[17]

Conclusion on virtue

The ancient poets revealed their religious attitudes in two ways that Plato found objectionable. First, they showed the gods taking actions that Plato regarded as unethical and therefore impossible for gods. From that he inferred that the poets' stories were false. Second, they betray ethical values in their treatment of human beings that clash with the values that Plato held dear.

The conflict is due partly to a difference of belief about the way gods and humans should interact. The poets hold that human beings should, with due reverence, eschew any ambitions to be or act like gods. They should, instead, remember their mortality and act accordingly. In any event, the gods of the poets are poor models for human beings because they can get away with crimes against humans and each other, owing to their immortality. Much as we might yearn to commit such crimes, we are too vulnerable to survive any attempt to live like gods. Plato, by contrast, holds that the gods are moral exemplars for humans.

The result of this conflict is that while poets tend to celebrate the virtues of imperfection such as reverence, good judgement, and compassion, Plato urges us to grow as close to moral perfection as we can. The poets' principal virtues fall outside his range of interest. Plato's perfectionism comes at a high price in ethical terms, as it wipes out crucial human virtues. Of these, the saddest loss is compassion, on which so much of human goodness depends.[18]

Notes

1. Some years ago, David Dean-Jones brought to my attention the language in this passage that is suggestive of theatre.
2. All translations are my own; from the *Phaedrus* they are based on my contributions to Alexander Nehamas and Paul Woodruff, *Plato: Phaedrus* (Indianapolis: Hackett Publishing Company, 1995).
3. *Theai* is used for seats in the theatre by writers contemporary with Plato (Aeschines the orator and Demosthenes). *Hapsis* means a circle or rim and is attested in later Greek writers for the uppermost rim of seats in a theatre; here we can be sure only that it refers to the circle at the top of heaven. 'Up and back (or to and fro)': the aisles must lead up and down, as the gods do not exit heaven or enter it; this theatre-space does not have the long aisles to either side that were a feature of ancient Greek theatres.
4. Translation from Peter Meineck and Paul Woodruff, *Sophocles: Oedipus Tyrannus* (Indianapolis: Hackett Publishing Co., 2000).
5. 'Jealousy has no place in the gods' chorus' (*Phaedrus* 247a7). We would not expect Plato to attribute any bad qualities to gods.
6. 'To describe what the soul actually is would require a very long account, altogether a task for a god in every way. But to say what it is like is humanly possible . . .' (*Phaedrus* 246a4–6).
7. I owe the point to Hallvard Fossheim.
8. See the poems translated in the Appendix to Nehamas and Woodruff, *Phaedrus*. On the topic, see Douglas Cairns, 'The Imagery of *Erôs* in Plato's *Phaedrus*', in *Erôs in Ancient Greece*, ed. Ed Sanders et al. (Oxford: Oxford University Press, 2013), 233–50. While developing new images, Plato continues to use old ones, as Cairns aptly explains.
9. The following quotations are from my translation in the Appendix to Nehamas and Woodruff, *Phaedrus*.
10. On Ibycus 286, see Vanessa Cazzato, 'Worlds of *Erôs* in Ibycus Fragment 286', in *Erôs in Ancient Greece*, ed. Sanders et al., 267–76.
11. I have discussed all three virtues in *Reverence: Renewing a Forgotten Virtue* (New York: Oxford University Press, 2001, 2nd ed., expanded, 2014). Their special features as virtues of imperfection are discussed in my 'Virtues of Imperfection', *Journal of Value Inquiry*, Special Issue, ed. Christel Fricke, 49 (2015): 597–604.
12. For a more detailed account of reverence in these dialogues, see my 'Wrong Turns in the *Euthyphro*', *Apeiron* 52, no. 2 (2019) https://www.degruyter.com/view/j/apeiron.ahead-of-print/apeiron-2018-0011/apeiron-2018-0011.xml?format=qINT.
13. On the subject, see David Konstan, *Pity Transformed* (London: Duckworth, 2001).
14. See Konstan's chapter 4 for a more nuanced account of pity and the gods. In the *Odyssey*, by contrast with the *Iliad*, the gods do show some capacity for pity towards their favourites.

15 On the many varieties of empathy, see the chapter under that title in my *The Necessity of Theater: The Art of Watching and Being Watched* (New York: Oxford University Press, 2008).
16 On this issue, see my *Ajax Dilemma: Justice and Fairness in Rewards* (New York: Oxford University Press, 2011), 105–9.
17 Reverence for truth is a virtue that we can share with gods, and I suggest that this displaces reverence for the gods – a virtue we would not expect to cultivate by emulating gods.
18 Thanks to Knut Ågotnes for helpful comments, and to an anonymous reader for the press.

Bibliography

Cairns, Douglas. 'The Imagery of Erôs in Plato's Phaedrus'. In *Erôs in Ancient Greece*, edited by Ed Sanders et al., 233–50. Oxford: Oxford University Press, 2013.

Cazzato, Vanessa. 'Worlds of Erôs in Ibycus Fragment 286'. In *Erôs in Ancient Greece*, edited by Ed Sanders et al., 267–76. Oxford: Oxford University Press, 2013.

Konstan, David. *Pity Transformed*. London: Duckworth, 2001.

Meineck, Peter and Paul Woodruff. *Sophocles: Oedipus Tyrannus*. Indianapolis: Hackett Publishing Co., 2000.

Nehamas, Alexander and Paul Woodruff. *Plato: Phaedrus*. Indianapolis: Hackett Publishing Company, 1995.

Woodruff, Paul. *Reverence: Renewing a Forgotten Virtue*. New York: Oxford University Press, 2001. 2nd ed., expanded, 2014.

Woodruff, Paul. *The Necessity of Theater: The Art of Watching and Being Watched*. New York: Oxford University Press, 2008.

Woodruff, Paul. *Ajax Dilemma: Justice and Fairness in Rewards*. New York: Oxford University Press, 2011.

Woodruff, Paul. 'Virtues of Imperfection'. *Journal of Value Inquiry*, Special Issue, edited by Christel Fricke, 49 (2015), 597–604. DOI 10.1007/s10790-015-9527-4. Access through http://link.springer.com/article/10.1007/s10790-015-9527-4?no-access-true.

Woodruff, Paul. 'Wrong Turns in the *Euthyphro*'. *Apeiron* 52, no. 2 (2019). https://www.degruyter.com/view/j/apeiron.ahead-of-print/apeiron-2018-0011/apeiron-2018-0011.xml?format=INT.

6

Gods, Giants and Philosophers: On Being, Education and Dialogue in Plato's *Sophist* 245e6-249d5[1]

Jens Kristian Larsen

The 'battle' between corporealists and idealists described in Plato's *Sophist* 245e6-249d5 is of significance for understanding the philosophical function of the dramatic exchange between the Eleatic guest and Theaetetus, the dialogue's main interlocutors. Various features of this exchange indicate that the Eleatic guest introduces and discusses the dispute between corporealists and idealists in order to educate Theaetetus in ontological matters. This chapter will argue that a close reading of the discussion between Theaetetus and the Eleatic guest in the light of these features reveals that the primary audience for the proposal advanced by the Eleatic guest in this passage, namely that being is power, is not any of the participants in the 'battle', as has been commonly assumed, but Theaetetus himself – a fact to bear in mind in any viable interpretation of the passage.

The dialogue form of the *Sophist*

To many it seems that the *Sophist* is the most dogmatic of all the Platonic dialogues and therefore, if one believes that dialogue and dogmatism are opposed to each other, the one where the dialogue form is least appropriate. Moreover, the contribution to the conversation by one of the dialogues two main interlocutors, Theaetetus, at times seems to be little more than a yes or a no. As Michael Frede puts it, 'no dialogue raises the question about the continued use of the dialogue form as clearly, and as urgently, as the *Sophist* does'.[2] In fact, the *Sophist* is commonly interpreted as a quasi-treatise meant to solve the problem how one should account for the possibility of false beliefs and false statements, rather than as a philosophical dialogue.

On the other hand, as the great variety of Platonic dialogues show, Plato uses the dialogue form for many different purposes and to many different effects. Some dialogues, such as the *Laches*, may indeed seem 'undogmatic' in that Socrates mostly tests the convictions of his interlocutors. But others contain what look like dogmatic assertions about the universe and the afterlife, advanced through certain 'myths', or seemingly dogmatic teachings about the sources and causes of all there is. Many dialogues contain complex analogies and similes that require careful interpretation. Some, such as the *Symposium* or the *Timaeus* and *Critias*, are not really dialogues, but rather speeches or collections of speeches. In some, the interlocutors are very active participants in the dialogue, in others less so. In many, we have dialogues within dialogues, where Socrates or others construe imagined dialogues with persons not present in the actual dialogue for different purposes.

It may therefore be prudent to say that what characterizes Plato's dialogues *as* dialogues is first and foremost that the dialogues are dramas in the simple sense that they are literary imitations of conversations between two or more characters. As such they unfold between specific dramatic characters with specific character traits, they take place at specific dramatic dates (although it is not always possible to determine when that is), and at a certain place, features that may affect how we should interpret the philosophical conversation they contain. And as such imitations, most of them unfold as 'real' conversations in the sense that the participants ask and answer questions, reach agreement, but also make changes to what was agreed upon earlier, and even misunderstand each other. If we look at the dialogues this way it is not the number of dogmatic assertions in a given dialogue, or the degree of active participation in the conversation by the dialogue partners, that turns Plato's dialogues into dialogues.

The *Sophist* may accordingly be said to be as much a dialogue as any other Platonic dialogue. This is perhaps particularly clear from its so-called outer part, often disregarded in interpretations of the *Sophist*. Here we find an introductory conversation between Socrates, Theaetetus, Theodorus and a certain Eleatic guest that in recent years has been at the centre of many interpretations of the dialogue that have sought to take its dramatic qualities into account. That the *Sophist* is a Platonic dialogue is no less true when it comes to the central section treating of questions about being and nonbeing, truth and *logos*. The philosophical conversation found in this section displays a number of dramatic features that has a bearing on the way we should understand what is proposed in it. To mention a few, we find a number of complex analogies used to explain the art or knowledge possessed by the dialectician that require real interpretative finesse, just as other images or analogies found in other Platonic dialogues. The Eleatic guest, when attempting to illustrate to Theaetetus the problems about non-being, uses what looks like Socratic irony. Mutually reached conclusions are revealed to be faulty or at least lacking. And the central section abounds with imagined dialogues with philosophers not present at the actual conversation. This last feature will be investigated in the present chapter.

An interpretation of the *Sophist* 245e6-249d5

The chapter offers a detailed interpretation of one passage in the central section of the *Sophist*, namely the passage running from 245e6-249d5.[3] In this passage, a dispute about the nature of being is discussed, which the Eleatic guest – or stranger, as he is often called – claims resembles the mythical battle between the gods and giants. I shall refer to this philosophical dispute as the Gigantomachy and to the passage in which it is discussed as the Gigantomachy-passage. In discussing this dispute with his interlocutor Theaetetus, the guest suggests that *dynamis*, which I shall translate as power, could be regarded as a distinguishing mark, or a definition, of the things that are.

The aim of the present chapter is to address the question, how we are to regard the *dynamis*-proposal, by looking at its significance for the dialogue between the Eleatic guest and Theaetetus. It will thus sidestep the question how we are to regard the proposal in relation to Plato's own understanding of being in order to focus on the role the proposal plays in what we may call the educative dimension of the guest's dialogue with Theaetetus.[4] Its thesis will be that it is Theaetetus, rather than the participants in the Gigantomachy – the philosophical 'giants' and 'gods' – who is the primary audience for the guest's proposal.[5] Accordingly, the guest's teaching about being should not be regarded as a general ontological or metaphysical claim about being as such, but rather as a teaching addressed to Theaetetus, meant to show him how being and our understanding of being, how *ousia* and *psychê* aiming at understanding *ousia*, must be understood as interrelated.

The dialogical context of the Gigantomachy

To understand the educative element of the Gigantomachy-passage it is important to understand the specific way the dialectical exchange it contains unfolds, the specific way the guest and Theaetetus pursue this part of their conversation. The best way to understand this aspect of the Gigantomachy-passage is to compare and contrast it with the way the dialogue between Theaetetus and the guest unfolds in the immediately preceding passage.

The Gigantomachy-passage falls within the middle (often referred to as the ontological) part of the *Sophist*, where the notions of being and non-being take centre stage in the discussion. In the first section of this part, after having discussed why utter non-being (*to mêdamôs on*, 237b7-8) is, as Parmenides had claimed, impossible to know, and indeed even to utter, the guest and Theaetetus turn to discussing what a number of previous thinkers have said about being or the things that are, about *to on* or *ta onta*, in particular Parmenides' view of being. This discussion unfolds by way of what Hegel might call an immanent criticism. By taking at their word these previous thinkers, who have all made claims about being, the guest shows Theaetetus that their teachings are self-contradictory. This criticism is developed dramatically, or 'enacted', via an imagined conversation with them during which the guest questions them and both he and Theaetetus answer on their behalf. The result of this conversation is that those who claim that the things that are, *ta onta*, are a plurality, are led to posit a single thing, namely being, *to on*, which is common to, or can be stated equally about, the things they claim truly are (243c10-244a3), whereas Parmenides, who claims that the one, *to hen*, alone is (244b9-10), is led to posit a plurality rather than a unity, in consequence of the fact that the one, according to Parmenides, is identical with being, *to on* (244b12-c2), which furthermore is claimed to be a whole, *holon* (244d14-15).

Parmenides thus implicitly posits a plurality, first of all, of names – 'one', 'being', 'whole' – and, if the names are to point something out, rather than be mere names of nothing, also a plurality of 'things', of beings. Whether this criticism reflects a fair interpretation of these thinkers is unimportant here; to be noticed is that it is based on claims advanced by these thinkers, rather than on assumptions about being made by the guest or Theaetetus. The guest's procedure reminds us of a Socratic *elenchus* carried out in discussion with imagined interlocutors rather than with real dialogue partners.

In one sense the dialogue found in the passage 245e6-249d5 continues this kind of imagined conversation with philosophers not actually present. But the conversation we find in it differs in at least two important ways from the previous conversation. First of all, the way the notion of being is discussed by the participants in the Gigantomachy is slightly different from the way it is discussed both by those who posit a plurality of beings and by Parmenides. Second, the way the participants are interrogated by the guest also differs from the way the pluralists and Parmenides were interrogated. Let us begin by looking at the participants in the Gigantomachy and their notions of being.

The battle referred to by the guest as a kind of *gigantomachia* (the philosophical version of the mythical battle between the gods and the giants) is a struggle about the nature of being, fought between two opposing parties. In contrast to the previously interrogated thinkers, the participants have what looks like a more refined position in regard to being. Rather than asking how many beings there are, they focus on the being or essence of the things there are, on their *ousia*, asking what it means to be a being.[6] One party in the discussion thus claims that only what is subject to our embrace or touch (*prosbolê kai epaphê*, 246a11) is, and defines being as body (*sôma*). These are the corporealists. The other party claims that true being is identical with 'certain thought-things (*noêta*) and incorporeal *eidê*'[7] (246b7-8) with which we connect through reasoning or calculation (*logismos*, 248a11). The guest at one point refers to them as 'friends of *eidê*' (248a4-5). So rather than asking which beings there are, or how many there are, the corporealists and the friends of *eidê* ask what characterizes these beings *as* beings, deciding this question on the basis of their understanding of the way beings are accessible to humans. According to the corporealists, beings are accessible through touch whereas the friends claim they are accessible through reason.

Who the participants are is a question we will turn to when we look at the way the discussion with them proceeds. Before we do that, however, we need to say something about the specific way the guest and Theaetetus enter into discussion with them. In the previous discussion with the pluralists and with Parmenides, the guest and Theaetetus answered jointly on behalf of their imagined interlocutors. Now the guest assigns different roles to himself and to Theaetetus: while the guest is to carry out the questioning, Theaetetus is directed to interpret what the philosophical antagonists tell him when questioned by the guest (246e3, 248a5). We confront a more complex dialogical situation, in which the guest poses questions to interlocutors who are not actually present, and whose answers are not simply to be reported by Theaetetus, but rather to be interpreted or translated by him for the sake of his and the guest's dialogue together.[8] This complex situation, which in itself may seem a bit strange, becomes all the more so in consequence of the fact that one side in the struggle, the corporealists, are never allowed to enter the dialectical encounter.[9] Before they can get a hearing, they are reformed into something else. When we now turn to the first half of the Gigantomachy-passage, where the notion that being is body is discussed, we shall have to consider who these reformed corporealists are and what their reform tells us about the ontological investigation carried out in the passage.

Interrogating the corporealists

In a short passage (246a4-246d9) that precedes the imagined interrogation of the parties to the Gigantomachy, the guest introduces these parties. A number of points about his presentation should be noted. First, when the guest describes the corporealists, Theaetetus exclaims that these are dreadful men (246b4-5). This echoes what he said on the previous day while engaged in discussion with Socrates, as related in the *Theaetetus*: there Socrates described certain men who only believe that what they can grasp with their hands really is, denying the reality of actions, coming-into-being (*genesis*) and all that cannot be seen. In the *Theaetetus*, as in the *Sophist*, Theaetetus expresses his distaste for such men (*Theat.* 155e4-156a1). Clearly, the young mathematician is unsympathetic to a corporealist outlook. In the *Sophist*, the guest suggests that the friends of *eidê* have a similar dislike. It is because (cf. *toigaroun* 246b6) the corporealists are so dreadful that the friends of *eidê* force (*biazesthai*) certain bodiless and intelligible *eidê*, forms, ideas or looks, to be true being (*tēn alēthinēn ousian*), while they declare that bodies are not at all being, but rather a kind of swept-along becoming (246b6-c2). We may thus suspect that there is a kind of spiritual affinity between Theaetetus and the friends of *eidê*.

The next thing to note is that the guest goes on to suggest that the corporealists, before Theaetetus will be able to interpret what they say about being, will have to be made better. Ideally, they should be made better in deed (*ergon*) but, if this is impossible, they should at least be made better in speech (*logos*), which means that he and Theaetetus should assume that the corporealists will answer in a more law-abiding manner than they are initially inclined to do (246d4-7). This is surprising. Why are the corporealists not to be questioned on their own terms, just as the pluralists and Parmenides were earlier? Stanley Rosen states that what the guest is really suggesting is that we need, in order to question a philosophical doctrine, to 'formulate' it 'in the best or strongest way',[10] and, as the corporealists are really philosophically rather crude, we need to improve them in order to get a coherent position out of them. This may be a true description of the way we should proceed if we are interested in discussing a philosophical doctrine on its own merits. But this can hardly be what the guest has in mind. For rather than suggesting that they should reformulate the corporealists' position for their sake, he proceeds to explain that what is agreed upon by better men has more authority than what is agreed upon by worse and, as he and Theaetetus are searching for the truth, they do not care about the corporealists (246d7-9). Indeed, at a later point, he explicitly points out that what Theaetetus agrees to on behalf of the corporealists is something the corporealists would themselves never concede (247c3-7).

At the beginning of the *Sophist* the guest claims that, in order to make something apparent in speech, in order to disclose the truth about it, those who seek the truth about it should reach a shared agreement about that matter through *logoi*, or accounts (218b8-c5). In this regard, at least, the guest shares Socrates' conviction that truth about something is reached through a shared search where it is essential that an agreement about the 'what it is' (*ti estin*), the being, of that which is sought, is established. At the same time, at least according to what the guest says at the beginning of the Gigantomachy-passage, such agreement is not merely a matter of being able to follow an argument. Better people, we may suppose, will agree on things that worse people will not concede, and just such agreement, the Eleatic guest leads us to understand, is more authoritative. The reason the guest claims that the corporealists must be reformed seems to be that he holds that only what appears to be the truth to people who are good – a truth reached through discourse and agreement – is in fact true. He thus might seem to have in mind something analogous to what Aristotle means when he states that what is really good only appears as good to those who are themselves good (*EN* 1113a17-26). If this is so, it means that what we disclose as true not only depends on our capacity for reasoning, but also on our goodness or virtue as men. And since the investigation about to commence concerns being, it seems that the guest holds this to be so not simply in our discussion of such matters as the good or the virtues, but also when we are discussing ontological matters. Moreover, as we shall see shortly, he seems to be of the opinion that a consideration of the nature of being cannot be complete if isolated from a discussion of such matters as 'justice and thoughtfulness and the rest of virtue' (247b1-2).

With these initial considerations in view, we may now turn to the hypothetical discussion with the reformed corporealists, the structure of which may be summarized as follows. The guest seeks to obtain from the corporealists the concession that a number of things which should be regarded as things that are, as *onta*, are not bodies. For if the corporealists accept that there are such things, and that they are not bodies, their account of all beings, *qua* beings, as bodily, must be wrong, which should lead them to look for a new account that can account for all the types of things that they now concede are.

The things the guest specifically cites as being, for the sake of this conclusion, are soul and the virtues. More precisely, he calls attention to a difference between just and unjust, and thoughtful and thoughtless souls (246e9-247a3), a difference that the corporealists, according to Theaetetus, acknowledge. The guest suggests that this difference should be explained by the presence or absence of justice and thoughtfulness (*dikaiosynê* and *sôphrosynê*)[11] in souls and suggests further that, what has the power to be present or absent in something else, that is the virtues, must be something that is (247a5-10). Again, Theaetetus accepts all this on behalf of the corporealists. Both souls and virtues are things that are.

But now the question arises whether the virtues or the soul can be said to be visible and bodily. We should note that a thorough-going corporealist might, like Democritus, accept that souls exist, but still claim that they, as composed of a certain kind of atoms, are bodies. He might furthermore accept that virtues are in some sense, while claiming that they only are by convention, or alternatively, like the proponents of the 'harmony' theory of soul in the *Phaedo*, he might hold that they should be regarded as being simply an epiphenomenal organization of the body's components.[12] But these alternatives do not occur to Theaetetus, who claims rather that the corporealists will answer that the soul *possesses* (*kektesthai*, 247b9; literally 'to have acquired') some body, which implies that it itself is not identical with its body.[13] He states further that they are ashamed to claim either that the virtues do not belong to the things that are or that they are bodily. In reply to this answer the guest says that the corporealists have indeed become better.

This means that what turns the corporealists into reformed corporealists is not simply that they acknowledge that soul and virtues are among the things that are. It is rather the narrower claim that the soul *has*, rather than *is*, a body, and the further claim that the virtues are bodiless, which suggest that the corporealists have been transformed into something else. It is important to bear this in mind in order to understand the full significance of the *dynamis*-proposal that the guest is about to advance, a proposal that offers a new account of *ousia*, purportedly in order to help the corporealists out of their dilemma. For the guest readily admits that true corporealists would not make the concession Theaetetus has just made (247c4-7) and further suggests that it will be enough if the corporealists should accept that something, no matter how small, is bodiless (247c9-d2), in order to drive home his point, which is that *ousia* cannot be identical with body. However, he offers no grounds at all why they should accept that some of the things are bodiless. It therefore seems likely that what the proposal is primarily intended to explain is what being, what *ousia*, is, provided we accept that not only what we can grasp exists, but that souls and virtues – which are bodiless – also are. In short, the proposal need not be offered to the real corporealists at all, but only to someone who, like Theaetetus, readily accepts that bodiless souls and virtues exist.

We may now turn to the proposal itself. It is meant to explain what characterizes bodily and bodiless beings alike, in so far as they *are*, and the guest clearly advances it in his own voice.[14] It reads as follows:

> I say, then, that what possesses any sort of power [*dynamis*] – whether for making anything at all, of whatever nature, other than it is or for being affected even the least bit by the meagerest thing, even if only once – I say that all this really is [*ontôs einai*]. For I set down as a boundary [*horos*] marking off [*horizein*] the things that *are*, that their being is nothing else but *power*.
>
> 247d8-e4[15]

In response to this proposal Theaetetus states that, since the corporealists themselves have nothing better to suggest, they accept it. The guest exclaims that they do well (*kalôs*) to concede this and, although he says that it may later appear differently to them all, he suggests that for now their agreement should be left as it is. It is this mutually agreed-upon *dynamis*-proposal that the guest will now advance against the other party in the Gigantomachy, the friends of *eidê*.

But before we turn to these, a few final considerations about the status of the *dynamis*-proposal are in order. As should be clear by now, the agreement that being is power is an agreement reached between the guest and the corporealists as interpreted by Theaetetus. This *dynamis*-proposal is motivated by the fact that the corporealists, who have been transformed into better men, now accept an ontology that clearly distinguishes between bodily beings, on the one hand, and bodiless and invisible virtues, on the other, which also seems to operate with the soul as some kind of intermediary being – connected with, or possessing, a body – that *may* connect with the bodiless virtues, but does not necessarily do so. It is possible that Theaetetus, by interpreting the corporealists, finds this ontology attractive because of what he learned when considering what knowledge is with Socrates in the *Theaetetus*. There he learned that Protagoras' teaching, that man is the measure of all things, a teaching he initially found attractive (*Theat.* 152b1-13), is false (183b7-c3). He also witnessed his teacher Theodorus accept an alternative view to the effect that there is a godly pattern independent of humans, to which we should try to assimilate as far as possible in order to become virtuous – a view to be preferred to the position of Theodorus' old friend, Protagoras (cf. 176a5-177c5). Furthermore, he himself came to the conclusion that one should distinguish between the activity of the soul when it perceives via the body, and its activity when it reaches for being (*ousia*), the beautiful, and the good (185a4-e2, 186a2-b1). Although no reference to virtues as independent beings is made in these passages, they do imply that the soul becomes virtuous when it directs itself towards a divine pattern that transcends human convention. They suggest further that the soul is able to understand this pattern only when it reasons about being, rather than when it perceives through the body. This seems to point in the direction of an ontology resembling the one implied by the position of the reformed corporealists. If the rudimentary ontology of the reformed corporealists may then be said to represent Theaetetus' own understanding, it seems likely that the guest is in fact offering his account of being to Theaetetus as something that may provide an ontological foundation for the insights he gained during his discussion with Socrates the day before.

We may finally note that Theodorus, when he introduced Theaetetus to Socrates on the previous day, mentioned that Theaetetus' wealth had been squandered by some trustees (*Theat. Tht.* 144d1-2). Now, the word for wealth used in this statement (*ousia*) is the same word used to mean being. Given Plato's way with words, it is perhaps not reading too much into Theodorus' initial remark to suggest that Plato is here playfully pointing out to the attentive reader that Theaetetus' intellectual trustees, Theodorus and especially Theodorus' friend and teacher Protagoras (cf. 161b9-10, 162a4-5, 164e2-165a3, 171c8-9, 179a10), whom Theaetetus has studied closely (152a5), have in fact impoverished Theaetetus' understanding of being.[16] If this suggestion is not entirely off the mark,[17] one might further suggest that the guest is offering to restore Theaetetus' 'wealth', his understanding of being, in a fatherly manner. This seems to be in harmony with the way the guest, at an earlier point in the dialogue, claimed that he, like all those present at the conversation, is attempting to bring Theaetetus closer to the truth about the things that are, that is, that he is trying to educate him (*Sophist* 234e5-7; see also 242b1-2). On this reading, the Gigantomachy-passage is a high point in a philosophical education that is pursued throughout the *Sophist*. With these considerations in mind, we may turn to the discussion of the friends of *eidē*, in order to see how the *dynamis*-proposal fares with them.

Power and *eidē*

As was the case with the corporealists, Theaetetus is to interpret the answers given by the friends of *eidê* to the questions posed by the guest. A question arises whether their notion of being is compatible with the *dynamis*-proposal advanced by the guest. Let us take a closer look at it.

The ontology of the friends is characterized by a basic distinction between being and becoming (248a7-8), which in turn corresponds to a distinction between two ways in which we align ourselves relative to these ontological regions. According to the friends we commune (*koinônein*) with becoming (*genesis*) by means of our body through sense (*aisthêsis*), whereas we commune with true being (*ontôs ousia*) by means of our soul through reasoning (*logismos*) (248a10-11). In the subsequent discussion of this basic distinction, to which Theaetetus seems to subscribe, the guest is primarily interested in gaining a clearer understanding of the notion of communion, to evaluate the friends' notion of being.

It has been a matter of controversy who these friends are. Most scholars have regarded them as representing Plato's hypothetically earlier position as expressed in for instance the *Phaedo*.[18] I cannot go into a full discussion of this matter here, but suffice it to say that it is only possible to identify the friends as representing Plato's earlier position if one disregards the dramatic dimension of the dialogue. The guest clearly states that Theaetetus is probably not too familiar with the friends' position, wherefore he may not be able to explain what they claim about our communion with being and becoming, but that he himself is familiar with it, because he has had habitual dealings with the friends (248b7-8). As a character in a Platonic dialogue the guest can hardly be familiar with views expressed earlier by Plato.[19] For this reason it seems more plausible to regard the friends as people somehow connected with the circle around Parmenides and Zeno of whom the guest is himself a part (cf. 216a3–4).

This suggestion gains further likelihood from the following consideration. At 246c2-4 the stranger states that the dispute about being is a boundless battle (*apletos machê*), taking place in the middle (*en mesôi*) between the two parties, a battle that is forever (*aei*) joined. Just as Theaetetus' reaction to the stranger's description of the corporealists echoes his reaction to Socrates' description of a similar group of people in the *Theaetetus* (*page 111 above), the stranger's description of the battle echoes Socrates' description of a similar battle at *Theaetetus* 179d3-181b5. Here Socrates described the doctrine that everything is really *kinêsis* as a teaching about 'being that's carried along' or in change (*pheromenê ousia*), a teaching that had instigated a battle (*machê*) among a great many people (179d3-5). He there described the party opposing the Heraclitean supporters of the moving being as people like Melissus and Parmenides (180e3). Socrates explained that he, Theodorus, and Theaetetus had fallen into the middle (*eis to meson*) between the two parties. If these parallel expressions are not coincidental, as seems doubtful, it is reasonable to think that the stranger's description of the two parties in the Gigantomachy are not meant to recall any specific philosophical schools, but should be seen as sketches of philosophical attitudes towards being, associated loosely with the names of Heraclitus and Parmenides.

If this is correct, these passages from the *Theaetetus* and the *Sophist* can be read as a continued dialogue with the ontological tradition preceding Plato. In the *Theaetetus*, Heraclitus and his followers are discussed at length and their understanding of being is eventually dismissed (183a2-c3) but when Socrates is asked to discuss the opposing party, the followers of Parmenides who claim that being is one and stands still, he refrains from doing so out of reverence for Parmenides (cf. 183c8-184b1). In the *Sophist*, by contrast, the Eleatic guest begins the entire ontological investigation of the middle section of the dialogue by questioning the Eleatic tradition, in particular Parmenides (cf. 237a4-b2, 241d3-e7), and the investigation ends when Parmenides' notion of being has finally been dismissed or at least modified into a richer understanding of being, which allows for non-being *somehow* to be (258c7-e5). On the reading suggested here, the passage 245e6-249d5 should be seen as a part of the Eleatic guest's overall discussion of his own Eleatic heritage, rather than as a dialogue Plato is carrying out with his own previous position.[20]

To the above considerations may be added that what the guest is about to state about the friends' understanding of our communion with being has a rather 'unplatonic' ring to it, by the usual standards. So, let us look more closely at what they say.[21] At 248b5-8 the guest suggests that this communion could in fact be the same as a being affected or an affecting, a *pathêma* or a *poiêma* that arises (*ek . . . gignomenon*) out of some power (*dynamis*) from a mutual coming together of different things (*pros allêla syniônton*). In other words, our communion with being as well as with becoming, as the guest suggests, may be viewed as an affecting or a being affected, arising out of a power from, on the one hand, the body and the sensibles coming together through sensing, and, on the other, from the soul and the intelligible coming together through reasoning.[22] As soon as he has made this suggestion, however, the guest assumes responsibility for interpreting what the friends say, asserting that they will reject this suggestion. The reason for this, he says, is that they will not accept the suggestion that being and power are the same (248c1-5), since they deny that true being takes part in any power to affect or to be affected (248c7-9).

To Theaetetus' mind, the friends may be onto something in claiming this. In what follows, however, the guest defends the *dynamis*-proposal against the friends,[23] and insofar as Theaetetus here seems to identify himself with these friends, we may say that he defends it against Theaetetus as well. The guest's primary intention thus seems to be to get Theaetetus to agree with him that being is power, that is, to make Theaetetus come to share the understanding of being he has put forward.

If Theaetetus finds attractive the suggestion that being can neither affect us nor be affected by us, it is hardly surprising that the guest now demands to know how the friends will explain the fact that the soul may come to recognize (*gignôskein*) being, and being may come to be recognized. For some such relation between the soul and being is essential if the ontological distinction between being and becoming is not to deteriorate into a sterile two-world theory where the real beings are left without a function for the soul that strives to understand them. If the friends cannot explain this relation, their ontology threatens to become devoid of meaning. However, the passage in which the guest defends his suggested notion of being against the friends is one of the more complex passages in the dialogue, which, since we are talking about the *Sophist*, is saying quite a bit.

In this passage Theaetetus takes over the role of interpreter for the friends whom the guest, at 248d4–7, proceeds to present with three alternative interpretations of the soul's and the forms' relation to each other.[24] The alternatives are set out as follows:

1. Recognition and being recognized are likewise an affecting or an affection or both, or
2. one is an affecting, while the other is an affection, or, finally,
3. neither has a share in either affecting or affection.

The first alternative itself yields three possibilities, namely (a) that both recognizing and being recognized should be regarded as affecting, that (b) both should be regarded as being affected, and finally (c) that both should be regarded as affecting and being affected at the same time. As Lesley Brown puts it, the two first possibilities are 'non-starters', since we need both affecting and affection to explain the relation between souls and forms – which makes it understandable why the guest and Theaetetus do not pursue them. The third is theoretically a possible explanation of this relation, but it, likewise, is not discussed.

The second alternative offers us two possibilities: either (a) recognizing is an affecting and being recognized is an affection or (b) recognizing is an affection and being recognized is an affecting. Apparently, it is only the first that is discussed. For when Theaetetus claims that the friends will have to choose the third alternative, namely that neither recognizing nor being recognized is an affecting or an affection, the guest states that he understands Theaetetus' reason for choosing this alternative. Otherwise, he suggests, the friends, in accepting that recognizing is identical with affecting, would have to admit that the beings that are recognized, since they would then be affected, would thereby also be moved. And this the friends will surely not admit (cf. 248a12-13). But what about the second interpretation, according to which recognizing the *eidê* would consist in being affected by them, whereas the fact that the *eidê* are recognized would amount to their affecting the one who recognizes them? If we look at what Plato has Socrates state about the relation between *eidê* and the soul in the *Republic* and the *Phaedo*, for instance, this would seem a rather attractive interpretation. In both dialogues, the soul is said to undergo a change as a result of recognizing or grasping *eidê* or true beings, which for their part are said to remain self-identical and unchanging, while they at the same time are depicted as powers or causes that may affect virtue in the soul that grasps them.[25] It is never stated explicitly in the *Sophist* that this would be the correct way to understand how the soul and the *eidê* relate to each other, but it is reasonable to read the final part of the Gigantomachy-passage as pointing in this direction.

A problem for this interpretation is the fact that the guest, when he and Theaetetus have concluded that the friends of *eidê* will have to maintain that the *eidê* cannot be affected by our recognizing them, seems at first to argue against the friends' understanding of the *eidê* as motionless, that is, to argue in favour of the first possibility within the second alternative. At 248e7–249a2 he suggests that the view expressed by the friends implies that motion, life, soul, and thoughtfulness, that is, *phronêsis*, are not present to that which completely, or perfectly is (*to pantelôs on*), a conclusion that both he and Theaetetus find disconcerting. However, before we look at the way this claim advanced against the friends unfolds, we should note that the expression 'that which completely is', *to pantelôs on* – from which life and motion seems to be excluded as a consequence of the friends' account of being – could be understood in two different ways. It could be seen as referring to the *eidê*, which the friends earlier described as truly, *ontôs*, or the true, *alêthinê*, being (246b8, 248a11). If we read it this way, the guest does indeed seem to argue that the *eidê* are moving or changing. On the other hand, it could simply refer to complete being, *whatever that may be*, in which case he might only be arguing that some things that move or change have to be regarded as belonging to the beings that completely are, an interpretation that has been defended by, for instance, W.D. Ross.[26] In short, he could in this case be arguing only that soul and mind should be elevated to the position of being, and not that the *eidê* are alive and moving. With this in mind, we now turn to the final part of the Gigantomachy-passage.

The friends, as well as the corporealists, are here left entirely out of the conversation. From now on, it is only the guest and Theaetetus who are engaged in discussion. Together they agree that, if complete being is to have mind, *nous*, it must be alive, and furthermore that life and mind must be in a soul. Finally, they agree that all this implies motion or change (249a4-b1). So complete being, if it is to include mind and thoughtfulness, must be characterized by motion, contrary to what the friends hold (249b2-3). But the guest can hardly wish to imply by this that the *eidê* posited by the friends are in motion and alive. For having reached the conclusion that complete being must include motion, the guest immediately goes on to claim that they will exclude *nous* from the things that are if they agree that everything is in motion (249b8-10). Mind, the guest explains, presupposes that there is something that is in the same respect and in a like manner and about the same, and such things cannot be regarded as moving (249b12-c1).[27] Although the full implications of this suggestion are not spelled out by the guest, it is reminiscent of a similar claim made by Parmenides in the Platonic dialogue named after him, where he concludes his criticism of the forms posited by the young Socrates by stating that one has to accept that there are, somehow, unchanging forms, if one is to be able to explain the activity of dialectical reasoning (135b5-c3). Seen in conjunction with this, what the guest is claiming seems likely to be that we have to accept a moving or changing being among the things that are, since movement and change characterize the soul, as well as motionless or unchanging beings to which the soul may be related, if our ontology is to make the fact of insight intelligible. Indeed, if motion is linked with being affected, as the guest claims at 248e3-4, the conclusion of the Gigantomachy-passage seems to be, not that the *eidê*, when recognized, are affected and in motion – they cannot be what they are, namely self-identical beings, if in motion – but rather that the soul must be regarded as moving, since being affected by the *eidê* is a way of being moved. So, it seems, after all, that the guest ends up defending the second possibility within the second alternative, that recognizing is a being affected and being recognized is an affecting.

One may still wonder what it means to include soul in complete being. Are we here talking about human souls? Or is it perhaps rather a divine soul, analogous to the one the Pythagorean Timaeus talks about in the dialogue named after him? The guest may well have both things in mind, but it lies beyond the scope of the present chapter to discuss this in any detail, since this would demand a discussion of the rest of the drama of this dialogue. Instead we shall end by trying to specify what the Gigantomachy-passage teaches Theaetetus about being and the soul. The guest has evidently advanced and defended his *dynamis*-proposal against both parties in the Gigantomachy in order to make Theaetetus accept it as well. The primary purpose of this proposal is to make intelligible the fact that the soul, which is moving, can be related to beings that are unmoved and invisible, so that these somehow become present to the soul. If one does not concede this, as the real corporealists do not, because they deny that there are invisible, self-identical beings, and as the friends of *eidê* cannot, since they deny the *eidê* any power, one not only denies that life, mind and motion truly are. One denies further that thoughtfulness, *phronêsis*, and knowledge, *epistêmê*, of anything whatever may come about at all, as the stranger points out at 249c6-8. At least from a Socratic point of view, this amounts to denying the possibility of virtue, since true virtue presupposes *phronêsis* or *epistêmê*, which Socrates elsewhere claims come about when the soul draws near to, or has intercourse with, the *eidê* or *ideai* (cf. *Phaedo* 65e7-66a8, 69a6-c3, *Resp.* 490a8-b7, 500b8-d3, *Symp.* 211e4-212a7). Perhaps it is the same view that is expressed in the guest's final remark in the Gigantomachy-passage. The philosopher, he states, who honours mind, thoughtfulness and knowledge above everything else, has to object both to the view that everything is in motion and to the view that everything is standing still, and, as the little child, when confronted with the question which hand it will choose, has to beg for both. Perhaps we should regard the insight the philosopher strives for as itself being a child, namely the offspring of the *erôs* of the soul and the generating power of the beings for which the soul longs.

In any case, it is the ontological preconditions for philosophical insight that the guest has sought to make Theaetetus understand through their mutual conversation. This conversation, we have seen, is not confined to a dialogue between the two of them but includes an imagined conversation with philosophers from the tradition not present at the actual conversation. Attention to the specific form of the dialogue we find in the central section of the Sophist thus allows us to see how the stranger uses different styles of conversation to educate Theaetetus about the soul's relation to being. If we had disregarded the dialogue form in our interpretation, we would not have seen that education was a central aspect of the action of the guest's argument. We might thereby have come to the conclusion that he was a dogmatic or even 'technical' philosopher preoccupied with ontological question and with little interest in the soul of his interlocutor. This has certainly happened to others.[28]

Notes

1 This chapter is a slightly expanded and revised version of the article 'The Virtue of Power', published in *The New Yearbook for Phenomenology and Phenomenological Philosophy*, 13 (2013): 306–17.
2 Michael Frede, 'The Literary Form of the *Sophist*', in *Form and Argument in Late Plato*, ed. Christopher Gill and Mary Margaret McCabe (Oxford: Oxford University Press, 1996), 137.

3 References to the Greek text are to *Platonis Opera*, volume I, eds. E.A. Duke, W.F. Hicken, W.S.M. Nicoll, D.B. Robinson and J.C.G. Strachan (Oxford: Oxford University Press, 1995).
4 That the *Sophist* as a whole can be regarded as an education of Theaetetus is strongly emphasized in Hans-Georg Gadamer, 'Dialektik ist nicht Sophistik – Theätet lernt das im *Sophistes*', in *Gesammelte Werke*, vol. 7 (Tübingen: Mohr Siebeck, 1990).
5 A similar reading is suggested in Fiona Leigh, 'Being and Power in Plato's *Sophist*,' *Apeiron* 43 (1) (2010): 78, though the implications of this are not worked out in her paper.
6 Cf. Martin Heidegger, *Plato's Sophistes, Gesamtausgabe*, vol. 19 (Frankfurt am Main: Vittorio Klostermann, 1992), 464–65; Mary Margaret McCabe, *Plato and his Predecessors* (Cambridge: Cambridge University Press, 2000), 81; Christian Iber, 'Kommentar', in Platon, *Sophistes*, trans. Friedrich Schleiermacher (Frankfurt am Main: Suhrkamp Verlag, 2007), 269.
7 Translations are from *Plato: Sophist or the Professor of Wisdom*, translation, introduction, and glossary Eva Brann, Peter Kalkavage and Eric Salem (Newburyport: Focus Publishing, 1996). The translation has been slightly modified at certain points without notice.
8 Noboru Notomi, *The Unity of Plato's Sophist: Between the Sophist and the Philosopher* (Cambridge: Cambridge University Press, 1999), 218 points to this difference in the dialogical situation, although he draws a conclusion along the lines of Rosen's, mentioned below, and unlike the one drawn in this chapter.
9 McCabe, *Predecessors*, 76 thus rightly describes the corporealists as 'missing persons,' as people who never turn up for the dialectical encounter in which they are supposed to take part. See also Kenneth Dorter, *Form and Good in Plato's Eleatic Dialogues* (Berkeley: University of California Press, 1994), 142.
10 Stanley Rosen, *Plato's Sophist* (New Haven: Yale University Press, 1983), 214.
11 In many Platonic dialogues, virtues such as justice and thoughtfulness are treated as Forms or Ideas, as instances of that which really is (*ta ontōs onta*). As it is a matter of controversy whether the *Sophist* operates with 'Platonic Forms' at all, and as the corporealists are in any case not adherents to a 'doctrine of Forms', I shall leave talk of Forms aside and refer to the virtues simply as 'beings', since this is how they are described in the text.
12 See Lesley Brown, 'Innovation and Continuity: The Battle of Gods and Giants', in *Method in Ancient Philosophy*, ed. Jyl Gentzler (Oxford: Oxford University Press, 1998), 188.
13 Brown, 'Innovation and Continuity', 188 regards this as equivalent to the claim that the soul *is* a body, in contradistinction to the virtues, which are said not to be bodies (cf. 247c2). In the reading suggested here, Theaetetus answers on behalf of the corporealists that the soul is invisible but *has* a body (while not thereby being identical with body), whereas the virtues and their opposites are both invisible and without a body.
14 This is rightly emphasized by Leigh, 'Being and Power', 65.
15 The passage is notoriously difficult to translate and to interpret. For a more detailed discussion of the formulation of the proposal, see Brown, 'Innovation and Continuity', 190.
16 Cf. John McDowell, *Plato: Theaetetus* (Oxford: Clarendon Press, 1973), 113.
17 For a similar play on *ousia*, see *Republic* 329e4 and 330d1-3, in comparison with 509b8-10. Note also that both Cephalus' grandfather (330b3-6) and Theaetetus' father (144c7-8) left fortunes, and both Cephalus' father (330b5) and Theaetetus' trustees (144d2) squandered them. I thank Hayden Ausland for pointing out these parallels.

18 Francis Macdonald Cornford, *Plato's Theory of Knowledge* (London: Routledge & Kegan Paul, 1935), 242; William David Ross, *Plato's Theory of Ideas* (Oxford: Clarendon Press, 1951), 107; Brown, 'Innovation and Continuity', 194; Notomi, *Unity of Plato's* Sophist, 219–20. For other suggested candidates, see Ross, *Theory of Ideas*, 105–6.
19 Cf. Alfred Edward Taylor, *Plato: The Sophist and The Statesman*, ed. Raymond Klibansky and Elizabeth Anscombe (London: Thomas Nelson & Sons, 1961), 44–5.
20 A full discussion of Plato's connection with the 'presocratic' tradition, in particular with Heraclitus and Parmenides, lies beyond the scope of the present chapter. A discussion of this complex and fascinating matter would require that one took the *Parmenides* and the *Cratylus* into consideration as well, and there is a further question to what extent the notion of Forms in the so-called middle-period dialogues can be regarded as 'Parmenidean'.
21 Even their understanding of our communion with becoming by means of our body through sense seems unplatonic. In the *Phaedo*, as in the *Theaetetus*, Socrates advances the view that we commune with sensibles, with becoming, through the *soul's* use of the senses (*Phaedo* 79c2-8; *Theat.* 184c1-9). In other words, the senses are not separate faculties, set over sensible things, but rather instruments through which the soul is related to sensibles. Brown, 'Innovation and Continuity', 195, note 23, acknowledges this difference, but, in contrast to the present reading, believes that this may be regarded as nothing more than the result of Plato's wish to 'state the Friends of the Form's theory in a bold and economical way'.
22 As is emphasized by Brown, 'Innovation and Continuity', 200, this 'theory' may remind us of the theory of perception developed by Socrates in the *Theaetetus*. It would be interesting to look more closely into this – in particular into the possibly close relationship existing between perception and knowledge in Plato – but it lies beyond the scope of the present chapter to go into this.
23 See Rudolf Rehn, *Der Logos der Seele* (Hamburg: Felix Meiner Verlag, 1982), 164, n 118.
24 The three alternatives have been carefully analyzed by Brown, 'Innovation and Continuity', 196–200, to whom the present interpretation is indebted. Brown's reading has recently been criticized by Leigh, 'Being and Power', 69–72, but Brown's suggestion remains the more attractive in respect of its understanding of the outcome of the Gigantomachy.
25 Cf. *Phaedo* 65c2-66a8, 69a6-c3, 80a10-b7; *Republic* 500b8-d9.
26 Ross, *Theory of Ideas*, 107–10. Brown, 'Innovation and Continuity', 203 takes the passage in the same manner.
27 For further discussion of this problem, and alternative solutions, see Brown, 'Innovation and Continuity', 190–2 and 197–200.
28 I wish to thank Lesley Brown, Vivil Valvik Haraldsen and Vigdis Songe-Møller who read an earlier version of this chapter and made fruitful comments. Thanks are also due to Knut Ågotnes who read the earlier published version and made helpful suggestions concerning the revision of the text. Special thanks are due to Hayden Ausland, who read the entire manuscript several times and made innumerable corrections and many valuable suggestions. The chapter was written as part of a postdoctoral research project financially supported by the Danish Council for Independent Research and later revised as part of a postdoctoral research project financially supported by the EU through the Marie Skłodowska-Curie Actions.

Bibliography

Brann, Eva, Peter Kalkavage and Eric Salem. *Plato: Sophist or the Professor of Wisdom*. With translation, introduction and glossary. Newburyport: Focus Publishing, 1996.

Brown, Lesley. 'Innovation and Continuity: The Battle of Gods and Giants'. In *Method in Ancient Philosophy*. Edited by Jyl Gentzler, 181–207. Oxford: Oxford University Press, 1998.

Cornford, Francis Macdonald. *Plato's Theory of Knowledge*. London: Routledge & Kegan Paul, 1935.

Dorter, Kenneth. *Form and Good in Plato's Eleatic Dialogues*. Berkeley: University of California Press, 1994.

Frede, Michael. 'The Literary Form of the *Sophist*'. In *Form and Argument in Late Plato*, edited by Christopher Gill and Mary Margaret McCabe, 135–51. Oxford: Oxford University Press, 1996.

Gadamer, Hans-Georg. 'Dialektik ist nicht Sophistik – Theätet lernt das im *Sophistes*'. In *Gesammelte Werke*, vol. 7, 338–69. Tübingen: Mohr Siebeck, 1990.

Heidegger, Martin. *Plato's* Sophistes, *Gesamtausgabe*, vol. 19. Frankfurt am Main: Vittorio Klostermann, 1992.

Iber, Christian. 'Kommentar'. In Platon, *Sophistes*. Translated by Friedrich Schleiermacher. Frankfurt am Main: Suhrkamp Verlag, 2007.

Leigh, Fiona. 'Being and Power in Plato's *Sophist*'. *Apeiron* 43 no 1 (2010): 63–85.

McCabe, Mary Margaret. *Plato and his Predecessors*. Cambridge: Cambridge University Press, 2000.

McDowell, John. *Plato: Theaetetus*. Oxford: Clarendon Press, 1973.

Notomi, Noboru. *The Unity of Plato's* Sophist: *Between the Sophist and the Philosopher*. Cambridge: Cambridge University Press, 1999.

Rehn, Rudolf. *Der Logos der Seele*. Hamburg: Felix Meiner Verlag, 1982.

Rosen, Stanley. *Plato's* Sophist. New Haven: Yale University Press, 1983.

Ross, William David. *Plato's Theory of Ideas*. Oxford: Clarendon Press, 1951.

Taylor, Alfred Edward. *Plato: The Sophist and The Statesman*. Edited by Raymond Klibansky and Elizabeth Anscombe. London: Thomas Nelson & Sons, 1961.

7

Philotimia. On Rhetoric, Virtues and Honour in the *Symposium*[1]

Knut Ågotnes

Introduction

When composing the *Symposium*,[2] Plato seems to have exerted himself in order to find ways to hide his 'true philosophical meaning'. Where we most of all expect to meet his thinking, in Socrates' speech, we find that the delivery is influenced by the demands of the rhetorical genre encomium, and by the language of initiation into the religious mysteries. Before we get that far in the text, however, Plato has given us several reasons to doubt that the text contains the exact words that Socrates spoke at the symposion. Since the drinking party is a fictitious event, nothing could have prevented Plato to give the impression that he had written down Socrates' speech word for word. Instead he makes up an intricate story about how the memory of what Socrates said was kept alive during the sixteen years that had elapsed between the event itself and Apollodorus' narration. Plato also alerts us to the question of the quality of Socrates' own memory since most of his speech is presented as a direct rendering of what he heard Diotima say twenty-four years before the – fictitious – symposion took place.[3]

Plato thus establishes a considerable distance between the reader and Apollodorus' account. Another kind of distance is created by Plato's choice of genre; he lets the speakers use the rhetorical genre encomium.

The impact of the rules and demands of the encomium genre

The core of the encomium is the praising of something or someone. To give a speech in praise is to give honour to the object or the person in question. Honouring is guiding the composition of the speech and it should show up emphatically in its peroration, its summing up. Honour may also accrue to the speaker himself. If he praises well, he will be honoured, and if the occasion is a speech competition, the winner gets the greatest honour. In the *Symposium*, Eros is the object of praise. Eros is praised for his inherent qualities and for the benefits he gives to man.

Andrea Nightingale writes: 'underlying all of the genres of eulogy is a basic binary scheme: what is praised is good (without, or with very few qualifications), and what is contrary to this is bad'.[4] She quotes Isocrates: 'It is necessary for those who eulogize a person to represent him as possessing a greater number of good qualities than he actually possesses.' Isocrates adds that this is something that everyone knows (*Busiris* 4 [222]).[5] In *Rhetoric to Alexander* we find this: 'To speak generally, the eulogistic kind [in contrast to the vituperative kind] is the mention of creditable choices, deeds, and words, and the attribution of qualities which do not exist'[6] (1425b35). A man's actions were praised, and so was his virtuous character, since his good actions or effects were supposed to follow from his character.[7] This creates a problem for the symposiasts, since 'everyone' knew that Eros (as well as Aphrodite) could have negative and even disastrous effects on human beings.[8] Eryximachus and Pausanias try to solve this problem by postulating two kinds of Eros, a good and a bad. Diotima has some such problems too. She gives Eros a few not so attractive qualities; 'a genius with enchantments, potions and clever pleadings (*sophistês*)' (203d).

Encomiastic speech is not supposed to be concerned with the truth in any strong sense. John Poulakos says 'that classical Greek rhetoric was informed by the ethic of competition and the aesthetic of exhibition and performance'.[9] Rhetorical and poetical proficiency would certainly be appreciated at a drinking party.[10] If the speakers could manage to make his speech 'ring true', however, it could augment the appeal of his performance. Socrates seemingly objects to the devaluation of truthfulness by pretending that he has misunderstood the rules of the game. He has thought that the idea was to present the good qualities of the object in question as well as its effects, but that only true information should be conveyed, he says. But Socrates must be pulling our leg here. If one presents only the true aspects of *erôs*, the speech as a whole will be misleading. Truthfulness, in the sense Socrates employs the concept here, will not save the encomium from falsehood.

'Socrates' elenctic method is diametrically opposed to the language of the encomium. It does not aim at gratification or glory, nor does it promulgate falsehoods that instill in the auditor a proud and stubborn ignorance,' Nightingale writes.[11] His elenctic method also belongs to a way of doing philosophy that is constantly investigating problems, perhaps without ever reaching any final answers. The rules of the encomium presuppose, however, that the speaker should imagine, or pretend, that he knows the answers, and Socrates pretends that he does, as his summing up, his peroration, at 212b-c shows.

Encomiastic speech does not exclude elements of other types of discourse. Plato lets Diotima use the language of initiation into religious mysteries, especially evident from 210a on. Christoph Riedweg shows how 'Verbindung und Überlagerung der mysterienkultischen und der philosophischen Ebene sehr konsequent durchgeführt sind.'[12]

Preoccupation with honour as displayed within a competitive rhetorical contest: five speakers

The drinking party is held in honour of Agathon. He has won the first prize in the competition for the best tragedy, and, according to Socrates' ironic praise,[13] has been honoured by the applause of the 30,000 strong theatre audience. Phaedrus and

Eryximachus propose that each of the symposiasts shall 'give as good a speech in praise of Love as he is capable of giving' (177d).[14] Agathon is looking forward to a new victory. 'Dionysus will soon enough be the judge of our claims to wisdom!' Agathon says to Socrates (175e). We are going to witness a competition in praising, and Agathon, who does not recognize any difference between successful poetry and wisdom, is confident about his chances. Agathon's concern with his honour is patent enough before the contest begins, and it will come through in his speech. Even if we are not to expect truthful accounts about Eros, we will see how his, as well as the other speakers' values are being revealed.

Agathon and Phaedrus: Eros deserves praise because he makes us strive for honour

Agathon explains the rules: 'Now, only one method is correct for every praise, no matter whose: you must explain what qualities in the subject of the speech enable him to give the benefits for which we praise him. So now, in the case of Love, it is right for us to praise him first for what he is and afterwards for his gifts' (195a). He begins his encomium by claiming that Eros is a god who is in possession of every virtue and every skill.[15] He then simply lends his own qualities to those he likes, which is beautiful young people of a soft and gentle character. He gives the poet wisdom and the ability to compose. If Eros touches a poet, he becomes a good poet, and he makes people in all kinds of artistic production good in the same way. 'And as for artisans and professionals – don't we know that whoever has this god for a teacher ends up in the light of fame (*ellogimos*), while a man untouched by Love ends up in obscurity?' (197a). It has been noticed by many that the picture Agathon paints of Eros is similar to his image of himself, and he obviously thinks that he has been 'touched'. When he says that he shall honour his own profession, which arises out of the virtue of wisdom, he is giving honour to his own work as well. In conformity with the rules of encomium, virtues are given a central role, but Agathon, as well as the other speakers – except Aristophanes[16] – see them as means for realization of values.[17] Most important for Agathon is that wisdom, as he understands it, makes him a successful poet. After Agathon has finished his speech, he is awarded with tumultuous applause from all present. He is honoured, again.

In Phaedrus' speech Eros represents 'loving', in a broad sense, including love between parents and children, and between comrades. Eros gives us the greatest goods or benefits. He is more efficient in this regard than family bonds, public offices or wealth. He makes us courageous, and courage is Phaedrus' most cherished virtue. The mechanism is this. Eros gives us a sense of shame at acting disgracefully. One would not like to be seen either by one's beloved or one's lover to act cowardly, and the abhorrence of this kind of shame will make one courageous. However, even if avoidance of shame saves us from dishonour, Eros seems to motivate us to seek honour even if we do not expect to be shamed, since he gives us a sense 'of pride in acting well' (178c-d). He makes warriors compete for honour (179a). Moreover, strong love can motivate courageous acts directly, as was the case when Alcestis gave up her life for her husband. She acted by the zeal and courage that come from Eros (179d). Apparently, she did not have honour consciously in mind. The gods, however, in admiration gave her the special honour (*timê*) of having her soul sent back from Hades. Eros, then, produces honour as an end result, even if we are not fully aware of the working of the mechanism, or consciously motivated by love of honour.

Both Agathon and Phaedrus give praise to Eros for what he produces in us by means of desires, emotions and virtues, and the end result is honour, which is seen unequivocally as a value, something to strive for as part of the good life.

Pausanias: the god Eros deserves praise for the sex he gives us, if it is honourable sex

Pausanias undoubtedly considers sex as a great good in life, and he would probably have praised it to the skies, if it had not been for the fact that the sexual practice he favours, constantly threatens a gentleman's honour. For Pausanias, then, Eros is not an honour-producing force. Pausanias loves honour, though, and he needs to reach a balance between his most cherished values. He does it in this way: there are two kinds of Eros, one vulgar and shameful, the other honourable (*kalos*). To practice sex according to the custom of homosexual love between an older and a younger man is honourable. This custom requires an interest in the cultivation of the virtues in the beloved,[18] and this concern figures prominently in Pausanias' speech. It seems that '[W]hat is done properly and in accordance with our customs' are virtuous actions (182a). There is no shame in having sex if one respects the conventional rules of the relationship between the lover and the beloved. The speech is almost obsessively concerned with what is honourable. He asks: what could be more honourable than to do anything for the sake of virtue? Eros does not by himself point us towards the virtues. Honourable sex, though, needs virtues, and we get them from law and custom. Here too, then, the virtues play an instrumental role, they are seen as necessary for honourable sex.[19]

Eryximachus: knowing how to control the mechanisms of Eros gives honour to the expert

The doctor Eryximachus starts by giving his own science (*technê*) pride of place (186b). He knows how the two types of Eros that Pausanias had described affect health and sickness. He then broadens the field; Eros directs everything that occurs, after the same pattern that applies to the body. He can thus talk with authority not only about medicine, but also about music, poetry, physical training, farming, the art of divination, and astronomy. Eryximachus is practicing amplification here. In this way he gives Eros a maximum of importance and dignity, and his own medical science as well. Agathon, at 196e, shrewdly notices that Eryximachus' speech honours his own profession.[20]

Diotima: *erôs* makes us 'desire to become famous and to lay up glory immortal forever' (208c)

Socrates' speech gives us a comprehensive account of human nature from the perspective of moral psychology, and of philosophy seen in light of this psychology. Plato lets Socrates pretend that he has got this material from a non-philosophical source, from the priestess Diotima, who possesses a 'mysterious, superhuman authority'.[21] In addition, she is well versed in attitudes and opinions found in the *paideia* of the *polis*.[22] Her speech turns out to be in tune with the other speakers on the most important points: *erôs* as the central force of life and virtues as instruments for honour. Moreover, the conventions of the encomium genre are framing her speech.[23] This makes it possible for Diotima to make strong claims, in sharp contrast to Socrates' proclamations of ignorance about substantial matters in other dialogues. Plato lets Socrates play the role of the admiring pupil and is thus eliminating any serious questioning on his part. And by letting Diotima speak at all, instead of Socrates himself, Plato establishes distance between himself and Socrates on the one hand and the content of the speech on the other.

According to *Diotima* Eros is not a god, but a *daimôn*, a 'spirit', in most translations. When presented in mythical language, demons appear as messengers between gods and men; they shuttle back and forth between these two realms. Notice that they travel both ways all the time. Eros is born of Penia (poverty, lack) and Poros (resource). Diotima soon drops the mythical allusions, however. *Erôs* operates on a human level. He is the almost universal motive and force behind our striving to become what we should be but are not. One reservation is made. Those who are ignorant (*amathia*)[24] about their lack are content with themselves (204a). Erotic natures are aware of their ignorance and other shortcomings.

Erôs dominates human striving, he is in general desire for what we think is good, but do not have, and therefore yearn for. He is 'being in love', but this is just one kind of *erôs*. Diotima needs to widen the concept in order to cover 'every desire for good things or for happiness ...' It can include love of making money, love of sport or love of wisdom (205d). *Erôs* must thus be understood as *spoudê*: 'the eagerness and zeal we call *erôs*' (206b). Philosophers are erotic persons: '*erôs* must be a lover of wisdom, and as such is in between *(metaxy)* being wise and being ignorant' (204b).

'What is the real purpose of love?' 'What do people do with the eagerness and zeal we call love?' (206b). Diotima is beginning to tell us what the human values are, here understood as the most important 'things' we strive for in life, things we want to have forever and which we would be inclined to include when asked what the good or happiness means to us. For Diotima the fundamental values are shaped by *erôs*, and she knows what they are.

The deepest impulse of *erôs*, in men and animals, is to seek immortality: 'For among animals the principle is the same as with us, and mortal nature seeks so far as possible to live forever and be immortal.' For animals this is only possible by reproduction (207d). An animal 'in love' gets excited about beauty and draws near to it. *Erôs*, however, does not want beauty, but reproduction in beauty (206e). Beauty is a means to the final end, not this end itself. Humans seek immortality also through deeds and intellectual works. 'it is for the sake of immortality that everything shows this zeal (*spoudê*), which is *erôs*' (208b).

Socrates is sceptical, but Diotima does not lack facts and arguments. She presents these 'in the manner of a perfect sophist' (208c).

Be sure of it, Socrates. Look, if you will, at how human beings seek honour (*philotimia*). You'd be amazed at their irrationality (*alogia*), if you didn't have in

> mind what I spoke about and if you hadn't pondered the awful state of love they're in, wanting to become famous and 'to lay up glory (*kleos*) immortal forever', and how they're ready to brave any danger for the sake of this, much more than they are for their children; and they are prepared to spend money, suffer through all sorts of ordeals, and even die for the sake of glory ... I believe that anyone will do anything for the sake of immortal virtue and the glorious fame (*aretês athanatou kai ... doxês eukleoûs*) that follows; and the better the people, the more they will do, for they are all in love with immortality.
>
> 208c-e

Diotima's best argument, she seems to think, is that the excessive love of honour we can see everywhere would be difficult to explain (it would be irrational) if we do not see it as caused by the desire for immortality. We brave danger, accept death, spend money and toil for this value, and we develop virtues in order to attain it. Virtue – *aretê* – is a means to 'glorious fame'. It is, however, a necessary means; our renown is based on the virtues we have shown that we possess.[25] So, how are the necessary virtues nurtured?

> When someone has been pregnant with these [the virtues] in his soul from early youth, while he is still a virgin, and, having arrived at the proper age, desires to beget and give birth, he too will certainly go about seeking the beauty in which he would beget; for he will never beget in anything ugly. Since he is pregnant, then, he is much more drawn to bodies that are beautiful than to those that are ugly; and if he also has the luck to find a soul that is beautiful and noble and well-formed, he is even more drawn to this combination; such a man makes him instantly teem with ideas and arguments about virtue – the qualities a virtuous man should have and the customary activities in which he should engage; and so he tries to educate him.
>
> 209b-c

Virtues are developed gradually, motivated by *erôs*, starting with a relationship between lovers, and by means of beauty and the use of language. The general picture here is in tune with the concept of how to become educated in the established *paideia*, as it is expressed in the homosexual relationship between the beautiful youngster and the older man who is pregnant with the things that are 'proper' (*prosêkei*, 209a). These suitable items are: 'Wisdom (*phronêsis*) and the rest of virtue, which all poets beget, as well as all the craftsmen who are said to be creative or inventive. But by far the greatest and most beautiful part of wisdom deals with the proper ordering of cities and households, and that is called moderation and justice' (209a). The activities that are most esteemed in the *polis* are mentioned here: poetry and politics. Homer, Hesiod, Lycurgus, and Solon are mentioned especially, as persons honoured for their deeds and virtues (209e).

Excursus: the relationship between the speeches and the *paideia*

Are the five speeches we have looked at so far pertinent representations of prevalent attitudes in Athens? Let us focus briefly on four items.

1. *The importance of philotimia.* Xenophon writes: 'Athenians excel all others not so much in singing or in stature or in strength, as in love of honour (*philotimia*), which is the strongest incentive to deeds of honour and renown' (*Memorabilia* III iii 13).[26] Aristotle: 'But people of superior refinement and active disposition identify happiness with honour; for this is, roughly speaking, the end of the political life' (*Nicomachean Ethics* 1095b22).[27]
2. *The attitude to (posthumous) renown.* Thucydides' 'Funeral oration' is a double encomium: on the men who have died for Athens, and on Athens herself. Here the general idea is that the individual soldiers have won honour and fame by their death in battle, 'the final confirmation of a life of virtue'. This glory is strongly augmented by their laying down their lives for Athens, who has her own renown, based on her great power. '[Y]ou should fix your eyes every day on the greatness of Athens as she really is, and should fall in love with her.' 'They gave her their lives, to her and to all of us, and for their own selves they won praises that never grow old … but where their glory remains eternal in men's minds' (*The Peloponnesian War* 2.43).[28]

    K.J. Dover writes about Demosthenes that he 'claimed that in his own political career he had been primarily concerned with the honour of Athens – not with her security or prosperity, though both were relevant to her capacity to perform what honour demanded of her, but with her reputation, in the world at large and in aftertime'.
3. *The role of competition.* With reference to Demosthenes, Dover says, perhaps a bit categorically: 'When someone is honoured, the honour is necessarily withheld from others who wanted it just as badly, no one can win unless someone else loses, and an honour shared with everybody is a doubtful honour. Hence the *philotimia* of individuals within the community as a whole took the form of 'a contest of good men.' Dover adds that the Greeks deliberately gave a competitive character to as many aspects of life as possible.
4. *The instrumentality of the virtues.* Dover sums up his citations on this point thus: 'these passages are entirely in keeping with many generalizations to the effect that the hope of praise is a major incentive to virtue'.[29]

Diotima: The greater mystery: what *erôs* does to the philosophers (210a-212b)

There is some continuity between the lesser (209e-210a) and the greater mystery.[30] The driving force of *erôs* is in place in the greater mystery too, as well as love of young bodies, the role of beauty as a catalyst, the gradual transition to souls, activities, customs and kinds of knowledge, all of which seem to produce speeches and thoughts. Keeping a constant eye on beauty, the philosopher arrives at the upmost end of the ascent, where he catches sight of 'something wonderfully beautiful in its nature; the very thing, Socrates, for the sake of which all the earlier labours were undertaken' (210e). This is beauty itself, unchanging and everlasting. The philosopher attains knowledge of this beauty in the form of 'seeing' (211e-212b). Then, when he has seen beauty itself, 'absolute, pure and unmixed' (211e), it becomes possible for him to give 'birth to true virtue (because he is in touch with beauty)' (212a).

Discrepancies between the lesser and the greater mystery

Diotima is teaching a *method* for gaining philosophical insight. The philosopher must follow a procedure. It is implied by Diotima's method of initiation that you must learn how to take one step at a time. You must proceed 'in the right order and correctly' (210e), using the beautiful things as if they were steps (212b). This must mean that you have to master one rung on the ladder before you can take the next. It is thus assumed that there is *one* way, *one* method, *one* ladder. It is also implied that if you have reached a rung on the ladder, you have gained a secure footing for going higher.

In 'the lesser mystery', virtues are a product of *erôs* as a means to attain honour, which again is causally connected to the final aim, immortality. The importance of nurturing the virtues is built into the *paideia*, and citizens are well aware of the usefulness of the virtues for acquiring praise and honour. Here, in the greater mystery, the virtues emerge as a by-product of the search for knowledge of beauty. It is even suggested that they appear by a 'touching' ('because he is in touch with the true beauty' (212a)). The philosopher does not seem to have the search for virtue consciously in mind. Rather, the seeing of *beauty* 'is the reason for all his earlier labours' (211a); 'one goes upwards for the sake of this beauty' (211c). Beauty plays a more important role in the greater mystery than in the lesser. Diotima said there that *erôs* does not want beauty, but reproduction and birth in beauty (206e). Beauty functioned there as a sort of catalyst, or as a prompter. It does so in the greater mystery, too, but now it is also the thing we consciously seek.

In her last sentence, when referring to the philosopher who has reached the top of the ladder, Diotima says: 'The love of the gods belongs to anyone who has given birth to true virtue and nourished it, and if any human being could become immortal, it would be he' (212b). This sounds plausible at first sight. Since immortality is the *telos* of *erôs* quite generally, it would be strange if this didn't hold for philosophers too. But if it does, we would expect the aim of immortality to show up as a concern in the account of the ascent. But it does not. Could it be that the philosophers are unaware of the fact that *erôs* points them towards immortality? According to Phaedrus, Alcestis died for her husband out of her strong love alone, without, it seems, thinking that the gods would honour her and make her immortal. Does *erôs* move in such mysterious ways with philosophers too? Diotima, however, says that Alcestis expected the memory of her virtue to become immortal (208c-e). Before she starts to expound the greater mystery, she seems to hold that the conscious desire for immortality is universal. One implication of the view that the philosopher is unaware of the final end is that he will be lacking in self-knowledge. In fact, Solon and Homer would have had more self-insight than him.

We can choose between two alternative interpretations here. According to the first, philosophers are keen on becoming immortal. In that they are like everybody else, and they have had immortality in mind during the ascent, but for some reason Diotima will not mention this fact. Moreover, honour is intimately linked to immortality in Diotima's scheme. That honour is not mentioned in the ascent of the greater mystery, may then be for the same unmentioned reason. This reading will strengthen the coherence of Diotima's speech.

In the other interpretation honour and immortality is of no (or little) value to the philosopher. His conscious aim is to know beauty as such, regardless of any attention he eventually would get from gods and men. This would constitute a divergence from Diotima's conception of human nature, as she developed it until she started to reveal the greater mystery.

Neither of these interpretations, however, suggests an easy solution to the questions of the relation between the *virtues* and the *telos* of the ascent. The virtues are the last things that are learnt, after the seeing of beauty. So why should not the whole endeavour be for the sake of knowledge of the virtues? However, if it is, it is strange that the mode of investigating moral insight is so scantily discussed. It is even stranger that the salient question of what happens when the true virtues appear after the touching of beauty, is left unanswered. Some would probably surmise, in accord with the first interpretation, that we see a case of the mysterious ways of *erôs* here too, that even if the real aim is the virtues, the conscious goal is beauty.

Diotima makes a significant move away from the lesser mystery here that takes us *away from* what we would expect a philosopher's work to be. In the lesser mystery the virtues are in focus as the things the soul shall 'conceive and bear' in beauty. Beauty is a catalyst here. In the greater mystery the virtues are referred to when the lowest step is described, and then not directly, but as: 'the kind of discourse that will make young men better people' (210c). After that virtues are not mentioned, until they pop up as a by-product of the seeing of true beauty.

It seems odd that Homer and Solon, who are mentioned as products of the education described by the lesser mystery, should be more preoccupied with virtue than the philosophers. But then, Diotima has declared the poets as well as the inventive craftsmen to be procreators of wisdom and virtue. The lack of an account of how the philosopher investigates and evolves his views on the virtues will of course be less problematic if a 'seeing' of beauty could give us knowledge of true virtue by 'touching'.[31] In the beginning of Diotima's first account of *erôs* and his role as a philosopher, where the *daimôn*-metaphor is developed, *erôs* is called a go-between, first between gods and men, then in-between (*metaxy*) need and resource. The philosopher is placed there too; he is 'a lover of wisdom through all his life' (203d). And he is in a middle state between a wise man an ignorant one (204b). 'He is *always* midway between the two' (203e). This in-between position, added to the back-and-forth movement suggested by the figure of the *daimôn*, grates against the methodical ascent up the ladder of the sure-footed and successful, but somewhat unaware, philosopher that the greater mystery presents to us.

Irony

> This, Phaedrus and the rest of you, was what Diotima told me. I was persuaded. And once persuaded, I try to persuade others too that human nature can find no better

workmate for acquiring this than Love. That's why I say that every man must honour love, why I honour the rites of Love myself and practice them with special diligence, and why I commend them to others. Now and always I praise the power and courage of Love so far as I am able. Consider this speech then, Phaedrus, if you wish, a speech in praise of Love. Or if not, call it whatever and however you please to call it.

212b-c

Here, in his peroration, Socrates is doing exactly what one should do according to the rules of encomium, namely to give a general assessment at the end of the speech where the object is glorified in an unambiguously positive manner.[32] It is tempting to maintain, however, that this overblown praise also indicates a general ironical attitude on Socrates' part to this whole praising business.[33]

Aristophanes, a dissenting voice: Eros does not give us virtues, and the value we hope he will give us is completion

Aristophanes' speech amounts to a repudiation of the moral psychology of the other speakers. However, he begins by praising Eros in strong terms. '... he loves the human race more than any other god, he stands by us in our troubles, and he cures those ills we humans are most happy to have mended' (189c). This is in accordance with the rules of eulogy, but Aristophanes does not mean half of it. For it soon turns out that the benefits of Eros are not very great. Humans are at the mercy of Zeus himself, who first punishes them for their pride by cutting them in half, and, when they are in danger of dying out, keeps them alive only because the gods do not want to miss out on the sacrifices that their vanity craves. *Erôs* comes into the picture late: *erôs* is the name for our pursuit of wholeness, for our desire to overcome Zeus' halving of us. *Erôs*, then, prompts us to look for our lost half. If we find her or him, 'as very few men do nowadays' (193b), life will be as good as it can get. There is no sign of any erotic drive towards virtues,[34] works or deeds. And most significantly, honour or fame is not part of the gifts of *erôs*. The aim in life is to find our significant other.

Aristophanes is looking for more than sex; the unity with one's other half seems to be psychologically complex (192b-d). But neither searching for him nor living with him does call for the virtues and values of the *paideia*, and still less a quest for deeper knowledge of these matters. The implicit criticism, if not mockery, in Aristophanes' speech of the pretensions of the cultural and political establishment, could be aimed at the present speakers too, something his hiccupping (185c) and his application of the Sneeze Treatment (189a) could indicate.[35]

Alcibiades: disrupting the encomiasts' harmony between virtues and honour

Alcibiades belongs to the Athenian elite. During his visit in Plato's text he acts out a hyperbolic manifestation of one of their main values, honour and its extension, fame.

However, by his frank and unembellished talk, as well as by his behaviour, he exposes the cracks in the edifice of the encomiasts.³⁶

Alcibiades arrives drunk and with a flute-girl in tow. He will give an encomium too, to Socrates, he says. Significantly, by ignoring its rules, he manages to give us a sincerer speech, where some truths seep out from his confused talk. Alcibiades is making an honest attempt to 'investigate' Socrates' nature. Alcibiades praises Socrates, and he attacks him, scolds him, calls him vile, etc. Some of the chaotic, irrational and negative aspects of *erôs* are displayed: jealousy, wounded pride, rage, violence and lack of control (213d). We are shown the affinity between *erôs* and drunkenness. As Alcibiades sees him, Eros is hardly working in a harmonious way.

Alcibiades wants all the good things, sex and wine, Olympic gold medals, honour and fame, victory and power; and first and foremost: praise and honour. Socrates had pinpointed his character accurately in *Alcibiades I*:

> What then *is* your real ambition in life? [Socrates asks Alcibiades] I will tell you. You think that as soon as you present yourself before the Athenian people ... you will show them that you deserve to be honoured more than Pericles or anyone else who ever was. Having shown that, you will be the most influential man in the city, and if you are the greatest here, you will be the greatest in the rest of Greece, and not only in Greece, but among the foreigners who live on the same continent as we do.
>
> 105a-b

Alcibiades knew from experience that he could win honour and fame without being virtuous, courage excepted. When he held his splendid rhetorical speeches in the assembly and when he led the Athenians to victory on the battlefield, he got the admiration and praise he wanted so much. He is, however, the only speaker in the dialogue who has a strong – even if bewildered – sense of the value of Socrates' way of life: 'my heart, my soul, or whatever you want to call it, . . . has been struck and bitten by philosophy' (218a); 'Nothing is more important to me than becoming the best man I can be' (218d). This wish is what has made their close, if eventually dysfunctional, relationship possible. In the *Symposium* Alcibiades realizes that he cannot harmonize the virtues of Socrates and the *philotimia* of the city: 'I know perfectly well that I cannot prove he's wrong when he [Socrates] tells me what I should do; yet, the moment I leave his side, I go back to my old ways: I cave in to my desire to please the crowd' (216b).

What is it that Socrates wants him to do? It cannot be anything else than to choose a virtuous life *instead of* a life built on the conventional values of the Athenian *paideia*. Alcibiades is not far off the mark when he says:

> Believe me, it couldn't matter less to him whether a boy is beautiful. You can't imagine how little he cares whether a person is beautiful, or rich, or famous in any other way that most people admire. He considers all these possessions beneath contempt, and that's exactly how he considers all of us as well. In public, I tell you, his whole life is one big game – a game of irony.
>
> 216d-e

Alcibiades sees that Socrates rejects the conventional values, but he feels that this is due to arrogance. Incongruously, in spite of Socrates' alleged contempt for people, Alcibiades claims that he is fully beautiful, wise and virtuous inside. He is like a Silenus statue that is beautiful inside and ugly on the outside (215b, 221d-222a). This reminds us of Agathon's self-portrait; Alcibiades sees Socrates as perfect and self-contained, living with his hidden possessions on the top of the ladder, so to speak.

Mary P. Nichols asserts that Alcibiades lacks any understanding of the necessity of striving in-between in the search for virtue.[37] He thinks that you are either full of virtue and wisdom or empty. And since Socrates is supposed to be full, Alcibiades cannot understand Socrates' refusal to share what he has. The only explanation for this must be that he is vile and arrogant. Alcibiades' attempt to get hold of some of Socrates' wisdom through sex is rebuffed, again to Alcibiades' utter astonishment, not to mention his wounded pride. The idea of a trade-off between sex and wisdom, which was the kernel of the conventionally accepted homosexual relationship between an older and a younger man, is obviously taken for granted by Alcibiades. In this respect he is following the other symposion speakers, including Diotima, but – again – excepting Aristophanes. Socrates' rejection of this quasi-institution as a frame for developing wisdom is a clear repudiation of some of the basic tenets of Diotima and her fellow travellers.

Alcibiades' fascination with Socrates' philosophical talk must have been due to an intuition of a deeper truth, however dimly he could have seen what it was. By sensing the special quality of Socrates' character, he shows that he possesses a certain self-knowledge. He surely embraces his desire for honour and fame, but with the self-consciousness of a sinner.[38] Thus, even if he figures in the text as an example of how the *philotimia* of the Athenians could look when freed from the restraints of convention, rhetorical and otherwise, it is he who opens up what is probably Plato's most serious problematics, the complicated relationship between virtues, values and desires.

Conclusion

You can develop virtue in yourself, but honour is given to you from outside, and you get it for something. There is a transactional aspect involved; you must please someone in order to get it, as Alcibiades knew too well. To be given honour is not per se morally questionable. It is the love of honour, the *desire* for honour, the motivational aspect of honour, which is problematic. In conventional Athenian discourse *philotimia* was usually not seen as a problem, except when it became so strong that it produced *hybris*. Honour, as well as other prevalent values could be pursued, but in a virtuous way – always acting justly, for instance. The symposiasts assume that they know the nature of the virtues, and they think they have discovered their origin; they are instilled in us by *erôs*, or in Pausanias case, by *nomos*. Plato's revealing exposition of moral conceptions among Athenians, and of the current mode encomium used for expressing them, shows that he had reason to insist on a great distance between himself, the author, and the views expressed in the text.[39]

Notes

1. This chapter is a substantially revised and expanded version of 'Philotimia. On rhetoric, virtues and values in the *Symposium*', *Norsk filosofisk tidsskrift*, 48, no.1 (2013): 59–73.
2. The translation used is by Alexander Nehamas and Paul Woodruff, in *Plato: Complete Works*, ed. John Cooper (Indianapolis: Hackett Publishing Company, 1997).
3. Apollodorus had heard the story from Aristodemus, who was present at the dinner party. They are both enthusiastic followers of Socrates. Apollodorus, an aristocrat and wealthy businessman, is described as a maniac (*manikos*, 173d); he is a fanatic follower of Socrates. He has been with Socrates for three years, trying to learn philosophy from him. Aristodemus is, in his own words, 'an obvious inferior (*sofou andros*) arriving uninvited at the table of a man of letters' (174c). The reliability of the text rests for the most part on the memory of Aristodemus. He admits to some memory loss, and to have slept through some of the conversation. The correctness of the text is also dependent on the quality of Apollodorus' retelling.

    Debra Nails stipulates that the frame story takes place around 400 and she places the dramatic date of the *Symposion* itself in 416. At some point during these sixteen years Apollodorus has heard the story from Aristodemus. He has 'checked parts of his story with Socrates, who has agreed with the account' (173b). Which parts, one wonders. Debra Nails, *The People of Plato. A Prosopography of Plato and Other Socratics* (Indianapolis: Hackett Publishing Company, 2002), 314, 440.

    David Halperin, 'Plato and the Erotics of Narrativity', in *Plato and Postmodernism*, ed. Steven Shankman (Glenside: The Aldine Press, 1994), 56 writes: 'Far from rescuing the memory of what was said and done at Agathon's from forgetfulness, far from securing the preservation of Diotima's precious teaching, the process of narrative transmission is evidently just as liable to dissipate as it is to save valuable knowledge.'
4. Andrea Nightingale, *Genres in Dialogue. Plato and the Construct of Philosophy* (Cambridge: Cambridge University Press, 1999), 102.
5. Isocrates, 'Busiris', in *Isocrates*, vol. III, trans. LaRue Vab Hook, The Loeb Classical Library (Cambridge: Harvard University Press, 1945), 105.
6. 'Rhetoric to Alexander', translated by E.S. Forster, in *The Complete Works of Aristotle*, vol. 2 (Princeton: Princeton University Press, 1995), 2278.
7. With reference to Aristotle's *Rhetoric*, Brian Vickers, *In Defence of Rhetoric* (Oxford: Clarendon Press, 1988), 55 writes: 'praise can only be given to noble acts made intentionally, as the result of a man's moral choice, where his actions are the product of his good qualities'.
8. Euripides' Hippolytus: 'He [Eros] ruins mortals and launches them among every kind of disaster when he visits them' (*Hippolytus* 540–3, David Kovacs trans.). Cf. Richard Hunter, *Plato's Symposium* (Oxford: Oxford University Press, 2004), 17–20.
9. John Poulakos, 'Testing and Contesting Classical Rhetorics', *Rhetoric Society Quarterly*, 36 (2006): 171.
10. See Hunter, *Plato's Symposium*, 48–50, for the festive and playful nature of sympotic discourse and its ambiguities. This helped to smooth over moral ambiguities, as in the case of Pausanias' speech.
11. Andrea Nightingale, 'The Folly of Praise: Plato's Critique of Encomiastic Discourse in the *Lysis* and *Symposium*', *The Classical Quarterly* 43 (1993): 113. Nightingale, *Genres in Dialogue*, 103–4 contends that the *Symposium* is written as an *attack* on this kind of

rhetoric. The *Symposium* 'is part of a philosophic critique of praise discourse in general', which again is part of Plato's politically motivated attacks on the rhetorical practice of the sophists. 'The genre of the prose encomium, in sum, permeated many areas of Athenian life in the late fifth and fourth centuries. Delivered at funerals, festivals, symposia, in the schools, in private residences, and at other intellectual gatherings, the encomium involved at core a conferral of value – a statement of who or what is good (and bad). . . . it played an important role in the schooling of future leaders and politicians, and was regularly harnessed in the construction and reinforcement of Athenian ideology.'

12 Christoph Riedweg, *Mysterienterminologie bei Platon, Philon und Klemens von Alexandrien* (Berlin: Walter de Gruyter, 1987), 28–9. Riedweg writes that 'Platon im Symposion Sokrates' Ausführungen über *Eros* den schematischen Ablauf einer Mysterieninitiation als Tiefenstruktur zugrunde legt, dass also die einzige Stelle mit eigentlicher Mysterienterminologie (209e5f.) im vollen Wortsinn gedeutet werden muss.'

13 Socrates is here, before the contest of speeches has started, performing a eulogy. The praise, however, is ironical. He is heaping still more ironic scorn on Agathon's head at 198b-d. Cf. Nightingale, 'The Folly of Praise', 120: 'Socrates' effusion in the *Symposium* are all too familiar to readers of Plato . . . How should we interpret Socrates' hyperbolic praise? What is the relation between this kind of praise and encomiastic discourse? And, finally, how do we distinguish the dissimulation inherent in Socrates' ironic praise from the lies of encomiastic rhetoric?'

14 Nehamas and Woodruff render *erôs* as Love when it refers to the god, and love when it is supposed to designate the passion.

15 Justice, moderation and courage are mentioned, and *sophia*, which here is close to skill. Agathon makes a point of asserting that Eros has nothing to do with violence (196b-c).

16 When the expression 'symposium speakers' or the like is used in this chapter, Aristophanes is most often not included.

17 The general drift of the speeches in the *Symposium* is to show how the desire *erôs* instils, results in 'goods' for us. Such 'goods' can be virtues or they can be immortality or honour and many other things. The love of honour is a desire, but it becomes a value if we embrace honour as something to strive for. Money, pleasure and power are other possible values. A virtue is neither a desire nor a value, but relates to character traits and behaviour.

18 Sometimes called 'the pederastic model of education'.

19 Leo Strauss, *Leo Strauss on Plato's* Symposium (Chicago: Chicago University Press, 2001), 67: noble *erôs* is constituted by *nomos*.

20 R.B. Rutherford, *The Art of Plato: Ten Essays in Platonic Interpretation* (Cambridge, MA: Harvard University Press, 1995), 190.

21 See Ruby Blondell, 'Where is Socrates on the "Ladder of Love?"' in *Plato's Symposium: Issues in Interpretation and Reception*, ed. J.H. Lesher, Debra Nails and Frisbee Sheffield (Cambridge: Harvard University Press, 2006), 174. Blondell writes: 'In the *Symposium* Plato takes advantage of the symposiastic setting, with its characteristic role-playing, self-parody, story-telling and games, to present Socrates in many different guises – all conjured up through several layers of narration – from the Socrates of the party itself, to the Socrates of Alcibiades' memory, to the 'hypothetical Socrates' who consorts with the quasi-fictional Diotima.' This is pertinent, I think, but not one of the implications

Blondell draws, that 'Socrates can be viewed more or less plausibly as occupying all of the steps on the "ladder of love".'

22 See 210a-212b. Diotima contends that she knows how to initiate people into the final and greatest mystery, and thereby presents herself as a priestess of some sort. Nonetheless, she is supposed to be Socrates' teacher of philosophy.

23 Diotima seems to have taught Socrates by means of questions and answers (201e ff.), but most of the lesson Socrates recounts, is presented in the encomium genre.

24 *Amathia* is often used by Plato in the sense of believing that you know when you don't. It is the most despicable form of ignorance. See *Alcibiades I*, 118a.

25 Suzanne Obdrzalek, 'Moral Transformation and the Love of Beauty in Plato's Symposium', *Journal of the History of Philosophy* 48 (2010): 423, writes that she 'wants to emphasize something odd: these lovers ['the lower lovers'] appear only to seek virtue for the sake of immortal fame. The virtue which they beget is supposed to be strictly analogous to the babies begotten by somatic lovers; virtue, like children, is intended to confer immortality upon the lover. They thus do not appear to pursue virtue qua final good, but rather, qua means to immortality.'

26 Xenophon, *Memorabilia*, trans. E.C. Marchant. The Loeb Classical Library, Cambridge: Harvard University Press, 2002.

27 Aristotle. *Nicomachean Ethics*, in *The Complete Works of Aristotle*, vol. II, translated by W.D. Ross, 1729–1867. (Princeton: Princeton University Press, 1984), 1731.

28 Thucydides, *The Peloponnesian War*, trans. Rex Warner (Harmondsworth: Penguin Books, 1962), 121.

29 All the citations from Dover are taken from: K.J. Dover, *Greek Popular Morality in the Time of Plato and Aristotle* (Indianapolis: Hackett Publishing Company, 1994), 228–31.

30 'The lesser and the greater mystery': Plato could have had the procedure of the Eleusinian Mystery in mind here, or some other mystery of the same type. The initiation into these mysteries was a process consisting of several steps. See Robert Parker, *On Greek Religion* (Ithaca: Cornell University Press, 2011), 253, and Riedweg, *Mysterienterminologie*, 28–9. Diotimas' expression 'final and highest mystery' suggests that what had gone before was also a mystery. She talks about initiation (*myetheins*) there too (210a1). What has gone before, however, from 208e to 210a, lacks the methodical procedure of the greater mystery.

31 Some commentators think that beauty here stands for the good, and they refer to 204e, where Diotima replaces beauty with the good. However, this replacement does not lead to a discussion of the virtues, but to a focus on the values in life, ending up in a desire for immortality.

32 Cf. Agathon's long peroration at 197c-198a.

33 However, Socratic irony is a complicated matter. For ironic praise, see Melissa Lane, 'Reconsidering Socratic Irony', in *The Cambridge Companion to Socrates*, ed. Donald R. Morrison (Cambridge: Cambridge University Press, 2011), 249–57, and Nightingale, *The Folly of Praise*, especially 119–23, for the relation between ironic praise and hubristic contempt.

34 Except for the virtue of piety, something that in this context means sacrificing to the gods. Cf. Mary P. Nichols, 'Socrates' contest with the poets in Plato's *Symposium*', *Political Theory* 32 (2004): 188–91.

35 Paradoxically, Aristophanes is afraid that his speech shall make him appear ridiculous (189b). He was bitter when the *Clouds* only got third prize at the Dionysian festival in 423. On a personal level, then, he is not indifferent to honour.

36 'The dialogue's structure argues that the ordering/disordering play of *erôs* cannot be ordered into a final stability. Socrates' attempt to dialectically transcend the erotic by transforming the private/political tension into a hierarchical ascent from the somatic to the philosophic is undercut by the action within the dialogue. Socrates' retelling of Diotima's speech looks like a conclusion that addresses and places the concerns of the preceding speeches into a hierarchy that philosophically unifies and transcends their plurality, but at the end of this speech the dialogue is wrenched from its apparent resolution by an unplanned intrusion from the larger world.' James L. Kastely, *Rethinking the Rhetorical Tradition. From Plato to Postmodernism* (New Haven: Yale University Press, 1997), 237.

37 Mary P. Nichols, 'Philosophy and Empire: On Socrates and Alcibiades in Plato's *Symposium*', *Polity* 39 (2007): 505–10. I draw on Nichols' portrait of Alcibiades here.

38 When Socrates tries to teach virtue to Polus in the *Gorgias*, he very reluctantly makes him accept that whatever goods we seek to obtain, power, for instance, we should seek virtuously. Then he takes the next, decisive, step, insisting that it is better – in all cases – to suffer injustice than to act unjustly. A necessary premise for this is that the virtuous life itself and the harmonious soul it cultivates is the highest value. To this, however, Polus' reaction is curt: 'these statements are absurd, Socrates' (480e).

39 I wish to thank Erlend Breidal, Hallvard Fossheim, Vivil Valvik Haraldsen, Jens Kristian Larsen, and Vigdis Songe-Møller for helpful discussions and comments during my writing of this chapter, and Jacob Howland for penetrating criticism of an earlier draft.

Bibliography

Aristotle. *Nicomachean Ethics*. In *The complete works of Aristotle*, vol. II. Translated by W.D. Ross. Princeton: Princeton University Press, 1984.

Aristotle. *The 'Art' of Rhetoric*. Translated by John Henry Freese. Loeb Classical Library. Cambridge: Harvard University Press, 1982.

Dover, K.J. *Greek Popular Morality in the Time of Plato and Aristotle*. Indianapolis: Hackett Publishing Company, 1994.

Euripides II. Translated by David Kovacs. Loeb Classical Library. Cambridge: Harvard University Press, 1995.

Halperin, David M. 'Plato and the Erotics of Narrativity'. In *Plato and Postmodernism*, edited by Steven Shankman, 43–75. Glenside: The Aldine Press, 1994.

Hunter, Richard. *Plato's Symposium*. Oxford: Oxford University Press, 2004.

Isocrates. *Busiris*. In *Isocrates III*, translated by LaRue Van Hook. Loeb Classical Library. 100–31. Cambridge: Harvard University Press, 1945.

Kastely, James L. *Rethinking the Rhetorical Tradition. From Plato to Postmodernism*. New Haven: Yale University Press, 1997.

Lane, Melissa. 'Reconsidering Socratic Irony'. In *The Cambridge Companion to Socrates*, edited by Donald R. Morrison, 237–59. Cambridge: Cambridge University Press, 2011.

Nails, Debra. *The People of Plato. A Prosopography of Plato and Other Socratics*. Indianapolis: Hackett Publishing Company, 2002.

Nichols, Mary P. 'Socrates' contest with the poets in Plato's *Symposium*'. *Political Theory* 32 (2004): 188–91.

Nichols, Mary P. 'Philosophy and Empire: On Socrates and Alcibiades in Plato's *Symposium*'. *Polity* 39 (2007): 502–21.

Nightingale, Andrea. 'The Folly of Praise: Plato's Critique of Encomiastic Discourse in the *Lysis* and *Symposium*'. *The Classical Quarterly* 43 (1993): 112–30.
Nightingale, Andrea. *Genres in Dialogue. Plato and the Construct of Philosophy.* Cambridge: Cambridge University Press, 1999.
Obdrzalek, Suzanne. 'Moral Transformation and the Love of Beauty in Plato's *Symposium*'. *Journal of the History of Philosophy* 48 (2010): 415–44.
Parker, Robert. *On Greek Religion.* Ithaca: Cornell University Press, 2011.
Plato: Complete Works, edited by John Cooper. Indianapolis: Hackett Publishing Company, 1997.
Poulakos, John. 'Testing and Contesting Classical Rhetorics'. *Rhetoric Society Quarterly*, 36 (2006): 171–9.
Riedweg, Christoph. *Mysterienterminologie bei Platon, Philon und Klemens von Alexandrien.* Berlin: Walter de Gruyter, 1987.
Rutherford, R.B. *The Art of Plato: Ten Essays in Platonic Interpretation.* Cambridge: Harvard University Press, 1995.
Strauss, Leo. *On Plato's Symposium.* Chicago: Chicago University Press, 2001.
Vickers, Brian. *In Defence of Rhetoric.* Oxford: Clarendon Press, 1988.
Xenophon. *Memorabilia.* Translated by E.C. Marchant. The Loeb Classical Library. Cambridge: Harvard University Press, 2002.

Part Three

Reason and Irrationality

8

The Significance of the Ambiguity of Music in Plato

Kristin Sampson

Plato's views on music (*mousikê*) and art are commonly portrayed as negative. It is well known how he warns against music and art as potentially dangerous, both for the soul and for society. According to Plato, *mousikê*, as all art, is imitative, and as such not attributed a high status within his thinking. It is not difficult to find instances in the Platonic corpus that support such a view.[1] What this chapter considers, though, is the other side of the matter. It aims to take into consideration also some of the other and quite different statements about *mousikê* that can be found in Plato, in order to evoke a more ambiguous image of Plato on this point. Attention has, of course, also previously been directed towards *mousikê* in Plato as something that on the one hand is warned against, and on the other as an important part of the education of the soul.[2] Within such a perspective, music emerges as valuable both for the human being in possession of this soul, and also for the political society to which he belongs as a citizen. The aim here is to investigate this ambiguity that surrounds *mousikê* in Plato, and to display how it functions as a *pharmakon* that can be both a remedy and a poison, in order to indicate how this ambiguity plays a significant part in Plato's philosophy. Bringing out this significance of the ambiguity of *mousikê* for Plato's philosophy will involve two main aspects. The first concerns placing *mousikê* into a wider scope than that which pertains to the pedagogical and political, by also taking into consideration forms of music that go beyond the human. This chapter will show how *mousikê* informs even the depictions of cosmos and time in Plato and argue for the significance of these portrayals. The second aspect takes into consideration the relation between *mousikê* and philosophy in Plato, and argues that the ambiguity of music, as both remedy and poison, can shed light upon the difficulties sometimes involved with discerning between philosophy and sophistry in Plato. That is to say, the aim of this chapter is to demonstrate how *mousikê* reverberates through Plato at several different levels, and to explore how the ambiguities surrounding *mousikê* illuminate not only the political and pedagogical in Plato, but even relates to ambiguities affecting cosmos, temporality and philosophy itself.

Before turning to Plato, a few words about the vast and important role of *mousikê* in ancient Greece is in order. This, which is the topic of the first part of this chapter, pertains not least to the important differences between the ancient concept and our modern concept of music. Turning to Plato, the ambiguous nature of *mousikê* will first, in the second part of this chapter, be considered in relation to his depiction of *mousikê* as *pharmakon*: namely as both remedy and poison. Then, in the third part, the relevance of this ambiguous nature of *mousikê* will be considered in terms of Plato's description of the generated world (cosmos) and temporality. This concerns what may be called the ontological implications of *mousikê* in Plato. In the fourth part, *mousikê* as an educational, although ambiguous, element of politics and philosophy will be considered, before finally, in the fifth part, the ambiguity of music, as well as its ontological implications, will be used to display some of the difficulties involved in discerning between philosophy and sophistry in Plato.

The importance of *mousikê* in ancient Greece

It has been claimed that music was ever-present and everywhere in the Greek world.[3] In his book *Greek Philosophy* (originally published in 1914), John Burnet claims that Greek thinking is dominated by 'the idea of harmonia or the tuning of a string' and that 'an elementary knowledge of the Greek lyre is essential for the understanding of Greek philosophy'.[4] Music in ancient Greece did not merely concern the musicians or the musically interested, but was an obvious part of the education and upbringing of the young members of the population, and had a place in relation to religion, politics and medicine.[5] The classical Greek concept of music – *mousikê* – or, as it is also called, *mousikê technê* is a highly extensive concept, related to the arts of the Muses.[6]

Plato's dialogues are generated in a time and a culture that differ widely from our own, also in relation to the concept of music. Many of the words that we use today in relation to music – such as 'rhythm', 'harmony', 'tone', and also of course the word 'music' itself – are derived from and originate from classical Greek language. Still, the concept of music and the musical that we find in ancient Greek language and culture diverges quite a lot, and in quite a lot of ways, from our more modern notions of music. *Mousikê* embraces song, dance and what we would term 'music', in addition to myths, tales and poetry.

Still, *mousikê* does not include all art and craft that in Antiquity could be named as creative *poiêsis* or art (*technê*). It differs from the plastic or mechanical arts that are placed beyond the domain of the Muses. *Mousikê* is more temporary and transient than more visible forms of art, such as for example architectural structures and sculptures that contain a greater element of permanence in that they produce lasting products. Nonetheless, as for instance Glenn R. Morrow points out in his book on Plato's *Laws*, although 'Greek music and dancing have left no enduring monuments comparable to those of poets, sculptors, and architects; ... the indirect evidence of the primacy of the musical arts is overwhelming and indisputable.'[7] When Morrow here mentions the work of poets as something other than music, this seems to be at odds with a classical Greek notion of *mousikê* that also includes myth and poetry. However, this might shed light upon some of the aspects that are specific to music. *Mousikê*, both in the form of song and dance, as well as in the playing of instruments, is inherently related to temporality, in the sense that it unfolds through time. Everything belonging to the auditive, to rhythm and to movement, such as dance, are embedded within the unfurling of time. When poetry – or music – is written down, the words or notes are frozen in the sense that they can be removed from the context of a specific resounding. This makes possible a transference for instance to a later historical period a couple of thousand years later. However, in order for the poem or the piece of music to be heard, it needs to be made to resound again. That is to say, it needs to be unfolded through time. Where the more auditive arts of *mousikê* are more dependent upon diachrony, the more visible arts, like painting and sculpture emerge as more synchronic, in the sense that they open themselves up to being grasped within an instantaneous look. There is thus a diachronic element belonging to *mousikê*, that does not emerge as necessary in the same way for more visible forms of art.

A large part of the population in ancient Greece was exposed to the musical enchantment of songs and dances. For instance, a great many took part in choruses of one kind or another, learned to recite poetry, and played one or more musical instruments.[8] What pertains to *mousikê* relates also to a notion of the musician or the musically creative as someone who is open towards divine inspiration from the Muses, and who lets herself be possessed, so to speak, and be set in motion and moved by the divine. The musical could be understood as a divine force that is transmitted through inspiration from the Muses. *Mousikê* thus concerns the transmission between gods and humans, and what is transmitted is related to primary powers of being, connected in the end to the harmony and unison of all being. Considering these wider aspects of *mousikê*, the vast, important and self-evident place of music (*mousikê*) in ancient Greece is not surprising.

In the following, this wide conception of music as *mousikê*, that emphasizes its importance in ancient Greece, will be put into play in relation to Plato, both in terms of its ontological implications, namely in the portrayals of cosmos and temporality, and in relation to philosophy itself. First, let us turn to Plato's description of the ambiguous nature of *mousikê*.

The ambiguity of music: *mousikê* as *pharmakon*

In the second book of the *Laws*, a comparison is made between *mousikê* and wine. Both can be considered as poisonous and as such something that ought to be avoided, but they can also be seen as something that one should not necessarily keep completely away from, but rather entities that need to be handled with care and used in the proper way and in right measure. As the Athenian Stranger says at *Laws* 672d, by other people wine is 'bestowed on us men as a punishment, to make us mad; but our own account, on the contrary, declares that it is a medicine (*pharmakon*) given for the purpose of securing modesty of soul and health and strength of body'. Like wine music also works like a medicine – *pharmakon* – in this way.

As *pharmakon* music is something that can work for both good and bad. Music is thus ethically charged.[9] In the second book of the *Laws* the Athenian Stranger claims that most people 'assert that the value of music consists in its power of affording pleasure to the soul'. He, however, calls such an assertion quite intolerable, and claims, 'it is blasphemy even to utter it'.[10] The good form of music is the one that is the best imitator of the beautiful,[11] and which 'attach[es] to the goodness of soul and body, or to some image thereof'.[12] This is not the kind of music that provides the most pleasure, but the one that is directed to what is right (*Laws* 668b).

The correctness and beauty of music is related to order, and the two principles that serve the ordering of music are rhythm and harmony. As the Athenian Stranger explicitly states, 'the order of motion is called "rhythm," while the order of the voice ... is termed "harmony," and to the combination of these two the name "choristry" is given'.[13] Both rhythm and harmony can be expressed mathematically, through numbers. The notion that the beauty and correctness of good music is related to its mathematical structure is intrinsic to the Pythagorean-Platonic tradition. Furthermore, due measure and the timely are inscribed into the very concepts of harmony and rhythm. A harmony where the various notes are not tuned in relation to each other, according to due measure and proportion, will not ring true.

In the *Laws* there is also an interesting recognition of the Dionysian elements of music. The theme of the Apollonian and the Dionysian in Ancient Greece, related to the principles of calm, order, harmony, on the one hand, and movement, ecstasy and transgression, on the other, is known for instance from Friedrich Nietzsche.[14] What is striking about *mousikê*, also in relation to Plato, is the tension between these two aspects. On the one hand, *mousikê* is orderly and related to harmony, but on the other it represents a potentially dangerous and destabilizing element in relation to both soul and society. There is thus in *mousikê* on one side a relationship with the order of the Apollonian, related to mathematics understood as something cognitive, thought related and fundamentally non-perceptual and non-corporeal. However, *mousikê* is also related to the movement of the Dionysian, and necessarily related to the perceptual and corporal through its relation to the auditive and to temporality. In the *Laws*, the significance and importance of the force of Dionysian intoxication and invigoration is recognized through the place that is given to the Dionysian choir of old men (*Laws* 665 ff.). This is, however, only made possible through a qualification in terms of the right manner and the right context.

The prescription of a Dionysian choir for old men is presented in the context of a discussion of wine, which stands as an illustration of how one should approach *mousikê*. The administration of wine is not one and the same for everybody, but should be different for people at different ages, according to the Athenian Stranger. In the second book he prescribes different practices for children under eighteen, the young man under thirty, and the man who has reached the age of forty. For the latter wine is bestowed by Dionysus as a medicine (*pharmakon*) 'potent against the crabbedness of old age'.[15] Similarly with choristry, this is not the same for all, but varies with age, according to the three different choirs: the Muses' choir for children, the choir invoking Apollo Paian (the healer) for those under thirty, and the third Dionysian choir for those between the age of thirty and sixty (*Laws* 664c-d). Sexual difference is also one of the qualities that come into play in terms of prescribing the right kind of music. The Dionysian choir is for old men, not women. Moreover, in the seventh book of the *Laws* the Athenian Stranger asserts how it is right for the lawgiver 'to set apart suitable songs for males and females', and how it is necessary for him 'to assign both words and music for both types of song as defined by the natural difference of the two sexes'.[16] Neither wine nor music is good or bad, as such. It all depends upon the way in which they are used, and in what measure, what context, what time in the lifespan and in relation to whom. Differentiation, between various ages, between men and women, plays an important part in the management of music.

It has been argued that in Plato *kairos*, in the sense of occasion (right moment) and due measure, unites the aesthetic and the ethical aspects of his thinking.[17] This also pertains to *mousikê*, in the sense that *mousikê* in itself is neither good nor bad, but is inherently dependent upon being administered in the right way. In the fourth book of the *Laws* the Athenian Stranger declares, 'chance (*tychê*) and occasion (*kairos*) cooperate with God in the control of all human affairs'.[18] Inherent to human life is that which is specific to a particular moment and context. Similar to a musical harmony, living – or a person's life – is tuned according to that in which it is embedded, and this always relates to something specific. The inherent particularity of life and music is the other side of the coin of both. They belong fundamentally to the realm of the transient. This will be considered further in the next part of this chapter.

Vital in the descriptions of how the city-state should be organized in terms of the laws, is *paideia*, the education of the population that is centred on gymnastics and music. This, however, also includes Dionysian intoxication, but induced in the right manner. As Morrow puts it: 'The wild Dionysian dances are perhaps to be excluded, but not the spirit of Dionysus. It seems that Plato still felt, as he did when he was writing the *Symposium*, that "enthusiasm," or intoxication with the divine, was the driving force underlying all insight and achievement.'[19] Like wine, *mousikê* is a *pharmakon* that can work as both a medicine and a poison. In this sense it is inherently ambiguous. On the one hand, *mousikê* is related to numbers and mathematics, and on the other, it relates to enchantment, emotions and the bodily perceptual. The danger that *mousikê* can become bad lies not in the fact that it belongs to the bodily, which it necessarily does, but in the potential lack of right measure and moderation with regard to the specificity of the context in question. This can make *mousikê* poisonous.

The significance of this ambiguity echoing through *mousikê* extends beyond the realm of the human. It also pertains to what can be termed the ontological implications of *mousikê*: its relation and relevance for nature, cosmos, being and temporality.

Music beyond the human: ontological implications of *mousikê*

In the *Phaedrus* we find an instance where *mousikê* is not related to music created or played by man, nor can it be said to be related to the soul in the way that has previously been described. For once, Socrates has ventured outside the walls of the civilized city-state of Athens, and into nature, together with his friend Phaedrus. Walking outside the city walls, Socrates directs the attention to the cicadas singing overhead: 'how lovely and perfectly charming the breeziness of the place is! And it resounds with the shrill summer-music of the chorus of cicadas' (*Phaedrus* 230c). Socrates is portrayed here, where even music is that of nature, as having, in many ways, stepped into the realm of the bodily, the sensuous and desire to a greater degree than in most other Platonic dialogues.

In stepping out into the scenery of nature outside of the city-walls, Socrates opens himself up to being subjected to the bewitchment of the song of the cicadas. The cicadas themselves are a result of a form of enchantment, namely of the Muses. Once these locusts were men, but 'when the Muses were born and song appeared, [they] were so overcome with delight that they sang and sang, forgetting food and drink, until at last unconsciously they died' (*Phaedrus* 259b-c). The cicadas are the descendants of these men.[20] This short myth could be seen as a story warning against the seduction of song generated by the Muses. There is an element of passivity in bewitchment, in the sense that you are being taken over, and possessed and consumed by something enchanting. This can prove dangerous to one's identity and autonomy, as in the case of the music-lovers who are turned into cicadas, and who were transformed into an entity that belongs outside of the political society of humans. It is indeed outside the city walls that Socrates and Phaedrus encounter the song of the cicadas and are subjected to the danger of their enchantment. Furthermore, the song of the cicadas is something Socrates and Phaedrus must beware not to be enchanted by, lest they doze off, 'lulled to sleep by their song...like sheep gathering around the spring in the afternoon' (*Phaedrus* 259a). Being turned into an animal-like state like this would prevent any philosophical discourse between them.

However, in the short myth Socrates also recounts how the cicadas, when they die, report to the Muses and tell them who have honoured them. This seems to imply that Socrates thinks the Muses ought best be honoured, as he also indicates in the *Phaedo*, when he speaks of his 'making music'. The song of the cicadas thus constitutes something both warned against as well as given credit by Socrates, to the degree that he places them as the inspirational source of the artistry of his speeches.[21] As something both potentially dangerous and potentially inspirational the influence of the song of the cicadas is given its due. To put this even more explicitly in terms of the ambiguity of *mousikê* as described above in relation to music as *pharmakon*: even the music of nature, represented by the song of the cicadas, that resides beyond the human *polis*, displays the double aspect of *mousikê* as both dangerous and beneficial.

The ambiguity towards philosophical conversation in relation to the *mousikê* of the Muses is featured within the story about the cicadas too. The songs of the Muses can lead one bewitchingly astray, but the Muses, at least some of them, are also devoted to philosophy. The Muses explicitly named by Socrates are choral Terpsichore, Erato the erotic, the philosophic Kalliope and Urania.[22] The cicadas are also said to 'make report of those who pass their lives in philosophy and who worship these Muses who are most concerned with heaven and with thought divine and human' (*Phaedrus* 259d). Listening in the right way to the song of the more philosophically oriented of the Muses will promote philosophy. Not all discourse is equally philosophical or good, however. As G.R.F. Ferrari points out, the 'unabashed delight in intellectual talk to which Phaedrus gives vent', and that Ferrari claims is 'a philosophical trait', indicates that Plato, through this myth of the cicadas, takes his stand against this tendency personified by Phaedrus.[23] Phaedrus is too enthusiastic and too indiscriminate towards the different types of intellectual discourse. He lacks the discernment necessary to recognize what is truly philosophical. Listening to, and letting oneself be inspired by, the cicadas is all right, as long as one does not doze off to sleep, or become sheep-like, being overwhelmed by their sound. And, listening to the *mousikê* of the Muses can also be educational and good, as long as it is not indulged to the degree that it takes over, and takes, your life. Right measure, right way, and the right time and place appear to be values that echo in the background. All forms of inspiration are not equally bad. There are divine forms of enthusiasm that is embodied in the true lover and in the philosopher, and that should be embraced.

This pertains to the difficulties connected to distinguishing between philosophy and sophistry. In the fifth and final part of this chapter this difficulty will be discussed further in relation to the ambiguity of *mousikê*. For now, let us continue with the music beyond the human and what is here termed the ontological implications of *mousikê*.

The examples from the *Phaedrus*, with the song of cicadas and the story about the birth of the Muses, point beyond the human both in the sense that it is an example of song chanted by creatures belonging to nature, and in the sense that it is divine music that resounds through these animal voices. The principles of *mousikê* are evoked by Plato also beyond the cicadas and Muses. The mathematical structure of rhythm and harmony reverberates through the world even on to the cosmic level, where we find harmony expressed through the regular, circular movements of the celestial bodies that in the *Timaeus* are called the choric dances (*choreiai*) of the stars and planets.[24] Through this planetary dance *mousikê* is inscribed into the very core of the cosmos.

The way that rhythm plays into the ordering of the cosmos becomes apparent also through the image of the receiving principle – *chôra* – as a winnowing basket. This image is introduced at a point where *chôra* is described as an unordered container of potentialities (*Timaeus* 52e). She is filled with potential power, but not evenly balanced, in that she 'sways unevenly' and is 'shaken' by the forms she receives. Presented as this uncontrolled, powerful force, she sounds both irrational and dangerous. This is the point at which the image of the winnowing basket is introduced, as an entity that through shaking and uneven movement imposes reason and measure upon the unordered elements.[25] By means of her unordered shaking the winnowing basket functions as an ordering principle, sorting the different elements contained within it. The shaking of the winnowing basket implies at least a certain amount of rhythm, and thus a certain amount of musicality. Like a *pharmakon* she emerges in a double guise, as both unordered and ordering, both potentially dangerous and potentially beneficial: *chôra* is inherently ambiguous in her musicality.

This ambiguity that emerges through *mousikê* can also be understood in relation to temporality. Firstly, music is of course inherently temporal in the sense that music necessarily unfolds through time. In this sense there is an essential connection between *mousikê* and the temporal transient cosmos. However, temporality is also portrayed quite literally as musical in Plato. Both in the *Republic* and in the *Timaeus* examples of this can be found. In the tenth book of the *Republic* the ordering of time is depicted by Plato as song, although in mythical terms. Here (*Republic* 617b-c), Socrates speaks of the music of the sirens. The context is that of a mythical story, about the three fates, daughters of Necessity, namely Lacheis, Clotho and Atropos, 'who sang in unison with the music of the Sirens, Lacheis singing the things that were, Clotho the things that are, and Atropos the things that are to be'. Past, present and future are portrayed here as something that is unfolded through song. What makes this particularly striking is not only the inherent temporality of music. Song and music are by necessity unfolded through time. This image of the three fates seems even to suggest that time itself – past, present and future – is intrinsically musical.

According to the description of time – *chronos* – in the *Timaeus*, it is an image of eternity that revolves according to number. This definition of time is even repeated twice. First at *Timaeus* 37d: 'He [the demiurge] made, of eternity (*aiônos*) that abides in unity, an everlasting likeness (*aiônion eikona*) moving according to numbers (*arithmon*) – that to which we have given the name Time (*chronon*).' The second time is at *Timaeus* 38a, where it is stated that time 'images (*mimoumenou*) eternity (*aiôna*) and revolves according to number (*arithmon*)'.[26] Time is here given several characteristics. It is related in an intrinsic way to mathematics, moving according to numbers. Furthermore, it is portrayed as inherently ambiguous, in that it is described as a moving image of eternity. One of the most important characteristics of eternity is that it is immobile. Time, however, is defined as moving: a moving image of the immobile eternity. All three of these characteristics – a relation to mathematics, movement and ambiguity – time shares with *mousikê*.

Mousikê is, as we have seen thus far, portrayed in Plato as ambiguous, like a *pharmakon* that can work as both a remedy and a poison. This ambiguity of *mousikê* reverberates far beyond the merely human. It resonates at the very core of cosmos and echoes through the depictions of time. In its fundamental ontological implications *mousikê* gives voice to an inherent ambiguity of our transient world, as depicted by Plato. This resonates also through to the human and the political life of the *polis*, as well as to philosophy itself. Let us now first consider the significance of *mousikê* in connection to the education of the souls of the citizens, looking also at the fibres and aspects that weave *mousikê* and the laws of the *polis* together, before turning to consider the ambiguity of *mousikê* in relation to philosophy.

Mousikê as an educational part of politics

The philosophical and political relevance of *mousikê* as it is portrayed in the second book of the *Laws* becomes obvious through the notion of *paideia*. Education is key to the political goodness of the state, and philosophy is key in Plato's understanding of education. Among those who put emphasis on the philosophical relevance of the account of music in the *Laws* is Morrow, who stresses the philosophical exposition of the effect of music upon the character to which Plato 'devotes the whole of the second book of the *Laws*'.[27] Furthermore, according to Morrow, the perfect musician 'is the philosopher, who knows how to harmonize temperaments in men, not strings of the lyre'.[28] The philosopher, who is key to the political goodness of the state, is depicted as a master of music. Where the musician knows about the proper harmonies of musical tunes (*nomoi*) and instruments, the philosopher knows about the attunement of the soul, which in turn is essential for instituting the right form of education. This in turn is vital to the politics and organization of the state, including the organization of the laws (*nomoi*) that are to be instituted. Both melodies (*nomoi*) and laws (*nomoi*) must be structured in the appropriate manner. And, the musician and the philosopher (here portrayed as the best lawmaker) share, as it appears through this comparison, in having knowledge about the right measurements and harmonies that need to be involved in both musical melodies and political organization through laws.

The Greek word for 'law' – *nomos* – also means melody. *Nomos*, in its second main sense, is used to denote both a type of early melody, for example as created by Terpander for the lyre as an accompaniment to epic texts (in the first part of the seventh century BC), and also, later, to denote a composition including both words and melody.[29] According to Seth Bernadete, who points out that *nomos* also carries the meaning 'musical tune', Plato's *Laws* – *Nomoi* – could just as rightly have been translated *Songs*.[30] Embedded within the word '*nomos*' resides a manifestation of an inherent relation between music and laws, which finds an expression through Plato's *Laws*.[31] The music in the *Laws*, that is, the good form of music, emerges in several ways that share similarities also with the philosophical *erôs* of the *Symposium*. Both are intermediary in the sense that they represent ways towards insight, and both are conducive with wine and intoxication, but needs to be restrained in terms of the right occasion and measure. The music of the *Laws*, that is, the song that good laws sing, brings order and right measure to the *polis* that constitute human society and life, not least through prescribing the right education, or choristry. Music in Plato's *Laws* thus resounds on several levels: in the songs and dances of the choirs, through the chanting resounding from laws, and perhaps also within philosophy as the highest form of music. This last point we shall return to in the fifth and final part of this chapter.

Plato's *Laws* speaks explicitly about music. In the second book a highly extensive definition of *mousikê* is presented, which is at least as extensive as that of his contemporary Greek context. As Morrows says: 'If music has the power that Plato thinks it has (and evidence as to its effect upon the Greeks is altogether in accord with Plato's estimate), the dithyrambic and dramatic performances at Athens were in fact an educational institution of great importance.'[32] The Athenian Stranger states that 'choristry (*choreia*) as a whole is identical with education (*paideusis*) as a whole' (*Laws* 672e). Choristry is divided into two parts: one directed towards the education of the soul and the other towards the cultivation of the body. The one that is concerned with training the soul in excellence, and which is said to pertain to the voice and the 'vocal actions', consists of rhythms and harmonies. This is named music (*mousikê*). The part concerned with the body also consists of rhythms, and is said by the Athenian Stranger to have been called 'playful dancing'. In so far as this pertains to the training of the body in excellence, this is named gymnastic (*gymnastikê*, *Laws* 673a). Choristry (*choreia*) as a whole is identical with education as a whole, both for the soul, through music, and for the body, through gymnastics.

The ordering that constitutes cosmos echoes within every living creature that is born into the world. In the second book of the *Laws*, this is explained by a description of the origin of music and gymnastics. This story is even mentioned twice. As the Athenian Stranger says, no living being is ever born in possession of the reason that properly belongs to it when fully matured. This lack of reason makes the newly born move as if in a frenzy, crying out and leaping wildly (*Laws* 672b-c). According to this story of the origin of music, 'almost without exception, every young creature is incapable of keeping either its body or its tongue quiet, and is always striving to move and to cry, leaping and skipping and delighting in dances and games, and uttering also, noises of every description' (*Laws* 653d-e). This depiction of the newly born children shares some similarities with the description of the unordered motion of the newly born cosmos, mentioned above. Just as the newly born children need *mousikê* to help ordering their motions, the winnowing basket helps ordering the elements at the birth of cosmos. In both instances the unordered movements, the raw material of music, so to speak, needs to become harmonized and regulated in the right manner.[33] As the creatures develop and mature, the movements become more ordered, or as we might say, more musically ordered, in terms of rhythm and harmony. However, according to Plato, it is vital that the ordering is done in the proper manner. Otherwise the potential remedy that constitutes *mousikê* can turn poisonous. Politically this can be disastrous.

Plato's broad designation of *mousikê* in the *Laws*, that through the notion of choristry is extended to involve also the part of education that concerns the body, points to its political significance. Education is crucial to the political organization and success of the *polis*, according to Plato, and when choristry is identified with education, this means that any well-organized and good state will have to be not only inherently musical, but ordered musically in the right way. *Mousikê* can be both beneficial and dangerous and this of course means that not just any form of *mousikê* will do if the *polis* is to be good and well-ordered.

Music is also, at least according to the description in the *Laws*, characteristic of human beings, in the sense that what separates human beings from other living beings is the ability to perceive rhythm and harmony, that is, 'the various kinds of order and disorder in movement'.[34] As we have seen, this is a view that does not run completely consistently throughout all of Plato's dialogues, at least if we understand this to mean that *mousikê* is something that exclusively relates to human beings. However, even if Plato ascribes *mousikê* and musical movement and song even to cicadas, the planets and stars, the cosmos and temporality, it is still possible to argue that it pertains to human beings in a specific way that differs from these others. According to Morrow, both dance and song have their roots 'deep in human nature, according to a "widespread theory" which the Athenian Stranger expounds at the beginning of the second book'.[35] The specific and unique ability of human beings to perceive the order and disorder of movement that constitute rhythm and harmony, induces the importance of educating this ability in the right way. Contrary to the singing cicadas, humans can perceive of *mousikê* in a reflective way. We can think. Or, more specifically, we can philosophize, that is to say, search for wisdom. This opens up a possibility for us to distinguish between good and bad music, and also create both dangerous and beneficial *mousikê*.

For Plato it is thus imperative that we order society in ways that promote the beneficial influence of the right form of *mousikê*, and avoid the possible poisonous effects of the dangerous forms to the best of our abilities. In the *Laws* the Athenian Stranger asks for agreement on the proposal that, as he says: 'it is the duty of every man and child – bond and free, male and female – and the duty of the whole State, to charm themselves unceasingly with the chants we have described'.[36] These are of course the good and right form of *mousikê*. To be subjected to the enchantment of this form of music is thus a political duty both for the state and all of its inhabitants, women, children and slaves included. It permeates the entirety of the political entity. And, in order to know and recognize what these beneficial forms of *mousikê* are, as distinct from the possible poisonous ones, philosophy is needed. In the final part of this chapter let us briefly consider the ambiguity of *mousikê* in relation to philosophy.

The *mousikê* of philosophy or philosophy as *mousikê*

An understanding of *mousikê* as related to philosophy carries a resonance with a famous place within the Platonic corpus, namely the *Phaedo*. Here Socrates does not speak of laws or the organization of the *polis*, but compares philosophy quite directly to *mousikê*. He explicitly speaks of philosophy as the highest form of music (*mousikê*). This dialogue is unfolded on Socrates' last day alive. He sits together with his friends discussing the immortality of the soul until he finally, as the sun sets, drinks the poison and dies. At the beginning of the *Phaedo*, Socrates tells the others who are present about a dream that has come to him often in his past life, in various forms but always saying the same thing: 'Make music and work at it.' Formerly, says Socrates, he thought it was urging and encouraging him to do what he was doing already, 'that is, to make music, because philosophy was the greatest kind of music (*megistês mousikês*)'. Now, however, while he has been waiting in the prison after the trial for his execution, he has, 'in case the repeated dream really meant to tell [him] to make this which is ordinarily called music', composed a hymn to the god of music, Apollo, and also turned a myth of Aesop into verse (*Phaedo* 60e-61b).

For most of his life, Socrates has thought of philosophy as the greatest form of music. It is only in his very last days he has made what is ordinarily called music, in case he has misinterpreted his recurring dream. At this point, it may be useful to keep in mind the various meanings of the ancient concept of music (*mousikê*), as already indicated. *Mousikê* was used in a more limited sense, which is more akin to our modern concept of music, but it also could carry much wider connotations. When Socrates alludes to music in *Phaedo* 60e-61b, there may be quite some irony in play, too. Nonetheless, within the context of Plato's works, Socrates' choice of understanding philosophy as the highest form of music, and spending his life making this, is not portrayed as mistaken. Furthermore, to posterity, and mainly through Plato's dialogues, Socrates is not remembered for his attempts at making hymns and verse. He is remembered for his philosophical activity. By placing this passage into the dialogue that unfolds the last day of Socrates' life, Plato manages to emphasize the relationship between *mousikê* and philosophy. He makes the musicality of philosophy, and perhaps also the philosophical aspect of music, understood as *mousikê*, resound.

Mousikê, according to Plato, can be both beneficial and dangerous. Having indicated the relationship between *mousikê* and philosophy, a crucial reservation needs to be stated, in terms of what kind of *mousikê* can be said to be philosophical. According to the *Phaedo*, Socrates has throughout his life, until his last day, thought of philosophy as the highest form of music. As we have seen above, not all *mousikê* is good, neither for the soul nor for the *polis*. Neither can all music be said to work in accordance with philosophy. Some similar principles need to be put to into play both to create good music and to make philosophy as the highest form of music. This is, as we have seen, connected to order and the rhythmical-mathematical, and that which pertains to harmonies and accord. That is to say, *mousikê* in itself is neither necessarily philosophical nor good. It needs to be shaped and shaken into the right form. This pertains to the difference between philosophy and sophistry.

Above we saw how Socrates speaks of philosophy as the highest form of music. Nonetheless, he also portrays sophistry in a highly musical way. In the *Protagoras*, Socrates describes the dancelike movements and choreography of the ambulatory Protagoras with his two companies, that include some of the native inhabitants of Athens, who are dancing attendance and participating in the dance (*en tô chorô*, *Protagoras* 315b). In this choreographically depicted dancelike walk, the participants are both moving about and talking. That is to say, Protagoras is talking and the others are listening. However, the speech of Protagoras is painted in musical terms and as enchanting his listeners. As Socrates says of Protagoras (at 315a-b),[37] he is 'enchanting them with his words (*kêlôn tê phônê*) like Orpheus, while they follow where the voice (*tên phônên*) sounds, enchanted (*kekêlêmenoi*)'. The audible, musical aspect of Protagoras' speech could be stressed even more than this English translation does. The Greek expression that is translated 'enchanting them with his words' are *kêlôn* and *phônê*. *Kêlôn*, from *kêleô*, means to 'charm, bewitch, or beguile' especially by music. It can also be used to signify 'charm by incantation'. Thus, it is the audible, enchanting sound of Protagoras' voice that is stressed in this description, not the content of his words. The Greek words that Lamb translates 'words' in the expression 'enchanting them with his words' is not *logos* but *phônê*, which means 'sound or tone', properly 'the sound of the voice', whether of men or animals with lungs and throat. These two words – *kêleô* and *phônê* – are even repeated twice in the same sentence when Socrates continues his description saying that 'they follow where the voice sounds, enchanted'. All of this underlines the auditory, musical effect of the speech of Protagoras. Comparing him to Orpheus strengthens this even further. As is well known, Orpheus, the son of the Muse Kalliope, was famous for his musical talent. The lyre was his instrument and his song was said to enchant everyone and everything, even wild animals, rivers, stones and trees. It is a dancing and singing Protagoras that Socrates manifests through his words. What is performed by the great sophist Protagoras is a musical form of movement, both visually, as dance, and audibly, as chant.

Within the Platonic corpus we consequently find both philosophy and sophistry depicted as music. Philosophy is named the highest form of music, and Protagoras, arguably the greatest sophist of all, is portrayed as enchanting his audience with song and dance. Here, as well, the ambiguity of *mousikê* emerges. In its highest form, as philosophy, it can be the best remedy, but it can also, as sophistry, be enchantingly poisonous. One important aspect that the descriptions in Plato of both philosophy and sophistry as music bring out, is how it is not always easy to determine the difference between the two. Just as it may not always be easy to determine whether an instance of *mousikê* functions as a remedy or a poison, it is not always clear who is practising sophistry and philosophy in Plato. The depictions of philosophy and sophistry as music, both made by Socrates, reveal the ambiguous relation between the two in a significant way.

This chapter has considered the significance of the ambiguity of *mousikê* in Plato, first with special attention to *mousikê* as *pharmakon*: both remedy and poison. Furthermore, the relevance of this ambiguity of *mousikê* was developed in terms of the ontological implications of *mousikê* in Plato, through the descriptions of the generated world (cosmos) and temporality. Subsequently, *mousikê* as an ambiguous educational element of politics was considered, before finally, the ambiguity of *mousikê* was brought out in relation to philosophy. Plato's philosophy is extended within the tension between the eternal and the temporal. As living human beings, we stretch towards something beyond our own transience, but at the same time we are embedded within a bodily existence that is our condition. *Mousikê*, not least in its mathematical properties, is a means to educate the soul in the attempt to move towards something eternal. At the same time *mousikê* resounds within the perceptual realm of the auditive, which is characterized by temporality in a way more specific than other senses. *Mousikê* belongs to the temporal world of the in-between where the transient cosmos of sense-perception is extended between eternity and chaos. It can lead us astray in bewitching ways but is at the same time also singularly able to educate, especially in its highest form. By making *mousikê* resound on numerous levels – in the soul of the particular person, in the pedagogy and laws vital to the political, in nature, cosmos and time – Plato sings a polyphonous song that is both enchanting and philosophically profound.

Notes

1 See e.g. Plato's *Cratylus* 423c-d: 'In the first place we shall not, in my opinion, be making names, if we imitate things as we do in music (*mousikê mimoumetha*), although musical imitation also is vocal; and secondly we shall make no names by imitating that which music imitates (*he mousikê mimeitai*).' Plato, *Cratylus*, trans. H.N. Fowler, The Loeb Classical Library, vol. IV (Cambridge: Harvard University Press, 1977). *Statesman* 288c: 'In all the imitations created by the use of painting and music (*mousikê mimêmata*).' Plato, *Statesman*, trans. H.N. Fowler, The Loeb Classical Library, vol. VIII (Cambridge: Harvard University Press, 1990). *Laws* 668a: 'We assert, do we not, that all music (*mousikên ge pasan*) is representative and imitative (*mimêtikên*)? ... Of course.' Plato, *Laws*, trans. R.G. Bury, The Loeb Classical Library, vol. X and XI (Cambridge: Harvard University Press, 1994 and 1984).
2 One of the more recent examples is the book by Francesco Pelosi, *Plato on Music, Soul and Body* (Cambridge: Cambridge University Press, 2010).
3 See for instance Warren B. Anderson, *Ethos and Education in Greek Music* (Cambridge, Massachusetts: Harvard University Press, 1966), 1.
4 John Burnet, *Greek Philosophy* (London: Macmillan, 1968), 44 and 36.
5 See for example Boethius, *De institutione musica II*, who talks about *musica instrumentalis*, *musica humane*, and *musica mundana*. Anicius Manlius Severinus Boethius, *De institutione arithmetica libri duo. De institutione musica: libri quinque: accedit geometrica quae fertur Boetii / Anicii Manlii Torquati Severini; e libris manu scriptis ed. Godofredus Friedlein* (Lipsiae: B.G. Teubneri, 1867).
6 Plato mentions music in connection with the Muses e.g. in the *Phaedrus* 259b-d: 'The story goes that these locusts were once men, before the birth of the Muses, and when the Muses were born and song appeared, some of the men were so overcome with

delight that they sang and sang, forgetting food and drink, until at last unconsciously they died. From them the locust tribe afterwards arose, and they have this gift from the Muses, that from the time of their birth they need no sustenance, but sing continually, without food or drink, until they die, when they go to the Muses and report who honours each of them on earth.' Plato, *Phaedrus*, trans. H.N. Fowler, The Loeb Classical Library, vol. I (Cambridge: Harvard University Press, 1990).

7   Glenn R. Morrow, *Plato's Cretan City: A Historical Interpretation of the Laws* (Princeton, New Jersey: Princeton University Press, 1993), 302.

8   Penelope Murray and Peter Wilson, eds., *Music and the Muses: The Culture of Mousike in the Classical Athenian City* (Oxford: Oxford University Press 2004), 2.

9   This is often called the ethos perspective on music. See for instance Warren B. Anderson, *Ethos and Education in Greek Music*.

10 Plato, *Laws* 655c-d. Such a view can be found several places in Plato. In *Greater Hippias* music is warned against in the sense that it pleases the senses or brings bodily pleasure (Plato. *Greater Hippias*, trans. H.N. Fowler. The Loeb Classical Library, vol. IV (Cambridge: Harvard University Press, 1977), 298a-e). Later in the *Laws* pleasure-inducive music is referred to as the common, 'honey-sweet' form of music, whilst the form of music that is called noble is the more sober and regulated form (*Laws* 802c-d). As Seth Bernadete writes in *Plato's Laws. The Discovery of Being* (Chicago: University of Chicago Press, 2000), 64: 'The Stranger denounces the most common view that pleasure determines what is right in music, for if that were the case the disparity in men's pleasure when it comes to songs and dances would occasion no surprise and obviate the need for the Stranger to pose his question.'

11 Plato, *Laws* 655b. In the *Republic* simplicity in music is termed good, that is to say, the one that brings sobriety to the soul, akin to the way gymnastics brings health to the body (Plato, *Republic*, trans. Paul Shorey. The Loeb Classical Library, vol. V and VI. (Cambridge: Harvard University Press, 1982 and 1987), 404e, 410a).

12 Plato, *Laws* 655b: '[T]he postures and tunes which attach to goodness of soul and body, or to some image thereof, are universally good, while those which attach to badness are exactly the reverse.'

13 Plato, *Laws* 665a. Expressions of the importance of order and regulation as characteristic of good music can also be found later in the *Laws*, e.g. 802c: 'In truth, every unregulated musical pursuit becomes, when brought under regulation, a thousand times better, even when honeyed strains are served up: all alike provide pleasure.' And also 802c: 'For if a man has been reared from childhood up to the age of steadiness and sense in the use of music that is sober and regulated, then he detests the opposite kind whenever he hears it, and calls it "vulgar"; whereas if he has been reared in the common honeyed kind of music, he declares the opposite of this to be cold and unpleasing. Hence, as we said just now, in respect of the pleasure or displeasure they cause neither kind excels the other; where the superiority lies in the fact that the one kind always makes those who are reared in it better, the other worse.'

14 Friedrich Nietzsche, *The Birth of Tragedy* (Oxford: Oxford University Press, 2000).

15 Plato, *Laws* 666b. As Plato writes at *Laws* 666b-c: 'But when a man has reached the age of forty, he may join in the convivial gatherings and invoke Dionysus, above all other gods, inviting his presence at the rite (which is also the recreation) of the elders, which he bestowed on mankind as a medicine (*ton oinon pharmakon*) potent against the crabbedness of old age, that thereby we men may renew our youth, and that, through forgetfulness of care, the temper of our souls may lose its hardness and become softer and more ductile, even as iron when it has been forged in the fire.'

16 Plato, *Laws* 802d-e. According to Monique Canto, 'The Politics of Women's Bodies: Reflections on Plato', in *Feminist Interpretations of Plato*, ed. Nancy Tuana (Pennsylvania: Pennsylvania University Press, 1994), 50–6, the political is treated in a very different manner in the *Laws*, as compared with the *Republic*. This becomes especially apparent when it comes to sexual difference. Canto goes as far as calling what is proposed in the seventh book of the *Laws* a feminist political manifesto. Crucial in her reading is the fact that time and the mixing of different elements, for instance in reproduction, is placed as constitutive for the political. According to Canto, Plato places difference outside the *polis* in the *Republic*, but inside the *polis* in the *Laws*. As Nancy Tuana points out in her 'Introduction' to *Feminist Interpretations of Plato*, ed. Nancy Tuana, 5: 'Canto argues that women represent two conditions necessary for political life: procreation and desire.' And on p. 6: 'Canto argues that the *Laws*, in making women the primary object and first principle of political regulation, is a true feminist political manifesto.' I would not go as far as Canto, in saying that the *Laws* is a feminist manifesto. According to my reading Canto's point that this dialogue emphasizes temporality, needs a further qualification in relation to what kind of temporality is invoked. The conception of temporality that opens up for difference here, as I see it, is one embedded within the concept of *kairos*.

17 Doro Levi, 'The Concept of *Kairos* and the Philosophy of Plato', *Rendiconti della Reale Accademia Nazionale dei Lincei Classe di scienze moralia* RV 33 (1924).

18 Plato, *Laws* 709b. As John E. Smith points out in 'Time and Qualitative Time', in *Rhetoric and Kairos*, ed. P. Sipiora and J.S. Baumlin (Albany: State University of New York Press, 2002), 55: 'In the fourth book of the *Laws* (709b ff.), Plato discusses the different factors that govern human life in connection with the question whether laws are explicitly and designedly made by man or whether external factors are involved. He declares, "Chance [*tychê*] and occasion [*kairos*] cooperate with God in the control of all human affairs." These two mundane factors are said to condition human action and also to be in harmony with each other.'

19 Morrow, *Plato's Cretan City*, 315.

20 The story continues in the following way: '[T]hey have this gift from the Muses, that from the time of their birth they need no sustenance, but sing continually, without food or drink, until they die, when they go to the Muses and report who honour each of them on earth. They tell Terpsichore of those who have honoured her in dances, and make them dearer to her; they gain the favour of Erato for the poets of love, and that of the other Muses for their votaries, according to their various ways of honouring them; and to Kalliope, the eldest of the Muses, and to Urania who is next to her, they make report of those who pass their lives in philosophy and who worship these Muses who are most concerned with heaven and with thought divine and human and whose music is the sweetest' (*Phaedrus* 259c-d).

21 Cf. G.R.F. Ferrari. For more on this point, see his *Listening to the Cicadas* (Cambridge: Cambridge University Press, 1990), 57.

22 Ferrari, *Listening to the Cicadas*, 30.

23 Ferrari, *Listening to the Cicadas*, 27.

24 Plato, *Timaeus* 40c-d: 'the choric dances (*choreias*) of these same stars and their crossings one of another, and the relative reversals and progressions of their orbits, and of which of the gods meet in their conjunctions, and how many are in opposition, and behind which and at what times they severally pass before one another and are hidden from our view, and again re-appearing send upon men unable to calculate alarming portents of the things which shall come to pass hereafter, – to describe all

this without an inspection of models of these movements would be labour in vain.' Plato, *Timaeus*, trans. R.G. Bury, The Loeb Classical Library, vol. IX (Cambridge: Harvard University Press, 1989).

25 As Timaeus says at *Timaeus* 52e-53a: 'the forms, as they are moved, fly continually in various directions and are dissipated; just as the particles that are shaken and winnowed by the sieves and other instruments used for the cleansing of corn fall in one place if they are solid and heavy, but fly off and settle elsewhere if they are spongy and light. So it was with the Four Kinds when shaken by the Recipient: her motion, like an instrument which causes shaking, was separating farthest from one another the dissimilar, and pushing most closely together the similar ... Before that time, in truth, all these things were in a state devoid of reason or measure.'

26 Plato, *Timaeus* 38a. Both examples here are from Francis M. Cornford's translation in his *Plato's Cosmology* (Indianapolis: Hackett Publishing Company, 1997).

27 Morrow, *Plato's Cretan City*, 302.

28 Morrow, *Plato's Cretan City*, 315.

29 On the second main meaning of the word *nomos*, see H.G. Liddell and R. Scott, *A Greek-English Lexicon* (Oxford: Oxford University Press, 1996).

30 Bernadete likewise points out that 'The word for law (*nómos*) also means a musical tune ...' Furthermore, Bernadete makes a comparison between Plato's *Nomoi* and Herodotus' *The Histories*, where at 1. 23–24 we are told the story about Arion, the best singer in the world, who is thrown overboard by his crew. Arion escapes, however, by singing a song – the *orthios nomos* – a song or hymn in honor of Apollo, whereupon he is rescued by a dolphin (Herodotus, *The Histories*, vol. 1, trans. A.D. Godley, The Loeb Classical Library (London: William Heinemann, 1946). According to Bernadete, philosophy is the song of the Athenian Stranger and the *Laws* is his dolphin. Bernadete, *Plato's* Laws, xvii–xviii.

31 A further reference in the Platonic corpus to such a use of the word *nomos* is *Minos* 318b. Here the word is used in relation to flute-playing: 'Now can you tell me who, in former times, has proved himself a good lawgiver in regard to the laws of flute-playing (*en tois aulêtikois nomois nomothetês*)?' Marsyas turns out to be the lawgiver here, but whether he is a lawgiver of the laws of flute-playing or a lawgiver of the melodies of flute-playing is not clear. The word *nomos* could here be translated both as indicating the laws of flute-playing and as the melodies of flute-playing. Plato, *Minos*, trans. W.R.M. Lamb, The Loeb Classical Library, vol. XII (Cambridge: Harvard University Press, 1986).

32 Morrow, *Plato's Cretan City*, 312. As Morrow also says, at p. 302 in the same book: 'In giving choreia this position of honour, Plato is not expressing merely a personal preference, but is reflecting the common opinion of his fellow countrymen.'

33 Morrow uses the expression 'raw material' in this context: 'This theory maintains that every young creature finds it difficult to keep still and is always leaping and skipping about, frolicking with his companions (dancing, as it were, in his games with them) and uttering all sorts of sounds. This is the raw material which, when reduced to rhythm (*rhythmos*), or ordered movement ... [here there is a reference to *Laws* 665a], produces dance and song. Besides rhythm, song involves harmony (*harmonia*), i.e. an ordering of musical sounds with respect to high and low tones. Again the rhythm of the dance is itself ordered into figures (*schêmata*), and the succession of musical sounds into songs (*melê*, 654e, 672e). Finally, this theory maintains that of all creatures man is the only one who has a perception of order and disorder in these various movements of body and voice, the only one capable, therefore, of enjoying the

movement of dance and song. This enjoyment is said to be the gift of the gods (654a). Apollo and the Muses, the authors of dance and song, are therefore the authors of education.' Morrow, *Plato's Cretan City*, 305.
34 Plato, *Laws* 653e-654a. The full quote reads like this: 'Now, whereas all other creatures are devoid of any perceptions of the various kinds of order and disorder in movement (which we term rhythm and harmony), to us men the very gods, who were given, as we said, to be our fellows in the dance, have granted the pleasurable perception of rhythm and harmony, whereby they cause us to move and lead our choirs, linking us one with another by means of songs and dances; and to their choir they have given its name from the "cheer" implanted therein.'
35 Morrow, *Plato's Cretan City*, 304.
36 Plato, *Laws* 665c. Plato continues in the following manner: 'constantly changing them and securing variety in every way possible, so as to, so as to inspire the singers with an insatiable appetite for the hymns and with pleasure therein.'
37 Plato, *Protagoras*, trans. W.R.M. Lamb, The Loeb Classical Library, vol. II (Cambridge: Harvard University Press, 1990).

Bibliography

Anderson, Warren. *Ethos and Education in Greek Music*. Cambridge: Harvard University Press, 1966.
Bernadete, Seth. *Plato's Laws. The Discovery of Being*. Chicago: University of Chicago Press, 2000.
Boethius, Anicius Manlius Severinus. *De institutione arithmetica libri duo. De institutione musica: libri quinque: accedit geometrica quae fertur Boetii / Anicii Manlii Torquati Severini; e libris manu scriptis ed. Godofredus Friedlein*. Lipsiae: B.G. Teubneri, 1867.
Burnet, John. *Greek Philosophy*. London: Macmillan, 1968.
Canto, Monique. 'The Politics of Women's Bodies: Reflections on Plato'. In *Feminist Interpretations of Plato*. Edited by Nancy Tuana, 49–67. Pennsylvania: Pennsylvania University Press, 1994.
Cornford, Francis. *Plato's Cosmology*. Indianapolis: Hackett Publishing Company, 1997.
Ferrari, G.R.F. *Listening to the Cicadas*. Cambridge: Cambridge University Press, 1990.
Herodotus. *The Histories*. Translated by A.D. Godley. The Loeb Classical Library. Cambridge: Harvard University Press, 1989.
Levi, Doro. 'The Concept of *Kairos* and the Philosophy of Plato'. *Rendiconti della Reale Accademia Nazionale dei Lincei Classe di scienze moralia* 33 (1924): 93–118.
Liddell, H.G. and R. Scott. *A Greek-English Lexicon*. Oxford: Oxford University Press, 1996.
Morrow, Glenn. *Plato's Cretan city: A Historical Interpretation of the Laws*. Princeton: Princeton University Press, 1993.
Murray, Penelope and Peter Wilson, eds. *Music and the Muses: The Culture of Mousike in the Classical Athenian City*. Oxford: Oxford University Press, 2004.
Nietzsche, Friedrich. *The Birth of Tragedy*. Oxford: Oxford University Press, 2000.
Pelosi, Francesco. *Plato on Music, Soul and Body*. Cambridge: Cambridge University Press, 2010.
Plato. *Cratylus*. Transated by H.N. Fowler. The Loeb Classical Library, vol. IV. Cambridge: Harvard University Press, 1977.
Plato. *Greater Hippias*. Translated by H.N. Fowler. The Loeb Classical Library, vol. IV. Cambridge: Harvard University Press, 1977.

Plato. *Laws*. Translated by R.G. Bury. The Loeb Classical Library, vols. X and XI. Cambridge: Harvard University Press, 1994 and 1984.
Plato. *Minos*. Translated by W.R.M. Lamb. The Loeb Classical Library, vol. XII. Cambridge: Harvard University Press, 1986.
Plato. *Phaedrus*. Translated by H.N. Fowler. The Loeb Classical Library, vol. I. Cambridge: Harvard University Press, 1990.
Plato. *Protagoras*. Translated by W.R.M. Lamb. The Loeb Classical Library, vol. II. Cambridge: Harvard University Press, 1990.
Plato. *Republic*. Translated by Paul Shorey. The Loeb Classical Library, vol. V and VI. Cambridge: Harvard University Press, 1982 and 1987.
Plato. *Statesman*. Translated by H.N. Fowler. The Loeb Classical Library, vol. VIII. Cambridge: Harvard University Press, 1990.
Plato. *Symposium*. Translated by W.R.M. Lamb. The Loeb Classical Library, vol. III. Cambridge: Harvard University Press, 1991.
Plato. *Timaeus*. Translated by R.G. Bury. The Loeb Classical Library, vol. IX. Cambridge: Harvard University Press, 1989.
Smith, John. 'Time and Qualitative Time'. In *Rhetoric and Kairos*, edited by P. Sipiora and J. S. Baumlin, 46–58. Albany: State University of New York Press, 2002.
Tuana, Nancy. 'Introduction'. In *Feminist Interpretations of Plato*, edited by Nancy Tuana, 3–11. Pennsylvania: Pennsylvania University Press, 1994.

9

Pleasure, Perception and Images in Plato

Cynthia Freeland

This chapter will examine various dialogues in which Plato explored ways of explaining pleasure, in particular, the *Phaedo, Theaetetus, Timaeus* and *Philebus*. Despite differences in subject, setting and style, in all of these works Plato's focus is on fundamental questions about morality and the good life. Pleasure is linked to questions about how to live. In the *Phaedo* Socrates treats pleasure as suspicious and to be avoided. He criticizes bodily pleasures like hunger or sex because they are mixed with pain and distract us from higher goals like philosophy and virtue. Socrates condemns perception and imagination as inadequate routes to knowledge. Nevertheless, philosophical activities can bring rich pleasures to a good person – pleasures that are not just acceptable but praiseworthy.

In Plato's many treatments of pleasure we can find two broad kinds of account.[1] On one view, pleasure is the replenishment of a lack or the scratching of an itch; it involves the restoration of a normal bodily condition. This *replenishment view* is broadly physicalist or reductionist in nature. This view is proposed in discussions in the *Phaedo* and *Gorgias,* which focus on appetitive pleasures. The restoration view presupposes a dualist picture according to which, as Socrates puts it in the *Phaedo,* the soul is trapped in the body as if sealed within a jar. This higher part of us seeks escape after death to the pure realm which is its native element. On the second view, pleasure is linked to perception, images and thought. Pleasure belongs to the soul as well as – or instead of – the body. On this view, pleasure has aboutness or intentionality. I will call this second picture of pleasure the *psychological view*. This view represents a more complex and less dualistic account of human nature.

At times, the replenishment and psychological accounts appear to be blended together. My explanation for this is that Plato first approached the analysis of pleasures within the framework of the replenishment view, which seemed to fit physical pleasures. But he struggled to make this view accommodate higher kinds of pleasure involving images or thoughts, like the pleasures of poetry, art, learning, or philosophy itself. To construct an adequate account of the role of pleasure in a good life, Plato needed to develop a satisfactory theory of the human self or subject – one that could incorporate both physical and psychological elements. Ultimately, I contend, Plato reached his most sophisticated analysis of subjectivity and pleasure in the *Philebus*.[2] This complex dialogue presents a new ontology and defends an account of the best life as a mixture of pleasure and intellect. It provides a more complex psychological account of pleasure, now classified into many types. There are even 'false pleasures', ones which typically involve psychological states incorporating false images or thoughts.

Like the pleasures of philosophy or of learning, the pleasures of art and poetry must be evaluated in terms distinct from those that account for the badness of physical pleasures. Since such pleasures have no obvious links to the body, they cannot readily be described using the replenishment view. The psychological account allows for a more refined differentiation between good and bad pleasures. Plato warns us about the dangerous pleasures of an artwork or tragedy by pointing to mistakes in its associated images or thoughts. But this entails that certain pleasures of art and tragedy may be acceptable – those associated with true images and thoughts. Thus, my examination of Plato's psychological theory of pleasure will also show that his view of art is more subtle and complex than generally claimed. Certain kinds of poetry and art are associated with valuable pleasures – just as is philosophy itself. These pleasures are not simply permissible but essential to a good life.

The replenishment account of pleasure

The pursuit of pleasure often gets treated by Plato as something animal-like and morally questionable. Even in a dialogue like the *Phaedrus*, which is devoted to erotic love, the bodily side of sexual passion is spoken of with dismay and even disgust. A person in the throes of desire experiences such bothersome states as fear, fever, shuddering, itching, aching, etc. (250e-251d).

Socrates shows a similar scorn for physical pleasures of the hedonist in his debate with Callicles in the *Gorgias*. Callicles is portrayed as ridiculous because he endorses what Socrates calls the 'leaky jar' theory of pleasures. Socrates presents this theory as 'an image' (*eikôn*) to Callicles (493d5), contrasting the self-controlled man with the undisciplined man. The former gathers up scarce resources and stores them in jars, whereupon he can relax. The latter, in contrast, has leaky containers that he has to keep filling day and night, or else he will feel pain. Callicles endorses the life of the hedonist with his leaky jar, saying that the disciplined man lives life 'like a stone' (494a6). He believes that 'living pleasantly consists in this: having as much as possible flow in' (494b2). Socrates objects that for Callicles to want a lot to flow in, he must also want a lot to flow out. Despite this, Callicles asserts that he wants his jar to be full of holes so that more pleasures can run into and through him. Socrates forces Callicles (who tells him he should be ashamed! 494e) to acknowledge that this point applies not just to hunger and thirst but also to sexual pleasure. As in the *Phaedrus*, erotic pleasure is compared with scratching an itch: if you scratch, you reduce the pain, but the itch will come back, just as sexual desire will return soon after having been satisfied. Socrates is critical of such pleasures because they depend on the body and presuppose pain as a necessary condition.

Plato's negative assessment of physical pleasures is tied to a negative evaluation of physical sources of knowledge through sense-perception. Our senses are faulty as a source of knowledge. In the *Phaedo*, Socrates shows that the senses confuse us because of their inevitable ties to pleasure and pain (65a-e). They distract us from the proper human goal of acquiring philosophical knowledge. Instead, we pursue desires and satisfactions more appropriate to animals. The body also blocks the pursuit of truth because it is vulnerable to illness and connected to the sort of greed that causes wars (66b). In the *Phaedo*, physical pleasures are described as 'rivets' that fasten the soul to the body (83d). The true philosopher longs for death as the separation of the soul from the body: 'The soul of the true philosopher thinks that this deliverance must not be opposed and so keeps away from pleasures and desires and pains as far as he can' (83b).

Interestingly, despite this general derogation of the body and the senses, in the myth near the end of the *Phaedo*, Socrates presents a story about *higher* forms of sense-perception, especially of sight and hearing, as modes of knowledge. These higher senses enable the souls of philosophers who have managed to reach the true surface of the earth to have access to superior kinds of objects – even to achieve a kind of awareness akin to what the gods have. These higher souls can meet and see the gods directly.

> Their eyesight, hearing and intelligence and all such are as superior to ours as air is superior to water and ether to air in purity; they have groves and temples dedicated to the gods in which the gods really dwell, and they communicate with them by speech and prophecy and by the sight of them; they see the sun and moon and stars as they are, and in other ways their happiness is in in accord with this.
>
> 111b-c

Since the higher senses provide happiness, we can safely assume that there are related pleasures associated with the mind or soul, and that these become available to the blessed people who separate their souls from their bodies in pursuit of philosophic wisdom. Of course, the details are missing. It is not plausible, however, to suppose that such higher pleasures fit into the replenishment model. The myth fails to provide a sophisticated account of the mind's involvement with the body or of the relationship between perception, emotions and pleasure. And, after all, this is just a story told by Socrates to help reassure his fearful friends about the afterlife; he himself admits that 'No sensible man would insist that these things are as I have described them' (114d1-2). What we can safely say of the *Phaedo* is that Plato mostly tends to associate both pleasure and perception, as commonly experienced in *this life*, with lower or animal-like bodily states.

It is not surprising, given Plato's attempt to apply the replenishment view to pleasures of learning and philosophy, that the critique of art in *Republic* X depends in part on the *unreality* or *illusoriness* of the objects of art. (There is, of course, a different critique focusing on artworks' – particularly tragedies' – power of emotional influence.) The pleasures of art, poetry and images within the replenishment view become associated with deficiencies of sense-perception. They too are faulted because their objects somehow lack reality or substance.[3] Art and poetry are ultimately unsatisfying because they fill up our souls with mere vapour or air – as if we were eating cotton candy or worse, paper. By comparison, legitimate pleasures provide genuine restoration or nourishment to the soul.

I have said that the replenishment view begins to break down in the later books of the *Republic* when the framework is stretched to encompass higher pleasures of learning, art, and poetry. The most fundamental differences between so-called lower and higher pleasures cannot reasonably be explained in terms of the reality or emptiness of their objects. The slide from the *truthfulness* of thoughts to the *reality* of their objects is odd. Plato needs an account of how the mind experiences pleasure that goes beyond the replenishment view.[4] My next sections will show that Plato had the outlines of a more subtle and satisfactory account of pleasure, the psychological account. In order to develop this sophisticated account of pleasure, he first had to work out a more detailed analysis of sense-perception and its role in knowledge.

Revisions of replenishment (A): pleasure as perception in the *Theaetetus*

The primary concern of the *Theaetetus* is how to define knowledge. The dialogue shows Plato's ongoing interest in specifying the respective roles – if any – of the senses and the mind in achieving true knowledge. Theaetetus, a bright young man, answers Socrates' initial question about knowledge with the proposal that knowledge simply is perception. Socrates follows up with a detailed series of questions about the nature of perception. This leads into discussion of topics such as how perception is related to the world and the roles the mind and senses play in perception. In working towards a more detailed analysis of – for want of a better term – the physiology of perception, Plato appears to recognize that more complexity is needed in his account of pleasure.

Theaetetus' first proposal is that *knowledge is perception* (*aisthêsis*), at 151e2-3, a thesis often referred to as 'P' (for Perception) – a practice I will follow. Although Socrates rejects this proposal, his critique is circuitous because he immediately links it to two others. The first is Protagoras' doctrine that 'man is the measure of all things' ('M' for Measure), and the second, Heraclitus' doctrine that all things are in flux ('F' for Flux).[5] Let us consider the analysis of sense-perception developed through the association of these three doctrines, in order to see how it bears on the replenishment view of pleasure.

Near the start of the discussion of P, Socrates gives as an example of sense-perception our vision of the colour white (153d-54d). Since M implies that everyone's perceptions are correct, then if two people perceive an object differently – say, as having different colours or sizes – each one of them will be correct. Socrates takes this to mean that the object itself is not stable but in constant flux, i.e., to amount to F. This part of the dialogue proposes an interesting, though most likely incorrect, metaphysics underlying perception. Socrates aim in tackling these three linked doctrines – P, M and F – is to get Theaetetus to see how implausible his definition of knowledge as perception really is.

First, Socrates helps Theaetetus set forth a modified version of the flux hypothesis in which there are two kinds of changes or changers: fast ones and slow ones. Using this distinction, Socrates differentiates the *subject* and *object* in any perception (designated as the 'slow changers') from the actual *experience* of perception (which involves two 'fast changers'). The experience is an interaction between a subject and an object (the slow changers) giving rise to two fast changers: one on each side of the exchange. For example, if Theaetetus sees a white daisy, then he and the daisy are the slow changers. The two fast changers are Theaetetus' seeing of whiteness along with the daisy's looking white. One side of the relationship is said to be passive, the other active.

After establishing this framework for the analysis of perception, Socrates asks Theaetetus (157e-160b) to consider cases of *mistaken* perception in dreams and illusions or due to the illness. The P thesis is finally refuted in a complex argument from 184b-186e arguing that perception cannot be knowledge because it cannot grasp being. There has been considerable commentary about what this final refutation presupposes and implies.[6] I do not need to resolve these issues now since I am more interested in how Socrates' examination of P relates perceptions to pleasures.

In his critique of the crude Heraclitean model of perception, Socrates suggests that more is needed in order to ensure the stability of both the subject and object that interact in a perceptual experience. His questions hint strongly that there must be a unified subject of perception, something we would call a mind or self. Thus, he critiques the Heraclitean model as implying that there would be a multiplicity of subjects involved in sensation, since every sense organ would itself be a perceiver at every moment of interacting with some sensory object.[7]

One surprising feature of Socrates' critique has not received much attention from commentators. To show it I begin with this passage in which Socrates describes the correlative changers in a sense-experience of a colour like whiteness:

> The eye is filled with sight; at that moment it sees, and becomes not indeed sight, but a seeing eye; while its partner in the process of producing color is filled with whiteness, and becomes not whiteness but white, a white stick or stone or whatever it is that happens to be colored this sort of color. *We must understand this account as applying in the same way to hard and hot and everything else; nothing, as we were saying before, is in itself any of these. All of them, of all kinds whatsoever, are what things become through association with one another, as the result of motion.*
>
> 156e-157a, emphasis mine

What does Socrates mean to include when he claims that the Heraclitean model of perception must apply 'in the same way to hard and hot *and everything else*'? Surprisingly, he extends the category of perception to include pleasures, pains, desires and fears. Indeed, he already has made just this extension in a remark just before the passage cited above, while discussing the idea that perception involves the 'twin birth' arising from an interaction between two things, perceived and percipient. He says there,

> For the perceptions we have such names as sight, hearing, smelling, feeling cold and feeling hot; *also what are called pleasures and pains, desires and fears; and there are others besides*, a great number which have names, an infinite number which have not. And on the other side there is the race of things perceived, for each of these perceptions perceived things born of the same parentage, for all kinds of visions all kinds of colors, for all kinds of hearings all kinds of sounds; and so on, for the other perceptions the other things perceived, that come to be in kinship with them.
>
> 156b-c, emphasis mine

The point not much noticed, in other words, is that in the *Theaetetus* Socrates counts pleasures, pains, desires and fears among things *perceived*. The replenishment view would not be able to encompass such a picture of these states, nor has Socrates said anything to defend this broadening of perception. But Theaetetus never demurs. Perhaps it seems natural and plausible to him – and to readers of the dialogue.

In fact, however, Socrates' casual extension of perception to encompass pleasure, pain and emotional states poses metaphysical puzzles. Perception, on the theory under consideration, always has dual aspects of *the subject* and *the object*, where the perceiver corresponds to the perceptible such as a colour or sound. But what would be the parallel object for cases of 'perceiving' pleasure or fear – for example, my pleasure in eating an apple, or my cat Gabriel's fear of thunder? The object of a desire or emotion cannot simply be the apple or the thunder itself. There must be *features of* the respective objects (in the theory, 'fast changers') that amount to the apple's 'pleasingness to Cynthia' or the thunder's 'scariness to Gabriel.' In the shifting Heraclitean world under consideration, remember, the subject has pleasure or pain at the same time that the thing tasted becomes pleasure- or pain-inducing. Bizarre as this sounds, I suppose it is not any stranger than saying that a daisy suddenly becomes coloured-white at the moment an eye sees it.

In the end, Socrates' point in all this is that the ontology presupposed by thesis P is bizarre and implausible, precisely *because* it requires our supposing that the world is filled with fleeting subjects and objects that come and go. This is what Socrates means by saying that given F, nothing can 'be' anything but must always be 'coming to be' (157d). But what is the intuition behind generalizing from sense-perception to pleasure, pain, and emotion? Socrates appears to think that when a subject has any mental experience such as fearing, enjoying or desiring, there is something *in the world*, and not just *in his or her thoughts*, that corresponds to the experience – something frightening, pleasant or desirable. If pleasures and emotions are perception-like, they may also have a sort of veridical or non-veridical status. Thus, what may lie behind Socrates' grouping is the recognition that pleasure, pain and other emotional states are types of *psychological experiences of the world*. This is an intriguing result of Socrates' extension of the category of perceptions. In the *Theaetetus*, Socrates seems to recognize what we would now call the intentionality of a range of mental states including sense-perceptions, pleasures, pains and emotions. By treating emotions and pleasure/pain as types of perception, Socrates assumes that such mental states have at least some sort of informational content – they are responses that register aspects of objects in the world.

Revisions of replenishment (B): mental pleasures in the *Timaeus*

Yet another and, I would argue, better developed account of perception as again including emotions, pleasure, and pain, is advanced in the *Timaeus*. Like the *Theaetetus*, this is a very complex dialogue which I cannot hope to study thoroughly here. I will examine some passages that confirm what seemed surprising in Socrates' grouping of a range of mental states, including pleasures, under the heading of '*aisthêseis*' (perceptions) in the *Theaetetus*. The *Timaeus* confirms Plato's awareness that pleasure and pain must be viewed as psychological states and not simply as physical states involving lacks or replenishments.

In the *Timaeus*, the spokesman who tells the 'likely story' (*eikôs mythos*) of the dialogue, the astronomer Timaeus of Locri, describes both mind or soul and sensation or perception in physicalist terms. Soul and body are each made up of a certain mix of materials with their own proper innate motions. But even so, his account is not reductive, because human souls have some distinct abilities that are not accounted for in terms of their bodies alone. Timaeus says that the higher, more godly or intellectual part of the soul, if left to itself (as it is in the case of the gods) would follow the orderly motions of the circles of the Same in the cosmos – motions which produce the regular paths of the stars and of the cosmos as a whole. But when various impure ingredients are mixed to compose the soul of a human individual and then placed in a body, the human mind becomes confused and disordered. Its own inherently orderly motions become subject to the physical forces and motions of the body, which is composed of fire, earth, water and air. 'The motions produced by all these encounters would then be conducted to the soul and strike against it. (That is no doubt why these motions as a group came afterwards to be called "sensations".)' (43c4-7). Despite these negative influences of the body, as the soul matures and its body stops rapid growth, it can become calmer and more able to adhere to its innate orderly motions (44b4-7). Thus people, if well brought up, are able to stay healthy and sane.

Sight and hearing are described in more detail in 45b-47e, within a larger teleological context in which sight is said to enable humans to see the stars, which inspires us to begin philosophizing (47a2-4). Seeing is defined as the transmission of motions from an external object through the body to the soul (45c-d). Hearing also promotes rationality and graceful rhythmic motions, because it enables us to perceive musical harmony (47c-e).

Timaeus provides a more detailed physiological account of sense-perception within the section of the work that follows his introduction of the forces of Necessity, which are materially based or grounded. He says he must assume a view of the body and soul, and of sense-perception, in order to begin describing details of the physical bodies and features such as cold, hot, heavy, light, hard and soft (61c-dff.). Presumably this is because we know the physical features of the world through our various sensory capacities. Timaeus quickly moves on into an account of pleasure and pain (64a-b). He regards physical feelings of pain or pleasure as causal results of sensory processes rather than as themselves types of sense-perception. A pain, for example, is a disturbance 'passed on in a chain reaction ... until it reaches the center of consciousness and reports the property that produced the reaction' (64b3-6). Sensation occurs only when a disturbance is made in the more mobile parts of the body that are suited to passing it along; we do not feel pain in our less flexible physical parts like hair or bone. Sharp or strong disturbances of the body are painful, while returns to normalcy are pleasurable. This sounds like a variation of the replenishment model of pleasure. And Timaeus sums things up by discussing pains as alienations of or restorations to a normal state (65a-b).

All of our psychological or mental experiences of sensation clearly involve bodily organs including taste (65-6), smell (66-7), sound (67) and colour (67-8 ff.). Timaeus seems to be working out a psychological theory of pleasure that is physically grounded in the body and closely tied to the replenishment view. The reason that sensation is so closely linked to pleasure and pain is that sensation itself is a physical process, one that is more disruptive at some times than at others. Taste, for example, occurs due to contractions or dilations of the tongue having to do with objects that are rough or smooth, or that can stir around or intrude into its vessels (65d-66a). The sense organs here include some non-obvious ones: not just the eyes and ears, for example, but even the liver can play a role. Its dense and smooth surface can supposedly receive and return visual images sent from the mind 'like stamps', at times causing dreams and nightmares, and also grounding the possibility of divination (71b-e).

However, not all sensory processes are accompanied by pleasure or pain. Vision, for example, involves neither pleasure nor pain: 'Its perceptions are the more vivid and clear the more it is affected and the greater number of things it encounters ... for there is absolutely no violence involved ...' (64e1-4). This fact about vision contrasts with other sensations involving bodily parts comprising larger particles, which are subject to greater disruptions and restorations. Sometimes we are not aware of the depletion of some part, but its restoration is still noticeable, and this makes it pleasant, as with pleasant smells (65a6).

In the *Theaetetus* as we saw, Socrates considered pleasure and pain, along with emotions, as *types* of sensation. The *Timaeus* does not offer the same view, but instead explains that pleasure and pain arise from special conditions of sensory experience. The *Timaeus* seems to uphold the replenishment theory of pleasure by saying that the mental side of the relevant perception is simply the *perception of* the restoration of a natural and normal physical state. On the other hand, though, the *Timaeus*, like the *Theaetetus*, makes room for a more distinctively intentional view of pleasure and pain as mental experiences that involve thoughts or images. The physical processes that produce pleasure or pain must be registered by the soul or in consciousness. Not all pleasure is explained in terms of the replenishment view, since the relation of soul to body has been described in a much more complex way.

The *Timaeus*' theory is, of course, presented by a visitor who propounds his theory as only a 'likely story' (*eikôs mythos*). Without attributing this story to Plato himself, we can still judge that the account of pleasure in this dialogue is superior to the one sketched in the *Theaetetus*. Some evidence for this is the difference in characterization of the two dialogues' key figures. As a respected older scientist, Timaeus, the narrator, is likely to have a more sophisticated outlook than the bright but naïve young Theaetetus. Plato seems to indicate this to us through the way Socrates takes Theaetetus through a long and patient critique of his definition of knowledge as perception. This proposal is inadequate because it cannot account for the stability of either subjects or objects of knowledge. Timaeus's account fixes both of these flaws: in his view there is a unified soul which serves as the subject of mental phenomena, along with independently described (fairly) stable physical objects. Timaeus describes the principles of how physical objects behave and are known or sensed by human minds and perceptual organs. All of this is explained in as much detail as possible within a larger framing context describing the universe – both its design and purpose and all of its parts, ranging from Forms to purely material 'stuffs'.

Revisions of replenishment (C): false pleasures in the *Philebus*

The *Philebus*, like the *Theaetetus*, draws a link between pleasure or pain and various states that we would be more likely to describe as emotions, such as hope, fear, love, envy, malice, anger and so on (40e). The *Philebus* represents Plato's most sustained examination of the nature of pleasure. As I see it, this dialogue goes further with the project of developing a psychological account of pleasure. Here Plato develops a more sophisticated framework that can better account for the pleasures of learning than the *Republic* IX's replenishment view. The *Philebus* continues the pattern shown in the *Timaeus* of acknowledging that while both pleasure and pain are related to the body, they are not just a matter of physical states such as the disruption or restoration of harmony. The *Philebus*, like the *Timaeus*, investigates the mind/body relation. Plato accounts for pleasures and pains as events in the soul that are caused by, and that sometimes represent, bodily states. In a new development, it emerges here that there are some types of more purely mental pleasures: this is because pleasure and pain, as well as emotions, often involve imagination and thought. This recognition in turn paves the way for an improved account of the 'higher' pleasures of philosophy, art and poetry.

The *Philebus* presents a debate about whether the best life involves pleasure or intellect. Surprisingly, perhaps, for Plato, it turns out that *both* are needed; no one would want a life that contained intellect with no pleasure, nor vice versa. Various kinds of both knowledge and pleasure are recognized as essential 'if in fact our life is supposed to be some sort of *life*' (62c3-4).[8] Socrates proceeds by leading his interlocutor, Protarchus, into a consideration of the very nature of pleasure. He develops a typology of pleasure in which some pleasures are said to be 'false' and others 'true'. The false ones are bad and belong to bad people. Protarchus resists the idea that a pleasure can be false. To persuade him, Socrates carefully builds an analysis of pleasure and ultimately differentiates four types of false pleasure: (i) false pleasures involving mistaken judgement, (ii) false pleasures due to size distortion, (iii) false pleasures involving incorrect theory, and (iv) false pleasures that are mixed with pain. My focus here will be primarily on the first type.

Before examining false pleasures, it is worth noting that the *Philebus* offers a variation of the replenishment view of pleasure and pain that includes an important refinement. Socrates distinguishes two types of pain. Some pains arise in the body, such as cuts and burns, whereas others occur in the soul, such as anger or grief. Bodily pain is explained through the replenishment theory in the sense that pain and pleasure are described as involving the disruption or restoration of natural harmonies. As in *Republic* IX, Plato insists that such pleasures are fulfilments of lacks.

> What I claim is that when we find the harmony in living creatures disrupted, there will at the same time be a disintegration of their nature and a rise of pain.... But if the reverse happens, harmony is regained and the former nature restored, we have to say that pleasure arises ...
>
> 31d4-10

However, pain involves more than just the physical disruption of harmony. It also requires a *perception* of the disruption – just as was claimed in the *Timaeus*, where perception is the transmission of a physical disruption of an organ to the soul. Here again we see something more like a psychological theory according to which the mind or soul is involved in experiences of pleasure and pain – even when the relevant kinds of pleasure or pain are explicable in terms of replenishments.

Since the experience of pleasure or pain involves an awareness of trends in the body, or of effects in it that reach to the level of the soul, then 'perceptions' of pleasure or pain can reasonably seem very similar to sense-perceptions. Thus Socrates comments, 'But when the soul and body are jointly affected and moved by one and the same affection, if you call this motion perception, you would say nothing out of the way' (34a3-5). This echoes the *Theaetetus*, where Socrates counted pleasures and pains within the broader category of sense-perceptions. In the *Philebus*, Socrates explicitly corrects the claim that the soul is 'oblivious' (*apathês*) in cases where it is unaffected by the body. He says we should instead call this state 'nonperception' (*anaisthêsian*, 34a1). The *Philebus* revises the *Theaetetus*' view. In the *Theaetetus*, pleasure and pain were treated as having coordinated objects in the world. My pleasure now in a particular apple co-exists with the pleasingness of this apple to me. Both sides of this interaction are momentary happenings or appearances that might fit into a Heraclitean world of flux. But in the *Philebus*, perceptions are described in a more complex way with a more satisfactory ontology. The direct experience of a sensory object that is transmitted via the sense organ to a person results in the *soul's registering* of an internal bodily state. Such states belong to a presumably stable subject – the person uniting both soul and body. There are orderly and predictable transmissions of *pathê* from objects through organs to the soul.

In rare cases an unperceived disruption can be followed by the pleasurable awareness of whatever provides the relevant kind of fulfilment. Socrates identifies a category that he calls 'pure' pleasures that do not require any prior pains for our experience of them. These are said to be pleasures related to the perception of special sensory objects such as pure colours or fine scents (51b-e). For example, if I suddenly smell a lovely lilac bush while walking down the street in spring, this does not imply that I previously was deprived of such a smell or had the pain of needing it. Similarly, Socrates gets Protarchus to acknowledge that there are also pure pleasures of learning. People can have pleasures of learning although their prior ignorance is not attended with (or experienced as) pain. In a remark that seems a direct denial of the *Republic* IX account, Socrates contends that 'there is no such thing as hunger for learning ... nor any pains that have their source in a hunger for learning' (51e7-52a3). Here Plato amends the mistake of trying to force the replenishment model to accommodate pleasures of learning in *Republic* IX.

Socrates uses the modified account of pleasure as *perception by the soul* of a bodily restoration to help build his account of false pleasures. He argues that pleasure has a complex structure resembling a judgement, an activity occurring in the soul. This is a key point in Plato's development of what I have called the psychological view of pleasure. Socrates draws an analogy between judging and being pleased. If the object of a particular judgement is misrepresented, then the judgement is false. A parallel structure results in false pleasures. Socrates says that, 'whoever has any pleasure at all, however ill-founded it may be, really does have pleasure, even if sometimes it is not about anything that is the case or ever was the case, or often (or perhaps most of the time) refers to anything that ever will be the case' (40d7-10). Protarchus, not surprisingly, resists this analogy. He responds to Socrates by saying that, 'it's the judgement, not the pleasure, that's false.' Socrates concedes that the person having a false pleasure *is* actually pleased – just as the person making a false judgement *is* actually judging. However, Socrates insists, there is still something amiss with the pleasure in cases where a person is pleased *at* or *about* something false or mistaken.[9]

In order to clarify the problematic nature of both false judgements and pleasure, Socrates compares them to errors of visual identification. A person who sees something from afar might ask himself what he's seeing and say, 'It's a man', or 'It's a statue'. He could utter this judgement in a statement. Socrates compares the soul to a book (38e7), saying that memory and perception write in our minds like a scribe in a book (39a1-5). When our inner scribe writes the truth, we acquire true judgements. But now a second craftsman, a painter, can accompany the scribe by 'providing illustrations to his words in the soul' (39b6). This painter's illustrations can be true or false, just like the scribe's statements: 'And are not the pictures of the true judgements and assertions true, and the pictures of the false ones false?' (39c3-4). Images thus play a key role in the experience of pleasures – whether true or false. This is because images help specify the *content* of a pleasure – what that pleasure is *in* or *about*.

Notice how this argument works and why it explains the inferiority of false pleasures. The person who makes a judgement is asserting something in his soul through either a type of mental statement (something written) or a mental image (something drawn). If the inner statement or drawing is false, then the person is still judging, but falsely so. In the same way, the person who is having pleasure is in effect pleased at something asserted in the soul either via a statement or an image. It is true that when the person's experience of pleasure involves an internal statement or image that is *false*, he is still actually pleased, but the pleasure, like the judgement, is a false one. And here a key point emerges. True pleasures, or pleasures involving true thoughts or images, are better than false ones, those involving mistaken thoughts or images. In other words, *images can be a part of true pleasures*, the pleasures good people have. This indicates that Plato is no longer asserting the general claim that an image must always be deceptive, illusory and bad, as he had in, for example, the *Republic*. The inferiority of a false pleasure is not explained here in terms of it having an inferior ontological status.

But why is it exactly that good people will have true pleasures, ones where internal images represent reality correctly, whereas bad people's pleasures involve images that represent reality incorrectly? Socrates argues that false pleasures can include pleasures about the future or hoped-for pleasures. He claims that a good person is less subject to false pleasures, especially ones about the future, than a bad person. This claim is hard to interpret. Socrates might conceivably mean that the gods will reward moral behaviour by making good people's wishes come true. But such an interpretation seems implausible. His point is probably instead that good people have more sensible anticipations than bad people, since they are less prone to making false judgements. Such people have reason to receive the gods' blessings, whereas someone who is bad is sure of the opposite.[10] Socrates puts the point by saying that good men, for the most part, have the truth written in their minds and bad men have the opposite: 'So wicked people as a rule enjoy false pleasures, but the good among mankind true ones?' (40c1-2).

Socrates generalizes from pleasure to other sorts of states we would call emotions ('like fear, anger and the rest', 40d7-e7 *passim*). Here he seems, as in *Theaetetus*, to be grouping pleasures with emotions. He implies that a good person's emotions will, like his or her pleasures, be true. We could say that emotions are similar to pleasures and pains through belonging to the category of mental experiences (or experiences of the soul). Although Socrates does not explain in detail how his point about the existence of false pleasures can apply to other emotional states like fear or anger, it is not too hard to infer. Presumably fear or anger, like hope, involve something one says or pictures to oneself. I might get angry that my friend stood me up for our coffee date and picture her doing something she thinks is more fun. If that is true, my anger is also 'true' (we might say, 'justified'). But my picture might be false – if, say, she has had a bicycle accident and been taken to the hospital. Then my anger was also false and unjustified, and I might later have reason to regret it. Similarly, I might fear something falsely if I picture it happening, but in fact it will not. Of course, in both situations I do still have or feel the respective emotion, but Socrates would call such an emotion false because it is *about* something false. Presumably, as with false pleasures, the good person is less prone to experiencing false emotions, and thus will have a good life (or be more 'favoured by the gods').

This treatment of false pleasures of judgement is not the whole of Socrates' account of false pleasures in the *Philebus*. Socrates discusses other kinds of false pleasure, some related to mistaken estimations of size and others resting on a mistaken account of the nature of pleasure.[11] I will not examine either type in detail here, but in those cases too Plato appears to assume that pleasures involve aboutness or intentionality.

The final sections of the *Philebus* work towards the conclusion that the best life for a human requires a mix of knowledge with pleasure, along with the acknowledgment that some pleasures – pure and true ones – are good. Even Socrates admits that no one would want any forms of knowledge without getting their associated pleasures (60d-3). Inexact forms of science or knowledge are also necessary for a good life (62b). The best life includes pure and intellectual pleasures along with more ordinary ones – such as the pleasure of being able to find one's way home. Socrates and Protarchus construct a recipe for the good life by finding the proper mixture of 'the fountain of pleasure, comparable to honey, and the sobering fountain of intelligence, free of wine, like sober, healthy water' (61c5-7). Of course, not every pleasure should be mixed with every kind of intelligence. Some pleasures, like some arts, are truer than others (61d). A well-off person needs to know not only the true definitions of concepts in geometry and astronomy but also about *human* spheres and circles as used, for instance, in housebuilding (62a-b). Next, Protarchus and Socrates allow in the true pleasures, followed by the necessary pleasures (62e-63a). The highest kinds of knowledge are asked, a bit fancifully, what kinds of pleasures they need or would welcome. Their answer is that they do not seek the most intense pleasures, which 'infect the souls in which they dwell with madness and even prevent our own development altogether' (63d4-e1). But they regard true pleasures as their 'kin' and also welcome the pleasures of health and temperance (63d-e).

Conclusion: pleasure, perception and images in art

I have surveyed some of Plato's accounts of pleasure, focusing on its relationship with perception, in order to trace certain changes he appears to make in his fundamental view. The dialogues I have considered – *Phaedo*, *Republic*, *Theaetetus*, *Timaeus* and *Philebus* – are, it goes without saying, very different from one another. Their subject matters vary significantly, as do their characters, settings, and mode of presentation. The *Phaedo* shows Socrates on the day of his death discussing the question of immortality. After engaging in various arguments intended to persuade his friends that we should not fear death, Socrates comforts his visitors in jail with a final 'swan song', his story about the afterlife, before bravely drinking the hemlock and dying. The *Theaetetus* is presented as a dialogue that occurred in the distant past between Socrates and the young Theaetetus, who became a distinguished geometer but is now dying after valiant service in war. Socrates gently leads Theaetetus to see mistakes in his proposed account of knowledge as perception. The *Timaeus* does not feature Socrates as its main spokesman, but rather Timaeus, a famous visiting astronomer. He presents a 'likely story' about the construction of the universe and creation of human beings. And finally, the *Philebus* recounts a debate between Socrates, proponent of the life of the mind, and Protarchus, who defends pleasure as the primary ingredient of the best life. After an extended examination even Socrates is forced to admit that both pleasure and intellect play a role in the best life.

Despite their many differences in subject and setting, these dialogues share three basic concerns: defining pleasure, assessing its role in the good life, and explaining how it arises in human individuals comprised of a soul and a body. Some scholars would account for their differences through a developmentalist theory, reasoning that these dialogues were composed at different times in Plato's life and that his ideas improved over time.[12] While I am not taking a definite stand on this issue, I do think that some of Plato's treatments of pleasure are more sophisticated than others. I have argued that the replenishment view breaks down when applied to the higher pleasures of philosophy, art, and poetry. The psychological account of pleasure is more complex and philosophically satisfying.

The *Phaedo* and the *Philebus* represent the more extreme variations of Plato's two views on pleasure, with the replenishment view predominating in the former, and the psychological view in the latter. In the two other dialogues I focused on, the *Theaetetus* and the *Timaeus*, Plato worked out a more complex psychological theory of pleasure as part of his pursuit of the question that is central to the *Phaedo*: what is the soul of a person, and what is its connection to a body? Despite the fact that the *Theaetetus*'s main topic is defining knowledge, it provides a thorough scrutiny of the nature of human perception. Socrates shows his young colleague that perceptions must be grounded in a unitary subject and achieve some stability in order to count as genuine knowledge. We could say that one account of the requisite sort of stability is provided by the astronomer Timaeus in the dialogue bearing his name. His 'likely story' narrates how human souls were created and placed in bodies with varied perceptual organs that would enable us to obtain genuine knowledge of Forms and the heavens, and to some extent also of the physical universe around us, if we live in accordance with virtue and order. The *Theaetetus* and the *Timaeus* provide a more robust framework to account for pleasure by scrutinizing how it is related to perceptions, sense-organs, emotions, and other sorts of psychological states such as dreams and hallucinations.

Plato's detailed examinations of pleasure result in a change in the way it is valued, along with how it is conceptualized. In the *Phaedo*, Socrates denounces physical pleasures because of their intrinsic links to pain. They threaten our soul's ability to focus on its true ends. But his story at the end indicates that there are better, more genuine pleasures – those associated with 'higher' forms of sight and hearing that we can aspire to in life after death or 'on the surface of the earth.' In the *Theaetetus*, pleasure is treated as a kind of perceptual experience. Its objects are fleeting and so it does not offer the kind of stability required for knowledge. Interestingly though, because it is a kind of perception, pleasure does appear to afford us some awareness of the external world. The *Timaeus* spells out a more complex mind-body relationship in which some sense-perceptions and affiliated pleasures are highly valued because they inspire our souls to obtain wisdom about the universe. Finally, the *Philebus* describes pleasures of true judgement – ones that involve an experience of something that is true. This claim can be interpreted in different ways, but of these, I think that the simplest is right: a true pleasure is the experience of being pleased at – having thoughts or images of – something that is really the case.

In the dialogues surveyed here I believe we can find evidence weighing against certain commonly accepted views about Plato's attitudes towards pleasure and images, particularly based on his account of tragedy in *Republic* X. It is not true that Plato always and in every circumstance denies the value of sense-perception, nor does he maintain that pleasure is always suspicious and untrustworthy because it is linked to bodily appetites. Finally, he does not argue that images are inevitably dangerous and misleading.

How does the psychological view of pleasures affect our understanding of Plato's critique of art and poetry in *Republic* X? I have not focused in detail here on the *Republic*, but its critique of art deserves another look. Jessica Moss has argued that Plato's critique of tragedy in Book X turns upon the appetitive nature of the interest and pleasure that we humans derive from poetic images.[13] On her view, Plato bans tragic art from the ideal state because the strong responses it can evoke, even in good people, derive from the lower parts of the soul. She takes it that spirit and appetite, the lower parts, have pleasure as their goal, in contrast to the rational part's desires, which aim at the good. The critique of art rests on the limited nature of the kind of pleasure it provides. Moss thus explains the moral criticism of tragedy's power in terms of the epistemic defects of spiritive and appetitive pleasures. Since artists and poets appeal to the senses and lack genuine knowledge, they create products that *Republic* X describes as illusions or mere appearances, in contrast to real truths. Moss claims that Plato regards 'desires for pleasures as slaves to appearances'. The lower pleasures do not have objects that are genuinely good.

Moss's argument seems prima facie plausible, but it has some significant weaknesses. First, it dissociates pleasure altogether from the good by treating all pleasure as appetitive or spiritive and hence as having illusory goods as their objects. But there are numerous passages in the *Republic* and elsewhere in which Plato recognizes some pleasures (and desires, we must presume) as being appropriate to a philosophical soul. I have mentioned such passages in *Phaedo, Timaeus, Philebus,* and elsewhere. The valuable pleasures of the rational part of soul cannot sensibly be understood to be confined to appetites or physical senses, nor interpreted as occupied only with illusions and appearances.

Second, Moss's account ignores the fact that not only does Socrates leave the door open for a defence of poetry in *Republic* X, but actually recommends the inclusion of certain types of poetry in the education of the young guardians in *Republic* III. Children should be entertained with stories of heroes acting virtuously because through imitating such people they will acquire virtue. They should be surrounded by poetry, images, and music that illustrate grace and nobility, 'so that something of these fine works will strike their eyes and ears like a breeze that brings health from a good place' (401c). The city will admit, then, 'the pure imitator of a decent person' (397d). These remarks from Book III are not anomalous. Even despite what I have criticized as the forced application of the replenishment account to the pleasures of learning in *Republic* IX, Socrates recognizes that there are both desires and pleasures appropriate to the rational part of the soul. The replenishment theory works better to explain bodily desires for 'mere' sensory gratification, but in Book IX Socrates applies it to the higher desires – even those associated with the love of philosophy. Pleasures of learning are said to be superior to bodily pleasures because their objects have more being or truth. Moss wants to say that all desire for pleasure is problematic because it (a) belongs to the lower parts of the soul, (b) derives from or is tied closely to sense experience, and (c) aims at objects qua pleasant, as opposed to good. But *Republic* IX describes pleasures that (a) belong to higher parts of the soul, (b) derive from or are linked to thoughts instead of, or in addition to, sense experience, and (c) aim at the good.

The *Republic*, then, clearly does allow for pleasure to belong to the rational part of the soul and to be associated with such positive objects as knowledge and truth. But can these objects include art and poetry? The natural response would be yes – so long as these present pictures or stories that are truthful and genuinely good. In the *Republic* IX, such goodness is equated with possessing large amounts of reality or being. But Socrates himself rejects the relevance of the replenishment model to intellectual pleasures in the *Philebus* when he denies that there is an actual 'hunger' for knowledge. The superiority of the objects of intellectual pleasure is not sensibly explained by their being more 'real' – as if they provide more nutriments to the empty stomach of the mind. Higher pleasures must be superior in some other respect. To explain this point is, I have argued in this chapter, precisely the motivation behind Plato's lengthy search for an account of pleasure to supersede the replenishment account. On what I have called the psychological account, Plato no longer has the same dualism of soul and body that results in a dualism of desires for the merely pleasant vs the good, as Moss alleges he has in the *Republic*. On the psychological account, more valuable pleasures are those taken in or about goods which are now not understood as having more reality (whatever that would mean), but as being more genuinely fulfilling to a human being. And when this human being is understood as a composite whole including soul and body, as in the *Philebus*, the valuable pleasures include true and pure ones of many types, including those associated with sensory experience, practical activity, the moral life, and learning. It is reasonable to suppose that the good and balanced life would also include pleasures we derive from truthful images presented to us by artists, tragedians, and philosophical authors like Plato himself.

Notes

1. There is a considerable literature on pleasure in Plato. I have benefited in particular from J.C.B. Gosling and C.C.W. Taylor, *The Greeks on Pleasure* (Oxford: Clarendon Press, 1982); Dorothea Frede, 'Introductory Essay', in *Plato, Philebus, Translated with Introduction* (Indianapolis: Hackett, 1993), xiii–lxxx; C.C.W. Taylor, *Plato: Protagoras,* translated with notes (Oxford: Clarendon Plato series, 1976); and Henrik Lorenz, *The Brute Within: Desire in Plato and Aristotle* (Oxford: Oxford University Press, 2006).
2. For further detailed arguments to this effect, see John M. Cooper, 'Plato's Theory of Human Good in the *Philebus*', *Journal of Philosophy* 74, no. 11 (1977): 714–30.
3. See Jessica Moss, 'Pleasure and Illusion in Plato', *Philosophy and Phenomenological Research* 72, no. 3 (2006): 503–35.
4. Plato needs what later thinkers will begin to distinguish as pleasures of process vs. pleasures of activity – Aristotle with his *kinêsis/energeia* distinction, the Stoics with the kinetic/katastêmatic distinction; for more, see Gosling and Taylor, *The Greeks on Pleasure*.
5. For an overview of the dialogue as a whole, see Zina Giannopoulou, 'Plato: Theaetetus', in *Internet Encyclopedia of Philosophy*; http://www.iep.utm.edu/theaetetu/.discussions, accessed 31 May 2014.
6. Whether the linkages among P, M and F are correct or not has been disputed among commentators, but I will not pursue the issue here. See John Cooper 'Plato on Sense-Perception and Knowledge (*Theaetetus* 184-186)', *Phronesis* 15, no. 1 (1970). 123–46; G.J. Fine, 'Knowledge and Logos in the *Theaetetus*', *Philosophical Review* 88 (1979): 366–97; and M.F. Burnyeat, 'Introduction', in *The Theaetetus of Plato*, trans. M.J. Levett (Indianapolis: Hackett, 1990).
7. See M.F. Burnyeat, 'Plato on the Grammar of Perceiving', *Classical Quarterly* 26 (1976): 29–51.
8. See Cooper, 'Plato's Theory of Human Good'.
9. Sylvain Delcomminette differentiates two aspects of a pleasure: 'the pleasure itself and what the pleasure is about (the content of the pleasure)', in 'False Pleasure, Appearance and Imagination in the *Philebus*,' *Phronesis* 48, no. 3 (2003): 215–37; see especially p. 219.
10. For more discussion, see Verity Harte, 'The *Philebus* on Pleasure: the Good, the Bad and the False', *Proceedings of the Aristotelian Society* 104, no. 2 (2004): 113–30.
11. See Cynthia Freeland, 'Nearer means Bigger: Artistic imitations and pleasure-illusions in *Republic* IX, X and the *Philebus*', *Norsk filosofisk tidsskrift* 43, no. 2 (2008)): 137–47; and also my 'Plato's *Philebus*: Pleasure, Imagination, and Poetry', *Norsk filosofisk tidsskrift* 42, no. 1-2 (2007): 54–62.
12. For one version of the developmentalist account separating strands of Plato's thought into various periods, see Gregory Vlastos, *Socrates, Ironist and Moral Philosopher* (Cambridge: Cambridge University Press, 1991). For critical discussion, see Charles H. Kahn, *Plato and the Socratic Dialogue* (Cambridge: Cambridge University Press, 1996); and Julia Annas and Christopher Rowe, eds., *New Perspectives on Plato, Modern and*

Ancient, Center for Hellenic Studies Colloquia 6 (Cambridge: Harvard University Press, 2002).
13 Subtle versions of these theses are defended by Moss in 'Pleasure and Illusion in Plato', cited above, and also in Jessica Moss, 'Pictures and Passions', in *Plato and the Divided Self*, ed. R. Barney, C. Brittain and T. Brennan (Cambridge: Cambridge University Press, 2011), 259–80. It would lead me too far astray to provide a detailed critique of Moss here. I believe that her interpretation is too oriented to a particular account of the *Republic*, according to which appetitive desire is necessarily linked to both deceptive sense-perception and the problematic pursuit of pleasure, while the higher part of the soul aims not at pleasure but at the good. Moss ignores the metaphysical critique in the *Theaetetus*, the more sophisticated psycho-physical views of the *Timaeus* and *Philebus*, and the ways in which sense-perception and images can function beneficially in both works. She also neglects altogether the revised estimation of pleasure's role in the best life in the *Philebus*.

Bibliography

Annas, Julia and Christopher Rowe, eds. *New Perspectives on Plato, Modern and Ancient*. Center for Hellenic Studies Colloquia 6. Cambridge: Harvard University Press, 2002.

Burnyeat, M.F. 'Introduction'. In *The Theaetetus of Plato*. Translated by M.J. Levett. Indianapolis: Hackett, 1990.

Burnyeat, M.F. 'Plato on the Grammar of Perceiving'. *Classical Quarterly* 26 (1976): 29–51.

Cooper, John M. 'Plato's Theory of Human Good in the *Philebus*'. *Journal of Philosophy* 74, no. 11 (1977): 714–30.

Cooper, John M. 'Plato on Sense-Perception and Knowledge (*Theaetetus* 184–186)'. *Phronesis* 15, no. 1 (1970): 123–46.

Delcomminette, Sylvain. 'False Pleasure, Appearance and Imagination in the *Philebus*'. *Phronesis* 48, no. 3 (2003): 215–37.

Fine, G.J., 'Knowledge and Logos in the *Theaetetus*'. *Philosophical Review* 88 (1979): 366–97.

Frede, Dorothea. 'Introductory Essay'. In *Plato, Philebus*. Translated with Introduction, xiii–lxxx. Indianapolis: Hackett, 1993.

Freeland, Cynthia. 'Nearer means Bigger: Artistic imitations and pleasure-illusions in *Republic* IX, X and the *Philebus*'. *Norsk filosofisk tidsskrift* 43, no. 2 (2008): 137–47.

Freeland, Cynthia. 'Plato's *Philebus*: Pleasure, Imagination, and Poetry'. *Norsk filosofisk tidsskrift* 42, no. 1–2 (2007): 54–62.

Giannopoulou, Zina. 'Plato: Theaetetus'. In *Internet Encyclopedia of Philosophy*; http://www.iep.utm.edu/theatetu/.discussions, accessed 31 May 2014.

Gosling, J.C.B. and C.C.W. Taylor. *The Greeks on Pleasure*. Oxford: Clarendon Press, 1982.

Harte, Verity. 'The *Philebus* on Pleasure: the Good, the Bad and the False'. *Proceedings of the Aristotelian Society* 104, no. 2 (2004): 113–30.

Kahn, Charles H. *Plato and the Socratic Dialogue*. Cambridge: Cambridge University Press, 1996.

Lorenz, Henrik. *The Brute Within: Desire in Plato and Aristotle*. Oxford: Oxford University Press, 2006.

Moss, Jessica. 'Pleasure and Illusion in Plato'. *Philosophy and Phenomenological Research* 72, no. 3 (2006): 503–35.

Moss, Jessica. 'Pictures and Passions'. In *Plato and the Divided Self*. Edited by R. Barney, C. Brittain and T. Brennan, 259–80. Cambridge: Cambridge University Press, 2011.

Plato: Complete Works. Edited by John M. Cooper. Indianapolis: Hackett, 1997.

Taylor, C.C.W. *Plato: Protagoras. Translated with Notes*. Clarendon Plato series. Oxford: Oxford University Press, 1976.

Vlastos, Gregory. *Socrates, Ironist and Moral Philosopher*. Cambridge: Cambridge University Press: 1991.

10

The Limits of Rationality in Plato's *Phaedo*

Hallvard Fossheim

Introduction

While most of Plato's dialogues reserve a place for irrationality as an irreducible aspect of human psychology, the *Phaedo* has in one way been treated as a rational cousin in the family. This is due to a focus on the sophisticated and complex nature of the arguments regarding soul, identity and causation, an overlapping series of topics that has provoked much interest. Matching these arguments on the dialogue's dramatic level, the serene nature of Socrates' death has caused us to extol the nobly rational nature of this martyr to philosophy, in discussions sometimes tempered by changing understandings of which drug was used and what are its actual effects.[1] Perhaps more importantly, the picture of the soul presupposed for the arguments is that of a unitary and pure entity, inherently active and in perfect alignment with itself.[2]

Together, these interests and perspectives amount to holding the soul in this dialogue to be a rational entity. Whereas the *Republic*, for instance, undeniably presents an irrationalism of the soul in that most of the soul is irrationally motivated as well as unreflective, the *Phaedo* can accordingly be thought to provide an antithesis of this picture. I aim to show that this text ultimately presents a vision of reason as weak, secondary and dependent on a framework of non-rational forces.

In what follows, I first establish that the text of the *Phaedo* primes the reader to focus on the centrality and ambiguous force of emotion, before I show how this connects with the text's foregrounding of its own status as a *mythos* or fable. A gradual reduction of reason is traced through indications of the underlying moral psychology limiting human access to knowledge, most notably the dialogue's notion of the 'child inside' and what I shall call a mimetic impulse. Together, these elements provide a re-orienting framework for the question of optimism or pessimism on behalf of human rationality in the *Phaedo*, and a basis for understanding the role of the so-called hypothetical method in this particular dialogue.

Ambiguous feelings

The *Phaedo* straddles two extremes in Plato's authorship. On the one hand, it offers a rather concentrated package of sophisticated arguments. On the other hand, in dramatizing the death of Socrates and the reactions of those present, the *Phaedo* constitutes what is perhaps the most violently emotional setting that we have from Plato. I will argue that this very contrast constitutes the *Phaedo*'s possibly most important philosophical contribution, in that the two elements – reason and the irrational – are juxtaposed in such a way that optimism on behalf of reason is undermined.

In building this argument, I will take as a point of departure that we cannot ignore the specific dramatics of the *Phaedo*. The drama in the dialogue shows how even the most abstract arguments take place in a particular setting, among a certain group of individuals, at a given point in their life stories. Beyond the general feature of being a dialogue with interacting characters, what is specific to the *Phaedo* is not least that it offers a dramatization of grief. Before looking into what this means for the dialogue, however, let us consider a couple of pointers provided early on in the framing dialogue. Before getting into the details of his story, Phaedo chooses to give Echecrates a rather special perspective on the significance of what happened the day Socrates died. Echecrates has not asked for it, but Phaedo articulates his own – that is, Phaedo's own – emotive reactions on the day.

> That is why I had no feeling of pity, for the man appeared happy both in manner and words as he died nobly and without fear, Echecrates, so that it struck me that even in going down to the underworld he was going with the gods' blessing and that he would fare well when he got there, if anyone ever does. That is why I had no feeling of pity, such as would seem natural in my sorrow, nor indeed of pleasure, as we engaged in philosophical discussion as we were accustomed to do – for our arguments were of that sort – but I had a strange feeling, an unaccustomed mixture of pleasure and pain at the same time as I reflected that he was just about to die. All of us present were affected in much the same way, sometimes laughing, then weeping; especially one of us, Apollodorus – you know the man and his ways.
>
> 58e-59a; G.M.A. Grube's translation is used throughout

Apollodorus of Phalerum is also known to us as the volatile person acting as one among several links to the reader for the tale of the *Symposium*.[3] For our present purposes, what I want to emphasize is only that emotion, analysed partly in terms of pleasure and pain, is introduced to us near the beginning of the text. On the face of it, nothing much is made of this. But remember that the whole of the *Phaedo* is about whether death is to be feared or not as the end of the soul, or perhaps even welcomed. All the arguments that follow are motivated by this concern on the part of those present.

The issues of emotive reactions, of grief, fear and pity in the face of death are brought on once more when the scene at the prison is introduced. After having waited around for much of the day, his followers are finally allowed to meet Socrates.

> We found Socrates recently released from his chains, and Xanthippe – you know her – sitting by him, holding their baby. When she saw us, she cried out and said the sort of thing that women usually say: 'Socrates, this is the last time your friends will talk to you and you to them.' Socrates looked at Crito. 'Crito,' he said, 'let someone take her home.'
>
> 60a

Once more, we are reminded not only that someone is about to die, but that grief is the reaction of the other characters to what is happening. Xanthippe's reaction is not the unacceptable troublemaking of a particularly mean-spirited person, but well within the range of a wife and co-parent's expected and understandable reactions.[4] A string of elements thus contributes to establishing a focus on emotive reactions. That tendency develops further with Socrates' first words. Without any obvious link to the content of the ensuing discussion, and without a cue from anything said by others, Socrates says the following.

> 'What a strange thing that which men call pleasure seems to be, and how astonishing the relation it has with what is thought to be its opposite, namely pain! A man cannot have both at the same time. Yet if he pursues and catches the one, he is almost always bound to catch the other also, like two creatures with one head.'
>
> 60b

To say that these passages form natural parts of a text about someone dying does not provide a sufficient explanation for their inclusion in the drama. Pain, pleasure, grief, pity, fear: there is no doubt that the episode could have been conveyed without mentioning any of them. Clearly, their presence is motivated on Plato's part. I suggest that at least part of the reason for their inclusion is to prime us to think of our status as emotive creatures. Plato is reminding us of, and at the same time activating in us, something pertinent to the dialogue as a whole.

A further element too has already been quoted but not commented on. This is the fact that the nature of pleasure and pain has, by Socrates' statement, been held up for us as the dialogue's first puzzle. Even though not much has been said at this point, Plato has made sure to include a puzzle among the few things that have been said. For notice that Phaedo had characterized his experience as a 'mixture of pleasure and pain'. And here is Socrates claiming that 'a man cannot have both [pleasure and pain] at the same time'. The two persons musing on their experiences of the situation seem to face us with mutually contradictory reports about basic emotive reactions. Certainly, Phaedo and Socrates providing conflicting claims about the phenomenology of pleasure and pain is part of a design that adds direction to the text without simply being dictated by the situation.

This is not to say that this particular question is the ultimate topic of the dialogue, or that the question receives a final answer in the course of the text. But by giving us a possible contradiction on the obviously central matter of emotions, one that seems to be significant for understanding what emotion is, the author has taken care to make us focus on and puzzle over it.

Fables and mimetic impulses

What is unfolding in these early parts of the *Phaedo* is not only argument, but fable and argument, to use Socrates' own distinction, at this very point in the text, between *mythos* and *logos*. Cebes asks what induced Socrates to write poetry after he came to the prison (60c–d). Socrates has indeed been 'putting the fables of Aesop into verse and composing the hymn to Apollo' (60d). Socrates explains this by referring to a recurring dream. He had previously taken it for granted that the divine dream's injunction to him to 'practice and cultivate the arts' had meant 'practice and cultivate the art of philosophy' – argument (*logos*). Now, in light of the presumably divine intervention causing the delay in his execution, he has begun to worry whether the god meant poetry – realized specifically as fables (*mythoi*) (60e-61b).[5] Again, we are given a seemingly accidental piece of information to help us see what is at stake; this time, it serves to highlight that what is of importance in the text is not only argument but also story.

Besides foregrounding the phenomenon of poetic composition as an art, the answer given by Socrates is at the same time among the most dignifying references to what we might call the production of fiction that exist in the Platonic corpus. Socrates is open to the possibility that the dream meant he should take up poetry, thus holding poetic production to be a believable runner-up to philosophy. His openness is an indication in its own right that drama is something to take seriously. It is difficult not to see this as also a comment on Plato's own activity in writing the *Phaedo*. As such, the foregrounding of poetic production serves as a reminder that one is reading a work of philosophy which is simultaneously argument and fable. From the very beginning, then, we are made to think of emotions, of pleasures and pains, and we are made to think of them as present in a story.

The use of a *mythos* to communicate emotion is also a way of activating emotion. Not only does the text of the *Phaedo* portray grief by creating a dramatic setting where Socrates' death causes others to lose themselves in sorrow. An analogous impact takes place on the level of the reader, in that the reader is made to experience an emotive reaction to the event along with exposure to philosophical arguments. While being exposed to arguments concerning the soul, and talk about the need to better one's soul in order to rise above irrationality, one at the same time experiences oneself both as an intellectual being, critically analysing the arguments, and as an emotive, irrational being, sensing the drama of Socrates' execution. Whether this is best thought of as a test of one's individual qualities or as a reminder of human limitations, the result is that as a reader of the dialogue, one experiences both aspects of one's dual nature as this is both expounded and dramatized in the text. In this elegant fashion, what is dealt with in the *Phaedo* is also activated in the reader. At the very least, this acts as a helper and reminder of the issues and of what is at stake.

The *Phaedo* also includes a specific illustration of a mechanism by which our irrational nature works. A crucial aspect of grief, as of other emotions, is its social power. In this respect, the *Phaedo* clearly displays the workings of what we might call a mimetic emotional impulse. 'Apollodorus had not ceased from weeping before, and at this moment his noisy tears and anger made everybody present break down, except Socrates' (117d). The setting apart of Socrates' response, while indicating an ideal beyond familiar human agency, also serves to emphasize the universality of the others' responses. Of particular interest in this respect is the claim that it is Apollodorus' display of grief and anger which makes the others enter into their own similar reactions. This adds to the picture of human agents as emotive, dependent and heteronomous. Overall, this mimetic impulse acts as one barrier among many to the ideal of rationality expounded by Socrates, and as a mode by which irrationality takes over the individual. The side of emotion made prominent in this sequence is not simply its function as a response to events or situations, but its spreading like some elemental force among people.

The emotive division between Socrates and all the others develops, on the moral psychological level, a seeming dualism in the *Phaedo*'s characters: rationality, controlling one part of their thoughts and behaviour, vying with irrationality, emotionally charged and partly mimetic in structure. Notice, however, that even the philosopher (Socrates) has an emotive presence, but one which renders him calm and friendly.[6] The dramatic dimension of the argument thus demonstrates how two principles, soul parts, or psychological aspects are activated together. Furthermore, the relation between reasoned argument and emotive reaction does not amount to the either-or of two independent and opposing systems. Their mutual dependence shows already in how the story or situation engenders an emotive reaction, which in turn dictates the theme as well as the tenor of the discussion. As we shall see, the radical infiltration of the two moral psychological principles is revealed also by other means.

Hypotheses and charms

Socrates famously states that practising philosophy in the right way is practising dying and death (64a, 67d-e). This means not only learning not to fear death, although this too is part of philosophy. The basis for not fearing death is not having reason to fear it, because one has managed to free one's soul from the body. Without this, one would still both *be* and *think of* oneself as an embodied being, that is, a being which will be destroyed upon death. Death is deeply unenviable for such a person. Depending on how one lives, one can further contribute to tying oneself – one's soul – to the body, through habits and modes of thinking and living, or one can live the life of a philosopher and hope to escape all that. The characters in the *Phaedo* have an ideal to live up to which they, with the possible exception of Socrates, do not manage to realize in the dialogue's drama.[7] The central virtues – moderation, courage, wisdom and justice – each have a shadow version which is bodily, and a real version that is proper to the perfected philosopher. The shadow version is the 'popular and social virtue' coming about by habit and practice in the case of, for instance, moderation and justice (82a-b). This is only to say that what apparently decent non-philosophers take to be central virtues are not really virtues, or not real virtues, because they do not properly involve reason (69a-c). Accordingly, even those who have practised such social virtue will often return to bodily form in a lower species. Similarly, mystic rites are evoked throughout as suitable similes to the process of perfection.[8] This points to transcending mere human life for an existence that in the *Phaedo* is divine and found, if ever, in death.

The fearful 'child in us'[9] is thus best understood as part of the non-perfected economy of what we might call the bodified (rather than merely embodied) soul. The figure of the child inside is introduced in order to uncover what motivates Simmias and Cebes to require insurances concerning what happens to the soul at death. The child's foremost explicit quality is fear of death and dying. In this, the 'inner child' is ruled by pleasure and pain, which is to say that the figure constitutes an irrational aspect of the non-perfected, bodified soul. Each pleasure and pain 'makes the soul corporeal' (83d), which in turn connects it further to pleasure and pain as its way of existing (e.g., 84a).[10]

Cebes introduces the 'child in us' in order to articulate the experience of still holding on to a fear of death, in spite of having been rationally convinced that there is no cause for such a fear. With the possible exception of Socrates, it seems we all have such an inner child in need of comfort.[11] What is particularly striking, however, is what form the comfort takes. Says Socrates, 'You should . . . sing a charm (*epaidein*) over him every day until you have charmed away his fears' (77e). Why is this charm necessary? One might think that the charm is necessary only because of personal weakness on the part of some minority of failed individuals. The text very clearly suggests another understanding. The famous, long myth (starting at 107d) is the dialogue's strongest candidate for a charm – an image as placeholder for firm arguments, and a vision of a just cosmos. That myth is not introduced simply because of specific individuals' weakness (although that too plays into it), but because arguments are not sufficient on their own (107a-b).

The dramatic progression, from argument to myth, is also a sort of psychological regression. This development has everything to do with what sort of argument – or, rather, what sort of methodological framework for arguments – is proffered. The approach in question, hypothetical method, is contested in the literature and seems to be displayed differently in the various texts where scholars have identified it. In the *Phaedo*, the approach usually identified with hypothetical method only arrives as an alternative once Socrates sees that he cannot discover the cosmic or universal causes of coming-to-be, existence, and destruction.[12] Socrates avows he 'was deprived and could neither discover it myself nor learn it from another' (99c-d), and only at this point did the method enter the scene as a second best way of searching. Its introduction already bears the mark of a forced resignation from the ambition of obtaining clear and direct access to principles and rational understanding.[13]

The forced move to a hypothetical method implies the following approach: 'taking as my hypothesis in each case the theory that seemed to me the most compelling, I would consider as true, about cause and everything else, whatever agreed with this, and as untrue whatever did not so agree' (100a). Further investigation is then needed to see whether a given hypothesis yields contradiction, and to provide an account of the hypothesis in terms of another hypothesis (100d).[14] As hypothetical arguments, they seem to be incapable of securing absolute and safe knowledge, in that the investigation can only reveal impossibilities or incongruities.[15]

Not only does the method arise as an alternative that is at best a second option. There are at least two related considerations leading one to suspect that the very nature of the method rules out the sort of certainty for which the interlocutors were originally hoping. First, considered in isolation, the logic of the investigation and its results do not inherently include any point of direct or naïve confirmation that one has actually grasped the truths about the objects in question. This principled insecurity is mirrored in Socrates' wording, as he does not speak of entailment from higher hypotheses – or ultimately from something non-hypothetical – but only of agreement or harmony.[16]

Second, and perhaps more disconcertingly, even this approach is not trusted to work on its own. One might think of the relations between experience of the world and intellectual development as being of such a sort that, having worked through the cumbersome process of tracing agreement and disagreement, whatever the world and the process in the end allowed to remain standing would indeed be the truth. The need for charms, however, would appear to undermine all of this. It seems one can have a hope of success, or even of moving safely in the right direction, only by embedding one's search in a vision of one's (popular-variety virtuous) wishes, articulated as one or several convoluted myths or fables. While this is not to say that humans cannot be rational, it does seem to imply that our argumentative rationality (with the possible exception of wonders like Socrates)[17] is embedded in and depends on something other than itself. If so, the trouble acknowledged in the *Phaedo*'s use of invocations and hypothetical method is not simply about some individual's psychological shortcomings, but finds its root in the fact that there are no non-hypothetical arguments, or approaches void of mythology, available which could do the job of securing knowledge for us.

Inspired by the metaphor of the 'second sailing' often invoked in articles about the *Phaedo*,[18] we can thus perhaps speak about two *waves* in enumerating what I take to be its two consecutive reductions of the place and power of reason and rationality. After first having been reduced to hypothetical status (the first wave), arguments must give way to fables because the former are powerless to provide a firm footing on crucial questions about causality or the soul (the second wave). The metaphor is apt, because while Plato does not present them in nautical terms, the reductions act as waves in the sense that they spread through the text in a way that quietly undermines the claims of reason proffered by Socrates and the others, and so the prospects for at least the broad majority of human beings as rational beings.

This state of affairs also suggests that the relation between reason and an irrational part comprising the 'child within' is universal, because reason – even Socrates' reason – is not capable of independently reaching truth on the most important matters. Reason *needs* techniques directed at the other aspects of soul in order to ground its domain of arguments. With the presentation of the myth, with its detailed geography and moral map of the world, we see Socrates reverting to what he, just previously, said no longer interests him: 'When I was a young man I was wonderfully keen on that wisdom which they call natural science' (96a). By the end of the dialogue, after what seemed like promises to leave such things behind, Socrates is back to speculating about the Earth's middle position in the cosmos (109a) without providing much by way of argument for it,[19] and even less for the claims that follow. The inner child is not some unfortunate psychological factor realistically to be overcome. On the contrary, it seems one is apparently forced to regress to it in order to move closer to truth and knowledge.

If so, it is no wonder that Socrates inserts a specific reminder not to let oneself turn into a misologue (89d) when one finds out that the arguments simply are not capable to do what they were supposed to do. This is a timely reminder, coming as it does before seemingly solid arguments give way to hypotheticals which again yield to myth. By the end of the dialogue, the moralizing myth is described as a *belief worth risking* – nothing more (114d). Put differently, the *Phaedo* is constructed so as not only to present arguments, but to put argument and reason in their place. The putatively sound, abstract arguments give way to hypotheses, which in turn depend on myth and charms to do their work, in the dialogue's final wave undermining autonomous rationality in catering to our inner child. Perhaps paradoxically, the conclusion of all of these considerations is not so much that there is some basic battle between reason and emotion, with emotion coming out on the winning side, but that reason is inherently dependent on those other forces and resources.

Conclusion

Plato's use of the dialogue form makes it impossible to be certain concerning which message is conveyed by the *Phaedo*'s combination of *mythos* and argument. What is striking, however, is that his depiction of the death of Socrates is also, on argumentative, dramatic, and reader levels, a highlighting of the limitations of reason in humans. The death of Socrates is at the same time suggested to be, if not the death of successful rational agency, then certainly a dramatization of its extreme rarity and of the demands placed on it if considered as an autonomous instance. At the same time, we can perhaps tentatively conclude that the *Phaedo* works as a reminder of the reader's moral psychological situation: a confrontation with oneself that is at the same time an occasion to engage reflectively with one's own motivational constitution. In the *Phaedo*, rational argument definitely has an important place, but one that is crucially embedded and dependent.[20]

Notes

1 Christopher Gill, 'The Death of Socrates', *The Classical Quarterly* 23, no. 1 (1973): 25–8, is a classic version including musings on the mismatch between what has been taken to be the known workings of hemlock and the portrayal of Socrates' death. Janet Sullivan, 'A Note on the Death of Socrates', *The Classical Quarterly* 51, no. 2 (2001): 608–10, is the latest response claiming that the hemlock variety used is *conium maculatum*, which does indeed have the symptoms described by Plato.

2 A nice exposition is Section 2 of Allan Silverman, 'Plato's Middle Period Metaphysics and Epistemology', SEP (available at https://plato.stanford.edu/entries/plato-metaphysics/#2). Gareth Matthews and Thomas A. Blackson, 'Causes in the *Phaedo*', *Synthese* 79, no. 3 (1989): 581–91, argued that the *Phaedo* constituted a turning away from definitions to *aitiai* like 'the beautiful', in a reaction to Gregory Vlastos, 'Reasons and Causes in the *Phaedo*', *The Philosophical Review* 78 (1969): 291–325.

3 *Symposium* 173d–e. The remark in the *Phaedo* about Apollodorus, indicating that he is an especially volatile character, is perhaps an added reason to worry about the accuracy of the *Symposium*'s tale.

4 Until her recent reevaluation, Xanthippe had usually been thought of as a particularly difficult person, and this bias had habitually been read into Plato's texts. That reading goes back at least to the bad press she received in Xenophon's *Symposium* (2.10). The poet Robert Graves provided an early and somewhat leftfield rehabilitation, in terms of values for which she then stands as emblem, in 'The Case for Xanthippe', *The Kenyon Review* 22, no. 4 (1960): 297–305.

5   Although his theory is based on *mimêsis*, a concept absent from the *Phaedo*, Aristotle in his *Poetics* gives voice to the opinion that it is not transferring something into verse which makes someone a poet, a sentiment perhaps analogous to the one Socrates expresses here (*Poetics* iv, 1447b9-16).
6   The notion that dialectical argument should take place in a certain emotive atmosphere characterized by graciousness and friendliness is explicitly invoked in the *Theaetetus* (168b).
7   As a potential comment on the stern requirements for the latter option, notice that the pleasures of sex are among the things the 'true philosopher' despises (64d-e), and that Xanthippe was just at the prison with her and Socrates' baby.
8   Cf., e.g., 69c-d. Kathryn Morgan, 'The Voice of Authority: Divination and Plato's *Phaedo*', *The Classical Quarterly* 60, no. 1 (2010): 63–81, provides useful comments and further references. Furthermore, in mystic initiation too, one must be shown things in non-argumentative ways and let them work on one in a manner that far transcends mere reason.
9   *tis . . . en hêmin pais hostis ta toiauta phobeitai*, 77d
10 Tripartition is not necessarily in play in the *Phaedo*, but if these descriptions smack of appetite (*epithymia*) as a principle of motivation, something like *thymos* too is strongly present in the later quote from the *Odyssey* (94d). Either way, a plurality of motivational forces is a requirement for human irrationality as theorized in Plato, and tripartition is its clearest expression.
11 While his arguments are different from the present considerations, an interpretation placing Socrates as something like a unicum and a contrast to the majority of humankind is J.T. Bedu-Addo, 'The Role of the Hypothetical Method in the *Phaedo*', *Phronesis* 24, no. 2 (1979): 111–32. Rui Zhu, 'Myth and Philosophy: From a Problem in *Phaedo*', *Journal of the American Academy of Religion* 73, no. 2 (2005): 453–73, takes an original position in agreeing that while argument does not come far on the question of death, this is still an apology of philosophy because the myth chosen by Socrates is *sôphrosynê*-inducing (469–72). If so, surely it is an apology also in the modern sense, as long as philosophy constitutes what can be achieved with reason.
12 For the scope of the cause(s) sought, cf. 97b.
13 Whereas one might argue that what is presented as hypothetical method in the *Republic*, e.g., is tied to a procedure for securing absolute knowledge, the *Phaedo* does not provide anything of the sort. The present reading considers the *Phaedo* as a single whole, without speculating on how what is there presented relates to apparently similar or analogous features in other dialogues.
14 For an investigation into the nature of the agreement required, cf. Jyl Gentzler, '*Sumfônein* in Plato's *Phaedo*', *Phronesis* 36, no. 3 (1991): 265–76.
15 This is well articulated by Samuel Scolnicov, *Plato's Parmenides* (Berkeley: University of California Press, 2003), who speaking about the *Meno* and *Phaedo* states broadly that the method 'does not *prove* the conclusion. It only shows *on what assumption or assumptions* the conclusion is possible' (9–10, italics in original).
16 One clear-headed suggestion as to how the various hypotheses and propositions relate was provided by Paul Plass, 'Socrates' Method of Hypothesis in the *Phaedo*', *Phronesis* 5, no. 2 (1960): 103–15.
17 Charles Blattberg, 'Opponents vs. Adversaries in Plato's *Phaedo*', *History of Philosophy Quarterly* 22, no. 2 (2005): 109–27, intriguingly but somewhat tendentiously argues that Socrates in the *Phaedo* is less a wonder than a monological freak.

18 *Phaedo* 85c–d; the expression is generally taken to refer to the hypothetical method as a second best, like taking to the oars when the wind fails. Cf., e.g., Donald L. Ross, 'The *Deuteros Plous*, Simmias' Speech, and Socrates' Answer to Cebes in Plato's *Phaedo*', *Hermes* 110, no. 1 (1982), at 20.
19 The general lack of ultimate insight might be acknowledged by Socrates' mysterious reference to the (proverbial) 'art of Glaucos' (108d). Diskin Clay, 'The Art of Glaucus (Plato *Phaedo* 108D4-9)', *American Journal of Philology* 106, no. 2 (1985): 230–6, argues that the Glaucus in question is no other than the Glaucus of *Republic* X: the imprisoned soul that is also, from another perspective, the human made immortal.
20 I would like to thank the attendants for their responses to an earlier version of this paper presented at a workshop organized by the Bergen Ancient Philosophy research group in Athens. Special thanks to Vigdis Songe-Møller, Jens Kristian Larsen and Knut Ågotnes for their written comments to later revisions of the text.

Bibliography

Bedu-Addo, J.T. 'The Role of the Hypothetical Method in the *Phaedo*'. *Phronesis* 24, no. 2 (1979) 111–32.

Blattberg, Charles. 'Opponents vs. Adversaries in Plato's *Phaedo*'. *History of Philosophy Quarterly* 22 no. 2 (2005): 109–27.

Clay, Diskin. 'The Art of Glaucus (Plato *Phaedo* 108D4-9)'. *American Journal of Philology* 106, no. 2 (1985): 230–6.

Gentzler, Jyl. '*Sumfônein* in Plato's *Phaedo*'. *Phronesis* 36, no. 3 (1991): 265–76.

Gill, Christopher. 'The Death of Socrates'. *The Classical Quarterly* 23, no. 1 (1973): 25–8.

Graves, Robert. 'The Case for Xanthippe'. *The Kenyon Review* 22, no. 4 (1960): 297–305.

Matthews, Gareth and Thomas Blackson. 'Causes in the *Phaedo*'. *Synthese* 79, no. 3 (1989): 581–91.

Morgan, Kathryn. 'The Voice of Authority: Divination and Plato's *Phaedo*'. *The Classical Quarterly* 60, no. 1 (2010): 63–81.

Plass, Paul. 'Socrates' Method of Hypothesis in the *Phaedo*'. *Phronesis* 5, no. 2 (1960): 103–15.

Ross, Donald. 'The *Deuteros Plous*, Simmias' Speech, and Socrates' Answer to Cebes in Plato's *Phaedo*'. *Hermes* 110, no.1 (1982): 19–25.

Scolnicov, Samuel. *Plato's Parmenides. Translated with Introduction and Commentary*. Berkeley: University of California Press, 2003.

Silverman, Allan. 'Plato's Middle Period Metaphysics and Epistemology'. SEP (available at https://plato.stanford.edu/entries/plato-metaphysics/#2) (2014).

Sullivan, Janet. 'A Note on the Death of Socrates'. *The Classical Quarterly* 51, no. 2 (2001): 608–10.

Vlastos, Gregory. 'Reasons and Causes in the *Phaedo*'. *The Philosophical Review* 78 (1969): 291–325.

Zhu, Rui. 'Myth and Philosophy: From a Problem in *Phaedo*'. *Journal of the American Academy of Religion* 73, no. 2 (2005): 453–73.

Part Four

Place and Displacement

11

Place (*topos*) and Strangeness (*atopia*) in the *Phaedrus*

Erlend Breidal

Introduction

This chapter sets out to investigate the significance of the terms *place* (*topos*) and *strangeness* (*atopia*) located in the prologue, and furthermore, how a philosophical relationship develops between them in the course of the dialogue. *Topos*, *atopia* and related terms occur several times in the prologue and reappear in significant passages in the main body of the text. This suggests that they signal a meaningful theme running through the dialogue. The morphological relation between *topos* and *atopia*, which designate some kind of conflict or incompatibility, is exploited and developed at a semantic level in the dialogue. Roughly, *topos* signifies a place of transcendence, namely the sacred grove where the interaction between Socrates and Phaedrus takes place, as well as the metaphysical place of the hyperuranian beings of the palinode. *Atopia* and its cognates occur in a context where image, forgetfulness and ignorance are the themes. Strangeness seems to signify the limitations in human cognition.

Anne Lebeck argues that the *Phaedrus* is constructed as a diptych, made up by the complementary pair *erôs* and *logos*.[1] Her further claim is that there are more of these divisions into complementary pairs manifest in the dialogue.[2] Thus, complementary pairs constitute an important framework within which the drama of the dialogue develops. I will try to show that *place* and *strangeness* is another such complementary pair, and that the interplay between *place* and *strangeness* is a metaphorical way of talking about the tension between transcendence and finitude in human being.[3] In the first part of this chapter, I try to map out the interpretative terrain where the two terms are situated. In the second part, I hope to display the philosophical significance of their interplay.

Part one: *place* and *strangeness* in the Prologue

Three of the four occurrences of *topos* and related terms refer to the geographical place where the speeches on love and the preceding conversations about rhetoric take place.[4]

That the place of the dialogue is meant to be significant is suggested by Plato's very detailed and prolonged description of it. Perhaps nowhere else in Plato do we get such a comprehensive account of the place of conversation. This geographical sense of *place* will take on a transferred and relatively abstract sense in the course of the dialogue.

Atopia and related terms occur three times in the prologue.[5] The literal sense of the term is 'without place', thereby implying 'out of place', and so perhaps alluding to the fact that this is the only Platonic dialogue where Socrates converses outside the city walls of Athens. An exception is perhaps *The Republic*, where the conversation takes place in Piraeus. Piraeus is a place that is somehow in between being in Athens and outside of Athens, since the harbour of Athens is within Athens itself only via the extension of the fortified city called the 'long walls'. One plausible interpretation is that such a setting is particularly suited for philosophical conversations. Philosophy is a potentially dangerous activity because of its critical disposition. Being among friends in an intimate setting, Socrates can speak more freely. The *Symposium* also has a similar setting, however within the city. In this dialogue, Socrates is very direct about the situatedness of philosophy. Eros is described as a *daimôn* and philosopher. The philosopher is situated between (*metaxy*) the wise and the ignorant, between ugliness and beauty as well as between human beings and gods. The parallels between Eros and Socrates are striking.[6] The philosopher's indeterminacy in being intermediate is experienced by Alcibiades as very out of place. In his encomium of Socrates, *strangeness* (*atopia*) is the key characteristic of Socrates 'in himself and in his speeches' (221d2).[7] The interplay between *topos* and *atopia* in the *Phaedrus* is set in motion when Socrates and Phaedrus are on their way out of the city.

The dialogue starts with the theme of *erôs*, when Socrates stumbles upon the beautiful Phaedrus in the city. In this encounter between the lover and the beloved, another major theme in the dialogue is prepared, namely a movement from concealment to disclosure: Phaedrus is hiding a speech by the famous rhetorician Lysias under his cloak. He wants to practise his memorizing of the speech on Socrates. But Socrates discloses both Phaedrus' intentions and the hidden speech. He will not let Phaedrus speak until 'you show me what you have in your left hand under your cloak. I'll hazard (*topazô*) it's the actual text' (228d6-8).[8] *Topazô* means 'guess' or 'aim at' (LSJ). There may also be a pun on the literal sense of 'putting in a place'.[9] Because, in a metaphorical sense, this is exactly what Socrates is doing. He is placing the speech in a particular place by disclosing its place of hiding.[10] The place of hiding (under Phaedrus' cloak) has a strong symbolic meaning, being a dialogue about love and rhetoric.

This same incident also playfully indicates another important and related theme: the one of image and original. Phaedrus is trying to trick Socrates into hearing his image of Lysias' speech instead of the original. But, as indicated above, Socrates exposes his intentions: '(...) bear in mind that, as fond of you as I am, I am not prepared to let you practice your speaking skills on me, not when Lysias is actually present among us' (228d-e). But this 'presence' of Lysias is in reality only another image in the form of a written speech. In the discussion of writing in the last part of the dialogue, writing is considered only an image (*eidôlon* 276a9) of the spoken word. The theme of image/original and presence/absence is set in motion.

Phaedrus and Socrates are now on their way into the countryside conversing. As they walk along the river Ilissus, Phaedrus brings up the myth about Boreas and Oreithyia. He asks Socrates whether he really thinks the mythic story is true. In his rather long response to Phaedrus, the first two instances of *atopia* occur. In the first part of his reply, Socrates makes an important distinction between himself and 'the wise':

> What do you mean? If, like the wise men (*hoi sophoi*) of our day, I didn't believe in these stories, I wouldn't be so out of place (*atopos*).[11] And in my wisdom, I would say that the Borean wind blew Oreithyia down from the rocks nearby while she was playing with Pharmakeia.
>
> 229c6–8

From the perspective of the wise in the city, Socrates is 'out of place' because he does not question the mythic stories in the same way as is conventional for 'the wise'. Thus, Socrates situates himself outside of the understanding of myths considered acceptable among a certain group of people. Socrates dissociates himself from the intellectual establishment in Athens, of which Lysias is a part. By contrast, Phaedrus obviously aspires to become a part of it.

Socrates distances himself from the wise concerning the way mythical stories should be interpreted and put to use. He characterizes the wise as people who 'make everything conform to the reasonable' (*kata to eikos* 229e2) and as 'employing some boorish sophistication' (229e3). In this way, Socrates presents himself to Phaedrus as the one with an 'urbane' understanding of the myths,[12] more sophisticated and inquisitive than the simpleminded intellectual establishment in Athens. Rather than engaging himself in a boorish and positivistic rationalization, which fails to see the human significance of the myths,[13] he wants to use myths and mythical figures as ethical metaphors in philosophizing. Socrates has no leisure for explanations that try to reduce the myths to naturalistic historical events.

> Although in some ways I find such explanations ingenious, Phaedrus, it's also true that they're the mark of a clever, hard-working, and not altogether fortunate man, if only because after these explanations he will then have to correct the mistaken beliefs about the shape of Horse Centaurs, and after that the Chimaira. Then mobs of Gorgon-like creatures, Pegasuses and other monsters will flood over him, not to mention other marvelously imagined oddities (*atopiai*).
>
> 229d2–e2[14]

To try to explain myths in this way is to make a mistake about the reality of myths. The rationalistic explanations also seem to presuppose a concept of reality in which everything can be explained. In creating this illusion, they cover up important philosophical problems; in this case the question 'Who am I?' To Socrates, however, the oddities or *atopiai* from the myths are an important resource for investigating this question. They are possible images with which he can look into himself. He claims that he is still not able to know himself (229e5-6) and needs the mythical monsters in his search for self-knowledge:

I believe whatever people say these days about those creatures,[15] and I don't inquire about them but about myself. For me, the question is whether I happen to be some sort of beast even more complex in form and more tumultuous than the hundred-headed Typhon, or whether I am something simpler and gentler, having a share by nature of the divine and the unTyphonic (*atyphou*).

230a

Because of the ignorance of his own nature, Socrates needs to investigate who he is. In his use of mythic creatures as *paradeigmata*, he asks himself whether he is like a beast more complex (*poluplokôteron*) than the Typhon, or something simpler and divine. By this distinction between simple and complex images, Socrates anticipates the difference between the images of the human and the divine soul in the palinode. In the palinode, Socrates presents the human soul as a team of two winged horses – one noble and one bad – and a charioteer.[16] The gods' teams however, are solely good and from good stock. In both the prologue and in the palinode, the unmixed is associated with something good and divine.[17] Being multi-formed or mixed involves a mix of both good and bad elements. The gods' teams, however, are also mixed in the sense of having three parts, but all the parts are good.

A key feature of the mixed images is strangeness (*atopia*). They are 'oddities' (*atopiai*) in being conglomerates of normally distinct animals. This mix makes the creatures abnormal, falling outside conventional expectations (*para doxa*). According to the wise, they would also be empirical impossibilities and in need of a rational explanation. The simple images, however, seem to be reserved for the gods, which are neither bad nor ignorant. The association between strangeness, ignorance and the mixed will be highlighted in the palinode. The image of the human soul is a mix of good and bad. This mixture will prevent it from a complete vision of the forms. Because of this ignorance, certain things will appear strange or out of place (*atopos*). Nothing will appear strange to a god with complete knowledge.

Socrates describes the place of the conversation, with its statues and images, as 'sacred, a haunt of the Nymphs and the river god Achelous[18] ... the gods do seem to occupy this place (*ton topon*)' (230b7-230c1). In both the prelude (230b2) and when they discuss the place of conversation once more in the interlude (between the palinode and the discussion of rhetoric),[19] Socrates designates the grove a 'resting place' (*katagôgê*). Literally, *katagôgê* means 'a bringing down from'. It alludes to the gods who have descended to the place and at the same time, it points forward to the myth of the palinode.[20] In this way, Plato signals a transcendent quality to the place, which prefigures the mythical journey beyond heaven to the hyperuranian place (*ton hyperouranion topon* 247c3).

Socrates' playful description of the place has another important aspect. As soon as they reach the grove, Socrates starts acting like a stranger to the region. He compliments Phaedrus for guiding them to such a beautiful place. Socrates is acting like a stranger out of place, feigning ignorance about his surroundings.[21] This imitation moves Phaedrus to characterize Socrates as 'someone most out of place' (*atopôtatos tis* 230c6).

Socrates is 'out of place' in the sense that, in imitating, he is not himself. Imitating means being other than oneself, and this is yet another way of being possessed. If you do not know what you are doing, possession can be dangerous and lead astray. However, as we will see in the palinode, it can also lead towards transcendence in the sense of metaphysical being and truth. Through his descriptions of the place (230b2-c5),[22] Socrates is communicating to both Phaedrus and the readers that there is a seduction taking place, and, as it turns out, a philosophical seduction carried out by way of imitations.

The themes indicated by *place* in the prologue can be summed up as consisting of three interrelated aspects: (1) the prologue plays out a movement between concealment and disclosure in a way that points to the relation between image and original. (2) The grove is potentially a place of transcendence, (3) and it indicates a theme of seduction, pointing forward to the divine madness of the philosophic lovers. All these aspects draw attention to the movement upward, to the divine.

Strangeness (*atopia*) is associated with ignorance, imitation and mixed images, elements that potentially represent a danger to the movement upwards. As such, these elements are the first intimation of a theme centred on human limitations and the limitations of philosophy. What follows from this is a tension manifest in Socrates' two paradigms of self-understanding: a beast more complex than the Typhon and something simple and divine. The two kinds of images – the mixed and strange as opposed by the simple and divine – are linked to the pair *place* and *placelessness* or *strangeness*. Part two will explore how this pair is an important doublet for the organization of the dialogue. More particularly, it will ask, is the interplay between *place* and *strangeness* an image of that interplay between image and original, which points to the limits and transcendence in human nature?

Part two: *place* and *strangeness* as recurrent themes in the *Phaedrus*

There are seven instances of *place* in the main body of the text.[23] All of them refer to some kind of divine place, either the sacred grove or some place in heaven. This can hardly be a coincidence and supports the view that Plato assigns a specific role to *place* in the *Phaedrus*. However, there is only one instance of *strangeness* in the dialogue apart from the prologue. One possible answer is that in this dialogue, Plato uses *atopia* with a certain thematic economy. It occurs in an important passage right in the middle of the palinode, which Plato has placed in the middle of the dialogue. Here, *atopia* concerns the experience of philosophical love described as a form of divine madness.[24] The experience of strangeness can make the philosophically disposed soul aware of its ignorance, an awareness that is the starting point for philosophy. But it also points to the paradox of philosophical activity, which is nourished by the tension between image and original. The philosopher desires to have knowledge of original being, but the embodied soul only has access to this being through images. From this perspective, it seems plausible to say that Plato highlights the theme of strangeness in the palinode.

Place in the palinode

In the palinode, the theme of *place* reaches a new level. Its function is to demonstrate that love – as a particular form of divine possession or madness – is good, for both the lover and the beloved. The palinode culminates in a claim that there is a connection between the soul's vision of true being and the sight of the beautiful beloved.[25] The sight of the beautiful boy induces a recollection of the vision of the forms in the lover. The lover will in turn 'lead the loved one wholly and entirely to resemble both themselves and the god whom they honour' (253b8-c2). This erotic relation is a 're-enactment',[26] a kind of imitation of the divine banquet and the soul's journey to 'the place beyond heaven' (*ton hyperouranion topon* 247c3). The important difference, however, is that the re-enactment is carried out by embodied souls. I will now trace this re-enactment back to its source to see what kind of place 'the place beyond heaven' is.

The soul's journey to 'the place beyond heaven' represents a peak in respect of transcendence, both in the dialogue itself and to the sense of *place*. By the simple fact that this is a journey made by the disembodied soul, the sense of place transcends a geographical or physical location. Paul Woodruff has described Socrates' vision of heaven as an inverted, revolving theatre.[27] His point is that it is not the physical design of the theatre itself that is inverted, but the location of the spectacle: When the gods 'reach the summit of heaven, they go to the edge and stand on the rim; there, the revolving motion carries them around as they stand and gaze on things outside the heavens' (247b6-c2). The spectacle is situated outside the theatre and thereby outside a mimetic relation in the ordinary sense of the word. We shall return to this issue of *mimêsis* shortly.

The emphasis on the transcendent character of the *place* in Socrates' description is very strong, almost hyperbolic: it is described as 'outside the heavens' (*exô toû ouranoû* 247c2, 'beyond heaven' (*hyperouranion* 247c3) and 'the place outside' (*ton exô topon* 248a3). The place and spectacle are bereft of any physical qualities: 'This is the place of Being, the Being that truly is – colourless, shapeless, and untouchable, visible to the mind alone, the soul's pilot, and the source of true knowledge' (247c6-d1). Socrates describes the place via a denial of features regularly present in the sensible realm. It is the place where the gods are feasting on the things that really are and the mythic source of true knowledge. The meaning of *place* has developed (ascended) from a physical place of transcendence and seduction into the metaphysical source of knowledge and the place of fulfilment for lovers of wisdom.

The problem of image and original in the palinode

In the palinode, Socrates seems actively to be undermining the metaphysical foundations for knowledge as recollection. The way Plato lets Socrates account for the human souls' vision of true being might very well contain an intended ambiguity. On the one hand, only the gods' chariots make this journey with ease. The human team is mixed with good and bad, which makes the chariot driving 'difficult and irksome' (246b4). Thus, the human souls fail to see what the gods envision with ease: 'all [human] souls, every one of them, leave the sight of Being, unfulfilled, and, once departed, feed on the food of conjecture (*trophê doxastê*)' (248b4-5). In a way contrary to that of the gods, the human souls obtain only a limited vision of the hyperuranian beings. When they fall into a body, they forget even that limited insight. On the other hand, when Socrates seems to be talking about his own experience in heaven, he appears to contradict this by saying that they were being 'fully initiated' (250c2-4). This indicates that only Socrates himself and a few others actually got a full vision of the hyperuranian beings in a godlike manner. This interpretation is supported by the context in which this statement occurs. Socrates has been explaining the phenomenon of recollection and the difficulties involved (249c ff.). He seems to conclude, however, that it is possible for some:

> There is no shine (*phengos*) in the images here on earth of justice and moderation and the other things honourable for souls, but through the dim organs of the senses a few people, and they with difficulty, approach these images and behold the original of the thing imaged.
>
> 250b1–5

Socrates says that just a few and these only with difficulty, can come to see the original behind the image. Socrates seems to be referring here to those fully initiated, himself included.

The tension between the possibility of a divine view of being and the difficulty of recollection, seems to be directed at implanting seeds of doubt and a critical attitude in the readers, or listeners. It should make us look very closely at what Socrates really says in his second speech. Socrates' introduction to his description of the hyperuranian being underscores the mythic origins of recollection: 'None of the poets here on earth have ever sung the praises of this place beyond heaven, nor will any ever sing of it adequately' (247c3-4).[28] If we take Socrates' interpretation of myths from the prologue as our guide, we should use the myth of the souls' journey as a mirror with which to investigate ourselves and our own limitations and possibilities as human beings.

The tension between the hyperuranian vision of being and the mundane process of recollection poses the difficult and pervasive philosophical problem of imitation, and, more specifically, the problem of the relation between original and image. To what extent can human beings have access to originals or hyperuranian being? How can a recollection of pure beings be possible when a direct vision of those beings is no longer fully accessible? If we assume that the difference between images and originals lies in the partiality of images in relation to their originals, a serious problem occurs for the activity of recollection. How can the viewer be sure that he recollects correctly? How can we be sure that we are not mistaking a false image for a true one and correctly identify the true?[29] The palinode does not solve the problem of original and image. On the contrary, it confirms that imitation poses a genuine philosophical problem within the dialogue. Even the genuine philosopher has no choice but to communicate with himself and others by means of verbal and visual images.[30]

Strangeness in the palinode

In the process of recollection, the problem of image and original is expressed as an experience of *atopia* or strangeness. In the passage 250e-252b Socrates describes in detail – using very concrete imagery – how the recently initiated (*ho artitelês*)[31] experiences recollection through a beautiful boy. Both the vision and the recalling of the beautiful boy are experienced as an intermixture of pleasure and pain. However, it is when the soul is separated from the beautiful that this intermixture of pleasure and pain has the greatest impact:

> When both sensations are intermixed, the soul is both greatly troubled by the oddity of the experience (*adêmonei te tê atopia toû pathous*) and raves, at a loss to understand it. Driven mad, she is neither able to sleep at night nor remain in one place by day, but, yearning she runs to whatever place she thinks she will see the boy who possesses beauty.
>
> 251d7–e3

What Socrates is describing here looks very much like a state preliminary to philosophy. The lover experiences strangeness and *aporia*,[32] caused by the intermixture of pleasure and pain. The image of the beloved makes the soul yearn for his presence, which is pleasurable, and his absence is experienced as painful. This mixture of feelings is strange and bewildering. To a philosophical soul, this bewilderment or *aporia* is an incentive to investigate or start philosophizing. This experience is different from the sight of the beautiful beloved, which induces a recollection of the form of beauty. The strange *aporia* of experiencing opposite feelings induces critical activity in the analysis of the *aporia* itself and its cause. The focus is turned inwards, on self-knowledge, and not on an abstract entity. The philosophical soul will be encouraged to investigate the simultaneous presence of two apparently opposite sensations, because such an appearance is experienced as strange and aporetic. The question 'how can two opposite sensations appear at the same time?' stimulates philosophical activity.

This figure – 'the strange mixture of opposite sensations' – also occurs in the *Republic* VII (524a-b), *Phaedo* (59a) and *Philebus* (49a). In other words, we here encounter a recurring Platonic theme, assuming a prominent place in four major Platonic dialogues.

In the *Republic* VII, in the introduction to the five mathematical studies, Socrates distinguishes between objects of sensation that summon the intellect, and ones that do not (523a ff.). Objects that summons the intellect causes simultaneous and opposite sensations in us, as for instance the soft and hard. The soul is then at a loss (*aporein* 524a7) to say what is indicated by the hard, if the sensation at the same time tells it that the same thing is soft. Glaucon responds reasonably, saying that these interpretations experienced by the soul are strange (*atopoi*) and require further consideration (524b1-2). According to Socrates, the strangeness caused by opposite sensations creates an *aporia* that should in turn initiate attempts to divide the object of sensation, and further make us ask the 'whatever is X?' question (*ti pot' esti* 524c11) of the soft and hard. The target of this process is to achieve 'clarity' (*saphêneian* 524c) and thus transcend the *aporia* by way of thought, rather than via the senses. The strange experience of opposite sensation occasioning an *aporia* leads by nature to intellection (523a1-3) and onto a philosophical path. The five mathematical studies are intended to imitate and cultivate this process that leads from the sensible to the forms.

In the beginning of the *Phaedo*, the natural version of this process is exemplified by the contrast between Phaedo and Socrates. Phaedo explains how he experienced being present at Socrates' last day on earth:

as I realized deep down that very soon that man was about to meet his end, a simply absurd feeling (*atopon ... pathos*) was present in me, an unusual blend, blended together from pleasure and from pain too. And all who were present were pretty much in this condition, sometimes laughing, sometimes weeping.

59a4–9[33]

Phaedo, and presumably the others present, experienced the blend of pleasure and pain as absurd or strange. The same collection of terms reappears a little later, when Socrates is released from his chains (see 60b3-c7). The crucial difference between the two situations is that Socrates engages in the philosophical work of investigating the *aporia* of opposite sensations, as this is prescribed in the *Republic*. Phaedo's report notes the strangeness of opposite feelings, but fails to recognize it as aporetic. He appears to lack a philosophical nature. By contrast, Socrates exemplifies an acute awareness of *aporiai* and a way to face and potentially resolve them in a philosophical way.

In the *Philebus*, Socrates deals with the *aporia* of pleasure and pain more directly than in the other three dialogues. He develops a remarkably elaborate dialectical analysis of pleasure and pain and their mixtures. The context is the problem of the best life. Initially, the competing alternatives are 'the life of pleasure' and 'the life of reason'. One of the questions Socrates and Protarchus must agree on, in order to decide on the issue, is a definition of pleasure. Socrates claims that what most people consider pleasures are not genuine pleasures. They are mixed with pain. Accordingly, he makes a division of pleasure into false (mixed) and true (unmixed) pleasures. Socrates admits that this division is a difficult one. He has always been amazed by the perplexities (*aporêmata* 36e2) involved.[34] Making his interlocutors aware of the serious difficulties involved in this matter, as Plato thereby also does his readers, Socrates goes on to explain pain as a kind of lack or destruction, and accordingly pleasure as a kind of filling or restoration. A condition of neither destruction nor restoration – no pleasure or pain – will be a godlike state of perfection.

Comedy was a genre mostly associated with the pleasures of laughter. To persuade Protarchus that pure pleasure in most cases is mixed with pain, Socrates chooses comedy because it is the least obvious examples. According to Socrates, this will make us able 'to understand more easily the mixture of pain and pleasure in other cases too' (48b).[35] Socrates tries to show that an element of pain is involved in the laughable. We laugh at our enviable neighbours when they are ignorant about themselves, when they think they are richer, more beautiful or wiser than they really are. We laugh at their ignorance. However, for ignorance to be laughable, it needs one more division. This is the context for Socrates' characterization of the mixture of pleasure and pain as strange: 'So we must continue with our division of ignorance, Protarchus, if we want to find out what strange mixture (*atopon ... meixin*) of pleasure and pain this comic malice is. How would you suggest that we should further subdivide?' (49a7-9)[36]

Socrates makes a twofold division of the ignorant into the strong and the weak. We cannot laugh at the ignorant who are strong, because they are dangerous. But we can laugh at the weak because they are harmless and incapable of revenge. Socrates tries to persuade Protarchus that in the comedy, a blend of laughter and envy is involved, a combination implying a blend of pleasure with pain. At first, Protarchus fails to see how this is possible (49c), but Socrates persuades him completely (50b). The strange mixture of pleasure and pain in comedy is revealed as a compound of pleasure and pain, caused by our laughter at self-ignorant, envious, and weak neighbours.

Why, however, is this mixture strange? It appears strange to most people because of the unconventional or unexpected mix of pleasure and pain in comedy. It is strange because we are ignorant or lack self-knowledge. The painful element in laughter is often not recognized because the pleasure of laughter covers it up. Sometimes people are also not aware of their envy or ignorance. In cases where such characters appear in comedy, members of the audience might recognize these weaknesses in themselves. In pointing at this, Socrates indicates a more serious and philosophical aspect of comedy. Comedy is not only about laughter and pleasure, but also about the painful process of getting to know oneself. We laugh at the characters in a comedy also because we recognize ourselves in them. It is easier to laugh at others than to do so at ourselves. If we are willing to look into the mixed feelings that accompany laughter, this can lead to increased self-knowledge.

It appears to be no coincidence that Socrates introduces the sequence on ignorance by referring to the inscription in Delphi: 'Know Thyself' (48c). Socrates ends his discussion of the mixture of pleasure and pain by admitting that he has chosen comedy in order to persuade and that the argument is incomplete: 'I will agree to give you an account of all these matters tomorrow' (50d-e). In other words, Socrates' intention is not to present a theory of ignorance, but to show how ignorance can show up where we do not expect it and that a philosophical analysis of what appears strange can help us to learn something about ourselves.

From these three occurrences a clearer picture of the theme of 'the strange mixture of opposite sensations' emerges. In all three dialogues, the main point is that this experience of opposite sensation creates an *aporia* that potentially can lead on to the path of philosophy. Things appear strange when something is unknown, unfamiliar, or seemingly absurd. In many cases, what seems strange also implies an *aporia* that can make us aware of our ignorance.

In the *Phaedo*, we see the contrast between Socrates and Phaedo's respective dispositions towards the aporetic strangeness of opposite sensations. In the *Republic*, Socrates demonstrates how opposite sensations can be used to stimulate the intellect and turn it from the sensible to the forms, a turn that is a necessary part of the education required for the philosophical rulers. In the *Philebus*, the mixture of pleasure and pain can seem strange in comedy, but then '... in the entire tragedy and comedy of life (as well as in thousands of different things), pains are blended together with pleasures' (50b). Socrates seems to say that if we are willing to look carefully into the matter, the *aporia* of the mixed pleasure disappears. On several occasions (47e1, 50c1 and 50d1), Socrates mentions *erôs*, among others, as a phenomenon exhibiting the mixture more obviously than comedy does. *Erôs*, then, leads us back to the *Phaedrus*. How can the analysis in the *Philebus* help us deepen our understanding of the strange mixture of pleasure and pain experienced by the lover in the *Phaedrus*?

In the *Philebus*, the painful had to do with a kind of emptying or destruction, and pleasure with a filling or restoration. Applying this 'theory' to the case of comedy is less than straightforward. It makes sense, however, that the painful feeling of envy is a destructive element. Being unable to enjoy your neighbours' success is unjust. But how can laughter be a kind of filling and a restoration? We might understand it as potentially a filling that consists of knowledge, provided that laughter can lead us to an awareness of ignorance and vanity in ourselves and human beings in general, and thus to increased self-knowledge and knowledge about human beings in general.

In the case of the *Phaedrus*, these connections seem immediately more applicable. The state of perfection, or the perfectly filled state, occurs in the mythic journey of the soul, when it has properly seen and taken in the spectacle of the hyperuranian beings. The journey to the place beyond heaven involves much toil and struggle, but the contemplating of the truth and the beholding of the forms is described as a banquet where the souls nourish themselves on and are filled with knowledge. This is a joyous experience (*eupatheô* 247d3). A soul who perceives something of the truth in the company of a god is free from pain or unhurt (*apêmôn* 248c4), until the next cycle begins. However, when the soul is unable to follow a god, it will not see the truth or follow the path. The soul 'gets weighed down burdened by forgetfulness and wrongdoing and in her heaviness sheds her feathers and falls to earth' (248c6-7). The fall of the soul into a body results in an emptying of the soul's knowledge. This emptying is associated with pain or harm.

This ascent and descent, as well as the relation between the human soul and a god, are mirrored in the relation between the lover and the beloved. For the embodied soul, the only way back up towards the vision of the hyperuranian beings goes through a recollection of this vision. This recollection is only possible through a form of divine madness. Socrates explains: 'The lover hit with this madness is called a lover of beautiful people and beautiful things' (249e3-4) and that beauty is the form that has the clearest earthly image. To those recently initiated into hyperuranian beings, an image of this beauty in a beautiful boy will initiate a recollection of the form itself. Such a lover, 'if he was not afraid to appear excessively mad, would sacrifice to his darling boy as if to a statue or a god' (251a). What the philosophical lover sees in the beautiful beloved is not so much a human being as a god and the beautiful in itself. The absence of this beloved causes pain because the desire is locked in, while the recalling of the beautiful is associated with pleasure or joy (251d). This is not only a one-way relationship. The beloved also experiences the filling, emptying, pain and pleasure, as well as the strangeness of this experience:

> The boy is then in love, but he is at a loss to say with what. He doesn't know what he has experienced, nor is he able to explain it, but just as a person who has contracted an eye-disease from someone is unable to name the alleged cause, so he does not realize that in his lover he is seeing himself as though in a mirror. When that man is near, his pain ceases, as it does for the man. But when the man is absent, the boy yearns and is yearned for, again in the same ways, as he experiences a 'return-love', an image or copy of love.
>
> 255d–e

Both the lover and the beloved experience the strange mixture of pleasure and pain. The beloved catches love from the lover and becomes himself a lover. The beautiful beloved is the only earthly symbol of heavenly truth. Through the beloved, the lover is filled with the presence of beauty itself, but at the same time, the vision of the beloved beauty is not identical with the hyperuranian form beauty. The earthly vision of beauty is also absence, and cause pain. The philosophical lover will experience the same mixture of absence and presence as in the recalling of earthly love, but at another level. The oddity of this mixture is due to the *aporia* of the interweaving of being and non-being, which is an essential feature of image as such, and accordingly of Platonic recollection.[37] The embodied soul's attempts to recollect the vision of the hyperuranian beings corresponds to a pleasurable filling or restoration towards the original state, but it is at the same time a painful destruction, in the sense that the recollection also represents an absence of being. The embodied soul does not have access to being itself through the process of recollection, only through images of being itself. In the reflection on the nature of image lies both the possibility of transcendence as well as our limitations in terms of knowledge.

The strange mixture of opposite sensations creates an *aporia* that is inducive to and the starting point for philosophical activity. As such, it is a valuable experience for those who are disposed towards philosophy. For those who are not, the mixture of pleasure and pain will remain unnoticed or a strange experience which they cannot explain.

The experience of strangeness also has to do with ignorance and lack of self-knowledge. The *Phaedrus* exemplifies that *logos*, *erôs* and image have a positive as well as a negative potential. It is in the same way with ignorance. It can have a positive value if you are aware of it, but is a vice if you do not. Awareness of ignorance or awareness of *aporiai* is *the* starting point for philosophy. Socrates has been aware of his ignorance and philosophical *aporiai* since he was a youth.[38] As a mature philosopher, Socrates is experienced as strange and one who creates *aporiai* in others. Experience of strangeness is a form of estrangement that has the potential of stimulating the intellect to philosophical activity. Strangeness becomes something that potentially induces investigation and introspection, and hence can lead to increased self-knowledge.

Conclusion: the strangeness of serious play

The soul's movement between the journey to heaven where it is feasting on pure Being, and its embodiment as ignorant human beings, constitutes a tension and a movement between *place* and *strangeness* in the *Phaedrus*. The estrangement the soul of the lover experiences in the simultaneous presence and absence of the object of desire directs the soul beyond the image itself. The tension between absence and presence characteristic of the image cannot be dissolved for the embodied soul. This tension discloses both the possibility of transcendence and limitations or finitude in the possibilities of human beings to acquire knowledge. We can construct images or myths as mirrors with which we can look into and investigate the human condition and ourselves. Plato's dialogues are such images. If we forget that the dialogues are dramatic images and try to disconnect them from their individuality and situatedness, we will find ourselves in the same situation as the sophist, who are trying to give a naturalistic explanation for every myth.

This tension between presence and absence is also present in the different configurations of Socrates, Plato's embodiment of philosophy. He is both ignorant, a poet and a knower of the truth about the place beyond. Socrates' knowledge of the truth about the place beyond heaven is a mythical truth. No one can give us an adequate account of this place. Socrates admits that his myth about the soul's journey to heaven is an incomplete image of our human condition.[39] No one has access to the originals. As an image and embodiment of the philosopher, Socrates is simultaneously absence and presence, sameness and difference, knowing and ignorant, both in and out of place. We see this perhaps most clearly in Socrates' relation to Athens. He is neither completely settled in Athenian culture nor completely outside of it. The configuration of presence and absence is also present in the paradox of writing, exposed towards the end of the dialogue.

In the last part of the dialogue, writing is presented as an image (*eidôlon* 276a9) of the spoken word, in the specific sense that the relation between written and spoken word is a reconfiguration of the image and original in the palinode. The spoken word of one who knows is the original of which a written version would be an image.[40] The knower is a speaker who employs *dialektikê technê*. This is a kind of speech that 'selects an appropriate soul, sowing and planting his speeches with knowledge' (*met' epistêmês* 276e6-7) in the soul of others. The qualification Socrates presupposes for this kind of dialectic speech[41] makes it a very difficult task. It implies that the speaker has knowledge of the individual souls as well as of the forms. Thus, because writing at its best is only an image of dialectical speech, writing is for play and one should not be serious about it (277e). If we take Socrates on his word in this matter, it is not much left to be serious about. The *Phaedrus* is a dialogue that in written form denounces writing as mere play and in doing so appears as a strange blend of seriousness and play.

The philosophical significance of *place* and *strangeness* in the *Phaedrus* lies in the way Plato connects these terms to original and image, and further, to transcendence and finitude in human being. *Place* is transferred from the place of seduction and conversation, inhibited by the gods, to the hyperuranian realm of original or true Being. Lastly, this realm descends to the spoken word of the knower in the form of *dialektikê technê*. *Place* represents a transcendence for which the philosopher is striving.

The experience of *strangeness*, however, is the experience of ignorance and points to the paradox of philosophy. The philosopher loves original or true being, but has only accesses to the images of this realm as long as the soul is attached to a body. Accordingly, the desire of the philosophical lover cannot be completely satisfied. For the philosophically inclined, the experience of strangeness can lead to awareness of ignorance and knowledge of one's own limitations. This awareness is the beginning of any philosophical investigation. Thus, philosophical activity operates in the tension between *place* and *strangeness*, between original and image, and between transcendence and finitude, tensions that cannot be resolved in the realm of human beings.

Notes

1   Anne Lebeck, 'The Central Myth of Plato's *Phaedrus*', *Greek, Roman and Byzantine Studies*, 13:3 (1972): 267–90.

2   As examples of such pairs, Lebeck refers to the following. The speeches of the rhetorician and the dialectician, the speeches on behalf of the non-lover and the lover, the written speech of Lysias read aloud and the oral speech by Socrates, the pure soul of the philosopher following the deities and the striving of the soul to regain its former state, the first part of the palinode that concerns the intelligible world (metaphysical) and the second part which describes the world of sense perception (physical) (268).

3   For a treatment of this theme in the *Republic*, see Drew Hyland, *Finitude and Transcendence in the Platonic Dialogues* (Albany: State University of New York Press, 1995).

4   230b5, 230c1, 230b2.

5   229c6, 229e1, 230c6.

6   See e.g. Richard Hunter, *Plato's Symposium* (Oxford: Oxford University Press, 2004), 80, and Allan Bloom 'The Ladder of Love', in *Plato's Symposium*, translated by Seth Benardete (Chicago: The University of Chicago Press, 2001), 133.

7   215a2 and 221d1.

8   All translations are by Stephen Scully, *Plato's* Phaedrus (Newburyport: Focus Publishing, 2003).

9   Its literal sense 'to put in a place' is not found in classical Greek (LSJ).

10 For a similar use of *topazô*, see *Theaetetus* 151b4 and 155d1. Joe Sachs uses the verb 'to place' in his translation of *topazô* at 151b4, and 'to have placed' of *topazein* at 155d1. See Joe Sachs, *Plato. Theaetetus* (Newburyport: Focus Philosophical Library, 2004), and in particular note 10, p. 28 (151b). His translations of *topazô* at these two instances are questionable.

11 Nehamas and Woodruff also translates *atopos* 'out of place'. See Plato, *Phaedrus*, translated, with introduction and notes, by Alexander Nehamas and Paul Woodruff (Indianapolis: Hackett, 1995).

12 According to Phaedrus, Socrates seems like a person who has never left the city (230d1). He is, however, in contrast to Phaedrus, interested in his surroundings, and it turns out that he is quite familiar with the area.

13 See Charles L. Griswold, *Self-knowledge in Plato's Phaedrus* (Pennsylvania State University Press, 1996), 38.

14 Nehamas and Woodruff translate these passages and the term *atopiai* somewhat differently from Scully: 'a whole flood of Gorgons and Pegasuses and other monsters, in large numbers and absurd forms, will overwhelm him' (229d7-9).

15 *Autôn* can be taken to refer back to *atopiai* at 229e1 and thereby pointing forward to 'some sort of beast' (*ti thêrion*) at 230a3. In this way *ti thêrion* at 230a3 seems to be connected with *atopia*.

16 Griswold notes the association between Centaurs and Pegasuses and Socrates' image of the tripartite soul in the palinode, Griswold, *Self-knowledge in Plato's Phaedrus*, 38.

17 The differentiation of souls as either simple or mixed/multi-formed is repeated at 270d1, 271a7 and 277c2-3, where requirements of rhetoric as a perfect *technê* are discussed. But the distinction between divine soul as simple and human soul as mixed is absent from the descriptions of artful speech. For rhetoric to be a *technê*, it must be able to recognize whether a soul is simple or multi-formed, but nothing is said about a simple soul being good or divine. The paradigm for the multi-formed is the figure of the body (271a), but no paradigm is set forth for the simple soul. The descriptions are purely technical, and there is no mention about a *telos* of the rhetorical art other than persuasion. An urgent question would be why Socrates completely avoids the

normative purpose of rhetoric at this point, a question which usually plays an important role in the discussion of rhetoric, for example in the *Gorgias*.
18 In this particular passage, Scully seems to have 'helped' the transition from Greek to English syntax a bit. In these two lines, *topos* does not occur in the Greek text, but refer to *ton topon* at b5. Therefore, I have omitted Scully's 'place' and used 'it', as I consider this more literal, still making good sense of the passage. Scully then instead omits 'place' at c1. His translation is as follows: 'And, if you permit me to go on, how adorable and delightful is the gentle breeze' (c1-2). A literal translation of the passage would insert 'the gentle breeze **of the place** (*to eupnoun toû topou*)'. Scully has probably made his choice of translation for aesthetical reasons and for the sake of clarity. It certainly does not change the meaning. But for my own purpose, it is of some importance to have as literal a translation as possible of the occurrences of *topos*. See Scully, *Plato's Phaedrus*.
19 259a5.
20 But we have already had a prolepsis to the soul's journey to heaven in the palinode by the abduction of Oreithyia.
21 Socrates corrected Phaedrus in locating the place of Boreas' abduction of Oreithyia (229b4-c4).
22 See note 6 above.
23 238d1, 247c3, 247d1, 248a3, 249a8, 259a5 (*to katagôgion*) and 274d3.
24 Lebeck analyses the palinode by a method adapted from its more regular application to choral lyric in tragedy. She ascribes pivotal importance to the central myth in the *Phaedrus*: 'The myth itself is an aggregate of images fused into an organic whole, the manner in which they are interwoven reflecting the theme and shape of the dialogue. The myth forms a central point to which every idea in the *Phaedrus* is related and should be referred.' Lebeck, 'The Central Myth of Plato's *Phaedrus*', 268.
25 This point is underscored by Socrates' prayer to Eros at the end of the dialogue (257a-b).
26 John Sallis describes philosophical love and the notion of recollection so: 'What the erotic engagement offers the lover, most fundamentally, is a way of re-enacting the divine banquet, of partaking mediately, through "memory," of that nourishment which is not available to him in the form of an immediate contemplation of being.' John Sallis, *Being and Logos* (Atlantic Highlands: Humanities Press International, 1986), 157.
27 See Paul Woodruff, 'Plato's Inverted Theatre: Displacing the Wisdom of the Poets', in this volume.
28 Griswold points out the discrepancy between what Socrates says in the myth and the myths own standards, the discrepancy between recollection as it is supposed to be acted out between a lover and beloved, and the relationship between Phaedrus and Socrates, Griswold, *Self-knowledge in Plato's Phaedrus*, 152.
29 I am indebted to Griswold, *Self-knowledge in Plato's Phaedrus*, 171–2, in my presentation of this problem.
30 There is a similar problem exposed in the *Theaetetus*. Here, Socrates explains his art as 'a kind of midwifery'. According to Socrates, this is not something people are aware of, so they experience him as 'most strange' (*atopôtatos*) and say that he 'makes human being perplexed' (*poiô tous anthrôpous aporein* 149a10). The main ability of Socrates' art as a midwife is to judge the soundness of other people's theories and opinions. But in wisdom he is sterile. Socrates does not have any positive doctrines. From this point of view, philosophy is a fundamentally critical activity. The question is then how the philosopher's art can judge between an image and something true if the philosopher

does not have positive measures or standards for truth as opposed to *mimêsis*. This sterility seems to force Socrates also to use images and pictures in his own investigations, since he is unable to produce true knowledge.
31 Those who have not been recently initiated or who have been corrupted are not able to recollect: 'When looking at beauty's namesake here, such a person fails to experience true reverence as he gazes but yields to pleasure and tries to mount and to spawn children according to the law of a four-footed animal. In company with wantonness, he shows no fear or shame as he pursues unnatural pleasure' (250e).
32 For the relationship between *aporia* and *atopia*, see Tormod Eide, 'On Socrates' atopia', *Symbolae Osloenses* Vol. LXXI (1996): 63–4, and Francois Makowski, 'Où est Socrate? L'aporie de l'atopicité chez Platon', *Revue de Philosophie Ancienne*, Vol. 12 (2) (1994).
33 The translation is by Eva Brann, *Plato. Phaedo* (Newburyport: Focus Publishing, 1998).
34 The pleasure-argument is far too long and complex to be properly reconstructed here. Whether Socrates succeeds in solving the *aporiai* involved is also a topic beyond the scope of this essay.
35 All translations from the *Philebus* are by Seth Benardete, *The Tragedy and Comedy of Life. Plato's* Philebus (Chicago: The University of Chicago Press, 1991), unless otherwise is noted.
36 Plato, *Philebus*, translated with an introduction by Dorothea Frede (Indianapolis: Hackett Publishing, 1993).
37 The strange interweaving of being and non-being is a theme that is treated explicitly in the *Sophist*. The Stranger and Theaetetus have agreed that an image both *is* and *is not* genuine. A genuine likeness is not genuinely being. Non-being is entwined in an interweaving with Being, and that is characterized as 'very out of place' (*mala atopon* 240c). An image is not identical with that which it imitates. Accordingly, an image consists of both identity and difference at the same time in the same respect. Supposedly, it is the contradictory statement 'nonbeing *is*', a statement inherent in the concept of image, which is the core of the Stranger's problem in trying to define the sophist.
38 See the *Parmenides* 130c ff.
39 See 247c. Socrates also claims that the speeches about love do not come from himself, but that he is possessed. Before Socrates begins his first speech, he covers his head and invokes the Muses (237a). He interrupts the speech and says that he seems 'to be caught in the grip of a divine passion' (238c). He warns Phaedrus that he might be Nymph-possessed, because 'the gods do seem to occupy this place' (238d). After the speech, he denounces it as being performed under a compulsion by Phaedrus (242d). He ascribes the speech to Phaedrus, 'which was delivered through my mouth while I was drugged and under your spell' (242e). In Socrates' introduction to the palinode, he says that 'the former speech belonged to Phaedrus . . ., but what I'm about to say belongs to Stesichorus' (244a). See also 265b-c for further 'palinodic' elements concerning his speeches.
40 Previously in the *Phaedrus*, *eidôlon* has been used of an image as related to an original (see 250d9 and 255d8).
41 See 271a–272b.

Bibliography

Benardete, Seth. *The Tragedy and Comedy of Life. Plato's* Philebus. Chicago: University of Chicago Press, 1991.

Bloom, Allan. 'The Ladder of Love'. In *Plato's Symposium*. Translated by Seth Benardete with commentaries by Allan Bloom and Seth Benardete. Chicago: University of Chicago Press, 2001.

Brann, Eva. *Plato. Phaedo*. Newburyport: Focus Publishing, 1998.

Eide, Tormod. 'On Socrates' *atopia*'. *Symbolae Osloenses* 71 (1996): 59–67.

Griswold, Charles L. *Self-knowledge in Plato's Phaedrus*. University Park, Pennsylvania: The Pennsylvania State University Press, 1996.

Hunter, Richard. *Plato's Symposium*. Oxford: Oxford University Press, 2004.

Drew Hyland. *Finitude and Transcendence in the Platonic Dialogues*. Albany: State University of New York Press, 1995.

Lebeck, Anne. 'The Central Myth of Plato's *Phaedrus*'. *Greek, Roman and Byzantine Studies*, 13:3 (1972): 267–90.

Makowski, Francois. 'Où est Socrate? L'aporie de l'atopicité chez Platon'. *Revue de philosophie ancienne* 12, no. 2 (1994): 131–52.

Plato. *Phaedrus*. Translated, with introduction and notes, by Alexander Nehamas and Paul Woodruff. Indianapolis: Hackett, 1995.

Plato. *Philebus*. Translated with an introduction by Dorothea Frede. Indianapolis: Hackett Publishing, 1993.

Sachs, Joe. *Plato. Theaetetus*. Newburyport: Focus Publishing, 2004.

Sallis, John. *Being and Logos*. Atlantic Highlands: Humanities Press International, 1986.

Scully, Stephen. *Plato's* Phaedrus. The Focus Philosophical Library, 2003.

12

Hunt: Method and Metaphor. A Reading of the *Sophist* 216a1–226a6

Gro Rørstadbotten

Introduction

How are readers to understand the Eleatic Stranger, the main speaker of the *Sophist*? Who is he? Or, what is he? For decades, it was commonly assumed that the Eleatic Stranger simply speaks for Plato,[1] a consensus about to dissolve.[2] For example, Seth Benardete argues that 'in the first half of the *Sophist*, the Stranger presents himself as a hunter of the hunter sophist ... and the Stranger is himself the model for the sophist.'[3] Jacob Howland claims at the outset of his reading, that the Stranger 'imitates the sophist in cloaking his method in the appearance of knowledge.'[4] However, he later 'faults the Stranger, ultimately, for employing this quasi-mathematical method in a ridiculously rigid manner and for neglecting Socratic concerns with Eros and the human soul.'[5] Victorino Tejera does not talk of the Stranger at all, but of the Elean Sophist.[6] He further identifies the Stranger as a sophist in the *Statesman* and accuses him for fabricating clever arguments in a pseudo-Socratic manner.[7] Eugenio Benitez reaches the conclusion that 'it appears as though the Eleatic *xenos* is a sophist. If he is Plato's mouthpiece, then Plato is a sophist.'[8] So, who is the Stranger? Is he Plato's mouthpiece, and thus a philosopher; is he a model for the sophist; is he an imitator of the sophist, or is he a sophist?

This brief introductory backdrop discloses that there are some severe ambiguities[9] connected to the Stranger. These ambiguities will serve as my point of departure when I intend to argue that in the prologue of the *Sophist*, the Stranger gives the impression of being a sophist. This appearance is exposed through his words and deeds, which in this context are notoriously confusing, and thus it seems like Plato invites the readers to enter an interpretative battlefield. I will state reasons for my argument through a two-step reading. First, the reading of the prologue is significant because it, like the prologues of most Platonic dialogues, sets the stage, and thus equips the reader with appreciated and relevant pointers (hints and clues, observations of twists and turns). The reading of the prologue intends to divulge the setting that the upcoming drama evolves from, and hence it provides the readers with the key to the whole dialogue.[10] Secondly, I will do a close reading[11] of the paradigm division and the upcoming three divisions. The paradigm division – modelled on the angler – is presented by the Stranger as the method that will enable him and Theaetetus to hunt down the sophist. The close reading of the following three divisions will reveal how the proposed method is gradually abandoned. Hence, by paying attention to what the Stranger is actually doing, I suggest that due to discrepancies between deeds and arguments,[12] he himself slowly but surely starts to look like a hunting sophist, and consequently Theaetetus starts to appear as the prey. The impact of this unhurried turnabout is progressively dawning on the reader: the hunting-method camouflages a hunting-metaphor, which conceals a threefold hunt. As a reader, I start hunting the Stranger in order to grasp who he is or what he is; Theaetetus thinks he is hunting the hunter-sophist, while the Stranger, in a deceptive hunt – in the end – is hunting Theaetetus. So, let us enter the prologue of the *Sophist*.

The Prologue (216a1-217b9)

When Theodorus introduces the newcomer to Socrates, he sets the stage of the prologue by his excited attitude and highly enthusiastic mode: 'Socrates ... we're bringing a Stranger, he's from Elea and ... he is very much a philosopher' (216a4).[13] Socrates' reaction to Theodorus' opening statement is noteworthy because it seems like he intends to tone down Theodorus' eagerness, and thus neutralize the atmosphere: 'Are you bringing a Stranger, Theodorus? Or are you bringing a god without realizing it instead, like the ones Homer mentions? He says gods accompany people who are respectful and just' (216a5-b1). In this response, we can identify a dual Homeric allusion related to Zeus, the protector of all travellers. The first allusion can simply be taken as an appeal to treat all visitors respectfully (*Odyssey* 9.269-71). The second transports us to a particular situation at the end of the *Odyssey*. After Antinous strikes down the still unrecognized Ulysses who at this point was disguised as a tramp, he receives a negative reaction from the others present:

> Antinous, you did ill in striking that poor wretch of a tramp: it will be worse for you if he should turn out to be some god – and we know the gods go about disguised in all sorts of ways as people from foreign countries, and travel about the world to see who does the right things.
>
> *Odyssey* 17.483-7

This allusion leads two ways. On the one hand, it could be read as a warning from Socrates to Theodorus. It is as if Socrates is asking Theodorus: Are you sure you know who the Stranger is? Or, are you sure the Stranger is what he appears to be? On the other hand, it could be taken as an ambiguous clue about the Stranger; a clue which is underscored twice by Socrates. First, when he questions Theodorus' judgement by indicating that he has brought 'a god without realizing it', and thereafter when he states rather ironically: 'Your Stranger might be a greater power following along with you, a sort of god of refutation (*theos ôn tis elenktikos*) to keep watch on us and show how bad we are at speaking – and to refute us' (216b7-8). This underlining hits the reader when

Socrates connects the Stranger to 'a god of refutation'. In Socrates' first reply to Theodorus, the dual Homeric allusion evoked Zeus; however, the allusion in his second reply points out quite another direction: here he evokes Hermes. Hermes, the god of transitions and boundaries, quick and cunning, who moves freely between the worlds of the mortals and the gods, a protector and patron of travellers, orators and wit, invention and trade, and more. In addition, he is a trickster and outwits others for his own satisfaction. The impact of Socrates' two replies indicates that he, through his allusions and ironic outburst, somehow suggests that he recognizes the Stranger, that he has met his kind before. He is a man reminiscent of a sophist, quick, cunning, sort of a trickster. Theodorus does not agree: 'That is not our Stranger's style (*tropos*), he is more moderate (*metriôteros*) than those who are eager to debate, or do combat with words' (216b7-8). Theodorus quickly adds that he does not hold the Stranger to be a god, but he is divine – as Theodorus holds all philosophers to be. Socrates now claims that the 'family' (*genos*, 216c3) of philosophers is as difficult to distinguish as the family of the gods. This, he explains, is because the 'genuine philosophers' (*ontôs philosophoi*, 216c6), by contrast to the fake ones, take on all sorts of different appearances due to the ignorance of people. Is Socrates, by these comments, implying that Theodorus is ignorant, or is this a hint related to the purported recognition of the Stranger? Or does he signal both?

Theodorus is not a philosopher but a well-known expert in geometry,[14] and it seems reasonable to infer that Socrates does not look upon him as a person who is able to tell the difference between a genuine philosopher and a fake one. However, Theodorus' rather vague differentiation between philosophers and the ones eager to debate – that the former are more moderate than the latter – points towards the *Euthydemus*. Here the two brothers from Thurii are presented as men 'eager to debate or do combats with words'. They practice the art of 'eristic' (combat), which literally means 'designed for wrangling'. No matter how one attempts to refute eristic arguments, one is doomed to fail. Due to the design of the arguments any means of refutation is in vain. When Socrates describes the expertise of the two brothers to his friend Crito, he says,

> They are both absolutely all-round fighters ... These two are first of all completely skilled in body, being highly adept at fighting in armor and able to teach this skill to anyone else who pays them a fee; and then they are the ones best to fight the battle of the law court and to teach other people both how to deliver and how to compose the sort of speeches suitable for the courts ... not a single man can stand up to them, they have become so skilled in fighting in arguments and refuting whatever may be said, no matter whether it is true or false ... They can make any other person clever at the same things in a short time.
> *Euthydemus* 271c8-272b4[15]

Could this be the kind that the Stranger differs from, according to Theodorus? And could this be the kind of man Socrates purportedly suspects? Before concluding, let us read the last section of the prologue.

After Socrates stated that the 'family' (*genos*, 216c3) of philosophers is as difficult to distinguish as the family of the gods, he proclaims that he would like the Stranger to explain what the people from his home town thinks about these things; i.e. sophist, statesman, philosopher. Theodorus interrupts: 'What, or what kind of thing, especially makes you consider asking the question? What special problem about them do you have in mind?' (217a4-5). How are we to understand this interruption? Theodorus knows Socrates' way, so is he anxious and concerned that Socrates will make the Stranger uncomfortable? Socrates elaborates: 'did they think that sophists, statesmen, and philosophers make up one kind or two? Or did they divide them up in three kinds corresponding to the three names and attach one name to each of them?' (217a6-8). Socrates' elucidating explanation makes Theodorus at ease: 'I don't think it would offend him to tell us about it. Or would it, sir?' The Stranger does not have any objection, and agrees to communicate what Socrates requested. Hence, in his last reply in the *Sophist*, Theodorus is again signalling the same kind of enthusiasm as he did in his opening line: 'Luckily, Socrates, you've gotten hold of words that are very much like the ones we happened to be asking him about. And he made the same excuse to us that he made to you just now – since he's heard a lot about this issue, after all, and hasn't forgotten it' (217b5-9).

Theodorus' words here actually give further clues about the Stranger. First, Theodorus comprehends the Stranger's answer as an excuse. Secondly, the Stranger spoke in the past sense. He stated that he *had heard* a good explanation which he still *remembered*. Both instances could suggest that the Stranger has nothing original to present and that he might be using a method which he has heard and still remembers. Thus, it will not be further developed during the upcoming conversation with Theaetetus. If Socrates at the outset recognized the Stranger's kind, the posed question could be understood as a test or a sort of trap, because, as we know Socrates we know that he already (and usually) knows the answers to the questions he puts forth. That is, Socrates probably already knows what they used to think about these things in Elea (note that Socrates also asks about these things in past tense: what *did* they think? how *did* they divide?). The reading of the prologue has exposed several hints indicating that Socrates recognized the Stranger's kind. Socrates' silence from this point on also corresponds to this alleged recognition.[16]

Paradigm for the hunting-method (218b6-219b7)

At this point the Stranger and Theaetetus set out to hunt down the sophist. As an introduction to the hunt, the Stranger presents a petition. Since it is 'hard to hunt down and deal with the kind (*genos*), sophist, we ought to practice our method (*methodos*) of hunting on something easier first. ... Do you want us to focus on something trivial and try to use it as a model (*paradeigma*) for the more important issue?' (218d3-9). Theaetetus finds the suggestion of practicing the method on something easy, agreeable. The Stranger then recommends the angler as a fitting, trivial issue because he is recognizable to everybody, and not worth being too serious about (218e4).[17]

Theaetetus' first task is to decide whether the angler is a kind of expert or not, 'Tell me, shall we take him to be an expert (*technitês*) at something, or a non-expert (*atechnos*) with another sort of capacity?' (219a4-6). Theaetetus states – quite confident – that the angler is certainly *not* a non-expert. If so, the Stranger continues – what sort of expertise does he possess? The Stranger now claims that 'expertise (*technê*) as a whole falls pretty much into two types (*eidê duo*, 219a8)': the 'art of production' (*poiêtikê* [*technê*], 219b11) and the 'art of acquisition' (*ktêtikê* [*technê*], 219c6). Agreeing upon the main categories of expertise, the first conclusion is reached: the angler is a kind of expert placed within the 'art of acquisition'. They now work their way through the first division which is supposed to be a paradigm for the method that eventually will enable them to hunt down the sophist.

The paradigm-division (219b7-221c3)

Section 1: The *manner* of the art			
Art of production	↔	Art of acquisition ↓	Cut 1: What kind of expertise?
Exchange	↔	Taking possession ↓	Cut 2: Where does it unfold?
Art of combat	↔	Art of hunting	Cut 3: How is it executed?
Section 2: The *object* of the art		↓	
Without name	↔	Art of animal-hunting ↓	Cut 4: What kind of object?
Land-hunting	↔	Aquatic-hunting ↓	Cut 5: Where is the object hunted?
Art of bird-catching	↔	Art of fishing	Cut 6: How is the object hunted?
Section 3: The *means* of the art		↓	
Enclosure-hunting	↔	Art of strike-hunting ↓	Cut 7: What kind of means?
Art of torching	↔	Hooking ↓	Cut 8: Where is the means used?
Spearing	↔	Angling	Cut 9: How are the means used?

The Stranger now presents a summary in accordance with the division's succession:

> Within expertise as a whole one half was acquisitive; half of the acquisitive was taking possession; half of possession-taking was hunting; half of hunting was animal-hunting; half of animal-hunting was aquatic hunting; all of the lower portion of aquatic hunting was fishing; half of fishing was hunting by striking; and half of striking was hooking. And the part of hooking that involves a blow drawing a thing upward from underneath is called by a name that's derived by its similarity to the action itself, that is, it's called draw-fishing or angling – which is what we're searching for.
>
> 221b2-c3

Because the Stranger launched this division as a paradigm for the method, and because they both agreed upon using it for hunting down the sophist, it is worth examining its structure in depth. The paradigm division falls into three sections, with three items in each section.[18] The bifurcations of the three sections follow the same procedure and thus establish a coherent pattern. Section 1 (cuts 1, 2, 3) deals with the *manner* of the art, and the first question asked is: *what* kinds of expertise are there? Expertise as a whole is usually divided into 'art of acquisition' (219c7) and 'art of production' (219b11), the Stranger claims when doing cut 1. Hence, at the outset he presents two main categories of expertise: production and acquisition. The dividing of the latter in cut 2 answers to the question: *where*, or within which areas, does the expertise unfold? The Stranger explains that it unfolds within 'exchange', which is mutually willing exchange through gifts, wages or purchase (219d6 f), and by 'taking possession', which denotes expertise in bringing things into one's possession by words or action/deed (219d7 f). When he divides the latter in cut 3, the third question posed is: *how* is the expertise executed? The Stranger elaborates. It is executed through the art of combat (*agônistikê*, 219d12) which is conducted openly, and the art of hunting (*thêreutikê*, 219e1) which is done secretly.

In section 2 (cuts 4, 5, 6) the Stranger establishes the *object* of the art. His point of departure in this section is the secretive 'art of hunting' (cut 3). From this outset we can ask: *what* kind of object is hunted for? Through cut 4 we learn that there is one kind without a name (220a2) where the hunter is pursuing lifeless things, opposed to animal-hunting (*zôothêrikê*, 220a4-5) where the hunter is pursuing living things. Thus, the main object is animals alive. But *where* is the object hunted? First there is the land-hunting (220a9), the Stranger claims, where the hunter hunts animals with feet, opposed to aquatic-hunting (220a10) where the hunter hunts animals that swim; this is displayed in cut 5. He further divides the latter and thus answers a new question: *how* is the object hunted down? Cut 6 shows that it is through the 'art of bird-catching' (*ornitheutikê* 220b5) or the 'art of fishing' (*halieutikê* 220b7).

In section 3 (cuts 7, 8, 9) the Stranger establishes the *means* employed to catch the prey hunted for and thus answers the question: *what* kinds of means are used in the hunt? The 'art of fishing' (cut 6) is now the point of departure. In cut 7 he divides this into 'enclosure-hunting' (220b12) and 'strike-hunting' (220d1). First 'enclosure-hunting' which denotes all that surrounds and encloses anything to prevent egress, such as twig baskets, casting nets, nooses, creels. Then 'strike-hunting' which is practised by a blow with hooks and three pronged spears. He divides the latter (cut 8) into night-time hunt which is done by the 'art of torching' (220d7) and daytime hunt which is called 'hooking' as a whole (220d10). This explains *where* the means are used, and when. Daytime hunt is further divided (cut 9), and the Stranger gives answer to the question: '*how* are the means used?' On the one hand there is 'spearing' (220d10) which is done by striking a spear downward from above; the spear strikes any parts of the prey's body. On the other hand, there is 'angling' (220d10) which is done with hooks; they are striking the prey's head and mouth and pulls it upwards from below. This is what they are searching for, the Stranger concludes.

What is the Stranger doing here? Apparently, he establishes a rather strict – and to a certain point inflexible – method. In addition, however, he also creates the ground for an interesting game which exposes parts of the Stranger's own identity. For instance, after having agreed upon cut 6 ('art of bird-catching' versus 'art of fishing'), and when he is about to perform cut 7 ('enclosure-hunting' versus the 'art of strike-hunting'), Theaetetus is asked if he has a better suggestion for the name 'art of striking'. 'Let's not worry about the name, that one will do', is Theaetetus' reply (220d4).[19] The Stranger does not pay attention to the reply, but continues and states without being contradicted that there actually *is* an 'art of striking', from which torching and hooking split off. According to Benardete,[20] an 'art (*technê*) of striking' did *not* exist as such in the empirical world, and hence, the Stranger at this point is 'laying himself open to the charge of making phantoms of the real'.[21] This point taken, it is reasonable to conclude that this is a kind of 'phantom-making', which is going on throughout the divisions and especially in the upcoming 'hunter-division' (221d7-223b7). In addition, it is pointing towards the dialogue's last definition which states that the sophist belongs to the 'blood and family' of 'imitation of the contrary-speech-producing, insincere and unknowing sort, of the appearance-making kind of copy-making, the word-juggling part of production that's marked off as human and not divine' (268c8-d3). Does the Stranger fit this description?

Maybe, because long before the sophist is explicitly set in the class of image-making, the Stranger himself already here appears to belong to 'the word-juggling part of production,' the kind who uses nets made up by imitation which he initially set in the 'art of production' at 219b11. As we shall see, the two main, originally mutually exclusive, categories of 'expertise' – 'art of production' and 'art of acquisition' – are blurred in the later exchange-division (223b8-224d3) which in turn undermines the paradigmatic function of the imperative paradigm division. In other words, the Stranger's 'phantom-making' at this point might not be accidental, but rather a hint pointing towards the game he is about to initiate; and thus, a sign for revealing his identity. Yet another significant element is his emphasizing of the movements concerning angling and spearing (cf. cut 9). *Spearing* was said to be done by striking downwards from above and aims to strike any part of the prey's body (220e). *Angling*, on the other hand, was done with a hook, striking the prey's head and mouth and pulling it upwards from below (220e-221a). Also in the summary these movements were underlined. First, when pinpointing the nature of angling as a method which involves a blow and drawing a thing upward from underneath, stating that it is called by a name which is derived by its similarity to the action itself, and, secondly, when concluding that the procedure is 'called draw-fishing or angling – which is what we're searching for' (221c1). Why this triple underlining of movements? The movement of the draw-fishing-procedure (angling) is in accordance with the movement of the 'Socratic dialectical method' as we know it from various dialogues: Socrates activates an upward movement, from the particular to the general.[22] The Stranger, however, advocates a method involving the opposite movement – from the general to the particular.[23]

In other words, when the Stranger performs the paradigm dividing, he underlines the angling-procedure, but performs the spearing-procedure. This emphasis on these opposite movements indicates not only a break with the familiar Socratic dialectics, but it also indicates that the art as the point of departure of his divisions might be illusive, because they do not allow a consistent method. Thus, the alleged outcome of the paradigm division, which was supposed to be an applicable method, is somewhat ambiguous and does not quite provide the simplicity which the Stranger anticipated, or pretended to anticipate. But still, it is the paradigm for the method. When the Stranger underlined the 'art of striking' as an art (*technê*) he went against the truth of the arts;[24]

and when making 'phantoms of the real' he simultaneously started to put on phantom-speeches.[25] Hence, Theaetetus now mistakenly believes that he is prepared to start the hunt for the sophist within the 'art of acquisition' where the Stranger placed him, but the Stranger is, in addition, starting a parallel hunt rooted within 'the art of production', which he set aside at 219b11. How does it develop?

Division 1 of 3: The Hunter (221d7-223b7)

```
                          Land-hunting (cf. cut 5 in the 'paradigm')

Section 1: The manner of the art     ↓

Hunting wild animals   ↔   Art of hunting tame animals       Cut 1: What kind of hunt?
                                       ↓
Violent hunt           ↔   Art of persuasion                 Cut 2: Where does it unfold?
                                       ↓
Persuasion in public   ↔   Persuasion in private             Cut 3: How is it executed?

Section 2: ?

       ↓                           ↓
Done by gift-giving (Cut 4.1)  Done by earning wage (Cut 4.2)
       ↓                           ↓
Art of love (Cut 4.1.1)        Art of private hunting (Cut 4.2.1)
                                   ↓                        ↓
                  Art of pleasing people (Cut 4.2.1.1)   Art of the sophist (Cut 4.2.1.2)
```

The subject for this division is the hunter and its outset is land-hunting, cut 5 in the paradigm division. Already at the start, at cut 1 'hunting wild animals' versus 'the art of hunting tame animals' (222c3), Theaetetus signals some kind of doubt, or surprise, when he asks: 'Is there any such things as hunting tame animals?' (222b6). The Stranger answers that 'there is if human beings are tame animals, at any rate' (222b7). He continues by giving Theaetetus some options, and tells him to decide,

> Either, there are no tame animals, or
> there are tame animals but humans are wild, or
> humans are tame but are not hunted.
>
> 222b6-7

These options are presented in a disjunctive form (either ... or), but the disjunction seems less than exhaustive of the possibilities. Is this something that requires a response? Is it a trap, or is it a test? If this can be read as a test directed towards Theaetetus, he at this point emerges quite clever. He chooses *none* of the options offered him. Instead he confirms the Stranger's first suggestion: 'I think we're tame animals and I'll say that humans are in fact hunted' (222c1-2). Without further remarks, they proceed from an agreement that there *is* a kinship between the angler and the sophist. The angler and the sophist are joined in the 'art of acquisition' but split off when the division reached animal-hunting. At this point the angler walked towards bodies of water and the sophist towards land. This premise suffices to allow the Stranger and Theaetetus to divide without further interruptions.

The 'art of hunting tame animals' is divided (cut 2) into 'violent hunting' (222c5) versus the 'art of persuasion' (222c9-d1). The former includes piracy, enslavement, tyranny and everything that has to do with the 'art of war', whilst the latter sums up arts such as legal oratory, political oratory and conversation. The 'art of persuasion' is further divided (cut 3) into 'persuasion in public' (222d5) and 'persuasion in private' (222d5).

So far, the Stranger has followed the method put forth in the paradigm dividing, hence section 1 (cuts 1, 2, 3) exhibits the *manner* of the land-hunting and the questions related to the manner of the art: *what-*, *where-* and *how-*, has been dealt with respectively. According to the proposed method in the paradigm it would now be reasonable to expect the Stranger to continue by displaying the *object* of the art.[26] However, he does not. Contrary to the reader's anticipation, he actually abandons the paradigm altogether. How? The expectation was that the 'art of persuasion in private' (cut 3) should have been cut off further, but instead the 'art of persuasion in public' and the 'art of persuasion in private' are cut off separately. Thus, it looks like he is starting to duplicate the structure of the paradigm within this hunter-division. This is obviously a major deviation from the proposed method, and the clarity these divisions were supposed to contribute to, is dissolving. Let us jump to the summary and see if it is in accordance with that of the paradigm:[27]

> According to this argument (*logos*), it seems that this sort of expertise belongs to the art of appropriation, the art of acquisition, the art of hunting, the hunting of the living, the hunting on footed animals, animal living on dry land, the art of hunting tame animals (cf. cut 1), human hunting (cf. cut 1), hunting privately (cf. cut 3), the art of wage-earning (cf. cut 4.2), the art of <u>money-changing</u>, the art of <u>opinion teaching</u> which is performed by the hunting of rich, prominent young men. And according to the way our account has turned out, it's what should be called the art of the sophist.
>
> *sophistikê*, cf. cut 4.2.1.2[28]

Theaetetus' reaction to the summary is total acceptance: 'Absolutely', he replies. But the Stranger's summary is not a summary of the argument. It just appears to be, and Theaetetus' lack of response is somewhat surprising. Why? The summary is presented as if the Stranger had just performed one division, but he does not take into consideration that he doubled the division after cut 3. In addition, there are several arrivals of terms in the summary which are not mentioned in the argument related to the division, such as the 'art of appropriation', the 'art of money-changing', and the 'art of opinion teaching'. Moreover, these arts do not have equivalents in the empirical world.[29] These denotations only exist in the Stranger's summary, so why does not Theaetetus comment on these alleged new arts? Why is he acting so defensively? What is the impact of these discrepancies?

When trying to answer these questions, let us start with the first characteristic given of the sophist, which was the kinship between him and the hunter. Believed to be equipped with a method, Theaetetus now apprehends himself to be a hunter hunting the hunter-sophist. However, as a pure hypothetical being, and because he has never experienced meeting a sophist,[30] he does not himself know exactly what kind of creature he is trying to hunt down. The result of Theaetetus' ignorance is that as a hunter he now believes he has captured the sophist for the first time and, as he also accepts the deviations of the hunter-division as well as the discrepancies between the presentation of the division and the summary, he simultaneously signals that he is not on track.

The result of the Stranger's hunt is that he appears to be a hunter – but now placed within the phantom-art of striking.[31] The Stranger displays, more and more, a grave discrepancy between his 'words and deeds'. He is not doing what he says he is doing. He has abandoned the method and his summaries do not encapsulate what he claims they do. By signalling total acceptance, Theaetetus' silence – at this point – makes him appear as a prey. In addition, due to Theaetetus' silence, it starts to dawn on the reader that Theaetetus is exposed to a kind of manipulation not recognizable to him. Nonetheless, this has an impact on the reader who recognizes the Stranger's phantom-speeches through which he is presenting phantom-arts with ridiculous names,[32] and further through the blurring of the distinctions he himself initially set forth (cf. the distinction between the two main categories 'production' and 'acquisition'). The manipulation is also recognizable because the Stranger now starts to move faster and faster. It is noticeable that the speed or tempo, *in* the summary, has increased compared to the summary of the paradigm division. This is visible through the disappearance of conjunctions.[33] From here on forwards, textual twists and turns become more frequent and the dramatic tempo increases rapidly. These incidents create a set of discrepancies, which give reason to suspect that the originally proposed method was abandoned almost at the outset. The methodical hunt, which the Stranger initiated, is now transformed into a metaphorical hunt where the hunted prey Theaetetus seems to be hit by the spear for the first time. What happens in the next division?

Division 2 of 3: Exchange (223b8-224d3)

		Expertise in the art of acquisition (cf. cut 4.2 in the Hunter-division) ↓	
Hunt	↔	Exchange ↓	Cut 1
Giving gifts	↔	Sale, commerce ↓	Cut 2
Art of selling	↔	Art of purveying ↓	Cut 3
Art of retailing	↔	Art of wholesaling ↓	Cut 4
Sale of body-nourishment	↔	Art of soul-wholesaling ↓	Cut 5
Art of display	↔	Art of knowledge-selling ↓	Cut 6
Expertise-selling	↔	Sophistry	Cut 7

The Stranger and Theaetetus now take a short break, and during the pause the Stranger creates a new situation where he seizes *kairos*.[34] The Stranger's seizing of *kairos* denotes a momentum which becomes visible as they move towards a new division. The point of departure is cut 4.2 in the previous hunter-division and the subject is exchange.

The structure of this division resembles that of the paradigm dividing, but the use of phantom-arts is similar to the previous, except this time the phantom-arts are introduced in the course of the division itself.[35] The 'art of acquisition' is once again established as a main category, and cut off into 'hunt' (223c7) versus 'exchange' (223c7). 'Exchange' is cut off into 'giving gifts' (223c10) versus 'sale and commerce' (223c10). The latter includes the 'art of selling' versus the 'art of purveying', that is purveying of things other people make (223d3). It is interesting to note that the former, 'art of selling', is sale of things the seller himself makes (223d2-3). The initial definition of the 'acquisitive art' included the clause 'the seller does not produce anything' (219c1-8). In other words, the Stranger then argued that to be acquisitive was to be not-productive, but now he seems to be arguing for the opposite. The 'art of production' and the 'art of acquisition' are no longer presented as mutually exclusive, as the initial definitions suggested. Why does not Theaetetus comment on this obvious contradiction? My suggestion is that by now he is so confused by the Stranger's many twists and manipulations that he is no longer able to follow him.

The Stranger moves to cut 4 where the 'art of purveying' is divided into the 'art of retailing' (223d5) versus the 'art of wholesaling' (223d6). The former is purveying within the city, whilst the latter is exchange between cities, which in cut 5 is divided into the 'sale of nourishment for the body in exchange for cash' (223d12-e2) versus 'soul-wholesaling' (224b4).

Let us take a closer look at bifurcation five and onwards. The Stranger now elaborates: 'Wouldn't the right thing to say be that the art of display is one part of soul-wholesaling? And don't we have to call the other part of it, the part that consists in selling knowledge, by a name that's similar and also equally ridiculous?' (224b4-7) We are by now used to Theaetetus' passive agreement, but what is he agreeing to this time? That the 'art of display' (224b4-5; cut 6) is one part of soul-wholesaling (cut 5), or that the name is ridiculous? The Stranger derives these names directly from an action, which obviously is an effective turn. Theaetetus becomes attentive and replies that he now has located the sophist for the second time. When noticing Theaetetus' partaking, the Stranger quickly presents the summary,

> We'll say that the expertise of the art of acquisition, the art of exchange (cut 1), the art of selling (cut 2), the art of wholesaling (cut 4), the art of soul-wholesaling (cut 5) dealing in words and learning that have to do with virtue – that's sophistry (cut 7) in its second appearance.
>
> 224c8-d2

The summary is again selective because it is lacking some essential elements. Especially is the lacking of the sixth bifurcation ('art of display' versus 'art of knowledge-selling') noteworthy due to the details given in the course of the division.[36] During this division and its summary, the reader is able to understand somewhat more of who the Stranger is by once again noticing what he is doing. This is a new illustration of how the Stranger is allowed to perform a sort of language-manipulation by mixing categories, twisting words and presenting it all in a speeding litany. The only indication of alertness is Theaetetus' relief for having located sophistry for the second time, but he himself has, simultaneously and metaphorically, been hunted down and hit by the spear for the second time.

An interlude (224d4-e6)

The Stranger's next step is fascinating, and signals another kind of turn. He says: 'I think you'd call somebody just the same thing if he settled here in the city and undertook to make his living selling those same things, both that he'd bought and the ones that he'd made himself; and thereby you have met the sophist for the third time' (224d4-8). Theaetetus agrees, but what happened here? According to the exchange-division and its summary, the sophist belonged to the sub-category of wholesaling. Just by transporting him into the sub-category of retailing, the Stranger here performs yet another turn, by picking up on a slightly altered definition of the 'art of acquisition'. Now he claims that the sophist 'makes his living selling things he'd bought and the ones that he's made himself'. Hence, the sophist does not only belong to the 'art of acquisition', he *also* belongs to the 'art of production'. Here, the mentioned contradiction is stated even more bluntly. The sophist belongs to both of the originally two main, mutually exclusive, categories. After having conducted the transport of the sophist from wholesaling to retailing, the Stranger concludes that they have encountered the sophist for the third time. So, subsequently he presents his summary in accordance with this turn,

> So apparently you'll still say that sophistry falls under acquisition, exchange, and selling, either by retailing things that others make or by selling things that he makes himself. It's the retail sale of any learning that has to do with the sorts of things we mentioned.
>
> 224d10-e3

This summary is a confirmation on the Stranger's manipulative strategies, and as such it is eye-opening in order to observe how the Stranger – by transporting the sophist – has managed to abolish the two initial main categories. In this summary, both are present, but mixed together. This turn simultaneously conceals the twist, which makes Theaetetus responsible for the conclusion: 'So apparently you will still say that ...' (224e3). Theaetetus' response at this point signals that he is rather tired,[37] and his acceptance of having come across the sophist again is rather submissive when he states that it has to be so 'since we need to stay consistent with what we said before'. But is this consistent with what they said before? No, this is a break with several things said before. And it is due to manipulation, twists and turns that Theaetetus admits the third encounter with the sophist, and by this act he is once again – metaphorically – hit by the spear, for the third time. They move on, and this time a new aim is set: by dividing the 'art of combat' they are now supposed to create the ground for later comparisons.

Division 3 of 3: The art of combat (225a1-226a6)

		Art of combat ↓	
Art of competition	↔	Art of fighting ↓	Cut 1
Art of violence	↔	Art of controversy ↓	Cut 2
Forensic	↔	Disputation ↓	Cut 3
Controversy	↔	Art of debating ↓	Cut 4
Art of money-waisting	↔	Art of money-making ↓	Cut 5
Art of chatter	↔	Art of the sophist	Cut 6

Prior to this division, Theaetetus and the Stranger decided that the 'art of combat' (225a2) was a part of the 'art of acquisition'. This is in accordance with its previous definition as open attempts at mastery;[38] which accordingly makes the sophist no longer a secret combatant or hunter.[39] The 'art of combat' is now cut off into the 'art of competition' (225a6) versus the 'art of fighting' (225a6-7). This is an opposition questioning how the contest is carried out, rather than what it is about. Cut 2 divides the 'art of fighting' into 'violence' (225a11) versus 'controversy' (225b1). The 'art of violence' denotes one body fighting against another and the 'art of controversy' denotes the pits of words against words. This refers to the means of the arts, which the manner of 'forensic speeches' and 'disputation' (225b10) is derived from. The former is a long public speech directed against another, which deals with justice and injustice; the latter is private discussions chopped up into questions and answers. 'Disputation' is by cut 4 divided in 'controversy about contracts' (225b12-c4) versus 'debating' (225c9). The former is not carried out in any systematic or expert way; the latter is done expertly and involves controversy about general issues, including what is just and unjust. It turns out that the 'art of debating' is the artful 'disputation'. However, according to Benardete, this is 'absurd since its anonymous opposite discusses contracts artlessly. Yet it is supposed to be a sub-division of the "art of acquisition".[40] The 'art of eristic' is cut into the 'art of wasting money' versus 'making money'. The latter is cut into 'chatter' versus the 'art of the sophist'. After the completion of this division, Theaetetus appears to be impressed: 'How could anyone go wrong in saying that the amazing sophist we've been after has turned up for the fourth time?' (225e3-5) The Stranger does not answer Theaetetus; instead he presents the summary – or again – what appears to be a summary,

> It seems his type is precisely the money-making branch of expertise (cf. cut 5) in debating (cf. cut 4), disputation (cf. cut 2), controversy (cf. cut 2), fighting (cf. cut 1), combat, acquisition.
>
> 226a1-3

The movement in the present division was, apparently, in accordance with the paradigm; downward from above (spearing-procedure). Nonetheless, the movement in the summary changes again. Now it moves upward from below. This entails that the Stranger for the very first time employs the draw-fisher-procedure, which is the procedure he initially announced they were searching for. It is also noteworthy that he activates it at this point when the hunt no longer is performed secretly. Thus, at this moment the draw-fisher strikes for the first time, and the impressed Theaetetus – metaphorically – swallows the hook, and is, like a prey pulled in, upward from below, in accordance with the primary aim of the hunter.

Towards a conclusion

On account of given hints towards the *Euthydemus*,[41] my conclusion will be framed with help from Socrates. In that context he observed, off stage, what happened on stage when young Clinias met the sophist Euthydemus: 'Euthydemus was hastening to throw Clinias for the third fall, when I, seeing that he was going down and wanting to give him a chance to breathe so that he should not turn coward and disgrace us, encouraged him …' (*Euthydemus* 277d1-3). Socrates stopped that combat, and consulted Clinias. He told him that when meeting a sophist, one must imagine oneself to be hearing the first part of the sophistic mystery, pay attention to the use of words, especially the correct meaning of words, and one must always think of the performance of the sophists as a game. After the first session – which involves several falls – the sophists will let one rest; in the pause they will doubtless display some serious things, before they start the game all over again.

Is Socrates' description of this sophistic performance somewhat similar to the Stranger's game in the *Sophist*? I think so, but contrary to Clinias, Theaetetus was not explicitly told to view his assignment as partaking in a game. Trained in mathematics he approached his task in a purely hypothetical manner, and hence, he did not pay attention to the meaning and use of words. Thus, the Stranger was offered the opportunity to set his game into play. In an alleged hunt for the sophist, Theaetetus did not comprehend that the Stranger gradually abandoned the proposed method. Therefore Theaetetus, the student of mathematics, did not grasp that it was he himself that was hunted, manipulated, and gradually started to appear as a prey. After three falls (stroked by the spear) he – metaphorically speaking – swallowed the hook and was pulled in by the Stranger.

Consequently, the readers' hunt of the Stranger revealed that the proposed hunting-method camouflaged a metaphorical hunt: Theaetetus thought he was hunting the hunter-sophist within the 'art of acquisition', according to the paradigmatic method. The Stranger pretended to do the same. However, his hunt was partly carried out within the 'art of production' which he set aside at the outset, but later transported the sophist into. Further, the Stranger, as a hunter working secretly, stroke his prey down three times with the spear, and when he no longer hunted secretly,[42] Theaetetus swallowed the hook and was pulled in.

Through this close reading of the prologue, and by the survey of the upcoming divisions, a specific problem concerning the Stranger has been revealed: There is a severe discrepancy between his words and deeds – that is, a discrepancy between what the Stranger said he was doing versus what he actually did. As the prologues of the Platonic dialogues, according to Gonzales, 'provides the foundation for the subsequent investigation by drawing our attention to specific problems … that have a bearing on the main subject of the dialogue,'[43] it is imperative to note this discrepancy – not only in the prologue – but throughout the dialogue. The Stranger will set his game into play over and over again, and due to his twists and turns he appears to act like a sophist more than the philosophical man Theodorus initially claimed him to be.

Notes

1 Some examples of scholars defending the mouthpiece theory (i.e. that the Stranger is speaking for Plato): Paul Friedländer, *Die Platonichen Schriften, Band 1-3* (Berlin und Leipzig: W. de Gruyter Verlag, 1929–30); A.N. Whitehead, *Adventures of Ideas* (Cambridge: Cambridge University Press, 1933); F.M. Cornford, *Plato's Theory of Knowledge: The Theaetetus and the Sophist* (London: Kegan Paul, 1935); J.R. Trevaskis, 'The Sophistry of Noble Linage (Plato, *Sophistes* 230a5-232b9)', *Phronesis* 1, no. 1 (1955); John Ackrill, 'Plato and the Copula: *Sophist* 251-259', *The Journal of Hellenic Studies* 77, no. 1 (1957); Gregory Vlastos, *Socrates, Ironist and Moral Philosopher* (Cambridge: Cambridge University Press, 1991).
2 Some examples of scholars questioning the mouthpiece theory: Stanley Rosen, *Plato's Sophist: The Drama of Original and Image* (New Haven: Yale University Press, 1983); Eugenio Benitez, 'Argument, Rhetoric and Philosophical Method: Plato's *Protagoras*', *Philosophy and Rhetoric* 25 (1992); Jacob Howland, *The Paradox of Political Philosophy. Socrates' Philosophical Trial* (Lanham: Rowman & Littlefield Publishers, 1998); Victorino Tejera, 'Plato's *Politicus*, an Eleatic Sophist on Politics', *Philosophy and Social Criticism* 5, no. 2 (1978), 'The Politics of a Sophistic Rhetorian', *Philosophy and Social Criticism* 5, no. 1 (1978), and *Plato's Dialogues One by One: A Dialogical Interpretation* (Savage, Maryland: Rowman & Littlefield, 1999); Seth Benardete, 'Plato's "Sophist" 223 B 1-7', *Phronesis* 5, no. 2 (1960), and 'On Plato's *Sophist*', *The Review of Metaphysics* 46, no. 4 (1993); Francisco J. Gonzalez, 'The Eleatic Stranger: His Masters Voice?', in *Who Speaks for Plato? Studies in Platonic Anonymity*, ed. Gerald A. Press (Lanham: Rowman & Littlefield Publishers, 2000); Lesley Brown, 'Definition and Division in Plato's *Sophist*', in *Definition in Greek Philosophy*, ed. David Charles (Oxford: Oxford Scholarship Online, 2010).
3 Benardete, 'On Plato's *Sophist*', 750.
4 Howland, *The Paradox of Political Philosophy*, 189.
5 Summarized by Catherine H. Zuckert, 'Who's a Philosopher? Who's a Sophist? The Stranger V. Socrates', *The Review of Metaphysics* 54, no. 1 (2000): 95 n 74.
6 Tejera, *Plato's Dialogues One by One*, 201. Tejera puts forth the same argument in 'The Politics of a Sophistic Rhetorian'.

7   Cf. Tejera, 'Plato's *Politicus*, an Eleatic Sophist on Politics'. The Eleatic Stranger is also the main speaker in the Platonic dialogue the *Statesman*.
8   Benitez, 'Characterisation and Interpretation: The Importance of Drama in Plato's *Sophist*', *The Sydney Society of Literature and Aesthetics* 6 (1996): 37.
9   This ambiguity is also mirrored through two manuscripts, which deliver two contradictory versions of the opening lines stated by Theodorus. First: 'Socrates, [...] we're bringing a Stranger, he's from Elea and he's *a companion (hetairos)* of the group who gather around Parmenides and Zeno.' This version is commonly used by commentators and scholars, a few examples are: George Kimball Plochmann, 'Socrates, the Stranger from Elea, and Some Others', *Classical Philology* 49, no. 4 (1954); Benardete, 'On Plato's *Sophist*'; John Sallis, *Being and Logos: Reading the Platonic Dialogues* (Bloomington: Indiana University Press, 1996); Noburu Notomi, *The Unity of Plato's Sophist. Between the Sophist and the Philospoher* (Cambridge: Cambridge University Press, 2007); Gonzalez, 'The Eleatic Stranger: His Masters Voice?'; David Ambuel, *Image and Paradigm in Plato's Sophist* (Las Vegas, Zuric, Athens: Parmenides Publishing, 2007). Second: 'Socrates, [...] we're also bringing this Stranger who comes from Elea, *but he's different from (heteros)* the group who gather around Parmenides and Zeno.' This version is strongly defended by Nestor-Luis Corderos, *Le Sophiste* (Paris: Flammarion, 1993), app. I, n 5, cf. Eyjólfur Kjalar Emilsson, 'Innledning til Sofisten', in *Platon. Samlede Verker*, vol. VI (Oslo: Vidarforlagets Kulturbibliotek, 2004), 231–47.
10 Cf. Gonzalez, 'How to Read a Platonic Prologue: Lysis 203a-207d', in *Plato as Author. The Rhetoric of Philosophy*, ed. Ann N. Michelini (Leiden: Brill, 2003), 16.
11 'Close reading' entails that I relate to reader response theory which recognizes the reader as an active agent; thus, the textual effects upon the reader are of importance. Cf. Jill Gordon, *Turning toward Philosophy: Literary Device and Dramatic Structure in Plato's Dialogues* (University Park: Pennsylvania State University Press, 1999).
12 Cf. Howland, *The Paradox of Political Philosophy*, 173: 'Plato leaves no doubt that the *Sophist* cannot be understood without attention to what the Stranger shows of himself in his *deeds* as well as what he says in *argument*.' I agree with Howland when he argues that the Stranger's deeds and arguments ought to be central issues when reading the *Sophist*, but our readings do not reach the same conclusion.
13 The English translation used in this chapter is *Sophist*, trans. Nicholas P. White, in *Plato. Complete works*, ed. John M. Cooper (Indianapolis: Hackett Publishing Company, 1997).
14 Theodorus is a teacher of mathematics. He knew Protagoras (cf. *Theaetetus* 161c, 164c, 179e-180c), and therefore the reader might expect that he has developed some convincing mixture of geometry and the partitive sophistic of his friend. Further, from the *Theaetetus* we learn that Theodorus does not give general cases by dividing oblong from square numbers. Instead he proves individual cases (147d) and furthermore, at 165a Theodorus confesses he turned too early from dialectic to geometry, and he hopes to analyse the problems of universal motion as if they were purely geometrical. Thus, he is unable correctly to apply his mathematics to the concrete philosophical situation (180c). Cf. Plochman, 'Socrates, the Stranger from Elea, and Some Others', 226.
15 The English translation used in this chapter: *Euthydemus*, trans. Rosamond Kent Sprague, in *Plato. Complete works*, ed. John M. Cooper (Indianapolis: Hackett Publishing Company, 1997). On the difference between eristic and elenchus, see Hugh H. Benson, 'A Note on Eristic and the Socratic Elenchus', *Journal of the History of Philosophy* 27, no. 4 (1989).

16 The assumed Socratic recognition can perhaps also be warranted through the fact that it is Socrates who sets forth the main issues discussed in the *Sophist*. This argument may find support in Notomi, *The Unity of Plato's Sophist*. Notomi argues that in the *Sophist* Plato addresses the problem of philosophy versus sophistry in order to set forth the worth of philosophy, which I also think is a theme in the *Protagoras*. Notomi claims: 'Plato found that, without serious criticism of the sophist, there could not be philosophy,' 301. This fundamental distinction is the backdrop of Socrates' upcoming trial. Thus, through the Stranger, Socrates seeks a defence against his Athenian accusers that can distinguish him from the teachings of the sophists. This last point is also made by Mitchell Miller, *The Philosopher in Plato's Statesman* (Hauge: Nijhoff, 1980), 2, 11; Sallis, *Being and Logos*, 464; Gonzalez, 'The Eleatic Stranger: His Masters Voice?', 163. And further, the difference between Socrates and the Stranger in this regard is, for example, commented on in detail by Rosen, *Plato's Sophist*, 20-28, and in *Plato's Statesman: The Web of Politics* (New Haven: Yale University Press, 1995), 2-4, 41-2, 50, 91, 154, and by Zuckert, 'Who's a Philosopher?', 97, and by Gonzalez, ibid, 168.

17 The angler 'not worth being too serious about', is a theme also touched upon in Book VII of the *Laws*. The Athenian Stranger sets out the rules for hunting – which he treats as the last part of *paideia*. His listing is reminiscent of the Stranger's paradigm division, except the items distinguished on. These items are, in the *Laws*, characterized as unworthy activities; and as such – the activities are not suitable for building the excellent character which the education in the *Laws* is aiming at. The practising of enclosure- and strike-hunting are regarded as the most damaging undertakings. When formulating the prelude to the law on hunting, the Athenian Stranger states that 'we hope you'll never be seized by a desire or passion to fish in the sea or to angle or indeed to hunt water animals at all; and don't resort to creels, which a lazybones will leave to catch his prey whether he's asleep or awake' (823e1-4). Thus, the subject in the paradigm division – the angler – performs an activity labelled unworthy by the Athenian Stranger, but the Stranger of the *Sophist* claims that the angler was chosen because his expertise is trivial, and 'not worth being too serious about'. Thus, in this regard, the two Strangers in the Platonic corpus contradict each other. The English translation used in this chapter is: *Laws*, trans. Trevor J. Saunders, in *Plato. Complete works*, ed. John M. Cooper (Indianapolis: Hackett Publishing Company, 1997).

18 Cf. Benardete, 'On Plato's *Sophist*', 758. Benardete suggests that the paradigm division falls into three sections where the manner, object and mean of the art are described, respectively. I found this suggestion to be very useful and have developed it further.

19 This quest which Theaetetus did not respond upon, can be read as a clue toward the Stranger and his 'phantom-arts' which he is about to create – and especially with regard to the 'art of striking'.

20 Benardete, 'On Plato's *Sophist*', 758, states that the Stranger here 'starts to duplicate the historical development of the ικὴ-suffix from being an ethnic to a skill'. That is, the discussions regarding 'art' (*technê*) that were going on in the fifth century denoted abilities such as 'striking' related to hunt, an ability generally known. For example, the knowledge of how to use a spear was a knowledge handed down from father to son (being an ethnic and an ability *generally* known), thus, not an 'art' which denotes an expertise, skill or a craft learned by a student from a master. The same instance we find if my father teaches me how to use a hammer and a spike, my father is teaching me a bit of general knowledge; but that kind of knowledge does not make me a carpenter (an expert within an art).

21 Benardete, 'On Plato's *Sophist*', 762. See also Robert W. Wallace, 'Plato's Sophists, Intellectual History after 450', in *The Age of Pericles*, ed. Loren J. Samons II (Cambridge: Cambridge University Press, 2007).
22 Plochman, 'Socrates, the Stranger from Elea, and Some Others', 230n17, points out that 'the whole problem of the nature of dialectic is so intricate that it would be folly to do more than offer a working definition of it here. We are given many accounts, a number of them highly figurative: a) dialectic is a way of beating up game (*Republic* 432b-e); b) dialectic is like a sight (*Republic* 532a); c) dialectic is a copingstone (*Republic* 534e); d) dialectic is of carving at the joints (*Pheadrus* 265e); e) dialectic is a net (*Sophist* 235b); f) dialectic is the harmless amusement of old men (*Laws* 820c). Nearly every utterance in the dialogues is dialectical in this sense: every main speaker seems to have a dialectic, even if it be foreshortened incoherent obscure.'
23 Cf. Platon, *Sofisten*; translator's remark, 323 n 21. Emilsson here comments on the method employed in the dialogue generally, and especially on the science of dialectic when mentioned at 253d1-4. Just prior to this point the Stranger is pondering: 'What if we, when hunting the sophist, have found the philosopher? [...] Aren't we going to say that it takes expertise in dialectic to divide things by kind and not to think that the same form is a different one or that a different form is the same?' (253c8-d4). Regarding the science of dialectic, Emilsson is in agreement with Plochmann, cf. note 22 above.
24 Cf. n 20 and n 21 above.
25 Cf. Benardete, 'On Plato's *Sophist*', 758–60.
26 Cf. section 2 in the paradigm dividing.
27 Regarding this summary there are some manuscript discrepancies, but 'all the original readings are defensible [...] it looks at first as if the summary (223b1-7) should show a progressive narrowing of the range within which the sophist is contained; but since it does not, the text has been changed to make it conform to our expectations', cf. Benardete, 'Plato's "Sophist" 223 B 1-7', 129. David B. Robinson, 'Textual Notes on Plato's *Sophist*', *The Classical Quarterly, New Series* 49, no. 1 (1999): 141, argues that in this summary 'confusion reigns ...: (i) terms are present which were not used earlier, and (ii) in the mss. text there is undoubtedly some redundancy; there are too many terms in this resume to fit the preceding division.' The explanation of these discrepancies is twofold: (a) Plato had varied his terminology in making the resume, but (b) some redundant terms were glosses added by scholiasts from the original terminology' (ibid.). One of the most spectacular cases of agreement with this judgement can be found in Cornford, *Plato's Theory of Knowledge*, 170. He omits to translate the division sections because 'the modern reader ... might be wearied'.
28 *Sophist* 223a12-b5. The translation of the summary is partly mine, and thus it differs slightly from Nicholas P. White's translation due to the Greek editions. I use the Greek text by Auguste Diès in *Platon. Werke in acht Bänden* (Darmstadt: Wissenschaftliche Buchgesellschaft, 1990). The terms underlined are the 'new arts' presented in the summary only.
29 Cf. n 20 above.
30 *Sophist* 239e1, cf. Benardete, 'On Plato's *Sophist*', 750, and Plochmann, 'Socrates, the Stranger from Elea, and Some Others', 226. They both argue that compared with the other youths we meet throughout various Platonic dialogues, Theaetetus – who has never seen a sophist – stands as the most innocent.
31 Cf. note 20 above. The 'art of striking' as such does not exist in the empirical world – thus it is denoted here as a phantom art.

32 The Stranger himself denotes some names as 'ridiculous', especially at 224b4 when referring to the art of soul-wholesaling, and at 227a4-5 when referring to the cleansing of nonliving bodies 'which have lots of specialized and ridiculous names'.
33 By 'disappearing of conjunctions' I mean that in the summary of the paradigm dividing the Stranger said, for example: half of the ..., and .... The impact of this was that the Stranger initially was patient and progressed so slowly that Theaetetus was able to follow him. In the course of the present summary the easy-going style has vanished – this summary is a rapid litany – hence the impact now is that the dramatic tempo increases.
34 As a concept rooted in time, *kairos* can signify the time in-between something and something else. *Kairos* is then the moment between processes, a moment which compels something extraordinary to happen. What this extraordinary happening *is* depends on the identity of the speaker or actor, and the way which the situation offers a change of perspective. When Isocrates in the *Panathenaicus* (30-32) describes the well-educated man, he connects practical wisdom (*phronêsis*) to *kairos* and claims the well-educated men are those 'who manage well the circumstances which they encounter day by day, and who possess a judgement which is accurate in meeting occasions as they arise and rarely misses the expedient course of action' (30). In a rhetorical perspective *kairos* also holds an element of force, and can be connected to actions like 'cutting', 'distinguishing', 'dividing', and 'judging'. Thus, when accepting most of the arguments placed before him, Theaetetus, by this acceptance, is offering the Stranger a momentum, or an opportunity to seize the moment (*kairos*).
35 Regarding this and the next dividing I will not comment upon the manner, object, or mean of the art because this pattern which was presented systematically in the paradigm dividing, is now abandoned pretty much in the same way as explained in the previous division.
36 Cf. *Sophist* 224a1-7 and 224b4.
37 Theaetetus indicated himself that this could happen, cf. *Sophist* 218b1-5.
38 Cf. *Sophist* 219e1-2, 225a2.
39 Cf. the paradigm division, third bifurcation where the 'art of hunting' (done secretly) was opposed to the 'art of combat' (done openly). See also Benardete, 'Plato's "Sophist" 223 B 1-7', 134.
40 Benardete, 'Plato's "Sophist" 223 B 1-7', ibid.
41 *Euthydemus* 277d1-278e1.
42 This was revealed at the outset of 'Division 3 of 3: The art of combat.'
43 Gonzales, 'How to Read a Platonic dialogue', 16.

Bibliography

Ackrill, John. 'Plato and the Copula: *Sophist* 251-259'. *The Journal of Hellenic Studies* 77, no. 1 (1957): 1–6.
Ambuel, David. *Image & Paradigm in Plato's Sophist*. Las Vegas: Parmenides Publishing, 2007.
Benardete, Seth. 'On Plato's *Sophist*'. *The Review of Metaphysics* 46, no. 4 (1993): 747–80.
Benardete, Seth. 'Plato's "Sophist" 223 B 1-7'. *Phronesis* 5, no. 2 (1960): 129–39.
Benitez, Eugenio. 'Argument, Rhetoric and Philosophical Method: Plato's *Protagoras*'. *Philosophy and Rhetoric* 25 (1992): 222–52.
Benitez, Eugenio. 'Characterisation and Interpretation: The Importance of Drama in Plato's *Sophist*'. *The Sydney Society of Literature and Aesthetics* 6 (1996): 27–39.

Benson, Hugh H. 'A Note on Eristic and the Socratic Elenchus'. *Journal of the History of Philosophy* 27, no. 4 (1989): 591–9.
Brown, Lesley. 'Definition and Division in Plato's *Sophist*'. In *Definition in Greek Philosophy*. Edited by David Charles, 151–71. Oxford: Oxford Scholarship Online, 2010.
Corderos, Nestor-Luis. *Le Sophiste*. Paris: Flammarion, 1993.
Cornford, F.M. *Plato's Theory of Knowledge: The Theaetetus and the Sophist*. London: Kegan Paul, 1935.
Emilsson, Eyjólfur Kjalar. 'Innledning til *Sofisten*'. In *Platon. Samlede Verker*, vol. vi, 231–47. Oslo: Vidarforlagets Kulturbibliotek, 2004.
Friedländer, Paul. *Die Platonichen Schriften, Band 1-3*. Berlin: W. de Gruyter Verlag, 1929–30.
Gonzalez, Francisco J. 'How to Read a Platonic Prologue: Lysis 203a-207d'. In *Plato as Author. The Rhetoric of Philosophy*. Edited by Ann N. Michelini, 15–44. Leiden: Brill, 2003.
Gonzalez, Francisco J. 'The Eleatic Stranger: His Masters Voice?' In *Who Speaks for Plato? Studies in Platonic Anonymity*. Edited by Gerald A. Press, 161–82. Lanham: Rowman & Littlefield Publishers, 2000.
Gordon, Jill. *Turning Toward Philosophy: Literary Device and Dramatic Structure in Plato's Dialogues*. University Park: Pennsylvania State University Press, 1999.
Homer. *The Odyssey*. Translated and edited by H. Rieu. London: Penguin, 2003.
Howland, Jacob. *The Paradox of Political Philosophy. Socrates' Philosophical Trial*. Lanham: Rowman & Littlefield Publishers, 1998.
Isocrates. *Panathenaicus*. Translated by George Norlin. [Online]: http://www.perseus.tufts.edu/hopper/text?doc=Perseus%3Atext%3A1999.01.0144%3Aspeech%3D12 (accessed 26.08.2018).
Miller, Mitchell. *The Philosopher in Plato's Statesman*. Hauge: Nijhoff, 1980.
Notomi, Noburu. *The Unity of Plato's Sophist. Between the Sophist and the Philosopher*. Cambridge: Cambridge University Press, 2007.
Plato. *Complete Works*. Edited by John M. Cooper. Indianapolis: Hackett Publishing Company, 1997.
Platon. *Sofisten*. In *Platon. Samlede Verker*, vol. vi. Translated by Eyjólfur Kjalar Emilsson. Oslo: Vidarforlagets Kulturbibliotek, 2004.
Platon. ΣΟΦΙΣΤΗΣ / Der Sophist. In *Platon. Werke in acht Bänden*. Griechisch und deutsch. Sonderausgabe. Sechster Band: *Theaitetos. Der Sophist. Der Staatsmann*. Griechischer Text von Auguste Diès. Deutsche Übersetzung von Friedrich Schleiermacher. Darmstadt: Wissenschaftliche Buchgesellschaft, 1990.
Plochmann, George Kimball. 'Socrates, the Stranger from Elea, and Some Others'. *Classical Philology* 49, no. 4 (1954): 223–31.
Robinson, David B. 'Textual Notes on Plato's *Sophist*'. *The Classical Quarterly, New Series* 49, no. 1 (1999): 139–60.
Rosen, Stanley. *Plato's Sophist: The Drama of Original and Image*. New Haven: Yale University Press, 1983.
Rosen, Stanley. *Plato's Statesman: The Web of Politics*. New Haven: Yale University Press, 1995.
Sallis, John. *Being and Logos: Reading the Platonic Dialogues*. Bloomington: Indiana University Press, 1996.
Tejera, Victorino. 'Plato's *Politicus*, an Eleatic Sophist on Politics'. *Philosophy and Social Criticism* 5, no. 2 (1978): 85–104.
Tejera, Victorino. 'The Politics of a Sophistic Rhetorian'. *Philosophy and Social Criticism* 5, no. 1 (1978): 1–26.

Tejera, Victorino. *Plato's Dialogues One by One: A Dialogical Interpretation*. Savage: Rowman & Littlefield, 1999.

Trevaskis, J.R. 'The Sophistry of Noble Linage (Plato, *Sophistes* 230a5-232b9)'. *Phronesis* 1, no. 1 (1955): 36–49.

Vlastos, Gregory. *Socrates, Ironist and Moral Philosopher*. Cambridge: Cambridge University Press, 1991.

Wallace, Robert W. 'Plato's Sophists, Intellectual History after 450'. In *The Age of Pericles*, edited by Loren J. Samons II, 215–37. Cambridge: Cambridge University Press, 2007.

Whitehead, A.N. *Adventures of Ideas*. Cambridge: Cambridge University Press, 1933.

Zuckert, Catherine H. 'Who's a Philosopher? Who's a Sophist? The Stranger V. Socrates'. *The Review of Metaphysics* 54, no. 1 (2000): 65–97.

13

Plato's *Sophist*: A Different Look[1]

John Sallis

The scene is much the same as that of the *Theaetetus*. This continuity is explicit in Socrates' final remark in the *Theaetetus*, taken together with the statement by Theodorus with which the *Sophist* begins. At the very end of the *Theaetetus*, Socrates proposes: 'But in the morning, Theodorus, let us meet here again' (*Theaetetus* 210d).[2] The site is near a gymnasium where Theaetetus and his young friends, including one named Socrates as well as at least one more, have been exercising and oiling themselves before coming upon Socrates and Theodorus at the site where the conversation is held. Here, at the same site, they are, according to Socrates' proposal, to meet early on the following day. The *Sophist* opens then, on the following day, with Theodorus' statement that this proposal has been carried out: 'In accordance with yesterday's agreement, Socrates, we ourselves have come in due order' (216a). It can be presumed that the words 'we ourselves' indicate that those who were present at yesterday's conversation are once more present; it is explicit that at least those identified by name in the *Theaetetus* – namely, Theodorus, Theaetetus, and the young Socrates – have come again duly, in due order (*kosmiôs*), that is, precisely as proposed by Socrates on the previous day. Thus, the *Sophist* takes place at the same site and with those present who were there at that site on the previous day. To this extent, the scene is the same; and the conversation that is about to commence is a continuation of the conversation carried out in the *Theaetetus*. In this respect it is part of a longer conversation; it belongs to one and the same extended conversation as that in the *Theaetetus*.

This very sameness, marked at the outset, renders all the more conspicuous the difference that sets the *Sophist* apart from the *Theaetetus*, that gives it a different look. The difference is twofold. The first is declared by Theodorus, who, to his opening affirmation, adds the following: 'and we are bringing along this stranger of sorts, who by birth is from Elea and who is a companion of those around Parmenides and Zeno – a very philosophical man' (216a).[3] Thus, to those present on the previous day, another is added. Not only does his presence render the scene other than that of the *Theaetetus*, but also the identification of him as a stranger marks his difference from the others present at the scene, all but one of them native Athenians.[4] He is different in kind, different in origin, different by birth – the word is *genos*. He is a foreigner; *xenos* designates one who comes from elsewhere, who by his lineage belongs somewhere else, even if he is being received as a guest. His character as an alien is emphasized by the fact that his name is never mentioned in the dialogue, that he is simply called *Stranger*. His presence makes the scene of the *Sophist* other than that of the previous day. The stage is thus set for the Stranger's discourse on the other, on otherness, in which the ontological core of the dialogue will culminate.

There is another difference that renders the scene of the *Sophist* other than that of the *Theaetetus*. Though never mentioned in the *Sophist*, it is revealed at the end of the *Theaetetus*. Just before Socrates proposes that they meet the next morning, he says: 'But now I must go to the Porch of the King to meet the indictment that Meletus has drawn up against me' (*Theaetetus* 210d). Thus, in the interval between the end of the conversation in the *Theaetetus* and the conversation on the next morning, Socrates will have appeared before the magistrate – in this case the King Archon – and Meletus' charge will have been officially brought against him. By the time the *Sophist* begins on the next morning, the decision will have been made that Socrates is to be brought to trial; and, most likely, the date of the trial will have been set. In other words, it will have been determined that Socrates must appear before the judges (those whom he calls 'men of Athens') in order to declare who he is, or rather, to differentiate himself from what he is taken to be in Meletus' indictment and, still more decisively, in the accusations or prejudices against him ingrained over the years. These accusations are that he makes the weaker *logos* appear the stronger and that he teaches this practice to others. Moreover, there is the general accusation that he is a *sophos anêr*, which, along with the other accusations, is tantamount to saying that he is a *sophistês*. When he appears before the 'men of Athens', his task will be to differentiate himself from the sophists, to distinguish between the philosopher that he truly is and the sophist that he is taken to be, that to these 'men of Athens' he appears to be.

This impending event looms over the conversation in the *Sophist*. It shapes the scene of the conversation and even, to some degree, the course that its *logos* follows. Thus, the very first exchange in the dialogue concerns the *appearance* of the philosopher, specifically that of the Stranger, this 'very philosophical man'. It is a question initially of his appearing to the other philosopher present, that is, to Socrates, who declares that perhaps he is a god who looks down in judgement of human actions or in order to refute those who are poor in *logos*. Assured by Theodorus that the Stranger is not a god, though, like all philosophers, he is godly, Socrates speaks directly about the appearance of the philosopher, about the difficulty of discerning this kind. This second occurrence of the word *genos*, now in the phrase *to genos ... diakrinein*, anticipates the task to which the ontological core of the dialogue will be largely devoted, that of discerning the kinds of being, the kinds in their community with being.

Asserting that the philosopher is scarcely easier to discern than a god, Socrates declares that on account of the ignorance of others, the philosopher appears in all sorts of shapes, sometimes as statesman, sometimes as sophist, and sometimes as though totally mad. Socrates' first question to the Stranger, relayed through Theodorus, asks about these differentiations: Do those in the region from which the Stranger hails regard sophist, statesman, and philosopher as one, as two, or, since there are three names, do they divide them into three kinds (*genê*)? If attention is paid to what Socrates has just said, then it is clear that this question is not just formalistic, that, in terms of what Socrates has said about the appearance of the philosopher, these are genuine alternatives. Indeed, in a sense, all three alternatives are correct. The three are one in that all three are just the philosopher appearing in different guises. They are also two if the emphasis is placed on the distinction between the philosopher's appearing as he is (as a philosopher) and his appearing as he is not (as a sophist or statesman). They are also three, as the dialogue and its sequel will attempt to establish and as the Stranger's fellow citizens, so he asserts, maintain.

The Stranger's very first speech in the dialogue answers Socrates' question directly: his fellow citizens hold that there are three kinds: sophist, statesman, philosopher – though, as the Stranger adds, it is not an easy task to distinguish clearly what each is. The way in which the Stranger thus restructures, yet retains, the configuration of appearances given by Socrates is highly significant. If the two statements are put together, then it will be said: though the philosopher is, as such, distinct from the other two kinds, the philosopher appears sometimes as a sophist and sometimes as a statesman. Then, the task is, first, to distinguish the philosopher from the sophist and, second, to distinguish him from the statesman. These are the tasks taken up, respectively, by the two dialogues that bear the names of these two shapes in which the philosopher can appear. In the transition from Socrates' statement to that of the Stranger, it appears that the other shape in which the philosopher appears, as utterly mad, has dropped out. In the immediate sequel there is no mention of how the philosopher appears as a madman or of how the philosopher and the madman are to be distinguished, of how philosophy differs from madness – or perhaps is akin to it. Only much later in the dialogue is madness mentioned, indeed just at the point where the Stranger proposes to turn against his 'father Parmenides' and to put his *logos* to the test, forcing it to say something utterly at odds with what in fact Parmenides said. The Stranger then says to Theaetetus: 'I'm afraid that on account of what I've said you'll suppose I'm mad (*manikos*)' (242a). The word *dokeô*, used here in its future form *doxô* and translated as *suppose*, means also *seem*, *appear*; one supposes something, has an opinion about it, depending on how it appears, on what it appears to be. Thus, the passage could also – indeed more literally – be rendered as: 'I'm afraid that on account of what I've said I'll appear to you to be mad.' In effect, the Stranger's fear is that to Theaetetus he will appear to be mad, that he, this 'very philosophical man', will appear in the shape of a madman.

In any case, whatever the kinds may be, it is a matter of discerning how they differ from the philosopher, how each is *other* than the philosopher. Thus, again, but now in direct reference to the philosopher, there is anticipation of the ontological discourse on the other.

The philosopher can appear as a sophist; that is, one who appears to be a sophist may be, not a sophist, but a philosopher, or he may actually be a sophist. To be able to distinguish these two kinds of appearance, the Stranger – this 'very philosophical man', presumably not lacking in self-knowledge – undertakes to delimit what a sophist is. By carrying out this delimitation, the Stranger – this 'very philosophical man' – demonstrates in deed what a philosopher is, demonstrates it to the philosopher Socrates, even aside from the instances in which, in the search for the sophist, the philosopher also – or instead – turns up. In the course of the delimitation, which, he warns, is not the easiest of all things, he will address also the question of appearance, the question of how something can appear as what it is not, of how it can appear as other than what it in truth is. Thus, from the outset, in the initial question of the appearance of the philosopher – as in the appearance to the 'men of Athens' that Socrates will soon seek to counter – the question of the other, of otherness as such, is already broached.

The reiterative exercise in division, which the Stranger proceeds to carry out in search of the sophist, yields multiple delimitations. Thus, Theaetetus observes finally that the sophist has appeared in so many guises that he, Theaetetus, is perplexed as to what the sophist can truly be said to be – or, in his words he is *aporos*, without passage, without a way through (231c). What blocks this way has to do with the structure of appearing (*phainesthai*). For, as the Stranger says, this appearing but not being – as the philosopher can appear as a sophist but also as an image or semblance (*phantasma*) can appear as something it is not – is now and always perplexing; one is left *aporos*, is caught in an *aporia*. The Stranger's next step is to identify precisely what constitutes the *aporia*. For something to appear – for instance, as being a sophist – yet not to be is, he says, a thing full of perplexity. It is likewise with saying something but not something true, saying something that is not. To think or say such things that are not is to be forced to acknowledge that nonbeing somehow is. To think or say this is to be trapped into asserting sheer opposites, to be caught between opposites. It is to be transposed into a state of *enantiologia* (oppositionality), to be turned into an *antilogikos*.

The word *contradiction* (from the Latin verb *contradico*) translates literally the Greek *antilogia*. However, the Latinate word comes subsequently to be so thoroughly determined by Aristotle's analysis and passed down in this form that there is much to be said for avoiding it in texts such as the Platonic dialogues that antedate the formulation of the so-called principle of contradiction. In fact, in the *Sophist* the Stranger ridicules those who maintain what sounds rather like this principle, namely, the thesis that it is impossible for the many to be one and for the one to be many. According to the Stranger, this would-be principle provides 'a feast for the young and the late-learners among the old', for those who 'through their poverty in the acquisition of intelligence are struck with wonder before things of this sort, and who go so far as to imagine they've discovered something superwise in this' (252b-c). Lest we appear to have joined this feast of fools, let us forgo reading the word *contradiction* and the corresponding principle back into the Platonic texts. Nothing is ever likely to be gained by transposing a conception back into the texts that first prepared the basis for it and that most likely harbor other possibilities that may subsequently have been marginalized.

In thinking and saying that nonbeing somehow is, one takes away, on the one side, what is posited, on the other. Except for the fact that it is sounded, such an utterance hardly differs from sheer silence. The perplexity is further compounded if the inherent self-referentiality is recognized. Those who declare that to assert that nonbeing somehow is can only leave one *aporos* and who would thus refute those who speak in this manner cannot avoid, in this very declaration, uttering the phrase 'nonbeing somehow is'. They will find themselves trapped in the same *aporia* as those they set out to refute. They, too, in stating their would-be refutation, would be forced to speak in opposition to what they say. They would be compelled to say opposites (*ta enantia . . . legein*) (241e).

There is only one way to escape the *aporia*, to see one's way through the impasse: in the Stranger's words, it is necessary to compel the *logos* 'to say that nonbeing in some respect is and, in turn, that being in some way is not' (241d). Likewise, in response to the Stranger's observation that an image is that which in its very being is not – thus, again the question of appearance – Theaetetus says: 'Nonbeing risks being entwined in some sort of interweaving (*symplokê*) with being, and a very odd one (*atopos*) too' (240c). Yet if being has nonbeing woven together with it, then perplexity arises not only about nonbeing but also about being. Thus, the Stranger poses the question as to what is meant when one utters *being*, and then adds: 'For it's manifest (*dêlos*) that you have known this for a long time, while we supposed earlier that we knew, but now are perplexed (244a).

To take up the question of being and, eventually, that of its intertwining with nonbeing, the Stranger launches a series of critical engagements. At this point he has already mentioned the *mythoi* told by the likes of Xenophanes and has alluded also to Heraclitus and Empedocles. The critical engagements, which also mark the beginning of the ontological core of the dialogue confront three figures: Parmenides, the giants, and the friends of the *eidê*. The most decisive results of these critical engagements lie in what they yield as regards the question of being. In each of the engagements there is one such decisive result.

The first of the three engagements puts the paternal *logos* of Parmenides to the test. Risking the appearance – or semblance – of patricide, the Stranger poses the question as to what those who say that the all is one (*hen to pân*) mean by being. If all that is, is one, then, as he says, it must be declared that one alone is, that is, only the one can be said to be. It is this *logos*, that being and one are the same, that the Stranger puts to the test, as he says, by forcing it to say such things as that nonbeing somehow is and that being somehow is not. He carries this out by demonstrating that being cannot be constrained to being one, that, regardless of how it is construed, the one being is exceeded and thus proves not to be one. There are two ways in which this is shown to occur. First of all, in that being is said to be one, there turns out to be two names for the same. But if there are two names, both being and one, then it is ridiculous, laughable, to say that there is only one, that being is one. Thus, the names of the one being exceed it. The same conclusion follows if the name, even a single name, is other (*heteron*) than the one, since in this case also there are two, the name and the thing named. If, on the other hand, the name is the same as the thing, then it is not the name of anything, that is, it is not a name at all; this supposition would render being unspeakable, and, recoiling on itself, would dissolve into silence.

What is shown, secondly, to exceed the one being is the whole (*to holon*). Since a whole has many parts, being – since it is one – is not a whole. All the parts that make up a whole will be, as a whole, more than one, and thus the whole will exceed the one being; and the one being cannot, then, be one, since there is also the whole. Furthermore, if the whole itself is, then there is something that can be said to be but that exceeds being. Thus, as the Stranger says, 'it turns out that being falls short of itself'. But then – decisively – 'being, since it is deprived of itself, will not be being' (245c). When the Stranger declares that in this connection myriad perplexities are inevitable, Theaetetus concludes: 'All that is now coming to light makes it quite manifest (*dêlos*): for an other (*heteron*) gets attached from something else' (245e). In other words, something – such as a name or a whole – that is other than being – and thus nonbeing – gets attached to being. Such is, then the result: through the effect of an other, nonbeing gets intertwined with being, so that each is, in some respect, the other.

The second engagement is with those who are identified as the giants (the word *gêgenês* literally means earthborn) who wage a battle (*gigantomachia*) with certain others whom the Stanger will soon engage. The giants delimit body (*sôma*) and being as the same. The Stranger counters their thesis by appealing to the soul and the things such as justice that come to be in it, which are irreducible to body. Yet the decisive result that emerges in this engagement is a direct and precise delimitation of being. The Stranger says: 'I propose to delimit beings as being nothing else but *dynamis*' (247e).

The verb *dynamai* means *to be able* or *capable*. Hence, the noun *dynamis* can, as such, be rendered as *power* or *capacity*, not to mention its more specific military and mathematical meanings. If, lacking other resources, powerless to render it more suitably, we translate *dynamis* as *power*, reservations are required, for the word has come to bear such an enormous weight of sedimented meanings. One must make the effort to set aside the Aristotelian determination, which counterposes it to *energeia*, as well as the transpositions involved in such renderings as *potentia, vis, Macht, puissance* and, instead, to hear *dynamis* with a fresh ear, determining its sense, insofar as possible, from the Platonic text.

Along with the delimitation of being as *dynamis*, the Stranger offers a significant indication as to how the word, as saying something like power, is to be heard. As power, it must be the power for something, a power through which something comes about. The Stranger identifies two such effects. One he calls *poieîn*, so that power would in this case be the power to produce or make something, of whatever nature, or to bring something to pass, to bring it about, to do it. The other he designates by the word *pathein*, so that in this case power would be the capacity to be affected. Thus, *dynamis* is the power to produce something or to be affected by something. Being – the Stranger proposes – is nothing else but such power.

The third engagement is with those whom the Stranger designates as the friends of the *eidê*. It is against these that the giants wage their battle. Indeed, in the description of this battle that he gives in speaking of the giants, the Stranger already identifies the position taken by their foes, the friends of the *eidê*: in his words, 'they force true being to be certain things that are thought [or intelligible – *noêta*] and disembodied *eidê*' (246b). When they focus on the tangible bodies that the giants identify with being, the friends of the *eidê* smash them up into small pieces and degrade them to the rank of becoming.

The friends of the *eidê* acknowledge that becoming involves powers of bringing something about and of being affected; this is to say that becoming has a certain share in being. What they deny is that power belongs to that which comes to be known, to eidetic, intelligible being; and on this basis they would refuse to accept the delimitation of being as power that the Stranger has proposed. It is this denial that the Stranger addresses critically, and it is through his criticism that he establishes the decisive result that emerges from this third engagement.

First of all, he establishes that the soul comes to know (*gignôskein* – from *gignomai*) and that being thereby comes to be known. On the one side, coming to know is a certain bringing about of something in relation to that which comes to be known; as *poieîn*, knowing produces something, does something, with respect to the known. Hence, on the other side, that which comes to be known is necessarily affected (*pathein*). The Stranger states then the decisive result: in his words, 'But, according to this *logos*, the being that comes to be known by the knowing, to the extent that it comes to be known, to just that extent is moved on account of its being affected' (248e). The decisiveness of this result is marked by the exclamation that follows almost immediately; the Stranger swears 'By Zeus (*pros Dios*)'. It is also marked by the reappearance of the philosopher, whom, in the *logos*, the Stranger brings upon the scene, as if at precisely this juncture it were being demonstrated what the philosopher is, how he appears when he appears as himself and not in the shape of a sophist or statesman. The Stranger declares that for the philosopher it is necessary to say that being is both motionless and in motion. It must be, in a certain way, motionless, unchanging, selfsame, in order – as the *Theaetetus* had demonstrated[5] – for knowledge to be possible; but in coming to be known, it is affected and thus is necessarily moved.

At this point the Stranger forgoes saying or even discussing what kind of motion is displayed by the *eidê*, as if the basis for such a determination had not yet been established. He circles back to this question only when the discussion comes to centre on *logos*. The decisive indication is given in the course of his consideration of how it is that certain words, spoken in succession, fit together; or, more precisely, of what, if the words do properly fit together to form a *logos*, they actually accomplish, this accomplishment, then, in turn, attesting that they fit together into a *logos*. The word that the Stranger uses to describe this accomplishment is a form of *dêloô*: to show, to bring to light, to make apparent, to make manifest (261e). Two occurrences of the corresponding adjective *dêlos* follow almost immediately. The Stranger observes that single words such as *lion*, *deer* and *horse* do not serve to put together a *logos*, for they do not make anything manifest (*dêlos*) (262b-c); whereas in saying 'man learns', something is made manifest about the being of which one speaks (262d). In speech, then, something is made manifest, brought to light, drawn forth so as to appear. Such coming to light, such being drawn into appearance, being brought from obscurity into manifestness – this is the way in which what is said is affected, is set into motion. But if speech brings it about that being is affected and thus in motion, then the same can be said of thought or knowing, since, as the Stranger goes on to say, thought and speech (*dianoia ... kai logos*) are the same, that is, thought is nothing but speech that the soul carries on in and with itself without sound (263e).

The conclusion is evident: insofar as eidetic being submits to being said or known, it is brought to light, set into the movement towards manifestness, and thus affected. The result is that the Stranger's delimitation of being as power is confirmed.

And yet, how is it when this power is deployed in such a way that something comes to be manifest otherwise than as it itself is? How is it when something comes to appear as something it is not – as when the philosopher comes to appear, not as a philosopher, but as a sophist or statesman? How, in the affection of being, can it happen that nonbeing comes forth? How is it that nonbeing can be intertwined with being?

This question of the nonbeing of being has been in play throughout the dialogue. It was launched with the appearance of the Stranger at the very outset, and it is the question that has animated the discussions of appearance and of images, as well as the prolonged search for the sophist. Finally, it is confronted head-on in the Stranger's discourse on the other (*heteron*). This discourse begins in the larger context of the discussion of the five kinds and eventually emerges as a distinct discourse and as most decisive for the question that has haunted the entire dialogue.

In the discussion of the five kinds, it is a question of the extent to which they mix and do not mix, a question of their participating (*metechein*) in one another in such a way as to form a community (*koinônia*). It will be precisely in the mixing, in a certain configuration formed by it, that the Stranger will finally track down the nonbeing that belongs to being.

The discussion of the community of kinds also marks an advance beyond the ontological reach of the *Theaetetus* in which the *eidê* were taken as the common (*koinon*) and as discrete, homogeneous units, not unlike the ones that are counted in arithmetic to yield numbers. With the transition from the common (*koinon*) to the community (*koinônia*), the *eidê* become uncountable, as indicated ironically by the Stranger's curious insistence on counting or numbering them.

The discussion of the five kinds traces the lines of the mixing and not mixing that form the configuration of the community. The Stranger points out, for instance, how motion is and is not the same. It is the same, as he says, 'on account of its participation in the same in relation to itself'. In other words, by its participation in the same, it is the same as itself, is selfsame. This can indeed be said of all the kinds: that each is selfsame by participating in the same. Yet – decisively – this selfsameness does not exclude otherness or difference, for, as the Stranger says, 'it is not the same on account of its sharing in the other' (256b). In other words, by its participating in the other, motion is other than the same, hence is not the same. This, too, can be said of the other kinds: that each is other than the others by virtue of its participation in the other. In particular, each of the others is other than being itself by virtue of their participation in the other. Thus, it becomes evident that it is the other that has the effect of installing nonbeing in being. The Stranger is explicit: 'So it is, after all, of necessity, in the case of motion and throughout all the kinds, that nonbeing be, for in each and every case the nature of the other, in producing each to be other than being, makes it nonbeing' (256d-e). Even being itself proves to be nonbeing: by participating in the other, being itself is other than all the rest of the kinds, and thus, as the Stranger concludes, 'being itself, to the extent that everything else is, to that extent is not' (257a). Finally, the Stranger states directly that it is the other that installs nonbeing in being. He says: 'Whenever we say nonbeing, we are not saying, it seems, something opposite (*enantion*) to being but only other (*heteron*)' (257b).

It remains only to observe the radical conclusion regarding the other that the Stranger goes on to draw. Since the other is a kind, it would seem that, like all other kinds, the other should be the same as itself by participating in the same. And yet, the Stranger twice says – most remarkably – that the other is *chopped into bits*. Since each kind is other than every other kind by virtue of its participation in the other, 'the nature of the other both *is* and is chopped into bits and distributed through all beings in their relation to one another' (258e).

The contrast with the same is striking. All kinds partake of the same so that each is selfsame and thereby set apart from the same, leaving it intact. If it can be said that the same partakes of itself, this would serve only to reinforce its integrity: by participating in itself, the same would itself be selfsame. But with the other the outcome is completely other. Since each kind is other than every other kind, each kind participates multiply in the other; each kind participates in the other with respect to every other kind. This proliferation of difference is what the Stranger refers to in saying that the other is chopped into bits. It is as if the other participated in itself so as to be other than itself, that is, dispersed, dismembered. In any case, in being the very kind it is, it would be devoid of the self-sameness definitive of kinds as such. It would undergo a kind of dissolution that, on the side of humans, would be akin to madness.

In any case, it is evident that the other, by which nonbeing is installed throughout being, is itself quite other than the other kinds or *eidê*. It is the *eidos* – let us say the *look*, translating literally – that injects difference into the community of selfsame looks, this look of difference that is also a very different look.

In conclusion, two points need to be mentioned. The first concerns the dual sense that being comes to have once nonbeing as otherness is installed within it. On the one hand, there is the *eidos* being itself; yet all other *eidê* participate in being itself and thus must themselves be said to be. Hence, being means both the *eidos* being itself and the totality of *eidê*.

But, finally, what about the appearance of the philosopher? In the search for the sophist and the ontological discourse to which it leads, does he ever really turn up? Does he come to be manifest in his difference from the sophist?

He does indeed appear to turn up on at least three occasions. The first comes near the end of the series of reiterated divisions in search of the sophist. Just before the search is broken off and the ontological discourse then begun, the figure that turns up is described as one who questions someone 'about the things about which he thinks he is saying something when he is really saying nothing' (230b). The description sounds remarkably like a description of Socrates' practice. What appeared as a sophist turns out, it seems, to be a philosopher.

The second occurrence comes at the threshold of the discussion of the community of kinds. Here the Stranger asks explicitly whether 'in looking for the sophist we have first found the philosopher' (253c). The philosopher would be, then, the one who – like the Stranger himself – knows how to discern the kinds in their community. Yet the Stranger acknowledges that the philosopher is difficult to see, not because of the darkness in which the sophist hides, but because of the brilliance of the place he inhabits; the word that the Stranger slyly slips in here is *chôra*.

The third appearance comes at the very end of the dialogue as the outcome of the final series of divisions. Two men show up, and the Stranger says: 'I see one who can dissemble in public and with long speeches before a multitude, another who can do it in private and in short speeches by compelling his interlocutor to say opposite things' (268b). Theaetetus agrees with the Stranger that the first man is to be declared a statesman and the second a sophist. The question is whether in what appears here in the shape of statesman and sophist, one can catch a glimpse of the philosopher, whether in either case there is a hint that it is the philosopher who appears in the shape of another. It hinges largely on the word translated as dissemble (*eirôneuesthai*), which can mean, in particular, to feign ignorance, to be ironic. Here, as in the first occurrence, there is only a glimpse of the philosopher appearing through the shape of another. It is only in the second occurrence that the philosopher fully appears and is explicitly announced as appearing – that is, only within the ontological core of the dialogue, only within the ontological discourse that allows the nonbeing in which the sophist hides to be dissolved into the light of the other.

The question is whether the discourse on the other suffices, in the end, to make the philosopher visible. Or whether something other than the other, another still more perplexing alterity, is needed to counter the brilliance of the place inhabited by the philosopher.

Notes

1. This text was originally published in *The New Yearbook for Phenomenology and Phenomenological Philosophy* 13 (2013): 283–91.
2. All translations are the author's own.
3. The Budé edition offers an alternative reading, replacing *hetaîron* with *heteron*. On this reading the sentence would be: '... and we are bringing along this stranger of sorts, who by birth is from Elea *but who is different from* those around Parmenides and Zeno – a very philosophical man'; see *Le Sophiste, Platon: Oeuvres Complètes*, vol. 8, part 3 (Paris: Société d'Édition 'Les Belles Lettres', 1925), 216a, n. If this reading were adopted, then – most significantly – the very first sentence of the dialogue would bear an explicit reference to otherness or difference.
4. Though Theodorus comes from Cyrene and so is not a native Athenian, he is represented in the *Theaetetus* as an established teacher in Athens; he has instructed Theaetetus and the young Socrates in geometry, and he is also a friend of Protagoras.
5. See my discussion in 'The Flow of Φύσις and the Beginning of Philosophy: On Plato's *Theaetetus*', in *Proceedings of the Boston Area Colloquium in Ancient Philosophy*, vol. 20, eds. John J. Cleary and Gary M. Gurtler (Leiden: Brill, 2005), 177–93, esp. 191–3.

Bibliography

Plato. *Le Sophiste*. *Platon: Oeuvres Complètes*, vol. 8, part 3. Paris: Société d'Édition 'Les Belles Lettres', 1925.

Sallis, John. 'The Flow of Φύσις and the Beginning of Philosophy: On Plato's *Theaetetus*'. In *Proceedings of the Boston Area Colloquium in Ancient Philosophy*, vol. 20, edited by John J. Cleary and Gary M. Gurtler, 177–93. Leiden: Brill, 2005.

Index

Achilles 8, 9, 31, 44, 51, 53–7, 72 n.20, 73 n.37, 74 n.48
Ackrill, John 223 n.1
Adeimantus 79, 81
Adkins, Arthur 46 n.9
Aesop 153, 182
affecting, affection 116–18, 170, 237
Agathon 15, 21, 24–6, 27 n.15, 27 n.20, 30, 39–43, 124–6, 134
Alcibiades 10, 132–4
Alcibiades I 133, 137 n.24
ambiguity 3, 10, 143–5, 147–50, 153–5
Ambuel, David 224 n.9
Anacreon 100, 102
Anderson, Warren 155 n.3, 156 n.9
anger (*cholos*) 57–67, 74 nn.48 and 49
Antigone 25, 96, 101, 103
Aphrodite 34–5, 80, 124
Apollodorus 123, 135 n.3, 180, 182, 186 n.3
Apollon 146
Apology 6, 8, 24, 39, 51, 53–8, 62–4, 66–7, 69 n.10
aporia 5, 11, 19, 22, 14, 189–200, 202, 234–5
aretê, see virtue
argument, argumentation 1, 4, 7, 8, 11, 16, 30, 43, 53, 63–4, 179–86, 187 nn.6, 8 and 11
Arieti, James A. 45 n.6
Aristophanes 8, 15–26, 26 n.5, 27 nn.12 and 21, 30, 39–43, 125, 132, 134, 137 n.35
Aristotle 2, 5, 112, 129, 176 n.4, 187 n.5
art (*technê*) 12, 18, 37, 79, 126, 144, 203–4, 213–22, 225 n.20, 226 n.31
Athenian Stranger, see Stranger, Athenian
atopia 11, 191–5, 197–8, 206 n.32
atopos 11, 193–4, 235
audience 45 n.6, 86–7, 95–8, 100, 104
Ausland, Hayden W. 1, 8

beauty 8, 10, 15, 25–6, 29–30, 33–4, 37, 39–40, 42–4, 82, 87, 90, 97, 127–31, 146, 192, 198, 201–2, 206 n.31
becoming (*genesis*) 111, 115, 116, 121 n.21
Bedu-Addo, J.T. 187 n.11
being 9, 10, 11, 12, 107–19, 120 n.11, 145, 147, 195–7, 201, 205 n.26, 206 n.37
Benedict, Ruth 69 n.8
Benitez, Eugenio 209, 223 n.2, 224 n.8
Benson, Hugh 224 n.15
Bernadete, Seth 151, 156 n.10, 158 n.30, 209, 215, 221, 225 nn.18 and 20, 226 nn.27 and 30
Birds 17–19
Blackson, Thomas 186 n.2
Blattberg, Charles 187 n.17
Bloom, Allan 72 n.21, 73 n.37, 74 n.49, 204 n.6
body (*sôma*) 37–8, 110, 111, 113–16, 120 nn.13 and 21, 145–6, 151–2, 161–3, 167–70, 173–5, 183, 196, 201, 203, 204 n.17, 211, 236
Boreas 193
Brandes, Georg 72 n.20
Braan, Eva 206 n.32
Brown, Lesley 117, 120 nn.13 and 21, 223 n.2
Brown, Norman 69 n.8
Buffière, Félix 47 n.25
Burnet, John 73 nn.37, 38 and 39, 144, 155 n.4
Burnyeat, M.F. 176 nn.6 and 7

Cairns, Douglas 68 n.8, 105 n.8
Callicles 162
Campbell, Joseph 71 n.11
Canto, Monique 157 n.16
Catherall, Sam 70 n.11
Cazzato, Vanessa 105 n.10
Cebes 181, 183–4
charm 152, 154, 183–6
cholos, see anger

chôra 149
chorus, choristry, choir 98, 100–1, 104, 105 n.5, 145–7, 151–2
chronos, see time
city of pigs 81
Clay, Diskin 1, 188, n19, 72 n.27
Clouds 16–18, 26 n.6, 137 n.35
comedy 3, 8, 15, 19–20, 24, 26, 199–200
compassion 102–5
contradiction (*antilogia*) 3, 234
Cooper, John 176 n.1, 176 n.6
Cope, E.M. 68 n.7
Corderos, Nestor-Luis 224 n.9
Cornford, Francis 158 n.26, 223 n.1, 226 n.27
corporealist 9, 107, 110–15, 118–19, 120 nn.9 and 13
cosmos 10, 19, 143–5, 147, 149–50, 151–2, 155, 167, 184–5
courage 21, 37, 39, 42–3, 46 n16, 88, 125, 132–3, 183
Critias 51, 108
Crito 63–4, 66–7, 70, 180, 211
Crito 9, 51, 63–7, 180

daimôn 98, 127, 131
dance 98, 144–5, 147–52, 154, 157 nn.20 and 24, 158 n.33, 159 n.34
Das Leben der Anderen 9, 79, 82, 84, 90
Delcomminette, Sylvain 176 n.9
Demosthenes 105 n.3, 129
Desjarin, Rosemary 1
dialectic, dialectical, dialectician 4, 29, 45, 90, 108–9, 111, 118
dialektikê technê 203
dialogue form 1, 2, 3, 6, 8, 29–30, 33–4, 39, 45 nn.4, 5 and 6, 107–8, 119, 179, 186
Diotima 8, 10, 17, 23, 25, 30, 43–4, 123–4, 126–31, 134, 137 n.22
divine madness 195, 201
division (as method) 209–10, 213, 215–23, 225 nn.17 and 18, 234, 239
Dodds, E.R. 69 n.8
von Donnersmarck, Florian Henckel 82, 84, 88–90
Dover, K. J. 47 n.20, 48 n.36, 129, 137 n.29
drama, dramatic 3, 6, 8, 11, 107–9, 115, 119, 179–84, 186
dynamis, see power

Echecrates 180
education (*paideia*) 7, 9, 10, 29, 31, 33–6, 38–9, 43–4, 67, 79–80, 82, 84, 107, 114, 119, 120 n.4, 128–9, 130, 132–4, 139 n.18, 143–4, 147, 149–52, 155, 175, 200
Eide, Tormod 206 n.32
eidôlon, see image
eidos, eidê, se Form(s)
Eleatic guest, see Stranger, Eleatic
elenchus, see refutation
Emilsson, Eyjólfur 224 n.9, 226 n.23
emotion 2–4, 7, 11, 31, 44, 95, 100, 126, 147, 163, 166, 168–9, 172, 174, 179–83, 189
encomium (see also eulogy) 10, 34, 123–4, 125, 127, 129, 132–4, 136 n.11
epistêmê 119, 203
Eros 30–5, 38, 40, 42–4, 100–2, 123–7, 132–3, 136 n.15
erôs 8, 10, 15, 17–25, 26 n.5, 27 nn.20 and 21, 30–45, 80, 86, 89–90, 119, 124, 126–34, 136 n.1, 151, 191–2, 200, 202
Eryximachus 8, 18, 37–9, 44, 124–6
euboulia, see good judgement
eulogy, see also encomium 30–4, 36, 39, 42, 44, 123, 132, 136 n.13
Euripides 96, 100
eusebeia, see reverence
Euthydemus 211, 222
Euthyphro 61–2, 66, 103

fable (see also story, myth) 11, 179, 181–2, 185
fame 54, 65, 125, 128, 129, 132–4
fear 53, 58, 65, 67, 165–6, 169, 172–3, 180–1, 183–4
feeling, see emotion
Ferrari, G.R.F. 1, 46 n.17, 148, 157 nn.21, 22 and 23
fiction 3, 29, 51–2, 63, 182
Fine, G.I. 176 n.6
finitude 11, 191, 202–3
Form(s) (*eidos, eidê*) 30, 97–100, 111, 117–18, 121 n.21, 168, 173, 194, 196, 198, 200–3, 239
Fossheim, Hallvard 45 n.6
Frede, Dorothea 176 n.1,
Frede, Michael 1, 107

Freeland, Cynthia 176 n.11
Friedländer, Paul 223 n.1

Gaskin, Richard 71 n.18
gender 9, 19–21
genesis, see becoming
genre 1–4, 8, 10, 51, 123, 127, 136 n.11, 199
Gentzler, Jyl 187 n.14
Gill, Christopher 186 n.1
Giannopoulou, Zina 176 n.5
Gigantomachy 109–15, 117–19, 121 n.24
Glaucon 79–84, 89–90
god(s) 9, 16–21, 23–4, 38–42, 54, 56, 59, 61, 80–1, 83, 88–9, 96–104, 107–10, 113–14, 125–7, 130–2, 145, 147, 163, 167, 171–2, 180, 182, 192, 194, 196, 201, 203, 210–11, 232
Goethe 56–7, 72 n.20
Gonzales, Francisco 223, 227 n.43
good, goodness 2, 4, 6, 9–10, 25, 30, 32–3, 35–7, 40–1, 43–5, 53, 81–2, 87, 98, 100, 105, 112, 114, 124, 127, 129, 146, 150–2, 161–2, 171–6, 196, 204
good judgement (*euboulia*) 102–4
good life (see also happiness) 2, 31–2, 41, 126, 132, 161–2, 172–3
Gordon, Jill 1, 224 n.11
Gorgias 51, 54
Gorgias 161, 162, 205 n.17
Gosling, J.C.B. 176 nn.1 and 4
grief 58–60, 104, 169, 180–2
Griswold, Charles 204 n.13, 205 n.28
Grubitz 85–9
guardians 79, 81, 84, 175
Gyges 79–83, 85, 88, 89
Gyges' ring, 9, 7, 9, 80, 82–5

Hackforth, Reginald 47 n.17
Hadot, Pierre 46 n.16
Halperin, David 48 n.39, 135 n.3
happiness (see also good life) 2, 16, 30–2, 34, 39–43, 83, 87, 127, 129, 163
harmony 6, 7, 37, 38–9, 113, 132, 144–7, 149–52, 154
Harte, Verity 176 n.10
Hecht, Jonathan 46 n.8, 47 n.20
Heidegger, Martin 120 n.6
Heraclitus 115–16, 121 n.20, 164–6, 170
hero, heroism 55–8, 65–7, 70 n.11

Hesiod 79
Hirzel, Rudolph 74 n.52
Hobbs, Angela 71 n.12
Homer 51–67, 72 n.24, 73 n.30, 74 n.48, 79, 80, 210
honour 2, 7, 10, 30–4, 119, 123–34
honour, love of (*philotimia*) 123–34, 136 n.17
hosiotês, see reverence
Howland, Jacob 1, 209, 223 nn.2 and 4, 224 n.12
Humbert, Jean 74 n.52
hunt, hunter 4, 12, 209, 210, 212–19, 220, 222–3
Hunter, Richard 135 nn.8 and 10
hybris 20, 89, 97–8, 103, 134
Hyland, Drew 1, 47 n.26, 48 n.38
hyperuranian 191, 194, 196–7, 201–3
hypothetical method 179, 184–5, 187 n.11

Ibycus 101
ignorance 11, 24, 127, 191, 194–5, 199–203, 218, 232, 239
Iliad 52–4, 56–67, 73 n.30
image (*eidôlon*, see also original) 2–4, 9, 11, 32, 38, 65, 88–9, 95, 97–8, 100–2, 108, 146, 149–50, 161–3, 168, 171, 173–6, 191–8, 201–3, 215, 234–5, 238
imagination 9, 81–3, 90, 161, 169
imitation (*mimesis*) 19, 86–7, 90, 108, 191, 194–7, 202–3, 215
immortality 10, 31, 43, 104, 127–8, 130–1, 153, 173
injustice 32, 55, 58, 63, 79, 80–4, 88, 90, 99–100, 121
in media res 5, 6
inner child 179, 183–6
Ion (Euripides) 100
Ion (Plato) 39
irony 3, 21, 108, 131, 133, 137 n.33
irrationality 10–11, 127, 179, 182–3, 187 n.10
Isocrates 67–8, 124, 227 n.34

judgement 169–72, 174, 210, 227 n.34, 232
justice 2, 4–5, 7, 35–6, 42, 58–9, 61–2, 66, 79, 81–3, 87, 97, 99–100, 103–4, 112, 120 n.23, 128, 183, 197, 221, 236

Kahn, Charles 176 n.12
Kallipolis 79–82, 84, 88–90, 91 nn.6, 7, 13 and 15
Kastely, James 138 n.36
King, Katherine Callen 74 n.49
knowledge 2, 4, 6, 8–9, 22, 33, 35–6, 39, 41–5, 51, 86, 88, 96–9, 103–4, 108, 114, 119, 129–32, 134, 151, 161–5, 168–75, 179, 184–5, 194–6, 198, 200–3, 219, 237
Konstan, David 105 nn.13 and 14
Kosman, Aryeh 45 n.4
Krüger, Gerhard 47 nn.19 and 22

Laches 107
ladder of love 8, 43–5
Lane, Melissa 137 n.33
law (*nomos*) 16, 35, 38, 44, 51, 61, 63, 80–1, 98, 126, 147, 150–1, 153, 155, 158 n.31
Laws 10, 47 n.24, 144–7, 150–2, 156 nn.10 and 13, 157 n.16, 225 n.17
Lebeck, Anne 191, 204 n.2
Leigh, Fiona 120 n.5
Lesky, Albin 71 n.18
Levi, Doro 157 n.17
Levinas, Emmanuel 91, n.9
Libanius 68
logos 8, 16, 30, 33, 83, 108, 111, 154, 181–2, 191, 202
Lorenz, Hendrik 47 n.24, 176 n.1
Love, see Eros
love, see *erôs*
lover, beloved (see also *erôs*) 18, 21, 23, 31–6, 41–5, 99, 125–6, 128, 149, 192, 195–6, 198, 200–3, 205 nn.26 and 28
Lysias 192–3

Makowski, Francois 206 n.32
Matthews, Gareth 186 n.2
McCabe, Mary 120 n.6
Macfait, Ebenezer 71 n.11
McCoy, Marina 1
Mead, Margaret 68 n.8
measure 38, 114, 145–7, 149, 151, 164
medicine (*pharmakon*) 38, 47, 126, 144–7, 155, 156 n.15
Mehmel, Friedrich 71 n.17
Melissus 115
melody 38, 151, 158 nn.30 and 31
Memorabilia 51–2, 68, 129

metaphor 4, 11–12, 33, 83, 90, 131, 185, 191–3, 209, 210, 218, 220, 222
Metcalf, Robert 69 n.10, 72 n.21
method (see also hypothetical method) 5, 11–12, 42–3, 124–5, 130–1, 179, 184–5, 209–10, 212–18, 222
Miller, Mitchell 225 n.16
mimetic impulse 179, 181–2
mimesis, see imitation
Minos 158 n.31
moderation 34–5, 37, 39, 43, 128, 147, 183, 197
Morgan, Kathryn 187 n.8
Morrow, Glenn R. 144, 147, 150–2, 156 n.7, 157 n.19, 158 nn.27, 28, 32 and 33, 159 n.35
Moss, Jessica 174–5, 176 n.3, 177 n.13
motion 117–19
mousikê (see music)
Murray, Penelope 156 n.8
Muses 144–6, 148–9, 155 n.6
music (*mousikê*) 4, 10, 38, 44, 80, 85, 126, 143–55, 155 n.6, 156 nn.10, 11 and 13, 167, 175
Myers, John 69 n.9
mystery 124, 129–31, 137 n.30
myth, mythical (see also fable, story) 3, 4, 9, 11, 19, 25, 41–2, 60, 79, 81–4, 89–90, 90 n.2, 91 n.10, 95, 98–100, 103, 107–8, 110, 127, 144, 148–9, 153, 163, 167–8, 179, 181–2, 184–6, 187 n.11, 193–4, 196–7, 202–3, 205 n.24
mythos, see myth

Nails, Debra 135 n.3, 136 n.21
narrative 1, 3, 6, 30, 56, 83
Nehamas, Alexander 46 n.10
Nichols, Mary 134, 137 nn.34 and 37
Nietzsche, Friedrich 146, 156 n.14
Nightingale, Andrea 123–4, 135 nn.4 and 11, 136 n.13, 137 n.33
nomos, see law, see also melody
non-being 11–12, 108–9
Notomi, Nobur 120 n.10, 224 n.9, 225 n.16
number 146–7, 150, 238

Obdrzalek, Suzanne 137 n.25
Odyssey 210
Oedipus Tyrannus 97–8

ontology 114–16, 118
Oreithyia 193
original (see also image) 1, 11, 17, 19–20, 22–4, 40–1, 88, 192, 195–7, 203, 206 n.39
ousia, see being

paideia, see education
pain 11, 161–3, 165–70, 172, 174, 180–2, 184, 197–202
palinode 191, 194–7, 203
paradigm 12, 20, 88, 195, 204, 209–10, 212–13, 215–19, 222
Parke, H.W. 69 n.8
Parker, Robert 137 n.30
Parmenides 109–11, 115–16, 118, 121 n.20, 231, 233, 235
Patroclus 53, 57–62, 65–6, 72 n.20, 73 n.30, 73 n.32
Pausanias 34–8, 44, 126, 134
perception 155, 161–76
Pharmakeia 193
pharmakon, see medicine
Philebus 198–9, 200
Pelosi, Francesco 155 n.2
Phaedo, 10–11, 67, 113, 115, 117, 119, 148, 153, 161, 162–3, 173–5, 179–86, 198–200
Phaedrus 8, 11, 30–6, 44, 95, 106, 125–6, 130, 148, 191–5
Phaedrus 9, 10–11, 29–30, 33, 36, 41–2, 147–9 155 n.6, 191, 195, 200–3
Philebus 15, 161–2, 198–200
philotimia, see honour, love of
philosopher 1–2, 4–6, 9–10, 12, 29, 52, 54, 56–7, 79, 82, 84, 88–9, 97, 99, 107–8, 110, 119, 127, 129–31, 149–51, 163, 183, 192, 196–7, 202–3, 209–12, 232–4, 237, 239–40
philosophical writing 1, 4, 7, 12 n.1, 30, 33, 36, 39, 41, 68, 182, 192, 203
phronêsis 117, 119, 128
pity 104, 180–1
place, see *topos*
pleasure 7, 10, 11, 42, 59, 83, 86, 146, 161–76, 180–2, 184, 187 n.7, 197–202, 206 n.31
Plochmann, George 224 n.9, 226 nn.23 and 30

poetry 3, 8, 15, 31–2, 39, 41, 43, 51, 53, 55–6, 63, 66, 80–2, 84, 86, 88–90, 95, 103–4, 125, 128, 144–5, 161–4, 169, 173–5, 181–2
poets 18, 21, 26, 30, 39–41, 52–3, 66, 81, 85, 87–9, 95, 97–105, 125, 128, 131, 144, 147, 197, 203
poison (see also medicine) 10, 143–5, 147, 150, 152–5
politics 10, 17–18, 21, 82, 84, 128, 144, 150–3, 155, 157 n.16
Polycrates 51–3, 67–8
Poulakos, John 124, 135 n.9
power (*dynamis*) 7–9, 12, 79–80, 82–7, 89–90, 91 n.7, 107, 109, 112–13, 115–17, 119, 236–7
presence 11, 192, 198, 202–3
Press, Gerald 1, 2
Protagoras 114, 154
Protagoras 154
Protarchus 199
psychê, see soul

rationality 8, 11, 167, 179, 181–3, 185–6
reason 1, 2, 10–11, 95, 110, 114, 151, 179–81, 183, 185–6, 187 n.11, 199
reasoning 63, 100, 110–12, 115–16, 118, 173
recollection 196–8, 201–2, 205 n.26
refutation (*elenchus*) 5, 53, 110, 165, 234
Rehn, Rudolf 121 n.23
remedy (see also medicine) 10, 143–4, 150, 152, 154–5
Republic 9, 10, 15, 39, 41, 47 n.24, 79, 82–3, 88, 90, 95, 97–8, 100, 103, 117, 149, 156 n.11, 157 n.16, 163–4, 169–71, 173–5, 176 n.11, 177 n.13, 179, 192, 198–200
reverence (*eusebeia*, *hosiotês*) 22, 98, 102–4, 106 n.17
rhetoric, rhetorical 3, 10, 18, 30, 33, 41–2, 52–3, 67–8, 95, 123–4, 133–4, 191–2, 194, 204 n.17
Rhodes, James M. 47 n.18, 48 n.37
rhythm 38, 144–6, 149, 151–2, 154, 158 n.33
Richardson Lear, Gabriel 48 n.38
Riedweg, Christoph 124, 136 n.12, 137 n.30

Robinson, David 226 n.27
Roochnik, David 1
Rosen, Stanley 11, 120 n.10, 223 n.2, 225 n.16
Ross, W.D. 118, 121 n.26
Rowe, Christopher 45 n.2, 46 nn.11 and 17, 48 n.36
Russell, D.A. 74 n.52
Rutherford, Richard 47 n.20, 136 n.20

Sachs, Joe 204 n.10
Sallis, John 1, 205 n.26, 224 n.9, 225 n.16, 240 n.5
Sappho 101, 102
Saxonhouse, Arlene 1, 70 n.10, 72 n.21, 74 n.49
Sayre, Kenneth 45 n.5, 47 n.27
Schadewaldt, Wolfgang 72 n.29
Schanz, Martin 51–2, 68 n.1, 68 n.4
self-knowledge 5, 23–6, 130, 193, 198, 200–2, 233
sexuality, sexual difference 17, 24, 146–7, 157 n.16
Shaftsbury, Lord 70 n.11
shame, shame culture 5, 32–7, 46 n.14, 53–6, 58, 60, 62, 65–7, 68 n.8, 87, 103, 113, 125, 126, 162
Sheffield, Frisbee 48 n.36
Sieland, Christer-Maria 84–7, 89
Simmias 183, 188 n.18
situatedness 4, 7, 192, 202
Smith, John 157 n.18
Snell, Bruno 55–8, 71 nn.14, 15, 16, 17, 18 and 19
Solmsen, Friedrich 69 n.8
sôma, see body
song 41, 144–52, 154–5
Sophist 5–6, 9, 11, 107–9, 111–12, 114, 116–17, 119, 209–29, 231–40
sophist 6, 12, 209–13, 215–23, 232–4, 237–40
sophistry 16, 143–4, 149, 154, 219, 220
Sophocles 96, 101, 104
soul (*psychê*) 7–11, 17, 22–3, 33, 56, 96–9, 100, 102, 109, 112–19, 120 n.13, 126, 128–9, 131, 133, 143, 145–7, 150–1, 153, 155, 161, 163, 167–76, 179–80, 182–5, 194–8, 201–3, 204 n.17, 209, 219, 236–7

Stasi 82, 84–5, 87, 89
Statesman 6, 209
story (see also fable, myth) 2, 4, 6, 11, 19, 79, 82–4, 89, 99, 148–9, 151–2, 163, 167–8, 173–4, 180, 182–3, 193
strangeness, see *atopia*
Stranger, Eleatic 5–6, 10–12, 107–19, 209–23, 225 n.16,
Stranger, Athenian 145–7, 151
Strauss, Leo 46 n.16, 47 n.29, 57, 72 n.21, 74 n.45, 74 n.49, 74 n.50, 136 n.19
Sydenham, Floyer 70 n.11
Symposium 8, 10, 15–26, 29–49, 108, 123–39, 180, 192

Taylor, C.C.W. 176 nn.1 and 4
technê see art
Tejera, Victorino 209, 223 nn.2 and 6, 224 n.7
temporality, see time
Theaetetus 107–19, 120 nn.4, 13 and 17, 210, 212, 214–15, 216–23
Theaetetus 111, 114–16, 120 n.21, 161, 164–6, 168–70, 172–4, 224 n.14, 231, 232, 237, 238,
theatre 9, 95–8, 100, 104, 105 n.3, 196
The Life of Others, see *Das Leben der Anderen*
Theodorus 210–12, 223, 224 n.14
Timaeus 6, 10, 37, 108, 118, 149–50, 161, 166–70, 173–4, 177 n.13,
time (*chronos*) 2, 4, 143–7, 149–50, 152, 155
topos 191–4
totalitarian 81–2
Trabattoni, Franco 47 n.17
tragedy 3, 8, 15–16, 19, 24–6, 102
Thrasymachus 79
transcendence 191, 195–6, 202–3
Trevaskis, J.R. 223 n.1
truth 2, 4, 6, 15–16, 96, 97–8, 163, 164, 171–2, 174–6, 184–5
Tuana, Nancy 157 n.16
Typhon 194–5
tyranny 80, 82, 91 n.7

value 2, 7–8, 10, 17, 30, 33–4, 44, 57, 95, 104, 125–8, 131–4, 136 n.17, 137 n.31, 145, 149, 174, 202

Vickers, Brian 135 n.7
virtue (*aretê*) 2, 4, 6–11, 30–6, 39–45,
    47 n.24, 54, 57, 69 n.9, 89, 97–8,
    102–51, 112–14, 117, 119, 119 nn.11
    and 13, 97–8, 102–5, 125–34,
    136 n.17, 138 n.38, 161, 175, 183,
    219, 238
Vlastos, Gregory 176 n.12, 223 n.1
Voegelin, Eric 72 n.22
Voigt, Christian 71 n.17
de Vries, Gerrit 47 n.17

Wallace, Robert W. 226 n.21
West, Grace Starry 58, 72 n.28, 74 n.46
West, Thomas 58, 72 nn.21 and 28, 74 n.44
Whitehead, A.N. 223 n.1
Wilson, Peter 156 n.8
wisdom 6, 9, 22, 24, 36, 42, 55, 79, 84, 88–9,
    95, 98, 102, 125, 127–8, 131, 134, 152,
    163, 174, 183, 185, 193, 196
Woodruff, Paul 1, 46 n.10, 105 nn.11 and
    12, 106 n.15, 196

Xantippe 180–1, 186 nn.4 and 7
Xenophon 51–3, 68, 74 n.52, 129

Zamyatin, Yevgeny 82, 90
Zuckert, Catherine 223 n.5, 225 n.16

www.ingramcontent.com/pod-product-compliance
Lightning Source LLC
Chambersburg PA
CBHW070029010526
44117CB00011B/1760